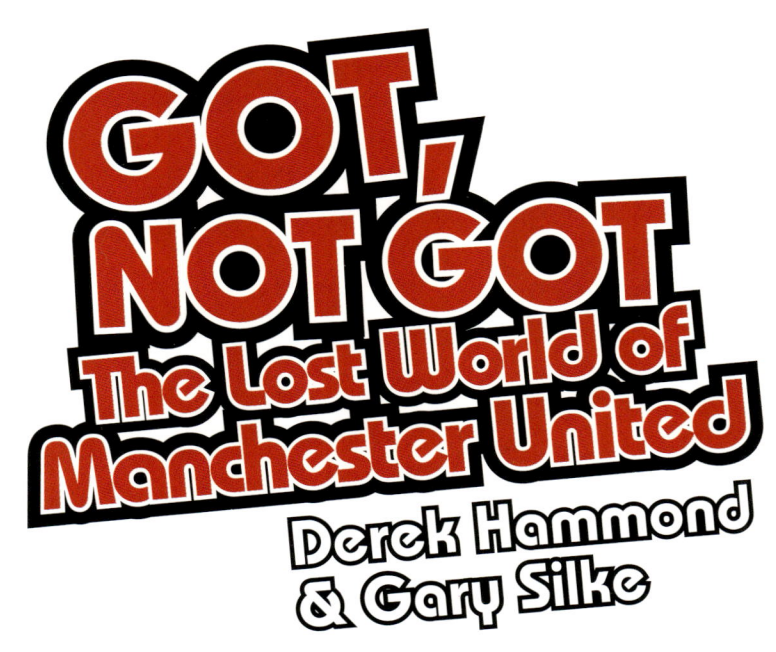

# GOT, NOT GOT
## The Lost World of Manchester United

### Derek Hammond
### & Gary Silke

Pitch Publishing Ltd
A2 Yeoman Gate
Yeoman Way
Durrington
BN13 3QZ

Email: info@pitchpublishing.co.uk
Web: www.pitchpublishing.co.uk

First published by Pitch Publishing 2013
13-digit ISBN: 9781909178755
Design and typesetting by Olner Pro Sport Media.
Printed in the UK by CPI Group (UK), Croydon CR0 4YY

*"When I first started I didn't mind the hard men too much because it gave me the chance to rubbish them with my skill. I'd go past them and they'd say, 'Do that again and I'll break your xxxxing leg'. And next time I'd do 'em again and they'd say, 'Right, I xxxxing warned you'. Next time I got the ball I'd stand on it and beckon them to me. I used to be like a bullfighter, taunting them, inviting them to charge me. They rarely got me. I was too quick. At moments like that, with the crowd cheering, I used to get the horn. Honestly, it used to arouse me, excite me…"*

George Best

*"Now Manchester United are 2-1 down on aggregate, they're in a better position than when they started the game at 1-1."*

Ron Atkinson

## A&BC

A&BC Chewing Gum of Romford, Essex, holds a special place in the hearts of millions of big kids. Back in the 1950s, it was Douglas Coakley (the 'C' in the company name) who came up with the idea of packaging football cards with a thin slab of chewy,

a combination which proved a natural winner. Throughout the 1960s and into the 1970s they produced a yearly set of football cards, as well as other stickers, tattoos and card series covering everything from the Beatles to *Star Trek* – and American sports and TV-related cards bound for the US via partner company, Topps.

Nowadays they're worth anything up to two or three quid each for the 1960s and early Seventies cards in excellent condition – though sadly that price drops off steeply for ones with edges chewed and worn, like ours. The 'crinkle-cut' extra photographs given away free with each pack in 1969 are even more desirable, and the little Action Transfers given away as extras in every pack in 1971 are worth anything up to seven or eight quid apiece. This for a small piece of paper which was given

away in a packet that cost thruppence.

Unfortunately, in 1974, A&BC lost a long-simmering legal battle and was taken over by Topps-Bazooka. End of story.

But, for some reason, it isn't easy to put out of your mind stray memories of football's long-lost people and places, the youthful obsessions and outdated rituals that seemed so important back in the day – and, in a strange way, still do. It might be a name on an email that you immediately associate with a recoloured kit on a card, and think: "Not got." Or just a vacant moment when you're driving at 80mph down the M6, when you find yourself wondering… whatever happened to Carlo Sartori?

It isn't everyone who could possibly understand.

### ROY OF THE ROVERS

Football's comic-strip heroes of the 1960s-80s split neatly into two categories. In one camp were the world-beating supermen in green-and-purple chevrons who scored pile-driving goals every week, on the way to Skillchester Athletic's 25th consecutive championship.

And then there were the more improbable heroes, the impossible underdogs aimed at kids who had realised early on that football would always be less about winning than about moaning and cursing and hoping.

In truth, Manchester United were always more of a Roy of the Rovers kind of team than, say, a Billy's Boots outfit like certain rival clubs.

Billy Dane out of *Scorcher* comic – your typical football-obsessed pre-teen, born with two left feet – was lucky

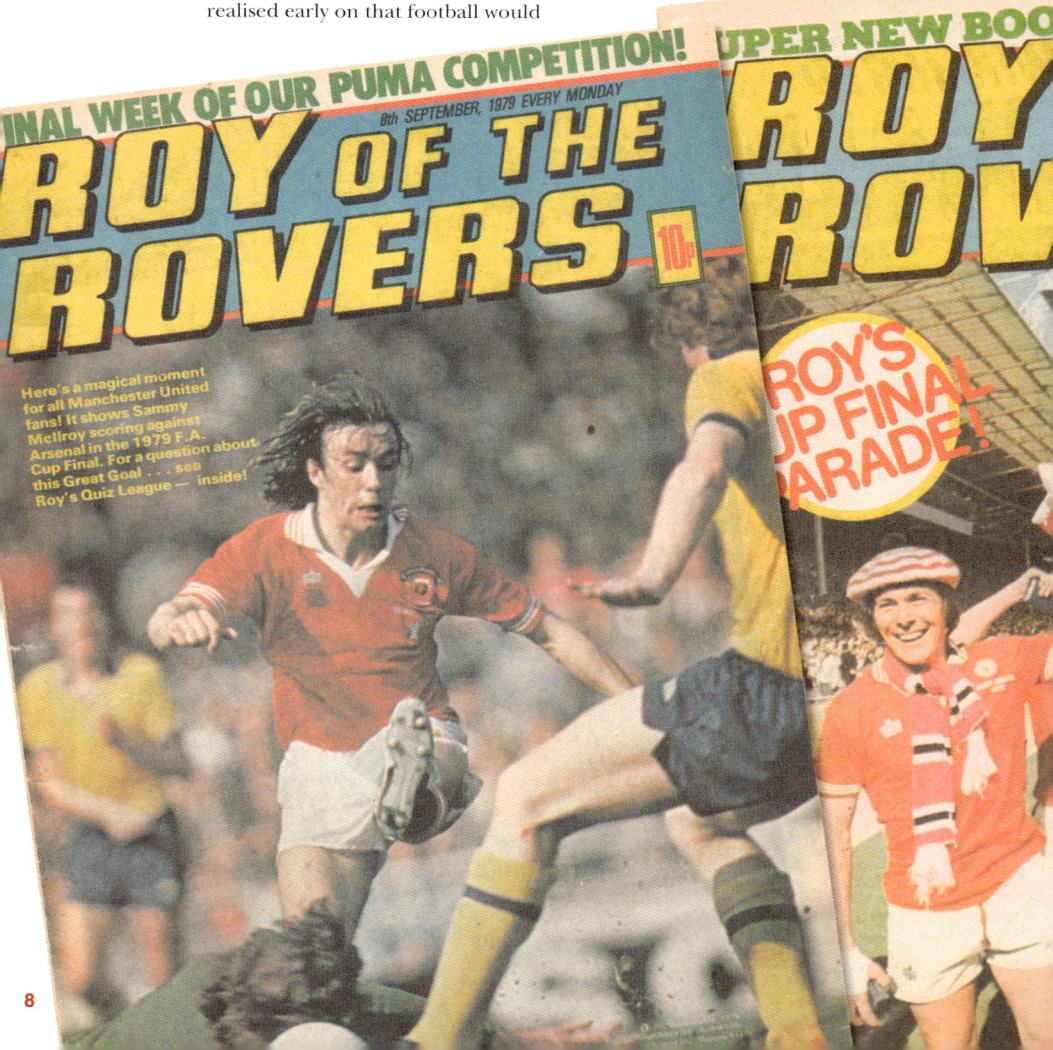

FINAL WEEK OF OUR PUMA COMPETITION!

**ROY OF THE ROVERS**

8th SEPTEMBER, 1979 EVERY MONDAY

10p

Here's a magical moment for all Manchester United fans! It shows Sammy McIlroy scoring against Arsenal in the 1979 F.A. Cup Final. For a question about this Great Goal . . . see Roy's Quiz League — inside!

SUPER NEW BOO

ROY ROV

ROY'S UP FINAL ARADE!

# E TALK-IN!

enough to find ex-England ace 'Dead-Shot' Keen's magical old boots in his gran's attic, and relied heavily on them to win the District Schools Cup Final every year.

Manchester United, meanwhile, were Melchester Rovers.

## Manchester United
provided the role model for Melchester Rovers.

T TO COLLECT!

7th APRIL, 1979 EVERY MONDAY

F THE RS 9p

BEGINS TODAY!

Collect our super Booklet over the next six weeks, showing scenes from top Cup Finals of past years. Here, Manchester United celebrate in 1977.

DAY: PART TWO OF OUR ROY RACE POSTER

2nd FEBRUARY, 1980 EVERY MONDAY

ROY OF THE ROVERS 12p

NAME THE PLAYERS!

The answer is in Roy's Super Quiz League inside!

a primary colour. Red socks and yellow waistcoats, for example, were only ever sported by show-offs, buffoons and variety acts.

So how to let it be known which side you were supporting in the big Cup game on Saturday? That's where red-and-white rosettes came in: they were the acceptable face of partisanship in more restrained times. You don't get them any more.

## THE ROSETTE

In the olden days, British males over the age of six were only permitted to wear brown, grey, greeny-brown, browny-green or, in moments of extreme flamboyance, navy.

If a chap had worn a football jersey anywhere other than on a football field he might well have been assumed to have taken leave of his senses, and arrested for causing a breach of the peace. And the same applied to sporting any item of apparel other than a school blazer in

## SUN SOCCERCARDS

Allow us to whisk you back to the tail end of the '70s, and one particular night beloved of many football card collectors. The night in question was notable for the long, gruelling, coffee-fuelled marathon undertaken by the anonymous Sun Soccercard artist, chained to his desk with a dozen packs of big bright felt pens and ordered to produce a set of nearly 1,000 player likenesses (or as near as possible in the

### It took a long, gruelling, coffee-fuelled marathon to produce this Gordon McQueen.

case of poor old Gordon McQueen).

The results speak for themselves. But just in case you don't recognise your heroes of yesteryear, here's... well, let's just hope their old mums don't recognise them either!

Anything to avoid paying image rights, eh? Even if the man with the felt-pen never did quite get the hang of eyes, their size relative to the human head, and the fact that they're usually pretty much on the same level.

SUN SOCCERCARD No 36 — S. COPPELL (England)

SUN SOCCERCARD No 89 — T. JACKSON (N. Ireland)

SOCCERCARD No 119 — S. McILROY (N. Ireland)

SUN SOCCERCARD No 120 — G. McQUEEN (Scotland)

SUN SOCCERCARD No 158 — J. RIMMER (England)

SUN SOCCERCARD N — B. CHARLTON (England)

SUN SOCCERCARD No 818 — J. GREENHOFF (Manchester Utd.)

SUN SOCCERCARD No 81 — J. HOLTON (Scotland)

SUN SOCCERCARD No 250 — D. EDWARDS (England)

SUN SOCCERCA — D. LAW (Scotland)

Atrocity Exhibition: Starring Denis Law as Worzel Gummidge, and Duncan Edwards' famous smirk.

## CHARLES BUCHAN'S FOOTBALL MONTHLY

It was the world's first monthly football magazine, unleashed on Britain's thrill-starved youth in September 1951 – and, despite missing the start of his debut season, Charlie Buchan's proved an instant hit.

Here, at last, was some colour to brighten the grey post-war landscape covered by the monochrome grown-up media. At least, bright pastel colours were daubed over black-and-white photos to vivid effect. And, in an era when kids were only expected to speak when spoken to, Charlie undid the top button of his sports jacket and did his best to address the herberts.

Even from the standpoint of sixty years on, the magazine's format is strikingly familiar, suggesting Charlie's editorial team got it pretty much right first time. There's analysis and tips from ex-pros and other enthusiastic scribblers; there's page-size posters for the bedroom wall, and interviews with players who aren't allowed to say anything.

Thumbing now through Charlie's back pages, he provides a unique window into an unrecognisable world of side partings and V-neck shirts, of rugby boots and weirdly recoloured violet irises.

From the magazine's perspective, football was steering into choppy waters when Buchan himself died in 1960, leaving the *Monthly* rudderless in the face of tidal changes such as footballers demanding a minimum wage, and suddenly not all agreeing to sport leather hair.

Although it limped on until 1974, *Football Monthly* never stood a chance against the new generation of marginally more readable comics and magazines put together by people who had heard of the Rolling Stones.

*Shoot! Goal.* Mud, even, eventually. Maybe they should have given Martin Buchan the job of editor – that might have stirred things up a bit!

If it proves anything, it's probably that in retrospect every age seems like a Golden Age, provided you were ten.

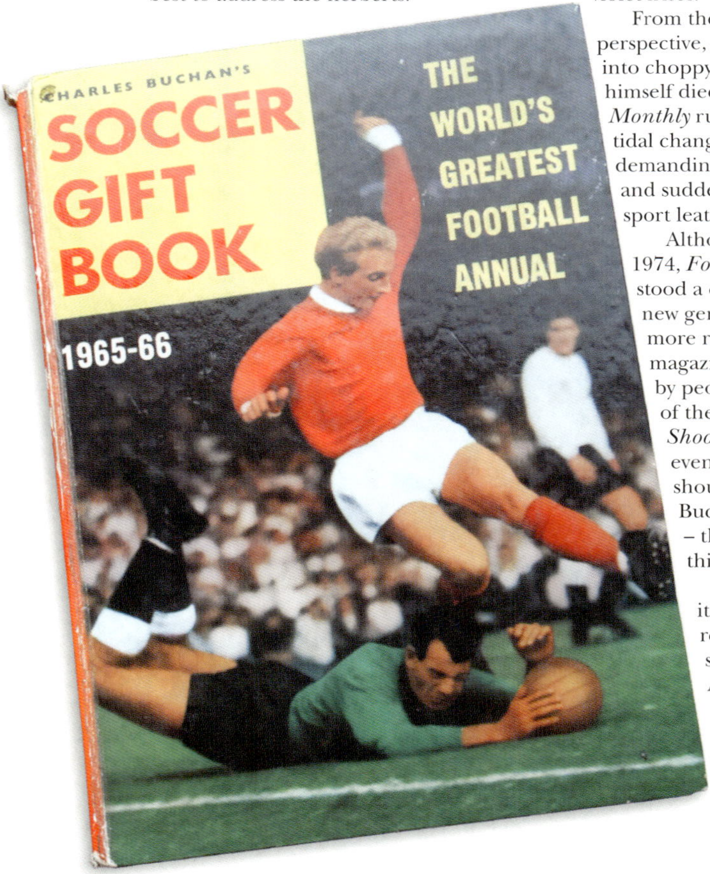

## THE CIGARETTE CARD

In the age of No Smoking – when anyone who fancies a tab is forced to stand outside their office in all weathers, and even crowd into a ramshackle lean-to hurriedly added twixt bar and beer garden – it won't be long until kids don't even recognise the reference to a good old-fashioned gasper, already obscured by the slick, sad euphemism of 'candy stick'.

The sweetie cigarette will soon be no more, like Bryan Robson's perm, mud and Ted MacDougall's promise of 30 goals per season.

Back in the day, however, they were clearly the best option for L-plate smokers, both in terms of their unique, chalky-sweet flavour and cunning

disappearing breed of oldsters.

No, not the stout men who smoked for England during the war only to be stamped out underfoot in the fallout from NHS cost-cutting exercises determined to make everyone live to 200. But us, the jammy-faced kids who remember the contents of Granddad's hand-me-down baccy tin: a length of string (now sneered upon as a throwback to the suspicious, militaristic Scout movement), a penknife (now

## We posed manfully with a sugary cig dangling from our lips,
## fooling absolutely everybody.

authenticity, courtesy of a dab of pink food colouring on the burning 'hot' end. And they came with a football card, too, if you were lucky – or a fat cricketer or lady tennis player if the dreaded mixed-sports set was in season.

Barratt's and Bassett's packs of sweet cigarettes were a throwback to the cigarette cards that had died out in the war; but we never realised that at the time. We were too busy posing manfully with our sugary cig dangling from our lips, fooling absolutely everybody.

Sweetie cigarette cards are already an obscurity to kids aged under 20 or 30. And the original pre-war mass cult of the cigarette card proper will soon be nothing but a memory clung to by a

banned), a Watney's Party Seven can opener ("puncture both sides to ensure even flow"), two shillings and fivepence in assorted, unfamiliar coinage ("Dad, what's a 'farting'?") and a small pack of cig cards in a perished and retied elastic band.

Guess Which Club:
The clue, as Jim Bowen
might have said, is in
the question.

13

## ACTION MAN

They don't make boys' toys like Action Man any more.

Kids aren't interested in peering through the back of a plastic doll's head and into his 'Eagle Eye' when the maximum thrill available is a slightly blurred view of the back garden. And as for realistic hair and gripping hands... they tend to pall into insignificance next to the Xbox's 3-D virtual world, where it's perfectly possible to drop in on Berlin in 1945 or Pluto in the year 4567, shredding Nazis and aliens alike with a sonic fire ray akin to a red-mist glare from Nobby Stiles. They'd call Action Man un-PC now – an eight-inch multi-skilled terrorist who thought nothing of changing out of his Nazi Stormtrooper uniform into that of a Navy frogman, a Canadian Mountie or an astronaut. And so into his Manchester United kit for a kickaround with your sister's Barbie in goal.

Unfortunately, that's when our vicious little accomplice became a complete bore. Whether you had one Action Man or 22, there just wasn't a game you could base around his non-existent ball skills. The specific types of 'action' mastered by 'the movable fighting man' were limited to bending at the joints and being blown into the air. There was only so much fun you could have dressing a doll in football kit, especially as it exposed his shattered-looking kneecaps. The final straw was the orthopaedic stand which he needed to balance on one leg, hovering over the ball in a sorry personification of inaction.

Because most Action Man enthusiasts kept their figures strictly military, the scarcity value of the football range has more recently seen eBay prices soaring. An original 1960s Man U kit recently sold on the auction site for £350, and the red Action Man team badge given away with the original kit pack can sell for over fifty quid alone. If only you'd kept them, Action Man's two-inch-long white socks could now pay for a decent night out. But don't get confused by the copycat 'spoiler' dolls that were floated out into the market back in the Sixties and Seventies, such as Johnny Goalgetter and this evil-looking Japanese Mintex soldier who's borrowed Action Man's Man U kit... or this curious penalty-kicking 'Shoot' figure from Germany, who did at least involve a modicum of 'Action'...

# Try painting 'Sharp Electronics' on a bloke who's two inches high.

## AIRFIX

Ever since 1955, when they released their 1/72 Spitfire model kit, Airfix had been satisfying little boys' unquenchable thirst for recreating World War II.

You could paint up a boxful of Commandos or Desert Rats and painstakingly put together a Hampden bomber, though how you were supposed to stop the 'cement' from clouding up the glass canopy of the cockpit was anyone's guess.

Even more satisfying than endless war was the 1/32nd scale Airfix Sports Series of Airfix Footballers – your chance to ditch khaki and grey for the far more exciting football colours of red, white and black, and maybe even a few of those other oppo colours like sky blue and canary yellow.

Up until the mid-Seventies it wasn't too much trouble recreating miniature versions of the kits of the day; but things got a lot trickier after that time.

Go on, you try painting an Admiral logo, Adidas sleeve stripes or a microscopic 'Sharp Electronics' logo on a bloke who's just over two inches tall.

Long boring Sunday afternoons were the perfect time for creating a pair of Admiral shorts, complete with the nautical and United logos on the front – right up until the double misery of *Last of the Summer Wine* and the parental enquiry: "Have you got any homework, son?" reminded you that Monday morning was nearly upon us once again.

Thanks to eBay you can still get that distinctive box through the post with England vs. Germany on the front. Old habits, like old enemies, die hard. And if you've got a steady hand and a couple of hundred hours on your hands, there's no more satisfying way to waste your time.

15

### THE TENACIOUS WARRIOR

1966 is remembered for glorious, golden images of a grinning, red-shirted Bobby Moore, carried on his team-mates' shoulders, holding aloft the Jules Rimet trophy. However, from a non-English point of view, the tournament saw world football reach a nadir of cynical foul play. It's known across the footballing globe as the 'Dirty World Cup'.

It was a time when defenders appeared to have free rein to hoof lumps out of strikers, who were given virtually no protection from referees. Full-backs had grown tired of being made to look like monkeys by the likes of Stanley Matthews and had discovered that there was more than one way to stop a tricky winger.

## Nob was no yob

he was a brave and loyal servant.

The nominated hard man of each club was almost as celebrated as the star strikers they sought to bruise: Ron 'Chopper' Harris of Chelsea; Liverpool's Tommy Smith, 'The Anfield Iron'; Leeds United's Norman 'Bites Yer Legs' Hunter (and a few more besides); Tottenham's Dave Mackay...

In other words, players you loved to hate – unless they happened to be on your side, in which case there was often room for a small amount of give-and-take. A healthy alternative perspective on their tendency towards ultraviolence.

Take Nobby Stiles, for example: he was a warrior, a loyal servant for 21 years, a man you'd want to go to war with, but certainly not against.

Oppo fans were often incensed by his high spirits, his tenacious, uncompromising tackling and never-say-die attitude, which was totally different in nature to the common yobs previously mentioned. Nob's real name was Norbert and he wore big glasses – he had to be hard.

There seemed to be a complicit understanding between a good old-fashioned hard man and referee whereby no one could be booked in the opening five minutes of a game. He was allowed one free, 'welcoming' clog on an opposing forward's calf, 'just to let them know I'm here'.

The second, Achilles-crunching challenge might warrant a brief word of warning from the ref. The third might occasionally earn a booking, at which the defender would present a picture of outraged innocence.

By this stage, the talented striker had completely lost:
1 – stomach for the contest; or,
2 – all feeling below the waist.

And the job was a good 'un.

## MITRE

Here's a cracking old ad from the manufacturers of Mitre footballs, complimenting United on their excellent taste in booting their muddy leathers around the country. We especially used to like the orange ones they used when the odd three inches of snow or a skating-rink frost presented something of an extra challenge.

It was only after the invention of namby-pamby under-pitch heating and the big spoilt girl's blouse Premier League that pitches became uniformly smooth and lime green, and splendid Football League balls like these were ditched for something more trendy and marketable.

...anufacturers of

## MITRE FOOTBALLS wish to pay tribute to MANCHESTER UNITED —

who have consisten... used thei... footballs

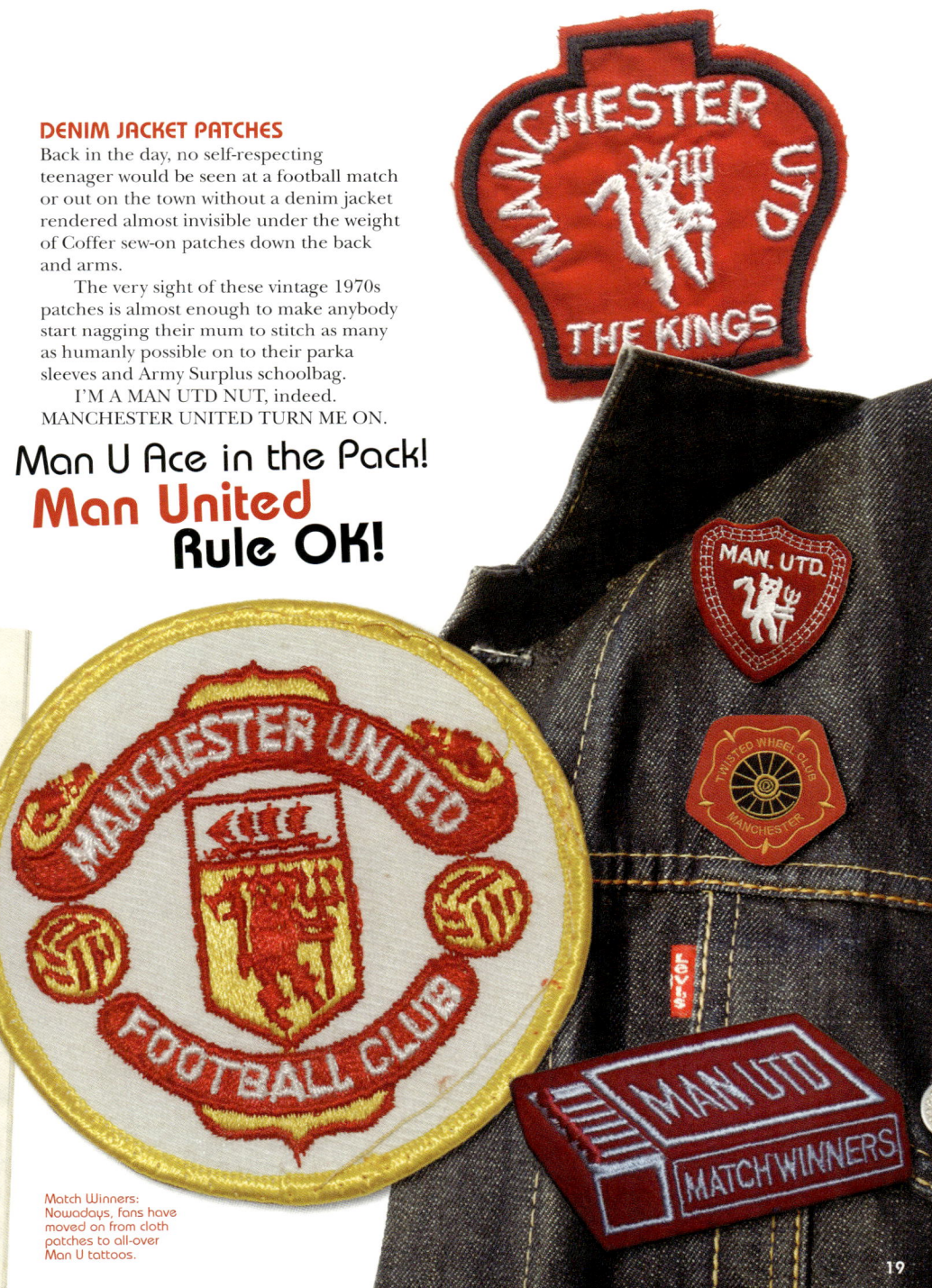

### DENIM JACKET PATCHES

Back in the day, no self-respecting teenager would be seen at a football match or out on the town without a denim jacket rendered almost invisible under the weight of Coffer sew-on patches down the back and arms.

The very sight of these vintage 1970s patches is almost enough to make anybody start nagging their mum to stitch as many as humanly possible on to their parka sleeves and Army Surplus schoolbag.

I'M A MAN UTD NUT, indeed. MANCHESTER UNITED TURN ME ON.

# Man U Ace in the Pack!
# Man United
## Rule OK!

Match Winners: Nowadays, fans have moved on from cloth patches to all-over Man U tattoos.

Cotton is perfectly soft and natural,
alternately warm and cool,
**and shrink resistant.**

## COTTON

It's the sensual associations that come bundled with cotton that make it such a rich source of minor, if largely subconscious, pleasure.

Ahh, the smell of a new cotton T-shirt being pulled on over your head on a Friday night. The slow fade of a favourite shirt, laundered a hundred times by your mum. Cotton next to the skin – warm against the winter cold, cool in summer... the pure smell of plain scarlet with a simple white collar and cuffs, and no other labels or logos smelling of a modern attempt to cash in.

In 150 years, the only negatives against cotton were an association with hippie cheesecloth and, ah yes, the institutionalised horrors of the slave trade.

Cotton isn't just perfect for clothes because it's easy to take care of and to wash. It's soft because it's made out of perfectly natural fluff. And it's cheap because the fluff grows on trees.

And so some tiresome bean counter inevitably decided to put about the idea that cotton is altogether second rate. Wear it for sports and it apparently now soaks up sweat in a way that you wouldn't want it to be soaked up. Cotton isn't stretchy enough, and it needs ironing, unlike a certain artificial wonder-fabric. They even tried to convince us that shell-suit bottoms were cooler and more comfortable than jeans.

Now, it just so happens that while cotton is cheap, polyester is cheaper. So much cheaper, it's practically free.

Polyester is an artificial plastic made from the acids and alcohol produced when you torch petroleum – in other words, from exhaust fumes.

Polyester is hard-wearing primarily because it's hard. It's rough to the touch, keeps you cold in winter and hot in summer. Wear it in summer, or for sports, and it will make you smell like you've been dead for a week.

Bring back cotton football shirts!

## BOBBLEHEADS?

Hmm, we quite like the old ones.

We're too old to fully appreciate the glory and power of the so-called Bobblehead. We just don't see the point.

The Corinthian statuette stands about two inches tall, collecting dust on your shelf, until you've got all 400 of the United players ever thus rendered in plastic – at a cost of about 1,000 quid – until such time that you decide to get rid on eBay and make yourself some beer money for your hobby of these past 10 years.

One big job lot should do the trick!

And, sure enough, you raise more than enough readies for a round of drinks at city-centre prices.

We quite like the old ones, mind.

Founded: 1902. Ground: Old Trafford. Manager: Tommy Docherty. League Champions: 908, 1911, 1952, 1956, 957, 1965, 1967. F. A. Cup: 909, 1948, 1963. European up: 1968.

# MANCHESTER UNIT

## THE WONDERFUL WORLD OF SOCCER STARS

How many sets of football cards and stickers do you reckon might have been pushed out into the UK market to mark the occasion of the 1966 World Cup? Ten? Twenty? The answer, you might be surprised to hear, is none. Not a one. Zero.

In recent years a limited test production of A&BC World Cup stamps has emerged, but these are priceless rarities that had no real impact. Even though pocket-size cardboard football cards had been successfully covering the domestic game since the end of the '50s, and European and South American manufacturers had produced trailblazing sticker books for the 1962 finals, it simply didn't occur to anyone to build on these trends.

It was only when England secured Monsieur Rimet's small gold trophy that the enthusiasm really rocketed, kick-starting the British football industry in the stands, in the shops and in sticker albums up and down the country.

In the second half of the '60s, playgrounds rocked to the tribal rhythm of "Got, got, got, *got, not got*" as kids flicked through their teetering piles in search of that elusive Seamus Brennan, perfectly willing to exchange 200 swaps to fill in the one remaining square left on their checklist.

If us Brits were slow off the mark seeing the possibilities in the market for cards and World Cups, it took even longer to get

### MANCHESTER UNITED F. C.

JOHN ASTON

GEORGE BEST

SHAY BRENNAN (LEFT MARKER OF WATERFORD).

FRANCIS BURNS

BOBBY CHARLTON

PAT CRERAND

TONY DUNNE

22

England Fi
1969

JIMMY RIMMER

DAVID SADLER

ALEX STEPNEY

the ball rolling on the Euro-led non-sticky sticker front.

In 1967, FKS's *Wonderful World of Soccer Stars* rolled into limited, regional production, reflecting a Golden Age when all you needed to start up a business in the football sticker market was a picture deal with an agency – no worries if the images were a season or two out of date, that's what retouching brushes are for – and a distribution deal around the corner shops of Britain.

The idea took off, and 1968 saw the first widely available sticker set, largely repeating the previous year's mugshot efforts. The following season's largely accidental mix of action shots and head-and-shoulders upped the excitement greatly and has rarely been bettered, still offering a real window into the Wonderful, and sadly Lost World of Football in the Sixties.

The business model was clear. Give any football-mad child a packet of (not really very accurately titled) stickers, an album and a pot of Gloy gum, let him stick his first sticker into the allotted slot, surrounded by another dozen blank spaces taunting him, and let nature take its course...

WORLD OF
STARS IN ACTION
"PICTURE STAMP ALBUM"

2'6

Founded:
Manager: To
pions: 1908,
1967. F.A. Ce
Cup: 1968.

ALEX FORSYTH

STEVE JAMES

MANCHESTER UNITED F. C.

GEORGE BEST

SHAY BREN

BOBBY CHARLTON

PAT CRERAND

TONY DUNNE

23

## UNITED WE STAND

Following on from the Seventies' music-led revolutions in DIY publishing, it took a while for football to catch up, but eventually fans took to their cranky old typewriters, hunting and pecking and ker-chinging out their frustrations, and learning all-new reprographic skills along the way.

They were tired of hearing 'The Fans' View' expressed second hand in the media, where the final word, the final edit, was always predictably happy and safe. Before the 1980s, every word written about football came from an industry perspective – tapped out by writers who were paid by newspapers, magazines, television companies or club programmes, which were in turn reliant on the FA, the League or the clubs themselves.

It's a tough job, running the back page of a local paper without access to news information, player interviews or pictures.

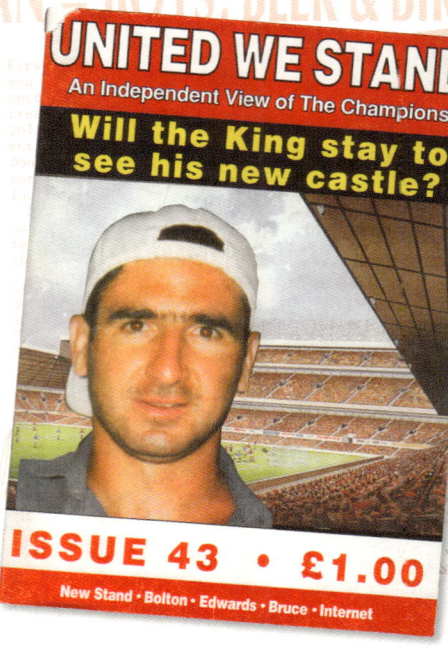

UNITED WE STAND
An Independent View of The Champions
Will the King stay to see his new castle?
ISSUE 43 • £1.00
New Stand • Bolton • Edwards • Bruce • Internet

*from titles such as Red News, United We Stand, Walking Down the Warwick Road and Red Issue.*

No such problem for the first wave of fanzine rebels, who offered an all-new diet of uncensored opinion cut with terrace humour, finally putting the majority view of 20,000 regulars above the handful of professionals and hired hands – the chairman, the players, the manager, the gentlemen of the press box – who were just passing through.

Suddenly your familiar old programme seller had a bit of competition on the streets from titles like: *Red News, United We Stand, Walking Down the Warwick Road* and *Red Issue.*

No matter if they were presented under headlines written using felt-pen, Letraset or John Bull Printing Outfit No. 7: here, for the very first time in print, were negative as well as positive views on our beloved clubs and teams, jokes at our own expense, better jokes at our local rivals' expense, album and gig reviews, stories of away trips, pubs and pies... always pies.

And, somewhere along the way, we discovered it wasn't just the fans in our corner of our ground who felt the same way about all-seater stadiums and ID cards, about the wreckers who came to football to chuck bananas and seats on the pitch, and the wreckers who came bearing calculators. And pies.

UNITED WE STAND
AN INDEPENDENT VIEW OF MANCHESTER UNITED
NUMBER 8
THE VOICE OF THE FANS
UP YOURS B SKY B!
BLOODY NORWICH ON A MONDAY NIGHT! YOU'RE MAKING THE CUP INTO A FARCE FOR US
INSIDE . . .
NIGHTMARE AT THE DELL • PREVIEW OF MONTPELLIER TRIP
• RED LETTERS • THE ATKINSON ERA
THE MANAGERESS CARTOON • REDS HOME & AWAY
ODD BITS • ANOTHER GREAT CARTOON & LOADS MORE
IN 32 GREAT PAGES!!
STILL ONLY 50p!

## THE FOOTBALL CARD ENGINE

Here's how to transform your humble pushbike into a revved-up, throbbing beast of a motorcycle, all too easy to mistake for a 750cc Norton Commando (provided you're only listening rather than looking).

### Turning heads, wobbling down the gutter
# with a guttural Vrrrrrrrrrrp.

All you need is:

1. One giant pile of football cards;
2. Two clothes pegs;
3. An anti-social desire to terrorise your neighbours like those cool Hells Angels you've seen on *Nationwide*; and,
4. A tragic disregard for your future financial security.

If you've got a teetering pile of cards, it naturally follows that you've got an even bigger pile of swaps, collected up over weeks of frustration while searching for the two or three you need for the set.

We recommend you use a Francis Burns 'orange-back' from A&BC's 1970-71 series. He's got a nice woody thrum.

All you have to do is use the pegs to secure the cards on to your bike frame so they stick a little way into the spokes. Then push off, taking note of the unusual sensation of slight resistance as you wobble down the gutter, turning heads with a guttural, engine-like *Vrrrrrrrrrrp*.

This way, in one afternoon you might easily burn through £100's worth of future sought-after collectables at 21st-century prices. But what the heck. You're only young once, eh?

It's 1-1 after 90 minutes in the 1968 European Cup final against Benfica...

## And 4-1 to United after 120 minutes.

## THE FOOTBALL LEAGUE REVIEW

Run from the back bedroom of secretary Alan Hardaker's Blackpool bungalow, the Football League was devoted to showing everyone what a big, happy family their 92-member club was. The *Football League Review* was a feelgood customer mag, given away free inside club programmes, where it bolstered many four- or eight-page lower-league efforts. The *FLR* was conspicuous in its absence from several larger League grounds, where power brokers were already wary of growing League influence.

However, in stark comparison to the petty politicking backstabbing

golf-clubbing small-minded scrap-metal merchant football-club owners of the 1970s, fans dug the freebies to bits – especially if Bobby Charlton featured on the cover.

The *Review* was 5 pence 'when bought separately'; which is to say never. It was full of behind-the-scenes peeks at the day-to-day running of all the League clubs, an article on the bootroom at Barrow being just as likely as a visit to the Arsenal trophy room. Then and now, its allure was almost entirely down to staff photographer Peter Robinson, who spent whole seasons travelling around snapping mascots at Mansfield and tea-ladies in Tranmere, thinking up ever more unusual formations for his teamgroups.

"I was conscious that I was different when I talked with other photographers at games," he told *When Saturday Comes*. Robinson never missed an angle, an expression, an oddity or a

1/- (5p)

# FOOTBALL LEAGUE REVIEW

1888

## A Frankenstein's monster
### of a football sticker...

location, showing more interest in football culture than the game itself. "I felt that you didn't just have to start photographing when the ref blew his whistle. I was interested in the whole build-up to the game."

### HASTILY RECOLOURED KIT

Although there was a lot less movement in the transfer market than today, the photo agencies that supplied the football card and sticker manufacturers in the Sixties and Seventies were rarely bang up-to-date.

Cue the burning of midnight oil as old shirts were hastily penned with new colours. Although, with this Ian Ure effort, they didn't even have to do that. We knew it was Highbury though. We knew the subtle difference between an Arsenal round-neck collar and a United one. And we knew he'd been transferred from Arsenal for £80,000

last season... they couldn't fool us.

FKS albums even carried a straight-faced 'guarantee': 'In order to maintain authenticity, some of the players have been photographed in clothing which is not necessarily their official club colours'.

But the filthiest trick in the sticker book has to be the unnatural horror of the head transplant.

First, an unsuspecting John Fitzpatrick is beheaded by the artist (or 'card sharp' in prison slang) who then sticks the offending appendage on to Shay Brennan's body in a disgraceful display of deceit and inappropriate forwardness.

The result of this unholy act: a Frankenstein's monster of a football card.

Ian 'Exercise in Minimalist Nomenclature' Ure: Are you Arsenal in disguise?

## ITV SUNDAY AFTERNOON FOOTBALL

*Doo-doodle doo-doodle doo-doo doo-doo-doo...*

Remember the theme tune from Sunday afternoon football on Granada – the *Kick Off* programme, presented by Gerald Sinstadt? It must bring back millions of mass memories of roast beef and Yorkshire puddings for the endless trail of nostalgic types who give it a spin on YouTube.

There was little room for manoeuvre in the editing suite, back then. The main game, however incident-packed or dull, ran for fifteen minutes up to a half-time ad break,

## Remember the theme tune **from Granada's Kick Off?**

followed by another quarter of an hour for the second half.

Part three brought fifteen minutes of a game from another ITV region, maybe yours. Hugh Johns was the smoky voice of ATV's *Star Soccer*, Tyne Tees was Kenneth Wolstenholme on *Shoot*, while LWT's *The Big Match* was fronted by Brian Moore...

After part four's brief highlights of another game – maybe Norwich or Ipswich from Anglia's *Match of the Week* with Gerry Harrison – and a round-up of results, the weekend seemed almost over.

Dozens of games went untelevised every weekend and that's why seeing your team was so special. With perhaps only a handful of TV appearances in a lean year, the novelty never wore off.

Which is why United fans lucky enough to work from home are always sneaking off to YouTube to find clips from the actual matches, as well as the great old pop-art titles.

*Doo-doodle doo-doodle doo-doo doo-doo-doo...*

Afternoon Delight: Roast beef, Yorkshire pud and Gerald Sindstadt.

## JAM JAR LIDS

Hartley's Strawberry Jam was already yummy enough, without them coming up with a further incentive for us to consume it even more greedily.

The introduction of footballers' faces to the lids during the 1971-72 season was marketing genius: Bobby Charlton, Geoff Hurst, Bobby Moore, Martin Peters, Alan Ball, Gordon Banks,

And if you were too full of Mother's Pride or Hovis for another sandwich but couldn't wait to get your hands on the lid with our Bobby you could always dip a spoon in and steal a couple more inches... nom nom nom.

## The more jam you slapped between your slices of bread
# the nearer you were to your next fantastic lid.

Colin Bell, George Best, Billy Bremner, Ron Davies, Jimmy Johnstone, Peter Osgood. A stellar line-up of football stars; twelve jars' worth to collect. That was a lot of jam – and a major expense for parents watching every half a new pee – but we ploughed through it somehow.

A 'jam samwich' was one of the few culinary treats you could prepare without parental guidance, and the more you slapped between the slices the nearer you were to your next fantastic lid.

31

## LEAGUE LADDERS/TEAM TABS

Wahey! Manchester United top of the League!

But there was more to your youthful flights of League Ladder-related fantasy than mere self-centred feelgood relish. There was also the bottom of Scottish League Division Two to consider (or maybe, if you were feeling generous, the bottom of the fourth division, and the basement trapdoor beckoning into non-League Hell). That's where a good old English emotion known as *schadenfreude* took over – and where you found clustered the likes of Leeds United, Manchester City, Liverpool and Everton. Not to mention every other side that had put one over on the Red Devils in the past three seasons.

Gifted to us in the build-up to the season's big kick-off by *Shoot!* or *Roy of the Rovers* or one of the old-school shoot-'em-up comics such as *Lion* or *Valiant*, the empty league ladders came first, closely followed over a number of weeks with the small cardboard team tabs designed to be poked into their ever-changing slot in the scheme of things.

In the days before computers, even before Teletext, the appeal of being able to stare at the league table was considerable. But, after the third or fourth week, updating your league ladders became a bit too much like hard work.

And that's when you could see what it would look like if East Fife were somehow suddenly transported to second in the League behind its natural eternal leaders. Ha! Swansea in the First Division, and Burnley in the Fourth! And all those lesser Lancashire clubs mysteriously close to going out of business – pointless, crowdless and hopeless, as God intended.

MANCHESTER U.
Ground:
Old Trafford,
Manchester 16.

Team tab:
Cut out and keep,
and collect the
whole set of 92!

THE "LION" FOOTBALL LEAGUE L

THE BATTLE FOR THE CHAMPIONSHIPS

| 1st DIV | | 2nd DIV | | 3rd DIV | | 4th DIV | | SCOT 1st I |
|---|---|---|---|---|---|---|---|---|
| 1 | EVERTON | 1 | STOKE | 1 | NORTHAMPTON | 1 | BRENTFORD | RANG |
| 2 | TOTTENHAM | 2 | CHELSEA | 2 | SWINDON | 2 | OLDHAM | KILMAR |
| 3 | BURNLEY | 3 | SUNDERLAND | 3 | PORT VALE | 3 | CREWE | PARTI |
| 4 | LEICESTER | 4 | MIDDLESBRO' | 4 | COVENTRY | 4 | MANSFIELD | CEL |
| 5 | WOLVES | 5 | LEEDS | 5 | BOURNEMOUTH | 5 | GILLINGHAM | HEA |
| 6 | SHEFFIELD W. | 6 | HUDDERSFIELD | 6 | PETERBORO' | 6 | TORQUAY | ABERI |
| 7 | ARSENAL | 7 | NEWCASTLE | 7 | NOTTS C. | 7 | ROCHDALE | DUND |
| 8 | LIVERPOOL | 8 | BURY | 8 | SOUTHEND | 8 | TRANMERE | DUNFER |
| 9 | NOTTS F. | 9 | SCUNTHORPE | 9 | WREXHAM | 9 | BARROW | DUN |
| 10 | SHEFFIELD U. | 10 | CARDIFF | 10 | HULL | 10 | WORKINGTON | MOTHE |
| 11 | BLACKBURN | 11 | SOUTHAMPTON | 11 | CRYSTAL P. | 11 | ALDERSHOT | AIRD |
| 12 | WEST HAM | 12 | PLYMOUTH | 12 | COLCHESTER | 12 | DARLINGTON | ST. MI |
| 13 | BLACKPOOL | 13 | NORWICH | 13 | QUEEN'S P.R. | 13 | SOUTHPORT | FAL |
| 14 | WEST BROMWICH | 14 | ROTHERHAM | 14 | BRISTOL C. | 14 | YORK | |
| | | | SWANSEA | 15 | SHREWSBURY | 15 | CHESTERFIELD | |

"Yeah, there's a bit of a dent, **but no one will ever suspect you, Bobby..."**

In 1972 United smashed the Third Division transfer record paying Bournemouth £200,000 for their lethal hitman Ted MacDougall. In an FA Cup game against Margate SuperMac had

# In 1972, United paid Bournemouth £200,000 when £200,000 was £200,000.

### LOWER-LEAGUE SIGNINGS

These days you'll seldom find a top club taking a punt on a lower-league signing. There are few potential stars left to be discovered as the Premier League scouting systems are as tight and effective as a purse seine tuna-fishing net: hardly anything of value can slip through the holes. In the modern game you're more likely to see players travelling in the opposite direction, sent out on loan from bloated top-flight squads to small-town lower-league clubs, just to get a game.

A few decades back, however, any chief scout worth his trilby would snoop around the Third or Fourth Division... or even lower than that, in the hope of a bargain.

found the net NINE times for the Cherries.

It didn't work out for Ted in what were times of turmoil at Old Trafford, with Frank O'Farrell being sacked and Tommy Docherty taking things in a new direction. After 18 games and 5 goals the Scot moved on to West Ham.

Sixteen years later United shelled out another £200,000, this time breaking the record transfer fee paid for a YTS player when they bought Lee Sharpe from Torquay United. This time the gamble paid off, with his United career being considerably more successful than MacDougall's.

## LEARN THE GAME

For hours at a time in the early Seventies, I would practise my skills out on the driveway, taking a break every couple of minutes to study the little diagrams on my Anglo Confectionery 'Learn The Game' football cards.

The only thing holding me back from performing the perfect scissor-kick was the slight disadvantage of never having seen Denis Law pulling off "the most spectacular of all kicks."

# Law contacts the ball with one foot
## while the other provides the scissor-like movement

Still, the basic idea was there for all to see, and never mind the niceties of cartoon conventions for body movement.

Law "jumps at split-second notice to the oncoming ball and contacts it with one foot while the other provides the scissor-like movement, his body outstretched in the air falling down to the ground."

So, I'd lob the ball up in the air, *wait for it...* then launch myself backwards, hanging upside-down in mid-air for graceful milliseconds before crumpling to the slabs.

It always came as some relief to connect with the ball, so I could move on to the next skill in my pack... Georgie Best and his big banana.

The Lawman: a scissor-kick so sharp it could cut defences to pieces.

## MIRRORCARDS

Back in the sunny 1971-72 season, the *Daily Mirror* was kind enough to give away a set of football cards featuring teamgroups of all 92 League clubs, plus the four Home International squads. The cards could be collected up and stuck on a large wallchart entitled 'Bobby Moore's Gallery of Soccer Sides'.

As if that weren't enough, it was then possible to order from the newspaper's HQ a special giant-size 'My Club' card to take pride of place in the middle of the poster.

# The big 'My Club' card
## is one of the rarest around.

To be frank, few punters made it this far down the line – making the United 'My Club' card (not to mention that of some of the smaller third and fourth division teams) one of the rarest around. Especially in mint condition, as those that were ordered were almost inevitably slapped straight on to Junior's wall!

*The Father Ted perspective challenge: the small card is big and the big card is far away.*

# MIRRORCARD

Back row (*l. to r.*): Greenhoff, Carrick, Connaughton, Rimmer, Stepney, Watson, James and Whelan.
Centre row (*l. to r.*): Lewis, O'Neil, Young, Donald, Edwards, Gowling, Ure, Sadler and Dunne.
Front row (*l. to r.*): Burns, Kidd, Best, Law, Fitzpatrick (inset), Crerand, Charlton (inset), Morgan, Aston and Sartori.
© Manchester United F.C.

## COFFER BADGES

In the days when no item of bling was complete without a little football badge or a cocky slogan, Northampton- and London-based Coffer Sports were the jewellers to a nation of kids.

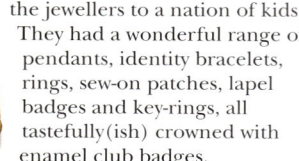

They had a wonderful range of pendants, identity bracelets, rings, sew-on patches, lapel badges and key-rings, all tastefully(ish) crowned with enamel club badges.

"Metal club badges are probably our biggest selling line," Arthur Coffer explained to the *Football League Review* in 1973. "For many fans the collecting of these lapel badges has developed into almost a cult. But rosettes are not far behind. We make more than half a million of them a year, in all sizes and all colours, and I cannot see them losing their appeal even though there are signs that the soccer souvenir market is slowly changing."

Slowly changing? Surely not.

You mean to say it's no longer the case that MAN U GOTTA LOTTA BOTTLE?

## Next to Ali, MAN UTD ARE THE GREATEST!

## THE SCRAPPER

In the six million-year interval between man first walking upright and the invention of the 24-hour kids' TV channel, the PlayStation, the Xbox, the Wii and the DS, kids were faced with a bit of a challenge. How to fill all those long, boring hours before it was time to blow their candles out? It was merely hundreds of years ago when the penny finally dropped, and pastimes such as needlepoint, pressing wild flowers and making your own scrapbook at last began to gain popularity.

Most young football fans had a go at assembling scraps devoted to their football team, but few persisted for very long. The first page of every scrapbook is filled, the last page hardly ever. After a few weeks, cutting your club's match reports and photos out of the paper tended to become a chore, enabling you to later track the ever-decreasing degree of care with which they were Gloyed onto the coarse pages. And then there was that final time you jumped the gun and Dad found a comedy hole in the back of his *Sunday Express* before he'd finished with it...

Charles Buchan's FOOTBALL MONTHLY

SOCCER SCRAPBOOK

96

Saturday. 26th. April. Old Trafford.

MANCHESTER UNITED 4·0 LEICESTER CITY

STAPLETON.
HUGHES.
OLSEN.
DAVENPORT-pen.

Attd.
38,840

SHARP

IND COO

# LATE UNITED BLITZ HITS CITY HOPE

A late scoring burst by Manchester United sent
cester City spiralling to a defeat much heavier than
y deserved at Old Trafford this afternoon.
ree goals in the last seven minutes made a mockery of City's sec
alf improvement and, just when they were sho
ould handle United's

Teams

UNITED: Turner; Gibson,
ston, Whiteside,

# Say cheese!
Posing for eternity in a million sticker albums.

## PANINI

Panini's first set of domestic League cards came out under the Top Sellers name in 1972, but it wasn't until later in the '70s that they hit their stride, producing uniform, trusted sticker sets which were actually sticky.

Under this onslaught, A&BC lost their way and were bought out by the American firm Topps, who temporarily brought a little baseball card razamatazz and glam-rock style to proceedings. Still, the days of cardboard were numbered – as were those of good old FKS, who responded to the Panini steamroller with their own sticky set of bizarre gold stickers in 1978 before quietly biting the dust.

The Panini Revolution stood for reliability, professionalism, mass popularity and a return to hundreds of near-identical head shots, albeit with little flags and team crests.

It seemed that everyone had a copy of that debut Football 78 album in their school bag, along with a pile of swaps held in place with a laggy band. Our new favourite thing was twice as hefty as its predecessor, weighing in at a fat 64 pages; each club spread over two pages instead of one, and in total there were 525 stickers to collect.

The stickers themselves were beautifully designed, clear head-and-shoulders shots with a club badge and a St. George or St. Andrews flag because, yes, the Scots had been included too. Clydebank's Billy McColl got to have his own sticker, and the English Second Division was also covered with a team group and badge

*Frank Stapleton throws some shapes, Football 83 style.*

for each previously ignored team.

Ah, those badges. There was a heartbeat jump when you ripped open your packet and saw a gold foil United badge nestling among the half-dozen stickers...

Panini reigned for a good fifteen years, never straying far from their '78 blueprint, producing a series of highly collectable and well-loved albums until they, in turn, were replaced by Merlin around the time the Premier League was launched and the licensing fees leapt up.

The Panini Football 1991 sticker album proudly bore the crests of the Football League and the PFA together with that of the Scottish League and pro body counterparts. What Panini didn't know was that Merlin (AKA good old Topps, if you read the small print) were waiting in the wings to scupper the comfy status quo with a deal already tied up with the brand-new Premier League.

In 1992, Panini's remaining PFA licence allowed them only to produce stickers without club colours or details. How sad it was to see official stats replaced by weedy 'captain's comments' and players trotted out in standard white PFA boiler suits – or else players' kit recoloured in lairy greens, reds and oranges in the utterly emasculated 'Super Players From Top Teams' of ' 96.

While Panini responded by skittering down the leagues for material, Merlin's Premier League 1994 debut featured PL badges, team groups, full info and players in kits, bright and beautiful. There was even a page for Sky TV cards.

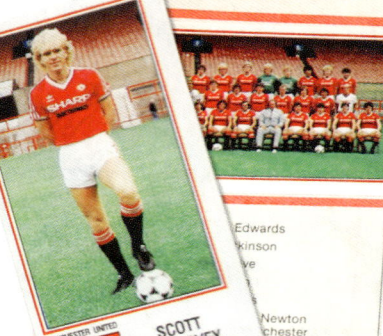

MANCHESTER
UNITED

1878

SCOTT
McGARVEY

MANCHESTER UNITED

GARY
BAILEY

Edwards

kinson

ve

Newton
chester

Div. Two Champions: 1935-36,
1974-75.
F.A. Cup winners: 1909, 1948,
1963, 1977.
European Cup winners: 1968
**Colours:** red shirts with white trim,
white shorts, black stockings
... and white hooped

... urs: White shirts with
... black shorts with red
... stockings with red
... ooped turnovers.

Goalkeeper. Born Ipswic...
6.1. Wt. 12.3. Age 24. A ...
England Under-21 and 'B' ...
tional who was playing fo...
University in Johanne...
before returning to Engl...
sign on for United in J...
1978. He made his League...
against Ipswich Town, wh...
father Roy used to be ...
keeper, in November 19...
has been the regular first...
'keeper ever since. By the...
last season he had ta...
career total of League ...
ances to 149.

ten years with
... fore and after
... eague, and spent
... Kettering Town
... and West
... fore taking over
... he 1981 in
... exton.

**FIGURINE PANINI**

Old
...ford

THE FOOTBALL LEAGUE
FOUNDED 1888

GMWU

MANCHESTER U

BRIAN GREE...

**DAVE SEXTON**
Born in Islington...
his playing career ...
in the Southern Le...
in 1951. Moved to ...
Leyton Orient in ...
and Crystal Palace...
rial experience ...
Tommy Docherty ...
briefly managed ...
coaching, first a...
nal. In October ...
manager at Che...
erable success w...
town to QPR in ...
Manchester Unite...
sudden departure ...
Docherty.

**ALEX STEPNEY**
Goalkeeper. Bor...
6.0. Wt. 13.3. Ag...
fonts with Milla...
with Tooting and ...
briefly in the 1...
ford that have...

**JIMMY NICH**
Defender. Bor...
Wt. 1... Ag...
the blo...
is Canad...

MANCHESTER UNITED

TONY YOUNG
Manchester Utd

earson
ER UNITED

## THE BEDROOM SHRINE

You can rebuild it, y'know – the bedroom shrine of your youth when you loved them all, even the dodgy old full-back on whom the adults would pour scorn and derision.

When you wanted to see their images last thing at night and first thing in the morning; arranged in teamgroup ranks, watching over you while you slept.

The thrill of opening a *Goal*, or *Shoot!* or *Tiger* and seeing a real actual United hero featured on a colour poster – or, even better, a team photo in the centre spread – might not be so keen now. But don't let that hold you back.

You can still get the horrible woodchip wallpaper we all had in our bedrooms, and paint it that turquoise light blue that was in vogue in the mid-Seventies. Someone will still have the recipe.

And there are people on eBay who make it their business to go through old magazines and annuals pulling out the United posters, flogging them by the dozen. The collection that took you seven years to accrue can now be obtained in a couple of days.

It won't have organically spread across your wall over the years like a fungus of devotion, but it will still look magnificent.

Almost certainly, the wife will understand.

FOOTBALL STAR
LOU MACARI
Manchester Utd.

MAN UTD.
CUP FINAL 1977.

GOAL

ALAN GOWLING
GEORGE BEST
Manchester United

**MORGAN** Manchester United

**MANCHESTER UNITED**

TEAM SET **MANCHESTER UTD**

| DENIS LAW | PAUL EDWARDS | NOBBY STILES |
| GEORGE BEST | BOBBY CHARLTON | JOHN FITZPATRICK |

● **START NOW! COLLECT THE WHOL**

**George Best** Manchester United

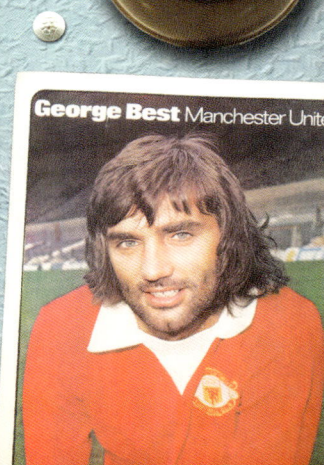

FRANCIS BURNS
MANCHESTER UNITED | RIGHT BACK

**MANCHESTER UNITED**
**FOOTBALL CLUB**

**JUST WHAT THE DOC ORDERED!**

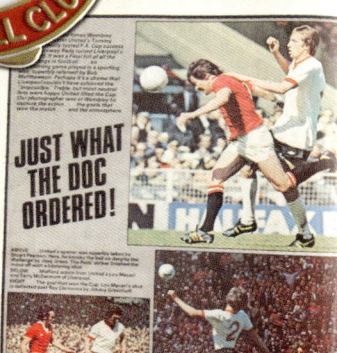

**MARTIN BUCHAN**
Manchester United

FOOT/GOAL

## THE AUTOGRAPH BOOK

Gone out of existence. Withdrawn from the field. Abandoned. Missed. Passed by.

Everything we come across on this journey through the Lost World of Manchester United is no more. They thought it was all over – and they were dead right.

The autograph book was unlike any other of its day. Its cartridge-paper pages were blank, devoid of words and lines, with the built-in compensation of alternate pastel shades – chalky blue, green, pink, yellow. The outer corners of the pages were missing, rounded off so as not to offend the hand of an honoured victim. The spine of the leather-bound booklet ran down the short side, so it lolled open invitingly. On the cover of the book there was no author's name or title, just a single, golden word in a curly typeface. And then there was the vital loop of elastic to hold the book closed in the owner's back pocket, either encircling the whole precious volume, or just stretching over a single corner.

Lost. Let slip.
No longer in our
possession.

It isn't just the autograph book that has bitten the dust in recent years, but also the crowd of small boys hanging around the locked double door marked PLAYERS AND OFFICIALS ONLY an hour after the match. The players are missing, too: men who didn't need a minder at their side to talk to a twelve-year-old about the afternoon's brawls and cannonballs. The kind of players whose personally signed message you'd want to treasure forever. Bryan Robson. Eric Cantona. Tony Dunne. Ian Ure...

The kind of players whose message

# you'd want to treasure forever.

The warning signs came when first two, then three, and now four of the five attackers in every team were phased out, goalscoring deemed surplus to requirement. Local heroes fell out of fashion. Red-faced stoppers failed to evolve with changing times, and so soon became extinct. And the best player in every team of the Sixties and Seventies became the first called up to the great kickaround in the sky.

All gone, but not forgotten.

Then as now, football magazines and club shops churned out sheets of pre-printed (quite literally auto-) autographs to help save the all-important stars time and hassle. It's all a question of supply and demand, see? But it's odd how much more charming the old sheets seem in comparison to today's handily pre-signed official postcards.

## BAB

The BAB Souvenir Company was known for just two, instantly recognisable products:

1   The lairy, you might say imaginatively, coloured football club crest sticker.
2   The star-player sticker, always carefully labelled in case of any doubt as to who was depicted.

The modern-day attraction to collectors is essentially down to the fact that, in the early Seventies, hundreds of thousands of children simply couldn't resist unpeeling the backs of the stickers and attaching them to their school bags, school desks, bedroom walls and younger siblings, testing to the limit the proud boast on the retail cards:

"GREAT! Collect ALL these football 'club' badges," shouted the old counter box. "Sticks to almost any surface."

## Children simply couldn't resist

### sticking the stickers on their school bags,

### school desks, bedroom walls

### and younger siblings.

It could almost have been a long-term strategy to boost values to collectors.

And then there's the sloppy way the company continually recycled their few sticker designs in new and unlikely colours, with endless minor variations, which appeals to the obsessive modern collector.

Admittedly, we mainly like them because they're funny. Is that the least flattering image of Nobby Stiles you ever did see? Bobby Charlton's doing his best to stifle a snigger... but he's no felt-pen painting!

The 'Heavyweight' figures of the Seventies had a stance that suggested they were

# well up for it.

## SUBBUTEO

Subbuteo was by far the most popular table-top representation of football, and its '00'-scale figures still hold a special place in the hearts of blokes across the globe. Part of the game's appeal was due to the huge range of accessories which, while unnecessary for the actual playing of the game, did prop up an illusion of realism and 'add to the big-match atmosphere'.

Plastic pitches were one of the ugliest developments in Eighties football. QPR, Luton and Oldham became unbeatable at home because they mastered the art of playing on a surface that had all the properties of lino – sliding tackles were out, except for players wearing motorcycle leathers under their shorts. Meanwhile, good old Subbuteo exhibited their usual dogged determination to keep up with the times, producing their own 'Astroturf' pitch – although, if their 'grass' pitch was made of green baize cloth, and the 'Astroturf' surface from slightly different baize cloth, it's unclear in what sense it was any more 'artificial'.

The rampant hooliganism of the time puts into stark perspective any complaints about plastic pitches, leading as it did to football attendances going down and spike-topped fences going up. Subbuteo didn't shirk its remit to mirroring the game and replaced its friendly green picket fences with prison railings and mounted police to keep any potential plastic yobboes off the pitch.

The actual Subbuteo playing figures of the late-Sixties to late-Seventies are known these days as Heavyweights, with their National Service haircuts, and a stance that suggested they were well up for it.

The Seventies also saw short-lived and unloved 'Scarecrows' and 'Zombies' figures, before the Eighties brought the more detailed, and more popular, 'Lightweights' which saw United through the Adidas era.

Although accessories such as the dugouts and the ambulance men, the TV tower with mini-Motty, the floodlights and VIP figures (including Queenie handing over a tiny FA Cup) were affordable and always welcome on a Christmas morning, the ultimate prize had to be the Subbuteo stadium, complete with a decent crowd of ready-painted spectators. Unfortunately, they were beyond the pocket of most kids' parents and you'd count yourself lucky to have a single, foot-long stand with a couple of dozen spectators dotted around it.

We used to buy packs of unpainted spectators – fifty per box, all as naked as the day they were moulded – and only after weeks of eye-damaging work on Polo-Neck Man, Fatty, Celebrating Man and his equally Celebrating Girlfriend, did we discover the ultimate irony: with stands on all four sides it was virtually impossible to play the game without nudging a stand and causing a mini-stadium disaster.

Oh, come on, let's go up the park and play football.

## SQUELCHERS

When it comes to 1970s petrol freebies, many fans of a certain age have their nostalgic favourites. It might be the miniature plastic player busts issued by Cleveland Petroleum in 1971, or the foil club badges that were given away every time dad bought four gallons of Esso 4-star. But it takes a special kind of purist to reserve a missionary zeal for the delights of Esso's set of Squelchers.

These were small, badly bound booklets full of facts of varying degrees of likelihood (and veracity, as it turns out), designed "to squelch arguments about football." Though of course, in pubs and playgrounds all over the country, all they really did was start arguments…

"Squelch!" you were supposed to butt into other people's conversations, fumbling open your blue plastic folder to recite: "When George Best scored his FA Cup record-equalling sixth goal against Northampton in 1970, he rounded goalie Kim Book and stood on the ball on the the goal line, saluting the United fans before kicking the ball into the gaping net."

There were 16 themed Squelchers in the set. And, even today, it's hard to do without them on a long away trip by rail.

"Don't be silly," you're invited to read aloud as a conversation-starter. "Denis Law wasn't signed from a Scottish side or from ex-club Manchester City, but from Italian club Torino!"

Woe betide any fan who should ever make a factual blunder within your earshot. The chance of a lifetime! An opportunity to whip out your Squelcher and humble a fellow football fan.

## "SQUELCH!
### Alex Stepney was signed from Chelsea!"

"SQUELCH!" you announce to your brand-new acquaintance in the snug at the notorious Twirling Star public house. "Manchester United goalkeeper Alex Stepney was signed from Chelsea, where he'd just moved from Millwall, and had only had time to play one match!"

Surely a fitting way to draw to a close any further discussion regarding the finest ever football giveaways. With an all-time classic collectable. And before anyone gets hurt.

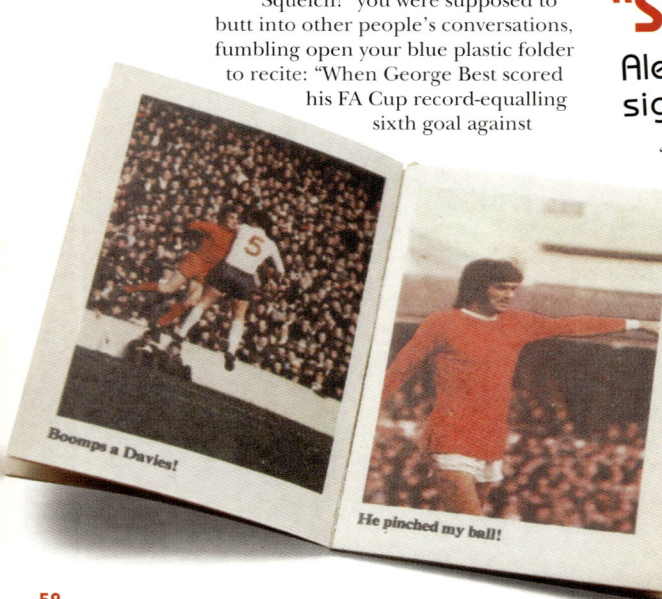

Boomps a Davies!

He pinched my ball!

## TEAMS THAT YOU CAN RECITE

When teams were teams rather than private contractors of fleeting acquaintance, the first-choice line-up would go unchanged for seasons on end, with the boss blooding a kid or adding perhaps one new face over the close season, but only to replace the arthritic right-back who had just enjoyed his testimonial year.

You knew your team was a team because they piled into a team bath after the match, rather than wearing flip-flops and initialled dressing-gowns and insisting on private shower cubicles. You knew they were a team because their surnames seemed to rhyme when you recited them.

Bailey, Nicholl, Albiston, McIlroy, McQueen, Buchan, Coppell, Greenhoff, Jordan, Macari, Thomas. What's the United team you can automatically recite?

Every year, you'd hear a news story about a fan who had named their firstborn after their whole beloved team. Take a bow, Gary James Arthur James Gordon Martin Stephen James Joseph Luigi Michael Blenkinsop. You'll be coming up 35, next birthday. And, of course, it's now a family tradition to name a little one after your heroes, even though it doesn't really work so well in the era of 30-strong Premier League squads.

So spare a thought for poor little David Rafael Patrice Philip Rio Jonathan Anderson Wayne Ryan Christopher Anders Javier Nemanja Michael Nani Ashley Daniel Robin Fábio Thomas Darren Antonio Shinji Federico Alexander Wilfried Guillermo Marouane Larnell Jesse Michael Benjamin Adnan Blenkinsop.

'Daffy' for short. Smashing little girl.

**Manchester United**

| | |
|---|---|
| STEPNEY | 1 |
| NICHOLL | 2 |
| HOUSTON | 3 |
| McILROY | 4 |
| GREENHOFF (B) | 5 |
| BUCHAN | 6 |
| COPPELL | 7 |
| GREENHOFF (J) | 8 |
| PEARSON | 9 |
| MACARI | 10 |
| HILL | 11 |
| | S |

**Colours**
Shirts: Red    Shorts: White

**TEAM CH**

**MANCHESTER UNITED CRYSTA**

Red Shirts, White Shorts

1  GARY BAILEY
2  JIMMY NICHOLL
3  ARTHUR ALBISTON
4  KEVIN MORAN
5  GORDON McQUEEN
6  MARTIN BUCHAN (Captain)
7  STEVE COPPELL
8  GARRY BIRTLES
9  JOE JORDAN
10  MIKE DUXBURY
11  MIKE THOMAS
12

Referee: Mr. J. E. Bray (Hin
Mr. D. D. Crone (Liverpool)

53

## SIDEBOARD SUPERSTARS

Not content with taking full advantage of the so-called freedoms hard won in the Sixties – the right to kiss each other after scoring; the right to take off their shirts at the end of the Cup Final – footballers then went right ahead, like PE's very own version of Che Guevara, and helped to normalise the newly relaxed social strictures of the Seventies.

Long hair. Groovy birds. Fat pay packets. It was argued that "a little bit of everything in moderation" was the order of the day. Pop and crisps. Chicken in a basket. Eight-track cartridges in the deluxe coupe dashboard, and reclining seats. Foreign holidays contributing to a higher standard of living at the expense of declining moral standards.

The one area where it's generally agreed that our heroes overstepped the mark, leading the working classes into one new-fangled fashion too far, was in the adoption of giant triangular sideboards.

## THE TESTIMONIAL MATCH

When was the last time you went along to pay your respects to a great old servant of your club, putting up with the prospect of a meaningless friendly against big local rivals – it's never quite the same, on their days off – in order to chip in to the loyal clubman's retirement nest egg as he looked forward to living in temporarily reduced circumstances and having to get a proper job? Eh?

There's no such thing as a testimonial match any more. Lining the pockets of a multi-millionaire with the proceeds of a kickaround against a team with the suffix 'XI' doesn't count. The vital elements of long service, need, mutual gratitude and respect are all absent.

## Long service, need, mutual gratitude and respect...

Did You Know? After 14 years of loyal service, Mike Duxbury moved on in 1990 to Blackburn Rovers.

**Manchester United**
Gordon Hill

| | |
|---|---|
| International Appearances | 5 |
| International Goals | 0 |
| League Appearances | 160 |
| League Goals | 49 |
| Height | 5'7" |

**Manchester United**
...rt Pearson

| | |
|---|---|
| International Appearances | 9 |
| International Goals | 5 |
| League Appearances | 251 |
| League Goals | 93 |
| Height | 5'9" |

**Manchester United**
Steve Coppell

| | |
|---|---|
| | 6 |
| | 33 |
| | 50 |
| | 295 |
| | 5'7½" |

**Manchester United**
Martin Buchan

| | |
|---|---|
| International Appearances | 27 |
| International Goals | 0 |
| League Appearances | 459 |
| League Goals | 12 |
| Height | 5'10" |

## TOP TRUMPS

Kids used to flip their cards at playground walls, either trying to get closest to the bricks or cover the oppo, and of course we jammed millions of pounds' worth of cards into the spokes of our bikes to get a groovily authentic engine noise.

Hence, Top Trumps were invented in the '70s to give card-owning a little more of a competitive dynamic:

Gordon Hill... challenge me on League Goals and you are going down in flames. Height, and he's all yours...

Martin Buchan... a whopping number of League Appearances, but a glass jaw when it comes to International Goals...

This head-to-head game-playing tradition was revived in the mid-'90s by Subbuteo Squads sets, and powers into the future with Shootout cards.

## WE ALL SCREAM FOR ICE CREAM

We're guessing the ice cream industry hasn't had a great time of it recently, given the drizzly nature of our rather rubbish summers (notlikewhenwewerekids). Well, maybe they should start giving football badges away with their ice cream, like they did in 1971. That would soon have us running to the end of the street every time we heard the chimes playing 'The Whistler and his Dog'.

Mister Softee issued their '1st Division Football League Club Badges' for the 1971-72 season, featuring the 22 top-flight clubs plus England and Wales... but not Scotland where, presumably, it's a bit chilly for ice cream and lollies.

Rarer editions of this set, which was issued for one more season, were branded 'Lord Neilson' and 'Tonibell'.

Was it just our dads that said: "You know when the chimes are going? That means they've run out of ice cream"?

## "Y'know when the chimes are going?

## That means they've run out of ice-cream."

## JOE MERCER'S GB SQUAD

Even back in the early Seventies, those corrupt jobsworths at FIFA were making noises about the home countries' historic standing as separate nations in international football (which we just happened to be pretty good at), while England chose to club together with our cousins from the Celtic fringes when it came to doing PE (which we always used to be pretty crap at) in the Olympics.

My, how we smirked when good old Cleveland Petroleum gave Man City boss Joe Mercer free rein to pick his fantasy GB squad, converting his wall picks into small but perfectly preformed plastic busts, in the classical tradition.

With the England side still ranked number two in the world behind Brazil (in our minds, at least) after the Mexico World Cup, it took barely any imagination at all to imagine a squad that included Charlton, Banks and Moore (England), Bremner and Johnstone (Scotland), Best and Jennings (Northern Ireland) and Ron Davies (Wales – just go with the flow, okay?) winning the next World Cup for fun.

In retrospect, it seems a bit of a shame we didn't do as FIFA suggested and thrash the blighters fair and square. Lord knows we had every chance when Mercer became caretaker England boss just three years later, in 1974.

# Just imagine. Charlton, Best and, er, Ron Davies
## in the same international team!

### GOAL HEROES AND COVER STARS

Modestly subtitled 'The World's Greatest Soccer Weekly', *Goal* launched on 16 August 1968, with a right posh do at the Savoy with dolly birds and everything. Well, it was the Sixties.

Its distinctive covers, with a bright yellow title on a red background and circular photo design, owed a nod to pop art, and they've stood the test of time, still looking fresh and bold to this day.

Between those glowing Technicolor covers was a good solid line-up of content, albeit on fairly cheap and rough paper prone to browning with age.

'Opinion' kicked things off: "There is no sitting on the fence with

# There is no sitting on the fence
## with Tommy Docherty...

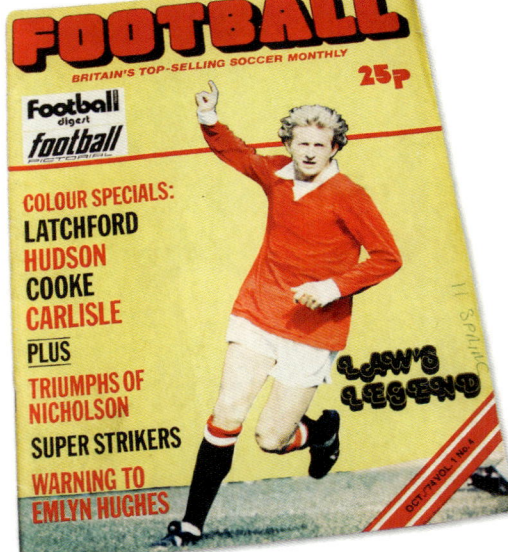

Tommy Docherty. You are either for him or very much against him."

'Bobby Charlton's Diary' was the star turn: "The withdrawal of clubs from the Warsaw Pact countries has given the current European Soccer competitions a very lean look…"

There were posters and features and 'Booter', a Beatle-haired footballer who starred in his own cartoon strip; and we even got to 'Meet the Girl behind the Man', Valerie McKinnon, "who passes the time when Ron of the Rangers is away by doing embroidery."

*Goal* perhaps became a victim of its own success because exactly a year later, encouraged by decent sales, IPC introduced a second football weekly… entitled *Shoot!*

Better still were the strip-packed comics such as *Roy of the Rovers* and *Tiger & Scorcher* and *Score & Roar* and *Scorcher & Score*. There was nothing again to ever touch that feeling of being blessed by the gods of the soccer pin-up and the cover star – though we'd have to say the cover appearance in *Tiger & Scorcher* was quite a biggie, if you were anything like 10 in 1975!

## FOCUS ON...

Back in 1975, United's Gerry Daly lay to shame every modern footballer who ever filled in a programme questionnaire namedropping property portfolios and £750 cocktails. Gerry didn't like bad referees or being relegated, but he did like signing for United, scampi and Switzerland. Give him a round of golf, a bit of Bee Gees and a Paul Newman film and he'd be a happy bunny.

### Chicken in a basket, gym teacher, Raquel Welch and Benny Hill.

And big Jock Stewart Houston tells it like it is. Or rather was.
**FAVOURITE FOOD:** Steak.
**FAVOURITE TV SHOWS:** Porridge and Kojak. **FAVOURITE SINGERS:** Andy Williams, Jose Feliciano.
**CAR:** Cortina GXL.
Stew hates smoking and injuries and was gutted about losing the League Cup semi-final to Norwich, but at least he's been to Greece.

Football's gain is civil engineering's loss, give him a round of golf with Tom Weiskopf, and possibly Sophia Loren carrying his clubs, and he'll be all ready for a tilt at the League title...

61

## MARSHALL CAVENDISH FOOTBALL HANDBOOK

Long before the age of YouTube or even the ubiquitous video recorder, there was no easy way to replay golden goals from the past – you just had to wait for them to be reshown on *Football Focus,* which could often prove quite a lengthy wait if you were waiting for a specific goal.

For most fans, there was some respite available thanks to the *Marshall Cavendish Football Handbook* ("in 873 weekly parts") and their smashing arrow-and-dot-laded diagrams which traced the build-up to a goal in stunning time-lapse ImaginationVision – complete with added slight confusion!

It is just like being there as Jimmy Greenhoff dumps Fulham out of the FA Cup. The Pearson twins outwit the Money twins out on the left wing before delivering a cross that flies over the diversionary runs of Macari, McIlroy and Thomas, before Greenhoff blasts a volley past Peyton which diverts in off the page fold into the back of the net...

### The Marshall Cavendish arrow-and-dot diagram shows every goal

### in stunning ImaginationVision,
### complete with added slight confusion!

**IMPROVE YOUR FOOTBALL**   Action replay... Action replay...

Action replay... Action replay... Action replay... Action replay...

## Jimmy's gem

'The two basics of target man play . . . in one move.'

**Graham Taylor's analysis**
A beautifully-taken goal, again showing the vulnerability of defences on the blind side. And note the way Pearson took those two passes from Buchan – with his back to goal so that his marker stood no chance of intercepting. Pearson laid off the first ball loyally, then, McIlroy would have been in possession and Pearson would have been looking for the short one-two or for the pass played into space behind the defence. But with the second pass, he turned and struck that excellent ball. The first-time lay-off and the quick turn – the two basics of target man play – illustrated in one move.

Manchester United had a long hard struggle to put Second Division Fulham out of the FA Cup this season. The London club held them to a 1-1 draw at Craven Cottage at the end of January, then took the replay by just 1-0 . . . thanks to a shot from Jimmy Greenhoff that was deflected off Fulham defender Tony Gale.

Yet, after weathering a series of convincing Fulham attacks throughout much of the first half, United had the inspiration of a spectacular goal from the same player to give them the lead in the first match at Fulham . . .

The move started when Richard Money gave away a free-kick just inside the Fulham half. Martin Buchan took the kick, knocking it forward and low to Stuart Pearson positioned to the left of centre in United's attack. Pearson laid the ball off to Sammy McIlroy, but the pass wasn't perfect . . . and McIlroy was forced to return the ball to Buchan.

Buchan patiently set about rebuilding the move with another pass forward to Pearson's feet. This time, though, the centre-forward, shielding the ball well from Money, turned inside and hit a long chip deep to the right of the Fulham penalty area.

The length of the ball caught out Fulham's defence. Despite Kevin Lock's despairing efforts, it fell beautifully for Jimmy Greenhoff's perfectly timed run . . .

Greenhoff's volley matched his timing, whipping past Gerry Peyton.

John Margerrison's header put Fulham back in the game but their hopes were dashed in the replay.

MARSHALL CAVENDISH

OTBALL
HANDBOOK

LAWRE
McME
Better
than

LEICE
CITY
Wag
Wal

Royle

MATCH
road

ODCOCK

In weekly parts
30p          THE MARSHALL CAVENDISH          PART 18

# FOOTBALL HANDBOOK

**JOE JORDAN**
Old Trafford
Investment

**DAVID PEACH**
Penalty King

**BOBBY GOULD**
Football
wanderer

**NORWICH CITY-BOND FOR GLORY**
**MICK CHANNON-'RUNNING AT DEFENCES'**

ATURES-MATCH ACTION-FACTS & FIGURES-PRIZE QUIZ.

In weekly parts
30p          THE MARSHALL CAVENDISH          PART 46

# FOOTBALL HANDBOOK

**MARTIN BUCHAN**
**Mystery man**

**DALGLISH v KEEGAN**
Who's better?

**FINAL FLING**
Last-gasp Cup
winner

**CHARLTON ATH.**
Youthful hopes

FEATURES-MATCH ACTION-FACTS & FIGURES-QUIZ

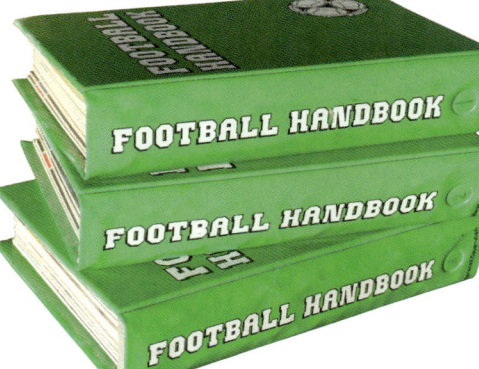

FOOTBALL HANDBOOK

FOOTBALL HANDBOOK

FOOTBALL HANDBOOK

Football Writers' Association

*

Annual Dinner

*and Presentation to the*

Footballer of the Year

*

*In the Chair:*
FRANK McGHEE, Esq.

CAFE ROYAL, London | Thursday 16th May, 1968

FOOTBALL ASSOCIATION CHALLENGE CUP
SEASON 1956-1957

Celebration
Dinner & Dance

*of the*
MANCHESTER UNITED
FOOTBALL CLUB

*

FINAL TIE
Manchester United
*versus*
Aston Villa

*
LANCASTER ROOM, SAVOY HOTEL, STRAND
4th MAY, 1957

MANCHESTER UNITED
FOOTBALL CLUB

*Football Association Challenge Cup · Season 1962-1963*

□

Semi-Final
Dinner and Dance

*Saturday, 27th April, 1963*

□

*Semi-Final Tie*

Manchester United
*versus*
Southampton

□

*Derby Suite, Midland Hotel, Manchester*

## POSH NOSH

Once the secret domain of heroic footballers, self-made chairmen and their respective blonde, understanding lady wives, the eBay explosion has opened up to us unworthy oiks a whole previously forbidden world of posh nosh at swanky Golden Age do's. That's right, with dicky-bows and long white gloves and *vol-aux-vents* and *hors d'oeuvres* and the whole cufflinks, cummerbund 'n' Corby trouser-press works.

Old-school menus aren't just collectable; it's brilliant to nose through and find out what the other half were nosebagging back in the day when the rest of us were restricted to Vesta paella ready-meals, volcanic crispy Findus pancakes, or Farley's rusks.

## "Bondy, steer clear of them volley vonts."

### Menu

| | |
|---|---|
| Amontillado Williams and Humbert | COCKTAIL DE MELON |
| Graves (White Bordeaux) | SUPRÊME DE SAUMON NEPTUNE |
| Volnay 1970 | CONTREFILET DE BOEUF POÊLE MODERNE HARICOTS VERTS AU BEURRE POMMES FONDANTES |
| | PÊCHE GLACÉE CARDINAL MIGNARDISES |

### Toast List

"THE QUEEN"

H.M. QUEEN ELIZABETH, DUKE OF LANCASTER

PROPOSED BY ... ... ... L. C. EDWARDS, ESQ.
(CHAIRMAN, MANCHESTER UNITED F.C.)

. . . .

"THE MANAGER, PLAYERS AND STAFF"

PROPOSED BY ... ... ... L. C. EDWARDS
(CHAIRMAN, MANCHESTER UNITED)

RESPONSE BY ... ... ... T. DOCHER
(MANAGE

Dancing to
THE RAY McVAY ORCHESTRA
and
LEE SCOTT DISCO

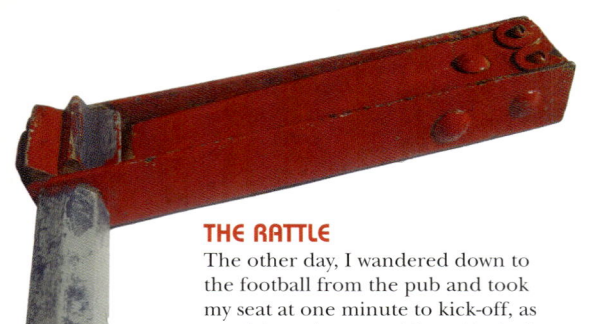

## THE RATTLE

The other day, I wandered down to the football from the pub and took my seat at one minute to kick-off, as usual, in order to avoid any kind of 'match-experience' shenanigans. Before I could sit down I had to extricate an object from the laggy band that secured it to my seat. It was a folded sheet of laminated card in club colours, called a 'clap-banner', which explained the horrendous noise that had assaulted my eardrums since I'd entered the ground.

Needless to say, I immediately took against it.

But when the frenzied clacking had died down a bit, I did at least concede that my age was partly to blame. For I once received a football rattle for my birthday that made a quite spectacular noise when I whizzed it round my head. So much so, that its use had to be rationed in the house.

One (young) person's great sound is another (old) person's unholy racket. That explains why the vuvuzela all but ruined the 2010 World Cup for me (along with England's risible performance), while some people thought they were such splendid fun, they started to take them to League games the following season.

The football rattle enjoyed its heyday in the 1960s, when they became as iconic a symbol of football-supporterdom as the scarf and bobble-hat.

They were nearly always homemade, employing the sort of engineering skills that only Dad could manage, and painted up in glossy club colours with the team name added as a finishing touch.

What modern day Health & Safety laws would have to say about spinning a fairly hefty chunk of wood at speed round your head in a tightly packed crowd, I don't know.

"You'll have someone's eye out," probably.

**What would Health & Safety laws have to say about spinning a chunk of wood around your head in a tightly packed crowd?**

## SPOT THE CLUBS

Back in the olden days of proper coppers with tit helmets and respect for your elders and attention spans hovering around the 30-minute mark even for kids with an Airfix-induced, as-yet-undiagnosed, as-yet-invented disorder, it was possible for any child to enjoy thousands of hours of fun with one of these fascinating Spot-the-Club quiz wheels, given away free with *Tiger* comic.

Enough of the sales claptrap, it was two circles of cardboard joined together with a rivet.

But hold on. Wheel the thingy around to Manchester United and – as if by magic –

you get to find out the name of the ground and the record attendance.

There's a badge, too. And the club colours. And the position achieved in the League last season. And the number of times the club has won the League (but only up to 1959, of course – plenty of time for improvement).

Let's all go on *Dragons' Den* and show those jumped-up twerps what for with one of these babies.

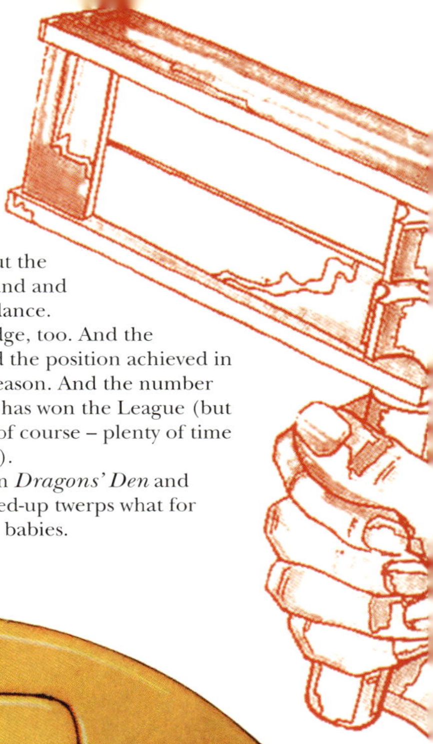

An early computer: or possibly think of it as a 'position last season' app…

SPOT the CLUBS
IN THIS FASCINATING FOOTBALL QUIZ-WHEEL

STUDY THE CLUES ON THIS CARD AND SEE IF YOU CAN NAME THE SOCCER CLUB WHICH USES THE BADGE SHOWN ABOVE

The Answer Appears on the Back Opposite this Number

SHIRT COLOURS

REDS

NICKNAME

POSITION IN LEAGUE LAST SEASON (1958-59)

LEAGUE CHAMPIONS

DIV. 1 (English)
DIV. 2
DIV. 3 (S-Southern N-Northern)
DIV. 4
DIV. 1 (Scottish)

HOME GROUND

OLD TRAFFORD
76,962

RECORD ATTENDANCE

CUP FINAL APPEARANCES

F.A. CUP RED
SCOTTISH CUP BLUE

F.A. CUP RED
SCOTTISH CUP BLUE

CUP WINNERS

Presented with TIGER

## SHOOT!

Allowed one comic a week, I'd already graduated from the entry-level *Beano* to *Scorcher*, but not until the summer of 1974, while immersed in the West Germany World Cup, did I consider myself man enough to step up to *Shoot!*

Eight pence was the price of admission, and I was soon in beyond the full-colour cover of Billy Bremner playing for Scotland against Brazil.

Now I could dive headlong into an article by Bobby Moore, chortle at the 'Football Funnies' chosen by United's Stewart Houston, and puzzle over the fiendish problems posed in 'You Are the Ref'; study up-close World Cup action featuring Australia, Scotland, Holland, Zaire, DDR and Yugoslavia; chortle at the 'Football Funnies'; 'Focus On' Paul Gilchrist of Southampton (Miscellaneous Likes: motor racing, oil painting, music), and realise there were people just like me all over the country, courtesy of the 'Goal Lines' letters page and 'Ask the Expert' readers' queries.

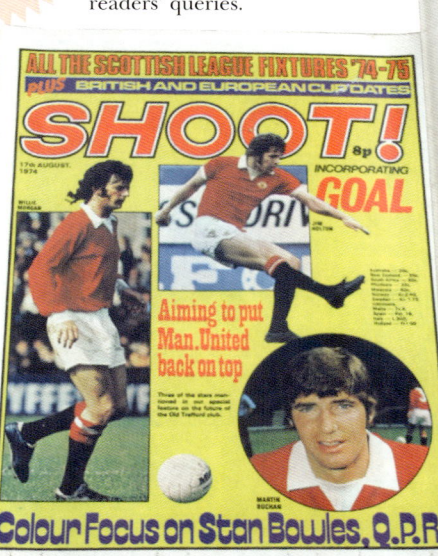

If I was lucky, there'd be a full-page star poster to add to my shrine, though this only happened once in a blue moon. It's difficult to explain now how a photo could be so prized, Blu-Tacked instantly up on your wall, but in the days of black newsprint papers and monochrome TV, the eight colour pages in *Shoot!* were like oases in a grey desert.

For five years my collection grew, filling several boxes, until 1979 when my head was finally turned by an attractive newcomer called *Match Weekly*.

I'm sorry I dropped you, *Shoot!*, and I'm even sorrier that we now live in a world where kids can't leg it down to the newsagents to eagerly pore over the latest issue.

## MOBIL BADGES

We love these silk badges given away with Mobil petrol in the early 80s.

When was the last time you visited a petrol station to be gifted a football collectable that you thought was worth holding on to for 30 years, fer chrissakes?

Made of pure 100% silk from a silkworm's bottom* and, as such, suitable for stitching on to your Sunday best anorak or parka?

Free with four gallons of 4-star.

The only downside, associated more with the free giveaway poster than the patches themselves, was the prospect of a giant Alan Hudson marauding down the country like King Kong or Godzilla or worse – Dribble of Destruction Horror Shock – stomping his way down the country and landing on your delightful suburban semi.

*probably not strictly true.*

70 Mobil

## UNITED CHOCOLATE BAR

Like many of the sweets of our childhood, the United bar is no longer produced, and is much missed. Crunchy honeycomb wrapped in chocolate, in three bite-sized pieces, available in Original and Orange... I'm actually salivating right now.

The TV advert from around 1980 reinforced the link with football with a cartoon cast singing along as they went to the match.

### "My name is Stan, I am a fan, And I'm delighted, to eat United."

"My name is Stan, I am a fan,
And I'm delighted, to eat United.
We are the fellas, the shouters and yellers,
And we never miss, this crunchy candy crisp.
I am the boss, and some things make me cross,
But even I'm delighted, to eat United."

Er, we take it these popular snacks were named after Manchester United, right? There aren't any other serious alternatives.

Hopefully McVities will bring back the jewel in the crown of our school packed lunches – though, admittedly, this could cause a little confusion as they are now owned by United Biscuits.

## QUIZ BALL

*Quiz Ball* was a staple of early-evening BBC Light Entertainment from 1966-72, originally reffed by David Vine before Stuart Hall took over en route to *It's A Knockout* stardom. The general knowledge quiz set club against club, each fielding teams of three stars plus one celebrity supporter.

There were four ways to score a goal, ranging from four easy questions to one decidedly difficult one, the routes to goal being illuminated in 100-Watt bulbs on a big board. The oppo could try to steal the 'ball' by answering the other team's questions – at the peril of giving away a goal.

The lasting legacy of the series was the phrase 'Route One', the direct but tricky path to glory; but the smarty-pants players and guests also stuck in the collective consciousness – young Alex Ferguson scored freely for Falkirk, Brian Labone for Everton and Gerry Queen for Palace. Bobby Charlton was such a star turn, he even got his picture on the book that accompanied the series, if not the lightbulb-sational boardgame!

Farmer-cum-quiz celeb Ted Moult (guesting for Nottingham Forest) was an all-time top-scorer, and Magnus Magnusson (Kilmarnock) showed some early quiz form. Among the countless other star guests were Percy Thrower (WBA, 1966), Harry Carpenter (Fulham, 1967), James Bolam (Sunderland, 1969), Peter Cook (Tottenham, 1970) and Jon Pertwee (Dunfermline, 1971).

Quiz night: Bobby Charlton and young Alex Ferguson were stars of the show.

FOR IAIN ????????

C
MU
M.U.F.C.

SOUVENIR
& LEISUREWEAR
SHOP
TELEPHONE
061 872 3398

CREDIT CARD
HOTLINE
061 848 8797

ClubCall
0898 121161

## MANCHESTER UNITED
### THE WORLD'S GREATEST FOOTBALL CLUB

EXCLUSIVELY SUPPLIED TO M.U.F.C. BY ☎ TEL: 061-859 5721

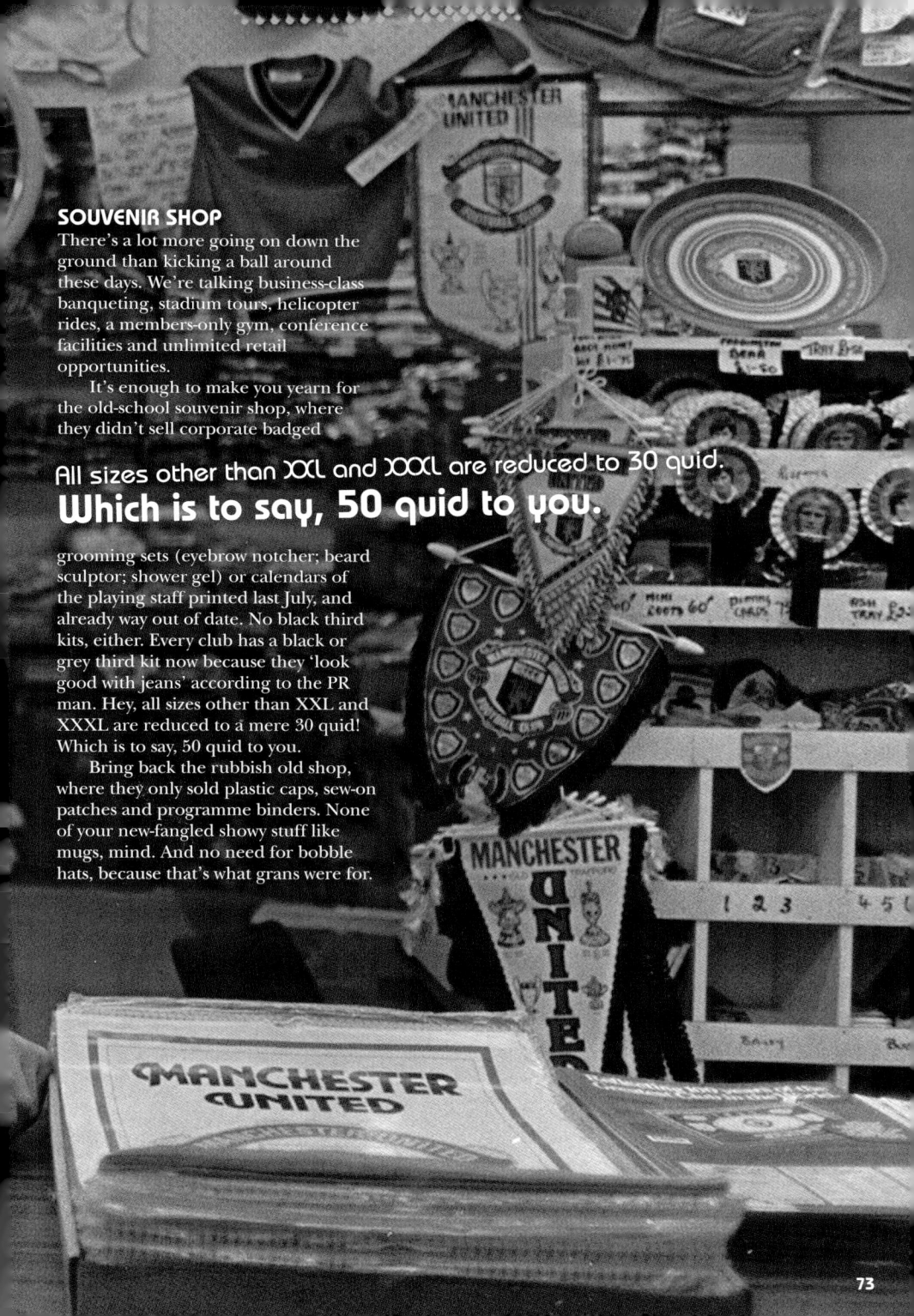

## SOUVENIR SHOP

There's a lot more going on down the ground than kicking a ball around these days. We're talking business-class banqueting, stadium tours, helicopter rides, a members-only gym, conference facilities and unlimited retail opportunities.

It's enough to make you yearn for the old-school souvenir shop, where they didn't sell corporate badged

**All sizes other than XXL and XXXL are reduced to 30 quid. Which is to say, 50 quid to you.**

grooming sets (eyebrow notcher; beard sculptor; shower gel) or calendars of the playing staff printed last July, and already way out of date. No black third kits, either. Every club has a black or grey third kit now because they 'look good with jeans' according to the PR man. Hey, all sizes other than XXL and XXXL are reduced to a mere 30 quid! Which is to say, 50 quid to you.

Bring back the rubbish old shop, where they only sold plastic caps, sew-on patches and programme binders. None of your new-fangled showy stuff like mugs, mind. And no need for bobble hats, because that's what grans were for.

## TOPICAL TIMES

Strictly speaking, the *Topical Times* wasn't the most topical of newspapers in the Sixties and Seventies, having gone under in the Forties... but that didn't stop them producing annual football books right into the new millennium.

Always a welcome addition to a Christmas morning pillowcase, the presentation was lively in design, picture led, and featured a seemingly never-ending supply of different fonts.

Apart from the punchy tabloid-style headlines and clippy titbits, 'Their Other Team' was always a favourite staple spread, enabling us junior peeping Toms to keep tabs on what star players, their wives and kids were getting up to, relaxing at home in suburbia. Here were huge rounded collars; kids in polo necks; flock wallpaper that has allegedly come back into fashion; velour sofas in a greeny-browny-goldy colour that no longer exists; and the sort of brick feature fireplace you could only attempt if you had a few quid.

And, best of all, there were glossy colour pages that showed up every stitch of the old cotton shirts and ragged badges. And Manchester United on the cover, in the particularly Golden Years...

There were glossy colour pages that showed up every stitch of the old cotton shirts and ragged badges **and Man U on the cover, in the particularly Golden Years...**

## FA CUP CENTENARY COINS

Good old Esso. Every year, they brought out something great for us to collect, and 1972 was no different. The handsome 'FA Cup Centenary 1872-1972' brochure and coin collection was such a must-have item for every young boy that silence must surely have descended on the forecourts of Shell garages while the offer was on, with tumbleweed blowing around between deserted BP, Jet and Cleveland pumps.

There were 30 of these "silver-bright, superbly-minted Centenary Coins" to collect, one per visit to the Esso station, the album to house them in representing a modest Dad Tax of 15p.

Swap yer 29 coins – from the Wanderers and Blackburn Olympic to the big gold-coloured centrepiece coin minted later, a week after Leeds United's Wembley victory over Arsenal – all for one United coin commemorating those three proud Saturday afternoons back in 1909, 1948 and 1963. United's greatest FA Cup moments in history... to date.

# United's greatest FA Cup moments in history **to date.**

The story of the F.A. Cup Winners 1872-1972

F.A. CUP CENTENARY MEDALS 1872-1972

F.A. CUP WINNERS 1972

Arsenal · Aston Villa · Barnsley · Blackburn Rovers · Blackpool · Bolton Wanderers
Bradford City · Burnley · Bury · Cardiff City · Charlton Athletic · Chelsea
Derby County · Everton · Huddersfield Town · Liverpool · Manchester City · Manchester United
Newcastle United · Notts. County · Nottingham Forest · Portsmouth · Preston North End · Sheffield United
Wednesday · Sunderland · Tottenham Hotspur · West Bromwich Albion · West Ham United · Wolverhampton Wanderers

1
MANCHESTER U.
£15,000

Wembley here we
come! Three cards from
Ariel's popular FA Cup
board game.

Manchester United

MANCHESTER UNITED

SIMON STEWART

## KIDS POSING IN YOUR KIT

Here's little Simon Stewart posing in his swanky Continental-style white-with-black-stripe Admiral replica kit, garnering jealous looks all over sunny Portsmouth and looking for all the world like little Stevie Coppell.

It was a magic feeling, pulling on your team's shirt, shorts and socks. And then looking down at the badge. It was the kind of occasion that warranted pestering your mother to get the camera out.

"Mam, take it now. Take it while I'm doing this..."

Waiting impatiently between shots while she 'wound it on'.

## "Mam, quick, take it now. Take it while I'm doing this..."

Standing up with your arms folded, with one foot on the ball, or crouched down holding the ball with splayed out fingers... it wasn't your mam anymore, it was the official club photographer on photocall day, taking the photo that would appear in *Shoot!* or on a football card. Or else you were your club's brand new signing, and a gaggle of snappers from the dailies were crowded round you.

"I think I've come to the end of the film," says Mam as her winder-onner meets resistance.

"Take it anyway!"...

## SCOTTISH SUPERSTARS

Up until twenty years ago, every great First Division team in football history had included at least one Scot, usually the brains of the operation – the ball player, the stopper who could do more than just stop, or the unstoppable goalscorer.

United had a brilliant boss in Busby, and a European Footballer of the Year in Law, the most insistent and inventive goalscorer of all time. Next came Joe

major championship this century; even back in the Home Internationals, so we can do our level best to beat their pasty bottoms.

Choose fitba.

MARTIN BUCHAN

## United had a brilliant boss in Busby,
## and a European Footballer of the Year in Law.

Jordan, Gordon McQueen and Gordon Strachan: so quake in your boots. And then there was Alex Ferguson – and he'd never have got away with saying he just wanted to "knock Liverpool off their ****ing perch" upon his arrival from Aberdeen, if he hadn't been Scottish.

For the twelve years between the World Cups of 1970 and 1982, all of Britain took a special interest in the Scots as, time and time again, England failed to take the baby steps up on the world stage. With so many familiar, gifted players, they became everyone's second team. Well, who were we supposed to support? Iran?

The Scots heap derision on our temporary switching of allegiances thirty years ago. In the same position, they now wear 'Anyone But England' T-shirts, and we wouldn't want it any other way. But how sweet it would be to see Scotland return to dynasty-building form and make their first

# UNITED REVIEW

### MANCHESTER UNITED FOOTBALL CLUB

6th ROUND
(REPLAY)
CHESTER UNITED
v.
STON
RTH END
ck-off 7-45 pm

WEDNESDAY
30th March

**6**d.

NUMBER 23

1965-66 SEASON

OFFICIAL PROGRAMME

## THE F.A. CUP

Here is a photograph of the F.A. Cup – actually the third to be competed for in the history of the competition. It was made originally by a Bradford firm in 1911 and coincidentally was first won by Bradford City! Its cost in those days was 50 gns. but it is insured for considerably more today. The first F.A. Cup was stolen in 1895 and the second was presented to Lord Kinnaird in 1910 to mark 21 years service as President of the Football Association.

Photograph from the Manchester Evening News Library.

# UNITED REVIEW

Winners of the European Champion Clubs Cup Competition 1968
**SEASON 1968·1969 · No 31**

THE OFFICIAL PROGRAMME OF MANCHESTER UNITED FOOTBALL CLUB LIM

## MANCHESTER UNITED
VERSUS
## LEICESTER CITY

AY 17th

West Ha
22nd April 1978 Kick-off

d by

NK
ROX

much more than
copier company

price 12p

78

MANCHESTER UNK
VERSUS
LEICESTER (

MANCHESTER UNITED
FOOTBALL CLUB

# UNITED REVIEW

The official programme of Manchester United Football Club Ltd
**NOVEMBER 20th 1971 · KICK OFF 3.00 p.m.**

The official programme of Manchester United Football Club Ltd

**MANCHESTER UNITED**
versus
**LEICESTER CITY**

MANCHESTER UNITED FOOTBALL CLUB

**UNITED REVIEW**

No. 3
5p

INSIDE!
PROFESSIONAL
PLAYING STAFF

AUGUST 23rd 1972 · KICK OFF 7.30 p.m.

**WELCOME T**
**OLD TRAFFOR**

Manchester United v Middlesbrough
27th March, 1976
Kick-off 3.00 p.m.

**UNITED**
**REVIEW**

10p

**MANCHESTER**
**UNITED REVIEW**

**WELCOME TO**
**OLD TRAFFORD**

Manchester
United    v. Liverpool
16th February 1977    Kick off 7.30 p.m.

Programme N
The Official Progr
of Manchester U
Football Club Ltd.

12p

**Manchester**
**United**
versus BOLTON WANDERERS

Programme No.22
11th
April 1979
Kick-off
7.30 p.m.

15p

MANCHESTER UNITED
FOOTBALL CLUB

STANDS F G H J K

& STRETFORD COVERED PADDOCK

SOUVENIR

79

**UNITED REVIEW**

Price 20p

FOOTBALL LEAGUE DIVISION ONE
1980-1981

VOTED PROGRAMME OF THE YEAR BY THE BRITISH PROGRAMME CLUB

MANCHESTER UNITED v CRYSTAL PALACE
Saturday, 4th April 1981
Kick-off 3.00 p.m.

**UNITED RE**

MANCHESTER UNITED FOOTBALL CLUB

CANON LEAGUE DIVISION ONE
United v Watford
Kick-off 3.00 pm

1983-84 SEASON

OFFICIAL

Sponsored by SHARP ELECTRONICS

PROGR

UNITED v A
United go d

**UNITED**

M
FOC

BARCLAYS LEAGUE DIVISION ONE
United v Norwich City

Kick-off 3.00 pm

OFFICIAL

Sponsored by SHARP

## PROGRAMMED TO EXPLODE

Even we are sometimes known to grudgingly admit that modern football has got something right, so it is good to see that ancient Old Trafford tradition – the player and supporter handshake masthead – return to its rightful place front and centre of the programme.

Times have changed somewhat since the days when the fan wore a grey suit and trilby and the background ball was made of brown leather. And obviously the player's kit now requires an annual update.

This metaphor for what the programme should stand for was first abandoned in 1967-68, obviously considered a bit old hat for the groovy times. Graphic images of an increasingly impressive Old Trafford, along with some rock n roll fonts were

UNITED FOOTBALL CLUB

**SHARP** ELECTRONICS (UK) LTD

Saturday
27th April 1985

**35p**

Volume 46, No. 31

1984-85
SEASON PROGRAMME

OFFICIAL

UNITED v LIVERPOOL, Goodison Park 13th April. United players join Bryan Robson to celebrate our opening
skipper was later to credit it to Mark Hughes after seeing an 'action replay' of his shot.

**TED REVIEW**

MANCHESTER
UNITED
FOOTBALL CLUB

Saturday
7th December 1985

**40p**

Volume 47, No. 15

1985-86
SEASON PROGRAMME

ARP ELECTRONICS (UK) LTD

UNITED v WATFORD, 30th November. Soon after substituting for the injured Kevin Moran, Alan Brazil
scored the goal that was to put United in front. The visitors replying with an equaliser in the 90th minute.

REVIEW

CLUB

Saturday
17th October 1987

**50p**

Volume 49, No. 7

PROGRAMME

CTRONICS (UK) LTD

WEDNESDAY
Hillsborough

used up to the late 70s. Then colour
photos of recent games were used, just
like every other club at the time.

Then, for the 1981-82 season the
masthead was revived – fans in fetching
brown jumper and beige Farahs, player
in Adidas.

This idea, with various tweaks in the
name of clothing fashion and graphic
trends, lasted right up to the end of the
2001-02 season before the introduction
of the square shaped
mega-prog.

After a decade's absence the
handshake returned in 2010-11, though
somewhat marginalised on the right
hand side, before 2013-14 saw it restored
to its old place.

Far from interrupted, but still the
longest handshake in football history.

## MATCH WEEKLY

*Match Weekly* was launched on 6 September 1979, three weeks into the 1979-80 season, by Peterborough-based publishers EMAP. Editor Melvyn Bagnall declared: "Our object is simple... to improve on anything currently available." By which, of course, he meant *Shoot!*, which had enjoyed a relatively unopposed decade of market dominance.

What immediately grabbed this 13-year-old about the newcomer on the newsagent's shelf was the way it was printed right to the edge, making *Shoot*'s white borders suddenly look very passé.

Inside there was a stellar line-up of writers: Keegan, Clough, Ardiles, Coppell, Atkinson and Jimmy Hill.

Sparky: Manchester United, 1980-86 and 1988-95. And let's just forget 2008-09.

## Magazine covers

**MATCH weekly** — Saturday June 4 1983 28p

**GLORY, GLORY, MAN UNITED!**

THE LIVERPOOL YEARS — NEW SERIES
KEEGAN v DALGLISH: THE VERDICT
...LUMP — THE MAINE ROAD FACTS

**match weekly IN COLOUR** — Saturday July 25 1981 30p

Super
STEVE
PERRYMAN
...t poster
...US
...NDERSON
...NSCOW
...UTCHISON
...RINER

*inside* ALAN BALL... EMLYN HUGHES
...TOMMY BURNS...STAN BOWLES

# A stellar line-up of writers:
# Atkinson, Coppell... Jimmy Hill.

Instead of 'Focus On' there was 'Match Makers', with loads more questions. There were more colour pages, and 'Match Facts' with marks out of ten for every player in every game. And, just in case anyone was still dithering about parting with their 25p, there was a free Transimage sticker album thrown into the mix.

After a five-year love affair with *Shoot!*, I jumped ship to *Match* in an instant. And I wasn't the only one. After a long battle, *Match* eventually won out with a higher circulation.

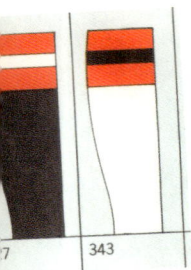

343

7

### ADMIRAL

In the mid-1970s, the first manufacturers' logos were beginning to appear on football shirts, and it was the Leicester-based Admiral company who seized on the possibilities of commercialising strips. Bert Patrick, chairman of Cook & Hurst, had formed an idea born out of England's 1966 World Cup win and the advent of colour TV. If kits could be uniquely designed and visibly branded then contracts with clubs could be signed, and the parents of young football fans would have to buy Admiral kit rather than the plain, generic shirts currently available.

Don Revie's fondness for making a bit of brass to supplement his salary at Leeds was a big help in the early days, as he cut a £16K personal deal for Admiral to clothe England as soon as he landed the national job. And Manchester United and many

The groundbreaking, bright, sexy and dare we say it **groovy United threads** supplied by Admiral between 1976 and 1980.

934 MANCHESTER UNITED ALL SIZES

MANCHESTER UNITED AWAY SIZES

other clubs quickly followed suit.

To the horror of a nation's dads and the delight of the kids Admiral's jaunty designs spread like wildfire from Southampton to Aberdeen. United's away kit with three black vertical stripes and all sorts of trimmings remains a big favourite to this day.

In every copy of *Shoot!* there would be a full-page colour advert showing their latest designs; you could send off for their posters displaying all the kits; and there was even an Admiral Annual which showed only photos of games in which both sides wore the approved brand.

They were never a big company, however, so inevitably Adidas, Umbro and Le Coq Sportif caught up with, and overtook, the pioneering Admiral; but for a few glorious years at the end of the Seventies, Admiral was boss.

# Admiral TOP TEAMS

## MANCHESTER UNIT[ED]

Manchester United first wore Admiral ki[t]
beginning of their successful 1975/76 se[ason]
when the Red Devils bounced back int[o the]
first division. However, a new away s[trip,]
white with black and red trimmings a[round the]
neck and sleeve and black and white [ ]
stripes - really caught the eye of the [ ]
public who were to be so impresse[d by]
United's performance throughou[t the]
season.

The Cup Final at Wembley also [saw]
the introduction of a new track[suit]
which was styled on the away s[trip]
with white jacket and black trou[sers.]

## Admiral

### Have you change[d]
### into Admiral kit y[et?]

## United, you're looking good.

**Admiral Sportswear**
AVAILABLE FROM YOUR LOCAL SPORTS SHOP

85

## MUD

Mud used to be as central to the game of football as the ball itself. Placed on a freshly repainted centre-spot. By the Man in the Middle. At Central Park, Cowdenbeath...

Mud was synonymous with football, a crucial factor in its tactics, skills and disciplines. We played in mud and paid to watch better players struggle to overcome mud – their control, balance and ability to dive and tackle like demons all dependent on mud.

From the terraces, football smelled of mud. On big occasions, we sneaked on to the pitch and helped ourselves to hallowed clumps of mud.

Mud was what George Best threw at the ref in a Northern Ireland v Scotland match to earn himself a six-week ban, and mud was what he skipped over to score six goals in a game at Northampton.

On Saturday morning, we picked
the dried, inverted mudprint out of
our studs – a perfect, stud-holed fossil
record of last weekend's 6-0 defeat –
tossed it on the changing-room floor
and started all over again, temporarily
clean and full of hope for what the mud
might bring.

## BARTHOLOMEW MAP

In the early 1970s John Bartholomew & Son produced the 'Football History Map of England and Wales' as part of their series of pictorial and historical maps… Created by John Carvosso, the stylised square kits and re-rendered club crests gave it an iconic look that remains hugely popular among football supporters. In the years just before more intricate kit designs arrived this was all that was required.

119

72

106

87
**MANCHESTER UNITED**
founded 1885
Old Trafford

It was a best seller among maps which gave a generation of football fans a solid foundation in geography… well, we knew where the towns with football clubs were, at least.

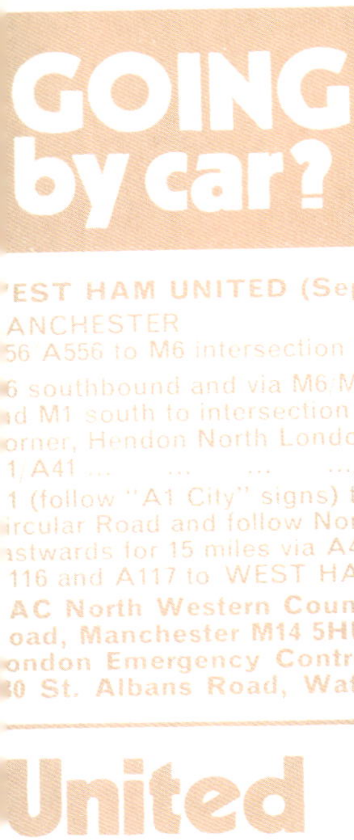

# GOING by car?

NW N NE
W E
SW S SE

'EST HAM UNITED (September 2nd).
ANCHESTER
56 A556 to M6 intersection 19 at Tabley     ... 15 miles
6 southbound and via M6/M1 Midlands link
d M1 south to intersection 2, Five Ways
orner, Hendon North London, junction with
1, A41 ...     ...     ...     ...
1 (follow "A1 City" signs)
rcular Road and follow Nor
stwards for 15 miles via A4
116 and A117 to WEST HA

AC North Western Count
oad, Manchester M14 5HU
ondon Emergency Contro
0 St. Albans Road, Watf

## United

## MOTORING AWAY

The sheer naivety of this waving Man U rosette whisks you back to a time when motoring away was a real expedition – an adventure and a treat on the A-roads of England when they were cluttered with transport caffs. Steering sensibly in your string-sided driving gloves, you were guided by the *AA Book of the Road*, stewed cuppas on glass-top tables – and, eventually, the beckoning of floodlight pylons.

It's time to rediscover the joys of a tactical teamtalk with salt and pepper pots in a giant puddle-strewn layby.

One of the most enjoyable elements of the away trip is the camaraderie shared with fellow supporters, so be sure to make yourself instantly

### Back to a time when motoring away used to be a real expedition.

identifiable as a motorised football fan. Car coats and bobble-hat combos are tops in this respect, with a silk or knitted scarf in club colours recommended to be trapped flapping from your rear windows or quarterlights. Knights of the road one and all, any fan on four wheels will be happy to assist a struggling fellow traveller with water for a boiling radiator or a pair of stockings for a make-do-and-mend fan belt.

So pack up your primus stove for a brew on a grass verge, stream your knitted scarf out of the back window, and set your waving-hand novelty boinging in the back window.

Happy motoring to one and all!

*Ladeez and gennulmen:*
*A big hand for*
*Manchester United.*

MAN. UNITED

On the record label (top right):

YOUNG BLOOD

J. J. K. R.
MUSIC

YB 1010 A
℗ 1970

ALL RIGHTS OF THE MANUFACTURER AND OF THE OWNER OF THE RECORDED WORK RESERVED · UNAUTHORISED PUBLIC PERFORMANCE BROAD...

YB 1
45-1

**BELFAST BOY**
(from B.B.C. Documentary "World of Georgia Best")
(Harris—Colton—Smith)
**DON FARDON**
Arranger: Johnny Harris / Tony Colton
Producer: Johnny Harris /
Tony Colton

## MADCHESTER

What's the finest United-related choon ever captured on record? One thing's for sure, it isn't 'Onward Sexton's Soldiers' by the Man U First-Team Squad of 1979.

Maybe 'Stars' by United fan Mick Hucknall and Simply Red? Howsabout 'I Wanna Be Adored' by big Reds fans the Stone Roses? Or could it be 'True Faith' or 'World in Motion' by lifelong Unitedites New Order?

Or how about 'It's Nice to be Out in the Morning' by local popsters Herman's Hermits? That's a proper groover, that is: "United's ground where the champions score / A hundred goals to the Reds stand's roar / United's ground where the champions score / Bobby Charlton, Best and Law…"

Or it could be 'Belfast Boy' by Don Fardon: "You move like a downtown dancer /

With your hair hung down like a mane / And your feet playing tricks like a juggler /

As you weave to the sound of your name…"

George Best speaks

George Best - his message
With compliments of

Tyne Tex

compliments of

*"I suppose you would say trendy, but not in a way-out sort of way": George on 45, flogging his Tyne Tex jackets and anoraks.*

GLORY, GLORY, MAN UNITED

UNITED, MANCHESTER UNITED
THE MANCHESTER UNITED FOOTBALL TEAM

# 'True Faith'. 'Stars'. 'I Wanna Be Adored'...
## 'Onward Sexton's Soldiers'

Back in 1970 Bobby Charlton was at the top of the charts on England's 'Back Home' 45. Right from the big cha-cha cha-cha-cha intro, the horn-driven romp epitomises everything a World Cup song should be. Jeff Astle's finest moment leading the line for England stirs and bonds: while we're watching Bobby and co on the box, they're thinking about us, the folks back home. Forget your arsey postmodern irony: jut your chin and fight back the tears.

Bryan Robson and Steve Coppell were heavily involved as front men and cage dancers on the 1982 England World Cup Squad's 'This Time (We'll Get It Right)'. When it comes to that particular brand of patriotic heroism best exemplified by a choir of thirty non-singers clenching their buttocks, it's England's last great moment. It's the very beginning of the record that does it – not the folkie opening bars with the twiddly accordion or the circus drum lead-in, but the squad's balled fist of a mission statement: "We're on our way / We are Ron's twenty-two..."

Sadly, 1986 proved a damp squib with 'We've Got the Whole World at Our Feet'. With the pack nervously following Captain Marvel's homicidally patriotic lead, no doubt anticipating

a disastrous sprained tonsil, the song casually ripped off 'We Got the Whole World In Our Hands' by Paper Lace & Nottingham Forest – but this slack, sad effort made Cloughie's mob seem like soulful poets. The end of an era.

SUN SOCCERSTAMP

ENGLAND STAR PLAYERS

Manchester United
Nobby Stiles

FOOTBALL
*Colour all your favourite teams
**Two Great Competitions inside

A. CAVERSHAM

THE Sun
ENCY
& SOCC
ALBUM

FLAGS OF WORLD
NATIONS · ENGLAN

CUP

1st DIVISI
TEAM

## COLOUR ME BAD

Back in the day, I spent many hours scribbling away at the coarse paper of *Caversham's Football Colouring Book,* tongue lolling out to one side in sheer concentration, transforming the black outlines into lifelike and vibrant living colour. As you can see, I hardly ever went over the lines and had an almost eerie command of every stroke.

Manchester United's crimson, West Ham's brilliant puce and blue, Hull's glowing amber and Liverpool's scarlet (achieved by pressing a bit harder than the crimson) were all portrayed to perfection under my artistic spell, now brought to life before your very eyes in a spectral rhapsody.

Just one tiny problem to prick my dreamlike bubble: "WHO'S GOT FELT PEN ON THE CARPET?!"

## SUN SOCCERSTAMPS

Long before the hilarious horrors of Sun Soccercards emerged at the end of the Seventies, *The Sun* newspaper bunged out a set of well-designed and sensitively considered collectables on an unexpected philatelic theme.

What we're trying to say is... they were stamps.

Sun Soccerstamps, to be precise. The equal best thing to happen in 1971, along with those Esso badges; but definitely more highbrow!

SUN SOCCERSTAMP
410
NORTHERN IRELAND STAR PLAYERS
George Best
Manchester United

Bobby Charlton
482
SUPERSTAR
SUN SOCCERSTAMP

SUN SOCCERSTAMP
252
Denis Law
Manchester United
SCOTLAND STAR PLAYERS

SUN SOCCERSTAMP
SUPERSTAR
Bobby Charlton
485

FOOTBALL
CLOPAEDIA
STAMP
1-72
WITH ALL THE FIXTURES FOR THE 1971-72 SEASON
10p

SUN SOCCERSTAMP
SUPERSTAR
George Best
480

1st DIVISION CLUB CRESTS
Manchester United
MANCHESTER UNITED FOOTBALL CLUB
13

When United used to take 10,000 away fans,

there wasn't always room in the ground for everyone who's made the trip...

**ham City**
unded 1875.
893, 1921, 48, 55.
L Cup 1963.
Royal blue

**Birmingham City**
Founded 1875.
Div 1 1893, 1921, 48, 55.
FL Cup 1963.
Royal blue

**Blackburn Rovers**
Founded 1874.
Div 1 1912, 14.
Div 2 1939. FA Cup 1884.
85, 86, 90, 91, 1928.
Blue & white

**Blackpool**
Founded 1887.
Div 2 1930.
Div 1 runners-up 1956.
FA Cup 1953.
Tangerine & white

**Bolton Wanderers**
Founded 1874.
Div 2 1909.
FA Cup 1923, 26, 29, 58.
All white

**Bradford City**
Founded 1903.
Div 2 1908.
Div 3 (N) 1929.
FA Cup 1911.
Claret & amber

**Brighton & Hove Albion**
Founded 1900.
Div 3 (S) 1958.
Div 4 1965.
Blue & white

**Bristol City**
Founded 1894.
Div 3 (S) 1955.
Div 4 1965.
All red

**Bristol Rovers**
Founded 1883.
Div 3 (S) 1953.
Sky blue & white

**Barnsley**
Founded 1887.
Div 3 (N) 1934, 39, 55.
Div 3 1966.
English 1947
Claret, blue &

**rton**
**Everton**
ed 1878. Div 1 1891,
28, 32, 39, 63, 70.
Div 2 1931.
Cup 1906, 33, 66.
Blue & white

**Falkirk**
Founded 1876.
Sc Div 2 1936, 70.
Sc Cup 1913, 57.
Navy blue & white

# Football Club Badges

The Esso collection of 76 famous football club badges.
When you've completed this card you'll have a permanent record of the most famous
football clubs in England, Northern Ireland, Scotland and Wales represented
by their unique and colourful insignias. Keep it safe – you will own what may become
a valuable collector's item.

EC European Cup. ECWC European Cup Winners' Cup. EFC European Fairs Cup. FL Football League. Sc Scottish. SLC Scottish League Cup

**STER CITY**
**Manchester City**
ded 1894. Div 1 1937.
Div 2 1899, 1903, 10.
47, 66. FA Cup 1904.
56, 69. FL Cup 1970.
VC 1970. Blue & white

**Manchester United**
Founded 1878. Div 1 1908,
11, 52, 56, 57, 65, 67.
Div 2 1936. FA Cup 1909,
48, 63. EC 1968.
Red & white

**FIELD UNITED**
**Sheffield United**
Founded 1889.
Div 1 1898.
Div 2 1953.
FA Cup 1899, 1902, 15, 25.
Red, white & black

**Sheffield Wednesday**
Founded 1867. Div 1 1903,
04, 29, 30. Div 2 1900.
26, 52, 56, 59.
FA Cup 1896, 1907, 35.
Blue & white

**Shrewsbury Town**
Founded 1886.
Elected to League 1950.
Welsh Cup twice.
All blue

**Southampton**
Founded 1885.
Div 3 (S) 1922.
Div 3 1960.
Red, white & black

**Stoke City**
Founded 1863.
Div 2 1933, 63.
Div 3 (N) 1927.
Red & white

**Sunderland**
Founded 1875.
Div 1 1892, 93, 95,
1902, 13, 36.
FA Cup 1937.
Red & white

**Swansea City**
Founded 1911.
Welsh Cup 5 times.
Div 3 (S) 1925, 49.
White & black

**Swindon Town**
Founded 1881.
FL Cup 1969.
Div 3 runners-up
Red & white

## ESSO CLUB BADGES

What was your favourite
set of freebies given
away with petrol back
in the day? Nowadays,
it's hard to imagine
anything but a form
for a mortgage being
handed out by the
garage man, as it costs the
same now to fill your tank as
it did to buy your first car. But
this hasn't always been the case.

While the likes of Texaco and Shell
seemed obsessed with making huge
amounts of money by flogging us the

world's
overflowing natural
resources, back in 1971 good
old Esso were only concerned
with making sure that small
boys had plenty of great
football stuff to collect.
First, there were
World Cup coins,
then 'Squelchers',
a series of little
booklets so named
because the info
contained in them
was enough to squelch
any argument. There
were FA Cup Winners
coins, and the Top Team
Collection of Photo-Discs built a
squad of Britain's best players... but best
of all was surely the literally titled 'Esso
Collection of Football Club Badges'.

## WEMBLEY METTOY BESTIE

Most of the experiences and objects within these covers relate to things that we knew first-hand or were at least aware of back in the day. But this Wembley Mettoy figure... never owned one, never even heard of them until recently. And yet it still manages to stir a certain something within my ten-year-old self which lurks just under the surface of my skin. I loved models, I loved football, I would *really* have loved one of these.

The English language doesn't seem to have a word for feelings of nostalgia for something you never knew. The Germans have *sehnsucht* (thoughts about facets of life that are unfinished or imperfect, paired with a yearning for ideal alternative experiences), while Portuguese has *saudade* (related to thinking back on situations

Esso even provided a splendid fold-out presentation card to stick them in and, frankly, if there was anything more exciting happening in 1971, we can't remember it now. It wasn't just the 20p blackmail job for the 'Starter Pack' of 26 otherwise unobtainable badges that made the heart beat faster. The little foil badges were irresistible. Everyone was collecting them. Have you still got yours?

of privation due to the absence of someone or something).

Somewhere in an alternative universe, this little Georgie would have been taken down from my shelf every week for a carpet-level kickaround with Billy Bremner, Charlie George, Martin Chivers and Bobby Moore – probably in slow-motion, with breathy crowd noise effects.

I would get one from eBay, as a sort of nostalgia experiment, but a Mettoy Best with no box or name label is going for £26.99... *saudade*, indeed.

## SUMMER SCHOOL TRAINING

The start of the school hols meant just one thing back in the day – nearly time for Butlin's Soccer Coaching! In the week leading up to the annual family sojourn, I would be meticulous that my kit was in optimum condition. Boots would be smothered in fresh dubbin, and both Manchester United kits (home and away in the classic '70s Admiral design) would be washed and pressed to perfection by my mum.

With the Hillman Avenger packed to the gills with essentials for a week's self-catering, we'd eventually roll into

## Butlins Soccer Coaching
# A 1970'S Summer Holiday
## Steve Mitchell is on a Hi-De-Hi...

Man U fan Steve Mitchell: so very chuffed to meet coach Gary Owen of Man City.

Pwllheli to meet up with a Redcoat and get hold of the week's programming. Suddenly it was there in front of me – Monday 10.00am Soccer Coaching with (insert name here) with the rest of the week's times to be confirmed. You always knew that at some point during the week a top-flight footballer would

arrive to assist in the coaching, but 1977 is the year that sticks out in my mind.

Our coach that year was a bronzed Adonis called Barry and it was also the year we took my best mate Paul along with us. It had been a magical year, United had beaten Liverpool in the Silver Jubilee Cup Final and I had recently been presented with some floodlights for my Subbuteo set, but life was to take a dramatic turn. Barry was a god to me and Paul – he was handsome, looked immaculate in his Adidas training kit and earned his living doing what we loved. But he was soon to turn Judas when on the second day of coaching he announced to our group that the two special guests later that week would be none other than Manchester City's young starlets Peter Barnes and Gary Owen.

Paul and I were devastated but after much deliberation, decided to stay for the remainder of the course. It was the big day and it was scorching hot. Owen and Barnes were to do a little coaching with us followed by the customary 5-a-side tournament. About an hour before the session was due to start, Paul, dad, and myself decided to take a stroll around the boating lake. As we walked along the water's edge my dad suddenly stopped, turned to me and said "Well, aren't you going to go and get their autographs?"

There in front of us, stripped down to just their city shorts were Mssrs Barnes and Owen. A broad grin swept across their faces as two young lads dressed in full United kit approached them.

"Can I get your autographs please?" I requested meekly. "Sure lads, no problem," said the dynamic duo. With the formalities completed, we started to walk away when Owen announced, "you can stay and chat for a while if you want lads."

The next 15/20 minutes were some of the most memorable of my childhood. City's finest turned out to be top, top blokes as they explained to two mesmerised young boys what it takes to become a professional footballer.

## BAG TAG

During our time at secondary school we invented a game that was so good we were convinced it would be adopted by every twelve-year-old boy in the land, sweeping across Britain like a forest fire; but somehow it didn't.

All you needed to make dinner-hour a time of high-octane excitement was a tennis ball. The rest of the equipment you already lugged round with you all day. Your bag.

the ball hit your bag you had one life left – a second hit and you were out of the game. You had to strike a balance between defending your own bag and forming alliances to attack someone else's. There was plenty of scope for subterfuge and double bluff and just as in *Macbeth* (which we would be studying later that day in English), overreaching ambition could swiftly lead to your downfall.

# All you need is an Adidas bag
## (with 'all day I dream about sex' added in felt pen).

Whether the cheapo variety with 'Sports' printed on the side; or a pricier 'Adidas' bag (with 'all day I dream about sex' added in felt pen) we placed them in a circle, the size of which was determined by the number of players. The rules were simple, as indeed were we. You could only touch the ball with your feet. Your bag was your own individual goal. If

## ACTION TRANSFERS

It isn't every club who got their own Letraset set, but United got lucky around the time of the Cup Final against Arsenal. Even so, the full glory of the Action Transfer isn't captured until you see them artistically applied to a scene...

This is easy. All you have to do is scribble the transfers off their greaseproof-paper backing on to the empty pitch in front of the Kop, and soon you'll have an action-packed Instant Picture™ of a match as good

© Paramount Picture Corporation, 1970.
Printed by Letraset Ltd., Patented.

## The full glory of the transfer isn't captured
# until they're artistically applied to a scene...

*Complete this scene using some of your instant pictures.*

# OOTBALL

## AN INSTANT PICTURE BOOK

as anything a photographer could produce.

Now then. Let's 'peel away backing paper' and kick off with one of the White-and-Violet team realistically booting the ball upfield. While his goalie jumps around out of his area. And one of the Turquoises throws a dummy on the edge of the box. While another one goes for a diving header sitting on his team-mate's shoulders.

It's no use the Letraset bods flagging up the deadly danger of failing to 'slide backing paper under other pictures to avoid accidental transfer' – it's already too late for the centre-forward's head. What we really need is more players just hanging around, like in real life, gossing and blowing on their hands and doing leg stretches…

ALAN MULLERY

ACTION TRANSFERS

GK 105/10    Patented. Printed in England by Letraset Ltd

*action's a*

Like
kit. Boots,
ma
match you

*Action! "C
match your act
Mitre jersey. F
fortable. Real
looking. Just p
in any one of
styles!"*

*. . . wet or dry.
Multiplex. Yo*

*Action ! "G
better control,
better support,
with so many
brand-new sty*

*Just for the record: Denis Law has scored more F. A. Cup competition goals than any other footballer. That's action for you!*

## BLACK BOOTS

Can you remember when football boots were mostly black, as nature intended?

They just looked right.

I'm not being puritanical about this, I like a well-designed splash of colour as much as the next man, such as you might find on a pair of beautiful late-Seventies Puma Mario Kempes Campeons, or the flashy red studs on Adidas's World Cup 78s. Or even the Woolworths two yellow stripes that I had to make do with.

I'm not suggesting we have no colour on boots, as happened in the 1974 World Cup when the Scotland players fell out with their boot suppliers and took a black felt pen to the distinguishing logos. Just that the base colour remains black. A dark canvas on which Puma and Adidas can paint their designs.

Just Say No to neon pink, luminous lime and those half highlighter yellow and half electric tangerine jobbies.

The FA have bundles of rules about tucking shirts in and pulling your socks up and base-layer clothing and even tape having to be the right colour, so why do they continue to allow this unseemly, giddy display of rainbow footwear?

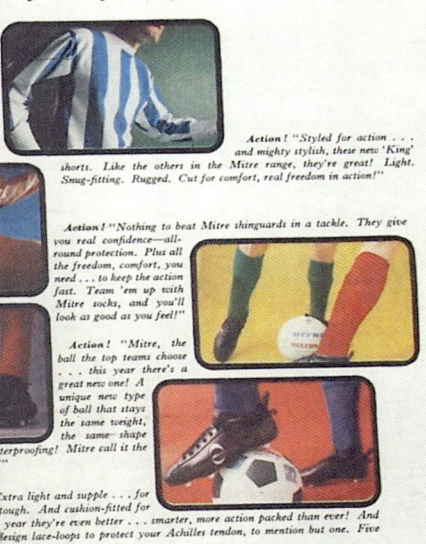

## MY FIRST BOOTS

The smell of fried onions at half-time; the whiplash weightlessness of a crowd surge; Double Decker vertigo, looking down on the Kop. They say sense memories are always the strongest, and my first boots are a sadly unforgettable example.

Making the big move up to junior school involved a similarly momentous step up from baseball boots to proper football boots for winter PE lessons. I could hardly believe my luck when the cheapest boots on offer in Oadby's Cut-Price Shoe Shop were George Best signature jobbies – "the world's first one-piece two-colour soccer shoe," it says here,

though I was blissfully unaware of my cutting-edge status at the time. Until I wore them for a match.

What it doesn't mention here is the reduced specs for the "sensational low-priced model." There was no nice comfy padding (as per the luxurious full-colour ad from 1968) – just a raw plastic edge which aligned perfectly with the bottom of my ankle bone.

While modern collectors fawn over the maroon-and-black side-laced George Best Matchmaker models, the first-boot sensations that stay with me are nagging pain, the weird clacking of studs on classroom cloakroom floor, and of suddenly teetering on inch-high platform soles.

## CUFF CLUTCHING

In the late Sixties and early Seventies, the trend for long-sleeved shirts led to an outbreak of cuff clutching.

Denis Law was mostly to blame. Whether straining to reach for a diving header, performing an acrobatic signature scissor-kick or saluting one of his many goals, Law always kept the white cuff of his red (or navy) sleeve stretched into his palm, clutched as tightly as a pushchair-bound infant grips his security blanket.

But a million mothers' chorused complaints of "You're STRETCHING it!" soon dried up when the cuff-clutching movement suffered two body blows: first, the trend for short-sleeved football shirts returned, and then chief protagonist, The Lawman, sadly hung up his boots after the 1974 World Cup.

Even the statue outside Old Trafford – the 'Holy Trinity' which set Law on a plinth with George Best and Bobby Charlton – portrays two inches of bronze cuff tucked under three fingers of his skyward-pointing hand.

## Setting Sons:
# The Holy Trinity overlook Old Trafford.

### THE ONE-MAN TEAM

Frank O'Farrell took the United job in 1971, installed on £15,000 on a five-year contract. "It was too big a job to turn down," he told us. "You're looking to improve yourself and here was a chance to win titles and play in Europe."

It was all going well until George Best was sent off at Chelsea.

"He was playing out of his skin at the time and we were top of the league up to Christmas. I'd brought Alan Gowling in to bolster up the midfield and George was scoring some brilliant goals and United were playing well again. But after Christmas George started running away and not turning up.

## "George was playing out of his skin at the time and scoring some brilliant goals. But after Christmas

# he started running away..."

GEORGE BEST
MANCHESTER UNITED & NORTHERN IRELAND

"The team wasn't good enough without him. We finished eighth, which wasn't bad considering the rebuilding job we had to do, but it was disappointing having been top."

How did O'Farrell get on with Best?

"He was a smashing person, a really likeable person. I liked him more than some of the people you feel you should like more. His shortcomings hung out for all to see, but he was so engaging and bright and was no trouble in training, when he was actually there. He'd stay after training to do some more shooting. But you never knew if he'd turn up the next day. I'd have him in the office and he'd be: 'Yes boss, no boss, three bags full boss.' And then he'd just go out and do the same thing the next week."

And so eventually Best was dropped.

"George had been missing all week. His landlady rang up to say that he'd returned from Ireland and could play. What George didn't know was that I'd been to his parents' house in Ireland that week to discuss bringing them over to Manchester to live with him, the club were so dependent on him having a stable life. So I knew he wasn't there. I knew he'd lied to me and there was no way I could play him."

And United lost 2-0 at Wolves.

"They just weren't good enough without him."

In December 1972 a letter was sent out to every First Division club, advertising Best for sale. But, just before Christmas, O'Farrell was sacked... and not paid off.

"It was almost an impossible job at the time. Managers were made scapegoats for what Matt Busby hadn't done in the latter part of his career. He'd been through the Munich Disaster with the likes of Bobby Charlton and perhaps that was why he let the team go on and on, getting older. The club was in a fragile state and it took a long time for them to recover. They had to go down to the Second Division under Tommy Docherty to rebuild."

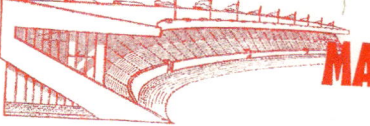

Manager:
F. O'FARRELL.

Secretary:
L. OLIVE.

Telegraphic Address: "STADIUM" Manchester
Telephone: 061-872 1861/2

**MANCHESTER UNITED Football Club Ltd**

OLD TRAFFORD, MANCHESTER,
M16 0RA

LO/IP
7th December, 1972

The Secretary
First and Second Division Clubs
- - - - - - - - - - - - - - - -

Dear Sir,

       We wish to **inform** you that we are prepared to receive offers for the transfer of registration of the following player:-

| | Age | Position |
|---|---|---|
| G. Best | 26 | Forward |

       This does not give you permission to approach the player and all enquiries should be made to our Manager, Mr. F. O'Farrell.

      Yours faithfully,

*L. Olive*

Secretary

109

## IN THE PINK

This same ritual went on up and down the country for decades, little kids and old blokes queuing up outside the paper shop at 6 o'clock on Saturday night, waiting for the sports final edition of the local paper – the *Green 'Un*, the *Pink 'Uns*, the *Blue 'Un* or the *Buff*. Any colour as long as it wasn't white. Here was sports journalism at its most demanding, where reports were phoned in on the hoof, assumptions were made before the final whistle, and last-minute goals were any editor's nightmare.

The MEN Pink Final match report **was vital reading** if you'd just left OT 80 minutes ago.

The *Manchester Evening News Pink Final* was vital reading for those fans who couldn't rest until they had read a report of a game that some of them had seen eighty minutes ago (unless they were after confirmation of a result they'd just heard played out on the radio).

The *Pink 'Un* gave you the chance to settle down in a favourite armchair, to check the pools and peruse the results and league tables at your leisure. In the days before Sky News and even Ceefax, it was either this or wait for the arrival of the Sunday papers.

Gradually the need for a Saturday evening sports edition lessened and then disappeared altogether. The internet was one blow – suddenly you didn't need to be standing out on the street in January – but the killer was the spreading of fixtures over the weekend due to the demands of TV.

One by one, the sports papers had to admit defeat and hold up their hands in surrender, in Manchester and Liverpool, Leicester and Coventry and Birmingham... although the Norwich *Pink 'Un* and Ipswich's *Green 'Un* are both websites now.

If you can't beat 'em, join 'em.

## UP FOR THE CUPPA

In the season before the 1966 World Cup, those nice people at Ty-Phoo Tea were running a smashing offer whereby any thirsty fan could collect up packet tops and send off for a large 10" by 8" teamgroup card of their choice.

And sometimes you'd even get a little picture of a player printed on the side of the box, which kids would inevitably hack out with scissors almost before mum could get the tea (note, that's 'tea', not your common-as-muck not-yet-invented 'teabags') into the tea canister.

Nice cup of Rosie Lee with your eggy soldiers in the morning? And a nice little Nobby Stiles on the side, with your triangular toast in a little metal stand to make it go cold extra quick...

**Nice cup of Rosie Lee with your eggy soldiers in the morning?**

## and a little Bobby Charlton on the side?

## THE KEY, THE SECRET

In the 1960s, keyrings were chiefly used for throwing into the pot at groovy wife-swapping parties attended by Swinging Manchester (to hell with London) people such as Georgie Best and several Miss World girlfriends, Mike Summerbee, the cast of Corrie, Sheilagh Delaney and Morrissey (he's older than he looks). No telling how you'd have got on, chucking in one of these rather suggestive expanding jobbies.

In the punk rock 1970s, the keys on rings just like these were chiefly used for making scratches down the sides of above-average sized cars.

In the 1980s, they carried the keys for those same above-average size cars.

And, in the 1990s, the keys to the executive box were added on...

Is that a multi-player mugshot concertina keyring in your pocket? Or are you just pleased to see me?

In the '60s, keyrings were chiefly used for throwing into the pot **at swinging wife-swapping parties.**

## DO'S AND DON'TS

Imagine a world where footballers were governed by grown-ups with the foresight to dissuade them from setting fire to £50 notes in front of people with proper jobs.

Almost incredibly, such a world did exist, and not so very long ago.

*Training Rules and Instructions to Players* was an official Manchester United publication containing emergency hotline phone numbers – including one direct to boss Matt Busby's bedside table – for the very purpose of steering potentially errant and/or red-faced Devils, out on the lash, back on to the straight and narrow.

A few simple rules might work a treat today at any Premier League club, reminding players of their responsibilities regarding driving a Baby Bentley at 160mph, and wearing electrical headphones during TV interviews:

### Training
All players will attend the grounds for training at 9.45am daily (except match days) and shall be under the orders of the management for the rest of the day.

### Motor Cars
Players are not prohibited from running a motor car, but it must be clearly understood that they do so at their own risk. Wages will be forfeited during the time of incapacity for any injury which is resultant through accidents in this pastime.

### Damage to Club Property
No loose balls will be allowed in the Gymnasium.

### Electrical Equipment
In no circumstances must any player use or manipulate any electrical apparatus or instruments. The operation of such equipment will be controlled and carried out by qualified members of staff.

MANCHESTER UNITED FOOTBALL CLUB PLC

1992-1993

PLAYERS

Manchester United Football Club PLC

SEASON — 1992-93

TRAINING RULES
AND
PLAYERS' INSTRUCTIONS

Ticket No. 23

## GOAL! LOLLIES

Interesting concept. Rather than littering the floor outside your local Co-op with your spent lolly stick, you take it home and "paint it to look like your favourite football star."

But what if you don't happen to be an artistic genius with an interest in micro-sculpture? And how can a lolly stick, no matter how well painted, be caught offside or take a goal kick, as promised? All is revealed in the sentence near the end, where the advertising copy becomes refreshingly honest: "It must all sound too good to be true. It is."

Oh well, maybe we should just put our trust in Lyons Maid and send them our 25p in any case. Best be quick, though: offer ends 30 December, 1978.

**When the loll the game's ju**

Whistles to the ready, and we'll start.

When you buy a Goal lolly, you not only get a terrific ice lolly with three crowd-pulling flavours, but a plastic lolly stick with a footballer on the top.

Two teams wort play in Kevin Keeg soccer game.

It's based on tru With tactical tips f Everything from a a goal kick.

So, just like the there'll be times w team is running ri the other. Or vice

It must all sou to be true. It is.

And so is the only 25p.

The sooner y coupon, the soc kick off.

Bet you can

You can paint it to look like your favourite star.

And after you've collected 10 of them, you'll have two teams.

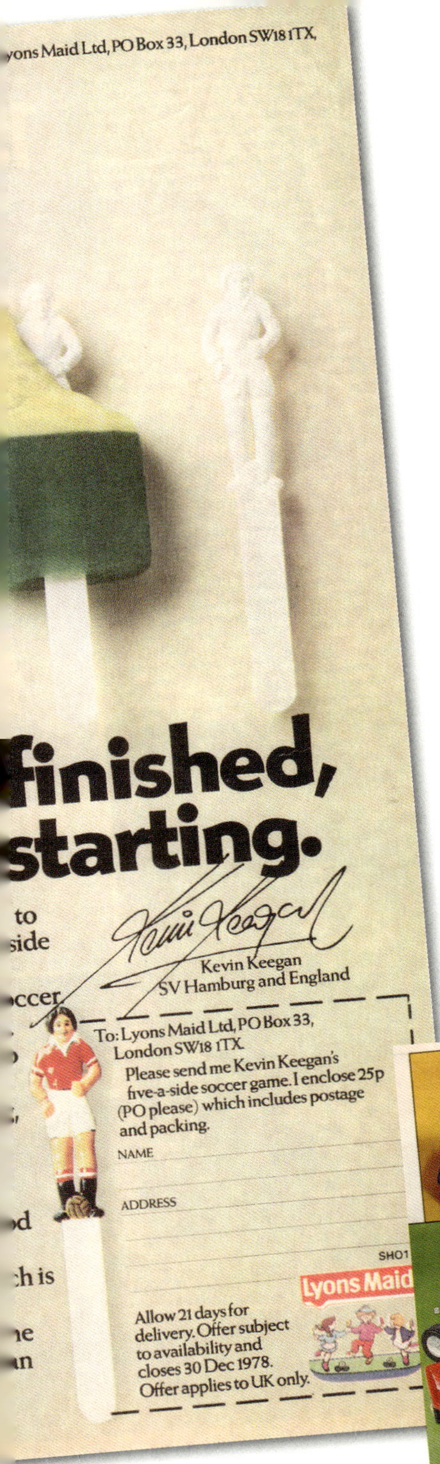

yons Maid Ltd, PO Box 33, London SW18 1TX.

*Our free gift and cut price offers always include free delivery and free credit.*

FREE! SOCCER DICE GAME WITH ITEM B

FREE! ZIPPED HEAD COVER WITH ITEM G

adidas

FOOTBALL

£1 OFF RECOMMENDED PRICE ON ITEM K

## NO CHOICE

Back in 1974, the John Noble catalogue brought in a splendidly sensible policy on football kit for kids: no choice except Man U! The toys section wasn't so clever, mind, the only footy game on offer being Striker; though the upright Hoover section was relatively well stocked...

finished, starting.

*Kevin Keegan*

Kevin Keegan
SV Hamburg and England

To: Lyons Maid Ltd, PO Box 33, London SW18 1TX.

Please send me Kevin Keegan's five-a-side soccer game. I enclose 25p (PO please) which includes postage and packing.

NAME

ADDRESS

SHO1

Lyons Maid

Allow 21 days for delivery. Offer subject to availability and closes 30 Dec 1978. Offer applies to UK only.

115

## I-SPY

Did anybody else out there used to be a 'Redskin' in a previous life – a member of that strange infant cult of I-Spy, where you sent off for membership packs to 'Big Chief I-Spy' at Wigwam-by-the-Water (London EC4)?

The idea was to keep kids occupied, though quite how they would have fared following Big Chief's instructions to the letter is anybody's guess. In the football edition of I-Spy he asked us to nose around our local football ground: did anybody actually try out any of these box-ticking fact-finding missions at Old Trafford, where the wrath of club officials would surely have been incurred within seconds:

## What else did you notice in the treatment room you saw?
### ... Score 80.

What else did you notice in the treatment room you saw? ... Score 80.

Which team have you watched training. And where? ... Score 40.

What other equipment have you seen the groundsman use? ... Score 40.

Other than a sponge, what else have you seen the trainer using while attending an injured player? ... Score 70.

I'm not sure it was ever possible to achieve the target of 1,500-points without suffering a thick ear or cartoon-style boot out of the main entrance, courtesy of the usually saintly Ron Atkinson.

**I-SPY FOOTBALL** 9p

## CASDON SOCCER

"Casdon Soccer – played by Bobby Charlton," the box proudly proclaims. And there is Bobby, resplendent in scarlet Slazenger V-neck pully, leaving his defence wide open as the little boy (representing you and me) launches an offensive.

Bobby's grinning in a convincing enough manner, and the blurb on the underside of the box reinforces his commitment: "Bobby Charlton says it is the nearest thing to English soccer it is possible to experience in one's own home, and has spent many hours playing with his own family."

What a delicious thought, brother Jackie coming round to play with Bobby.

No arguments about who would be white and who would be red.

This system of pirouetting players, ball-bearing ball and wildly undulating pitch surface was a big seller over the years, and Casdon's 'Item No. 150' went through several rebrands. Kenny Dalglish put his name to it after Bobby's retirement, and then in the Eighties it became the England Squad Soccer Game with Paul Mariner, Kevin Keegan, Bryan Robson and Garry Birtles challenging the rules of perspective by crowding round the playing surface along with two small children on the box photo.

THE OFFICIAL

CASDON **ENGLAND SQUAD SOCCER GAME**

A GAME FOR ALL THE FAMILY

According to the online Casdon Toy Museum, "Some say it was probably the best football game of all time" – although that bumpy pitch and the crude one-colour players both intruded into the game's proudly touted 'realism'.

I'll admit that a pitch consisting of dramatic troughs and peaks wasn't something that taxed my imagination too much. Our school pitch was sited on a field that had been employed for strip farming during medieval times. Several centuries after the enclosure of England's land our field of dreams still stubbornly consisted of ridges and furrows. A charge down the right wing was literally an up-and-down experience, and particularly small full-backs standing in particularly deep furrows could almost be hidden from view. A useful, if underhand, ambush tactic.

I don't think Bobby would have endorsed that.

*The Greatest Casdon Rip-off: Note Kevin Keegan, airbrushed casually into the background.*

119

## ADIDAS

Taking over from Admiral in the summer of 1980, German company Adidas produced kits for United for 12 years.

The first design was a simple but classy affair that lasted for two seasons.

After that things got a bit more complicated as the designers faced the challenge of producing a different-looking strip every two seasons, armed with pin-stripes and shadow weave.

The Adidas Era saw three FA Cup wins, a League Cup and a European Cup Winners' Cup, but not the League title that United had chased for so long. That came as soon as they changed to Umbro...

When Adidas parted company with United they also made the incredibly brave, or foolhardy, decision to drop their globally recognised trefoil logo they had used since 1972 – it was like Disney sacking the Mouse or Coca Cola plumping for an Arial font on their cans – and launched the new Adidas Equipment three-bar logo.

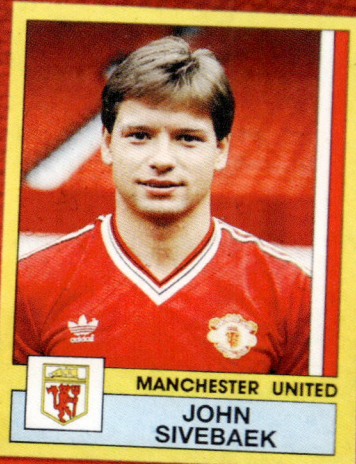

MANCHESTER UNITED
JOHN SIVEBAEK

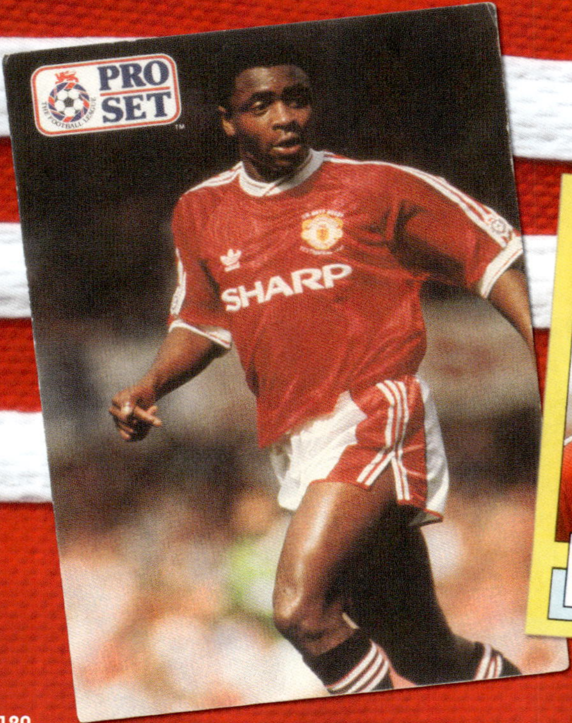

PRO SET

SHARP

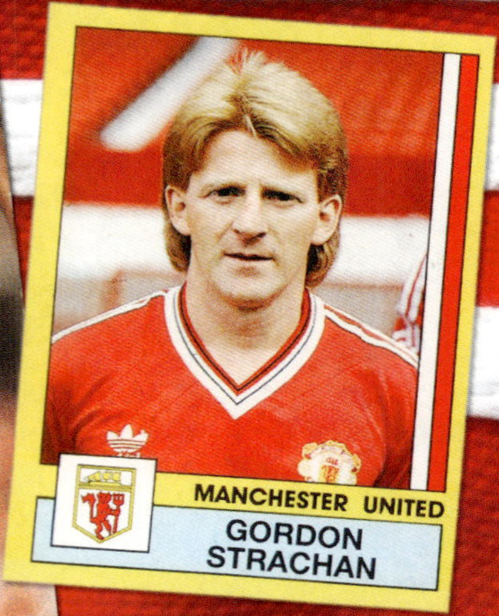

MANCHESTER UNITED
GORDON STRACHAN

# Adidas United

Aberdeen (Away)

Aberdeen (Home)

Birmingham (Home)

Brighton & Hove Albion (Home)

Crystal Palace (Home)

Crystal Palace (Away)

Dundee United (Home)

Dundee United (Away)

Ipswich Town (Home)

Ipswich Town (Away)

Northern Ireland

Luton Town (Home)

Manchester United (Home)

Manchester United (Away)

Middlesborough (Home)

Notts County (Home)

Notts Forest (Home)

Notts Forest (Away)

...ark Rangers

Welsh F.A. (Home)

Welsh F A. (Away)

West Ham United (Home)

MANCHESTER UNITED

VIV ANDER...

NORMAN WHITESIDE

MANCHESTER UNITED

adidas

The mark of a winner

121

## MIND THE GAP

Pity the poor old modern pro, who must occasionally feel like a talented younger brother brought up by cantankerous parents in the shadow of a favourite elder son.

"Look at me, Dad. I've got football skills that weren't dreamed of back in the 1990s, and I've got a girlfriend who models fake all-over tan."

"Ah, you wouldn't have caught *Our Bobby* earning your kind of obscene money. I don't know, with your diamonds stuck all over your mobile phone and your little nicks cut out of your eyebrows."

JOE JORDAN

JOE JORDAN

Heineken refreshes the parts other beers cannot reach.

"But Dad, I've been voted into the UK's Top 50 Eligible Celebrities by readers of *Eligible Celebrities* magazine."

"You know *Our Bobby* could down a gallon and then do a hundred press-ups on the bar? He was a proper head-turner was Our Bobby, especially when he put his teeth in..."

Fact is, today's pro can never compete with the players of even ten years ago precisely because he's so wealthy and talented, so polite and well turned out.

You wouldn't have caught Joe Jordan spending £50,000 on a pearl-white set of Gangsta gnashers. Joe had his four front teeth kicked out in a Leeds United reserve-team game: all the better to terrorise any unfortunate sod going up against him for a header, when he earned the horror-flick nickname of 'Jaws' without once resorting to cannibalism.

While on the way to Old Trafford from Elland Road during the 1978 World Cup, Joe was the star of a Heineken ad, where a pint of lager 'refreshed the parts other beers cannot reach'. Joe's teeth grew back, temporarily, while fresh graffiti across the north of England claimed: 'Joe Jordan kicks the parts other beers cannot reach'.

Once he'd slipped out his false front teeth, Joe had nothing left to lose. Stripped for action, he stood outside any real-world concerns such as the desire to find a mate, or to eat an apple.

Compare and contrast with, ooh, let's say Ashley Cole...

## SADISTIC GAMES MASTERS

Although the legions of mean-minded PE teachers that stalked the corridors of Britain's schools in the Sixties and Seventies created genuine misery for countless pupils, the definitive cinematic version was played for laughs.

Ex-pro wrestler Brian Glover's debut role, Mr. Sugden takes up only ten minutes' screentime in *Kes*, the film adaptation of Barry Hines' 1968 novel

*A Kestrel for a Knave*; but it remains a landmark performance in British cinematic history.

Sugden nurtures a deep dislike of the film's central character, the scrawny Billy Casper, due to his recurrent lack of PE kit. He bawls at Billy and bullies him physically on a regular basis.

We soon learn that Sugden is the biggest kid on the football field and, after the ritual humiliation of picking sides,

# "Denis Law," explains Mr. Sugden, "is in the wash."

leaving the duffers until last, he strips off his tracksuit to reveal his Bobby Charlton number 9 shirt.

"Denis Law," he explains, "is in the wash."

Sugden is the star of his own Manchester United v Spurs FA Cup tie, and in his imagination the Barnsley school playing field is Old Trafford.

In his desperation to win, he dives for a penalty which, in his dual role as ref, he awards to himself. When the keeper easily saves it, he demands a retake. His second shot narrowly evades the goalie, sparking a celebratory charge.

"And that, boys, is how to take a penalty!"

Despite sending off the opposing captain for complaining about being mown down, Sugden's United somehow concede a late goal and lose 2-1.

"Spurs are in the sixth round now, sir!"

"Sixth round?" seethes the defeated captain. "I'll give you six of the best!"

## THE PARK DRIVE BOOK OF FOOTBALL

"In this book we pay tribute to many of the finest footballers in the country. It is not suggested in any way that mention of any individual implies that he is a smoker or in favour of any brand of cigarette."

Having cleared up any potential misunderstanding, we were left to plough into the 1968, 1969 and 1970 editions of the *Park Drive Book of Football*.

# George Best was pictured measuring up a young lady
# for a pair of leather trousers.

As I inherited all three at once, many years after they were first published – in 1973 – to me they were a wonderfully nostalgic read, before players all started to have modern-day long hair, sideburns and V-neck collars.

United were one of the big movers and shakers at the time, winning European Cups, titles and FA Cups along with Leeds and Everton, while Liverpool had stopped winning trophies but still had plenty of coverage lauding Bill Shankly and the Kop.

'United – Kings of Europe' was penned by Paddy Crerand in which he reveals that Nobby Stiles is scared stiff of thunder and lightning; while *Sun* columnist Arthur Walmsley's 'Salute to Sir Matt' reveals that in his very first board meeting Busby was expected to hand over his team selection for the approval of his directors and said: "That is my team gentlemen, if it doesn't play on Saturday you will need a new manager."

'Player of the Season' was a feature on George Best, who was pictured in action on the field and also measuring up a young lady for a pair of leather trousers in his boutique.

## A BIT OF A BELTER

Here's a smashing Man U belt from back in the Seventies, when the practice of wearing your trousers around your backside simply wasn't an option.

The idea was, you assembled the belt yourself and wore the United players of your choice around your hips all day, having carefully threaded the little slotted pictures along the length of the belt.

Someday, it seemed at the time, all belts would carry this trendy and happening feature...

But ironically, nowadays, the curious American fashion of wanting to look like a convict has infected our wardrobe sense, leading us back into the trouser-related Dark Ages of bum-cracks and trousers dragging on the ground.

It's time for us trendsetters to get busy and set a groovy example!

# Without the towering beacon of four majestic floodlight pylons
## how are away fans supposed to find their way to the ground?

## DIY

DIY is all about originality, personalised team colours and sending out an individual message. Like hot pants, mini-skirts and cotton football tops, it's not just a sad old nostalgia kick but a groovy retro look for the 21st century. You dig?

Knitting was an ancient craft not dissimilar to today's recycling craze, and just as popular in the olden days. It involved taking a pile of fluff found on a sheep's back, twisting it into 300 yards of yarn and then painstakingly twisting this single length into a giant knot shaped like a bobble hat.

Why buy a baseball cap 'off the shelf' (or off a dodgy stall outside the ground) unless you're attempting to mimic the street style of an octogenarian Alabaman redneck? Get yourself a nice bobble instead. You might not be able to knit it yourself, but your gran will set you up with two cardboard rings and another 300 yards of wool and you can feel the DIY joy of spending seven creative hours winding yourself a giant fluffy bobble as big as your head.

Don't throw away those football socks, shorts and shirts just because they're ripped or worn out. Get darning with a needle and some not-quite-the-right-colour thread, and your mum will soon reassure you that they're 'as good as new'.

Why buy a nylon scarf emblazoned with an 'unofficial' version of a Red Devil? Instead, get knitting and purling

# You too can look a proper bobby-dazzler
## in a big stripy scarf with a message direct from your heart.

(ask Gran) and you too can look a proper bobby-dazzler in a big stripy scarf with a custom message direct from your heart. Something like 'Up' in one white stripe, and 'For The Cup' in another. The sky's the limit. You'll probably end up crocheting yourself a complete adult football romper suit in your club colours.

## POCKET-MONEY ENDORSEMENTS

There's just one welcome side effect of every British professional footballer owning a private island off the coast of Cheshire with a helicopter pad and a retractable Olympic-size swimming pool with a football pitch secreted underneath. Mercifully, football mags, programmes and comics are no longer cluttered up with embarrassing ads for cringeworthy products which the players have clearly never used in real life, but are still willing to put their name to in order to earn an extra 300 quid to throw away on the greyhounds.

Nowadays, the crowning achievement for any footballer is to make the final ascension to the fashion pages. That's where your football royalty is to be found: Wayne Rooney is among the select few who gets to strut in swimwear, barwear and awardswear. Oily abs, booted and suited, a nice cravat. Leave the sportswear to the losers with nothing but boot contracts to their names.

Ryan Giggs is pretty hot on the catwalk, too; but that's not to say he'd turn down the chance of a spot of extra pocket-money if someone offered to slap his fizzog on a box of chocolates.

Having said that, we're not so sniffy we wouldn't shove small children out of the way to get a go on Gordon Strachan's thrilling Centapost innovation, which he personally invented in his free time while at Manchester United. Disinterested observers from the United Nations have since backed up Gordon's claim that

the apparently cumbersome yet oh-so-easily portable device, which lit up and made a bleeping noise when you kicked the ball against it, was indeed "the most exciting football invention since the ball." Which is why, even today, you rarely come across a park or a beach without a posse of young pros benchmarking their new-found skills on a futuristic digital scoreboard. Available any time now, yeah?

Mover 'n' shaker: Nowadays, 99 per cent of all football goals have a left, a right and a centre post.

MILK CHOCOLATE PICTORIALS

## A PIECE OF THE ACTION

Sorry to say we've had to censor the action on this footy sticker jigsaw.

The composite puzzle picture came as part of Top Sellers' 'Football 72' series, and featured two Ipswich players lunging into a desperate joint tackle on George Best – or, as the original caption put it, "Georgie Best flashes his popular aggressive form in a scramble for the ball" – with a pitch-side invalid carriage waiting ominously in the background.

Quite interestingly, Top Sellers was a front used by Panini in their first attempt to grab a corner of the British sticker market.

## PLAQUE ATTACK

Collect the Big Names Now!

And, with all due respect to Darlington and Southport, some of the smaller ones, too.

Once you'd cut out your first token from this *Shoot!* advert, ripped another off a fish-finger box and painstakingly assembled 25 new pee, then you were ready to send off and claim your embossed football club plaque from the Co-op.

But was your club on this seemingly random list of 31 large, medium and frankly tiddler-sized clubs?

# Collect the big names *now!*

## EMBOSSED CLUB PLAQUES

### Only 25p and 2 tokens from special Co-op packs

And getting the tokens is as easy as doing the shopping because they're on all kinds of Co-op products from cream crackers to fish fingers. To help you get started here's your first Football Plaque Token free! Full details of where to post etc., are on all the special Co-op Football Token packs. Watch out for them. The large plaque shown here is actual size, and the full list of plaques available is:

| | | | |
|---|---|---|---|
| Leeds | Wolves | Notts. Forest | Oldham |
| Manchester United | Birmingham | Hull | Peterborough |
| Arsenal | West Brom. | Portsmouth | Shrewsbury |
| Chelsea | Millwall | Coventry | Darlington |
| Liverpool | Sheffield United | Charlton | Southport |
| ... | Newcastle | Bristol City | Stockport |
| ... City | Sheffield Wednesday | Luton | Middlesbrough |
| | Southampton | Lincoln | |

...lub is not listed, write to the address on Co-op label ...tion)

**YOUR FIRST ONE FREE!**
(Only 1 free token accepted per plaque)

## Co-op now!

It's All at Your Co-op... NOW!

However, somewhat oddly, these vital tribal territory markers were also presented as a Ty-Phoo Tea promotion a year later, in the 1972-73 season, with a similar wedge of two tokens and 25p required.

Stick this to your bedroom door with four foam Sellotape sticky fixers and that baby is never coming off in one piece...

# TRIUMPH IN EUROPE

BRIAN KIDD

**M**ANCHESTER UNITED were the first English team to enter for the European Cup competition, in 1956, and, at Wembley in 1968, they made history by becoming the first English club to win it!

The European Cup dream came true for Mister Manchester United, manager Matt Busby.

BOBBY CHARLTON

ALEC STEPNEY

GEORGE BEST

NOBBY STILES

JOHN ASTON

DAVID SADLER

## THE SHORT ROAD TO EUROPEAN GLORY

Many thanks to the unknown kid who, in 1968, diligently cut out all the instalments of *The Hornet* to complete this *Bernard Briggs' Album of Football '68…*

Thanks to the magic of eBay it found its way to us, and from its many (well, 14) varied pages celebrating the achievements of the 1967-68 season, we bring you this spread which shows you the carefully cut-out stars of Manchester United's successful tilt at European Cup glory…

But compare and contrast the games played with the monstrous, sprawling number of fixtures that have to be played today.
*1st Round: United 4:0 Malta Hibernian (agg)*
*2nd Round: United 2:1 Sarajevo (agg)*
*QF: United 2:1 Gornik (agg)*
*SF: United 4:3 Real Madrid (agg)*
*Final: United 4:1 Benfica.*

Job done, champions only need apply, get on with your lives.

MANCHESTER UNITED v. ZABRZE GORNIK ZABRZE

FINAL
**MANCHESTER UTD. 4**
*Charlton 2, Best, Kidd*
**BENFICA 1**

QUARTER FINAL
**MANCHESTER UTD. 2**
*Florenski (o.g.), Kidd*
**GORNIK 1**
*Aggregate.*

PAT CRERAND

SEMI-FINAL
**MANCHESTER UTD. 4**
*st, Zoco (o.g.), Sadler, Foulkes*
**REAL MADRID 3**
*Aggregate.*

BILL FOULKES

2nd ROUND
**MANCHESTER UTD. 2**
*Aston, Best*
**SARAJEVO 1**
*Aggregate.*

1st ROUND
**MANCHESTER UTD. 4**
*Sadler 2, Law 2*
**MALTA HIBERNIAN 0**
*Aggregate.*

SHAY BRENNAN

ONY DUNNE

**MANCHESTER UNITED**

EUROPEAN CUP
19 68
SEMI·FINAL

**REAL MADRID**

WEMBLEY · ENGLAND

**EUROPEAN CUP FINAL 1968**

**MANCHESTER UNITED**
**versus LISBOA e. BENFICA**

133

**Don't we look smart?**

An image more 1970s than the Wombles being arrested by Starsky & Hutch for stealing a Chopper.

## UMBRO

Umbro had been making fantastic football kits since 1924, when the HUMphreys BROthers Harold and Wallace set up a workshop in Wilmslow, Cheshire. In those less ostentatious days labels were worn on the inside of clothes, not the outside, so their prestigious list of classic kits remained largely anonymous.

Blackpool's famous FA Cup triumph of 1953, Tottenham's 1961 Double, England's World Cup glory in 1966, Celtic's European Cup win in Lisbon in '67 and United's the following year were all achieved in Umbro kit, with not a visible diamond in sight.

Umbro were the first to produce a full set of football kit replicas for kids in 1959, which became hugely popular when Denis Law endorsed them in the mid-Sixties.

# It's going to be a sparkling season…
## just look at all those diamonds!

By the time I was taken into our local sports outfitters for my first football kit, circa 1973, they were called the 'Umbroset' and came in a box with a cellophane front, affording you a tantalising glimpse of the shirt, shorts and 'hose' contained within (as they weren't interchangeable, you had to be 'average' size and keep your fingers crossed).

By the mid-70s, branding was beginning to creep in and the little diamond logo appeared on shirts, until, on the eve of the 1976-77 season, an advert appeared in *Shoot!* proclaiming: "It's going to be a sparkling season… just look at those diamonds!"

Six years after Brazil had won the 1970 World Cup in Umbro without a single diamond showing, the new range of Umbro kits now sported dozens, with multi-logoed tape down the sleeves and shorts.

United's decade in Umbro from 1992 to 2002 was their most glorious.

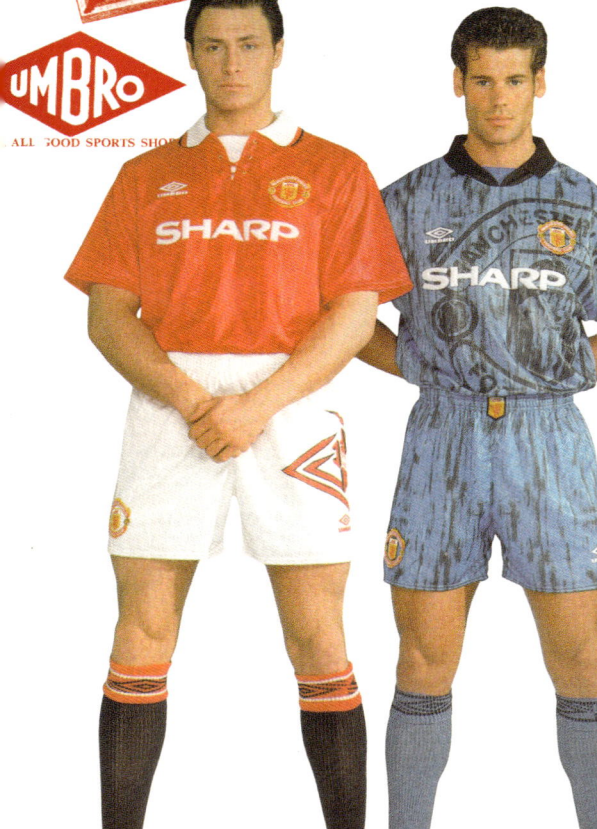

It spanned Eric Cantona's turned-up collar and the return of the long-lost League title; through to David Beckham's diamonds down the sleeves and the 1999 European Cup triumph in Barcelona.

It would be churlish to even mention the charcoal grey kit.... which United wore at Southampton in April 1996. 3-0 down at the Dell by half-time Alex Ferguson demanded a change for the second half claiming the players couldn't see each other.

They lost 3-1, so Fergie might have been right, and never wore the grey again. They still won the title though.

Sadly, having been swallowed up and spat out by American giants Nike, Umbro's future looks to be in some doubt.

It's probably just as well that Harold Humphreys – described as "the Dior of the football world" by the *Daily Express* in 1963 – isn't still around to witness the demise.

## XMAS MORNING

Our 1970s Christmases, in our terrace front rooms and boxy housing-estate semis, weren't quite the same as the sumptuous Victorian festivals portrayed on Christmas cards and chocolate boxes, in TV ads and cartoons.

We didn't have stockings hanging from huge holly-bedecked fireplaces. We had striped pillowcases stuck on the end of our beds.

We didn't have gaily laughing guests – gentlemen in top hats and ladies wearing furry muffs – we had bald men round in their new V-neck jumpers, and they hardly spoke.

And we had, to be frank, shite artificial Christmas trees, not those towering, richly decorated spruces portrayed on the cover of the *Radio Times*.

A Merry Christmas from everyone at Old Trafford

From us to you: Have a very happy Christmas, and a splendid New Year in 1967.

## We never had sleds and holly-bedecked fireplaces
### but, then, they never had Subbuteo Team No. 100, did they?

As for the romantic notion of a White Christmas, it never snowed round our way; though sometimes it rained.

Christmas dinner was the same as normal Sunday dinner, except with turkey instead of roast beef, and with added parsnips and sprouts. Rather than the mouthwatering spreads portrayed ... well, you get the idea.

But somehow, on Christmas morning, with Noel Edmonds visiting children in hospital as a televisual backdrop, we still managed to reach a goosebump-inducing level of excitement.

And it was all because we knew that, concealed in cheap Woolies wrapping paper, piled up under the shite tree, there lurked *Shoot!* annuals, Wembley Trophy footballs, full football strips and Subbuteo accessories housed in their pale green boxes.

So we never took a horse-drawn sled down to the pine forest to chop down the tallest tree to place by the main staircase like those privileged Victorians... but then, they never had Subbuteo Team No. 100, did they?

61662

GET YOURSELF A
MAN U LIFESTYLE

140

## Authors

Gary Silke and Derek Hammond are the authors of *The Lost World of Football* (Pitch, 2013); *What A Shot! Your Snaps of the Lost World of Football* (Pitch, 2013), and *Got, Not Got: The A-Z of Lost Football Culture, Treasures & Pleasures* (Pitch, 2011).

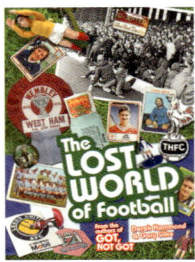 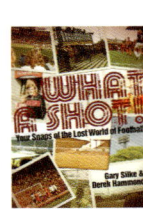 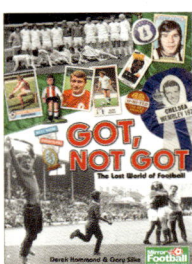

## Picture Credits

Neville Chadwick Photography: Front cover, 42, 86, 96, 134.
Getty Images: 16, 20, 26, 34, 54, 64, 72, 116, 126, 137.
Vectis Auctions – collectible toy specialists, www.vectis.co.uk: 58 (ice-cream van), 91 (Austin Countryman), 99 (boxed Mettoy figures).
Mike Schorah: 66, 98.
Simon Stewart: 76.
Steve Mitchell: 100.
Tony Smith: 106.
Steve Marsh: 111.
Chris Andrews: Plaque on front cover and 131.

# Acknowledgments

Grateful thanks to Iain McCartney, prolific Manchester United author and collector, for letting us photograph his incredible array of United memorabilia. Read his blog at imccartney.wordpress.com.

And to Jonathon Wheatley, whose luscious matchworn Admiral shirt collection can be viewed at freewebs.com/weedosenglandgear.

Further thanks to Paul Woozley, the proprietor of the excellent oldfootballgames.co.uk website, who let us take photos of, and even play with, all his great stuff.

Nigel Mercer for his jam-jar lids, *Lion* league ladders and Letraset. Check out his ace, encyclopaedic football card and sticker website at cards.littleoak.com.au. And, if you're a Letraset fan, the SPLAT Archives at action-transfers.com.

Gary James, author of *Manchester — A Football City* and many other bestsellers, for the George Best letter.

Andy Ormerod for his Sun Soccerstamps album.

David Tossell, Michael Dixon and Neil MacLeod for Christmas stuff.

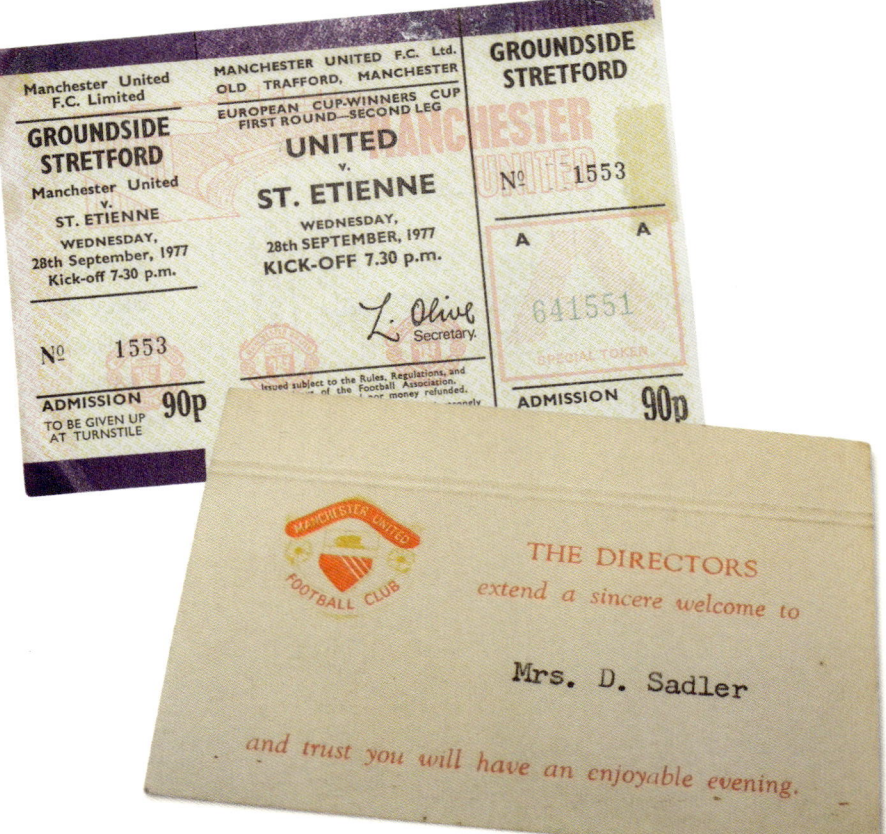

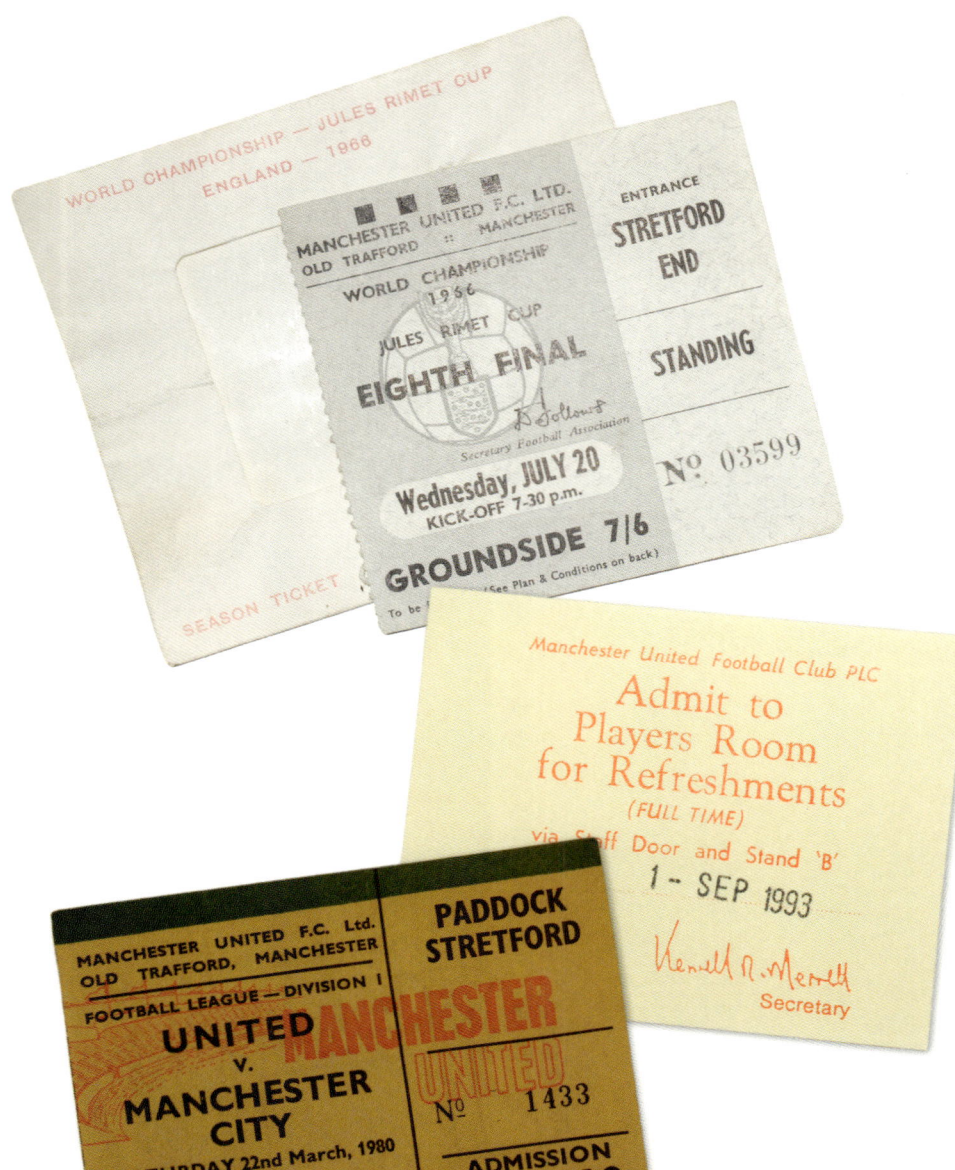

WORLD CHAMPIONSHIP — JULES RIMET CUP
ENGLAND — 1966

SEASON TICKET

MANCHESTER UNITED F.C. LTD.
OLD TRAFFORD :: MANCHESTER

WORLD CHAMPIONSHIP
1966

JULES RIMET CUP

EIGHTH FINAL

Secretary Football Association

Wednesday, JULY 20
KICK-OFF 7-30 p.m.

GROUNDSIDE 7/6

To be (See Plan & Conditions on back)

ENTRANCE

STRETFORD
END

STANDING

№ 03599

Manchester United Football Club PLC

Admit to
Players Room
for Refreshments
(FULL TIME)

via Staff Door and Stand 'B'

1 — SEP 1993

Secretary

MANCHESTER UNITED F.C. Ltd.
OLD TRAFFORD, MANCHESTER

FOOTBALL LEAGUE — DIVISION I

UNITED
v.
MANCHESTER
CITY

SATURDAY 22nd March, 1980
Kick-off 3.00 p.m.

L. Olive
Secretary

Issued subject to the Rules, Regulations and
Bye-Laws of the Football Association.
No Ticket exchanged nor money returned.

This portion to be retained

PADDOCK
STRETFORD

MANCHESTER
UNITED

№ 1433

ADMISSION
£1-40

As a capacity attendance is
expected, it is strongly
recommended that patrons
ENTER THE GROUND
not less than 30 minutes
before kick-off.

## More Critical Acclaim for *Got, Not Got*

"This exquisite book is a homage to the game of 40 years ago – not just the mudheaps and the mavericks but a celebration of its wider culture [which] rises above lazy, modern-life-is-rubbish nostalgia… The design is so sumptuous and the stories so well chosen and written that it's hard to resist the authors' conclusion that much – call it charm, character or even romance – has been lost in the rush for cash. Regardless of whether it really was a golden age, this is a golden volume, as much a social history as a sports book. If you've not got *Got, Not Got*, you've got to get it."
*Backpass*

"I can guarantee that virtually anybody who flicks open this magnificent book will immediately want to have it."
*The Football Trader*

"For further reminders of the long-lost game of the 1960s, '70s and '80s, the illuminating new book *Got, Not Got* does a very fine job."
*Sport* magazine

"If, like myself, you are an unashamed nostalgia junkie, this book is for you. It's more than just a book on football collectables, including memories and experiences from the golden age – a time before the FA Premiership and TV money took us through a pound-sign portal and into a parallel, but much less likeable, universe. Some of my favourite experiences/memories are included – I found myself saying either 'did it' or 'remember it' – and there's a heck of a lot to choose from."
*Programme Monthly*

"A huge success and an epic tome for lovers of football nostalgia everywhere."
*The Football Attic blog*

"It's an absolute beauty."
*Adrian Goldberg, BBC Radio WM.*

"An absolute gem of a book – part brilliantly written lament for an earlier age, part opportunity to reminisce about a time when you hankered after a Garden Goal ('Every Boy's Dream!')… football's relentless commercialisation comes, naturally enough, at a cost. It's brought us everything from the Stalinist-style obliteration of the game's pre-1992 history to the modern player, kissing the badge, logo and sponsor's name after scoring. A purer, less cynical era is depicted throughout *Got, Not Got*. Buy it – you will not be disappointed."
*SportsBookoftheMonth.com*

"The best dose of retro football nostalgia ever. I can't put it down!"
*footballcardsuk.com*

"It's a beautiful book – a smorgasbord!"
*John Keith, City Talk FM, Liverpool*

"An exhaustively researched collection of football programmes, stickers, badges and memorabilia, a coffee table book you can dip in and out of at any time. Some of the advertisements from old programmes are classics – 'Bovril – hot favourite for the cup!' Or culinary advice to players: 'Full English – eat up your fried bread now, it's full of energy.' Eat your heart out Arsene Wenger."
*Christopher Davies, Football Writers Association Book Reviews, footballwriters.co.uk*

"The wonderful book *Got, Not Got* – more of the same can be found on their equally superb blog."
ThreeMatchBan.com

"It is far more enjoyable to think about football in times past, and it is a seam that is
tapped so richly by authors Derek Hammond and Gary Silke, who have written a wonderful
A to Z of lost football culture, treasure and pleasures."
*The Blackpool Gazette*

"A book exploring the lost culture of the game when pitches were mudbaths, managers wore
sheepskin coats and players were too embarrassed to dive - a bygone age that seems a far cry
from the profit-driven game today played in the main by overpaid primadonnas."
Paul Suart, *Birmingham Evening Mail*

"Kampprogrammer, fotballfrimarker, fotboltegneseriert… smakfullt illustrert. Just get yourself one!"
*PIN* magazine, Norway

"This was in WSAG's Christmas stocking and it's fantastic.
Co-written by one of our fanzine chums Gary Silke, editor of The Fox, it is an amazing collection of
half-forgotten things and much loved memories. It covers mainly the 1970s when football itself seemed
more innocent (probably only because we were all still at school back then).
But if you're the same age as us then this book has your name all over it.
Admiral kits, football Action Men, League Ladders, Esso badges. On and on we could go…
Buy it. Well worth it."
*When Skies Are Grey*

"Outstanding."
Miniboro.com, the Middlesbrough FC, art and interviews website

"A great read with fantastic visuals, the book reflects on how football used to be before the sanitisation
of the Premier League. Amusing and quirky, this book captures the spirit of football from the terraces.
This book is an absolute must for any footballing household."
*King of the Kippax*

"*Got, Not Got* is wonderful. I'm feeling quite emotional leafing through it!"
Nick Alatti, The Bridge 102.5FM in the Black Country

"In an imaginary Victorian boozer in a sepia-tinted corner of the globe, old blokes gather to talk about
football back when it was good. It is a tempting retreat, with some fantastic flagship vehicles such as
*Got, Not Got* and 500 Reasons To Love Football using modern media to hark back to a glorious past."
theseventytwo.com

"It would have been easy to just produce a book of nostalgic memorabilia.
It's something else to have a book that captures the heart and soul of the time.
I didn't just look back fondly, I had flashbacks full of excitement!
A wonderful journey back into our childhoods…"
God, Charlton and Punk Rock blog

"A real treat – the ideal Christmas gift for anybody who loves their retro football.
With a page dedicated to Hull City, 'Fer Ark' and all, this is the perfect football book for this time of year."
Hull City FC official website

"Whatever the football fad that accompanied the era that you got into football, you'll find it all revisited in
the wonderful book *Got, Not Got*. It's a great book, every page has a throwback memory for any football fan
over 30 and you'll dip in and out of it for months on end as I have done."
Nick Sports Junkie blog

INTERNATIONAL POLITICAL ECONOMY SERIES

General Editor: Timothy M. Shaw, Professor of Political Science and International Development Studies, and Director of the Centre for Foreign Policy Studies, Dalhousie University, Halifax, Nova Scotia

*Recent titles include*:

Pradeep Agrawal, Subir V. Gokarn, Veena Mishra, Kirit S. Parikh and Kunal Sen
ECONOMIC RESTRUCTURING IN EAST ASIA AND INDIA: Perspectives on Policy Reform

Deborah Bräutigam
CHINESE AID AND AFRICAN DEVELOPMENT: Exporting Green Revolution

Steve Chan, Cal Clark and Danny Lam (*editors*)
BEYOND THE DEVELOPMENTAL STATE: East Asia's Political Economies Reconsidered

Jennifer Clapp
ADJUSTMENT AND AGRICULTURE IN AFRICA: Farmers, the State and the World Bank in Guinea

Robert W. Cox (*editor*)
THE NEW REALISM: Perspectives on Multilateralism and World Order

Ann Denholm Crosby
DILEMMAS IN DEFENCE DECISION-MAKING: Constructing Canada's Role in NORAD, 1958–96

O. P. Dwivedi
DEVELOPMENT ADMINISTRATION: From Underdevelopment to Sustainable Development

Diane Ethier
ECONOMIC ADJUSTMENT IN NEW DEMOCRACIES: Lessons from Southern Europe

Stephen Gill (*editor*)
GLOBALIZATION, DEMOCRATIZATION AND MULTILATERALISM

Jeffrey Henderson (*editor*), assisted by Karoly Balaton and Gyorgy Lengyel
INDUSTRIAL TRANSFORMATION IN EASTERN EUROPE IN THE LIGHT OF THE EAST ASIAN EXPERIENCE

Jacques Hersh and Johannes Dragsbaek Schmidt (*editors*)
THE AFTERMATH OF 'REAL EXISTING SOCIALISM' IN EASTERN EUROPE, Volume 1: Between Western Europe and East Asia

David Hulme and Michael Edwards (*editors*)
NGOs, STATES AND DONORS: Too Close for Comfort?

Staffan Lindberg and Árni Sverrisson (*editors*)
SOCIAL MOVEMENTS IN DEVELOPMENT: The Challenge of Globalization
and Democratization

Anne Lorentzen and Marianne Rostgaard (*editors*)
THE AFTERMATH OF 'REAL EXISTING SOCIALISM' IN EASTERN
EUROPE, Volume 2: People and Technology in the Process of Transition

Stephen D. McDowell
GLOBALIZATION, LIBERALIZATION AND POLICY CHANGE: A Political
Economy of India's Communications Sector

Juan Antonio Morales and Gary McMahon (*editors*)
ECONOMIC POLICY AND THE TRANSITION TO DEMOCRACY: The Latin
American Experience

Ted Schrecker (*editor*)
SURVIVING GLOBALISM: The Social and Environmental Challenges

Ann Seidman, Robert B. Seidman and Janice Payne (*editors*)
LEGISLATIVE DRAFTING FOR MARKET REFORM: Some Lessons from
China

Caroline Thomas and Peter Wilkin (*editors*)
GLOBALIZATION AND THE SOUTH

Kenneth P. Thomas
CAPITAL BEYOND BORDERS: States and Firms in the Auto Industry,
1960–94

Geoffrey R. D. Underhill (*editor*)
THE NEW WORLD ORDER IN INTERNATIONAL FINANCE

Henry Veltmeyer, James Petras and Steve Vieux
NEOLIBERALISM AND CLASS CONFLICT IN LATIN AMERICA: A
Comparative Perspective on the Political Economy of Structural Adjustment

Robert Wolfe
FARM WARS: The Political Economy of Agriculture and the International Trade
Regime

---

**International Political Economy Series**
**Series Standing Order ISBN 0–333–71708–2 hardcover**
**Series Standing Order ISBN 0–333–71110–6 paperback**
(*outside North America only*)

You can receive future titles in this series as they are published by placing a standing order.
Please contact your bookseller or, in case of difficulty, write to us at the address below with
your name and address, the title of the series and the ISBN quoted above.

Customer Services Department, Macmillan Distribution Ltd
Houndmills, Basingstoke, Hampshire RG21 6XS, England

# Bureaucracy and the Alternatives in World Perspective

Edited by

## Keith M. Henderson
*Professor of Political Science*
*Department of Political Science*
*State University of New York College at Buffalo*

and

## O. P. Dwivedi
*Professor of Public and Environmental Administration*
*Department of Political Science*
*University of Guelph*

Foreword by Ferrel Heady

Published by
PALGRAVE MACMILLAN
Houndmills, Basingstoke, Hampshire RG21 6XS and
175 Fifth Avenue, New York, N. Y. 10010
Companies and representatives throughout the world

PALGRAVE MACMILLAN is the global academic imprint of the Palgrave
Macmillan division of St. Martin's Press, LLC and of Palgrave Macmillan Ltd.
Macmillan® is a registered trademark in the United States, United Kingdom
and other countries. Palgrave is a registered trademark in the European
Union and other countries.

*Outside North America*
ISBN-13: 978–0–333–73354–7
ISBN-10: 0–333–73354–1

*Inside North America*
ISBN: 0–312–22097–9

This book is printed on paper suitable for recycling and
made from fully managed and sustained forest sources.

A catalogue record for this book is available from the British Library.

Library of Congress Catalog Card Number: 98–54699

Printed and bound in Great Britain by
Antony Rowe Ltd, Chippenham and Eastbourne

# Contents

# List of Tables

# Foreword

This collection of studies of 'alternative administration' has been assembled by the editors O.P. Dwivedi and Keith M. Henderson as a sequel to their *Public Administration in World Perspective* (1990) and Dwivedi's *Development Administration: from Underdevelopment to Sustainable Development* (1994). The notion of 'alternative administration' entails *choices* as to national systems of public administration that go beyond the usually accepted models to include less-conventional options more suited to the needs of developing countries in various regions of the world.

The key motivation here is a search for alternatives that are indigenous rather than imposed or copied. The objective is to nurture the growth of public administration systems that are better suited to the differing patterns of history, culture, economics and politics, as seen from a global perspective.

The editors and their collaborators have arranged their contributions in three main categories. The initial grouping starts with two overview chapters. In the first, Dwivedi traces use of the concept of 'development administration' that has largely shaped the evolution of contemporary administration in Third World countries. As he views it, a 'developmental creed' emerged, necessitating that 'in order to attain development, a country's administrative structure should conform to the standards of the most advanced industrial countries'. The task of these countries was 'perceived to be the supplier of external inducements to change through technical assistance and transfers of technology and institutions'. Disillusionment with the results has meant that political leaders and administrators in the developing countries now recognise that they must be more self-reliant in developmental objectives, using mostly their own very limited resources and employing a variety of indigenously devised administrative alternatives.

In the second chapter, Dwivedi and Henderson explore in more detail a new 'realistic unity through diversity concept of development', stressing that development must be 'human-needs-centred' and 'sustainable'. They examine some recent models offering possibilities of moving in the right direction – including the Sarvodayan movement inspired by the teachings of Gandhi, Islamic fundamentalism, and Liberation theology – but conclude that they sound better in theory than they have proven to be in application, and that other options are needed to transform rhetoric into reality.

The remaining chapters in this group focus on some of these possibilities for alternative forms of public administration, and are in my opinion the most novel and innovative contributions in this volume. These include greater use of NGOs (non-governmental organisations), written by Henderson; more attention to feminist, native and cross-cultural considerations, advocated by Reeta Tremblay; and increased emphasis on ecological principles in the formation of organizations, formulated by Jean Mercier. These are obviously not mutually compatible objectives, but as a group these chapters offer an array of possibilities from which choices can be made that are deemed responsive to differing circumstances. These chapters differ markedly in tone and approach. For example, in contrast to the more balanced presentations of the other authors, Tremblay argues ardently that the 'imported discourse' of public administration 'also brings with it the patriarchal and gendered discourse underlying the state and its structures', with the consequence that each society in the Third World 'may have to develop its own deconstruction of the gendered bureaucratic discourse and its relationship to indigenous institutionalised patriarchal structures and construct its own strategies for the empowerment of women'.

One of the most thought-provoking of these pieces is Mercier's 'Ecological Principles, Emerging Organisational Forms and Post-Modernism'. His thesis is that the use of ecology as a starting point shows promise of 'replacing unsustainable development patterns with environmentally sound and sustainable development'. Based on familiarity with the literature, answers to questions posed to ecological leaders, and analysis of characteristics of ecologist and environmentalist organisations, he identifies several institutional or organisational principles derived from ecological thinking: diversity (or avoidance of standardisation); self-regulation (implying decentralisation); human scale (indicating a tendency towards limitation of organisation size); and finality (discarding an excessively segmented view of reality); plus a megaprinciple of 'thinking globally and acting locally'. He also suggests that an ecological counter-principle is opposition to excessive specialisation, and a related tendency to be skeptical of bureaucratic or technocratic organisation. Underlying these views is a preference to view organisations through biological rather than mechanical metaphors. Mercier draws parallels between ecologist thought and 'postmodernism', particularly in their joint antipathy to the ideas of uniformity and standardisation, their preference for the ideas of diversity and variety, and their questioning of the notion that there is a uniform and standardised model of development. Finally, he points out that although there are common patterns between ecologists' views and other forms of alternative administration, there are also important points of difference. Moreover, in many types of organisation, none of these emerging alternative administrative designs may be applicable.

The second category of chapters in the volume consists of regional studies, offered by authors with expert direct knowledge of the regions treated: East and West Africa; Southern Africa; the Middle East; South Asia; Southeast Asia; Latin America; and the Caribbean. As might be expected, these treatments vary considerably in approach and coverage, but at least to some extent each of them deals with the historical evolution of existing administrative arrangements in the region, as well as with the evaluation of potential reform proposals.

The concluding segment consists of one chapter with a more international perspective. Gerald Caiden speculates about the future of public administration and the administrative state, appropriately considering the contributions of the United Nations and other entities representing the international community.

As this survey of its contents suggests, this compilation offers a generous range of options available for experimentation that might be helpful to developing countries in dealing with the complicated problems that they confront as the result of the interface between domestic factors and external interventions.

FERREL HEADY
*Professor Emeritus*
*Public Administration and Political Science*
*University of New Mexico, Albuquerque*

# Preface

Bureaucracy is a term used both to characterise a particular type of organisational structure (centralised, hierarchic, specialised) and to criticise it (slow, inefficient, cumbersome). Bureaucracy and the alternatives to it in the developing world is the theme of this book of readings. The focus is government bureaucracy (more kindly labelled Public Administration) and a full range of options to the status quo, many of them outside the realm of conventional thinking. The purpose of the book is to extend the concern with bureaucratic reform based only on New Public Management, World Bank/International Monetary Fund, and other Northern thinking stressing private sector models, to a fuller range of ideas and practices. Towards that end, grassroots movements and non-governmental organizations, Islamic revivalism, feminist administration, ecological administration, Liberation theology, and other modes of administration are discussed.

In 1990, we edited a volume entitled *Public Administration in World Perspective*[1] which included country/ regional studies; perspectives; and a section on 'Internationalization'. More recently, O.P. Dwivedi has published an important book in the Macmillan International Political Economy series.[2] In the former volume, we attempted to anticipate academic research requirements and the impact of indigenous scholarship. Dwivedi, in his book, explores development administration and its dilemmas emphasising bureaucratic morality and administration for sustainable development. In this volume, we emphasise the same concerns but with a more ambitious, more practical goal: to alert students and enlightened Third World officials to new frameworks for understanding and new case studies that move beyond centralised, hierarchical approaches which are Eurocentric, male-dominated, value-neutral, and non-ecological.

What a difference a near decade makes! No updating or modest revision of a 1990 or even 1994 text will do justice to the contemporary world of Development Administration or the broader, more descriptive, field of Comparative Public Administration. The context in which administrators function has changed dramatically: the communist alternative has largely disappeared; a Northern consensus model of administration is being exported not just by the World Bank and International Monetary Fund but by individual northern governments; external resources are scarcer; and the state has retreated as a problem-solver in deference to the private and even voluntary sectors. At the same time, an information age has raised enormous new opportunities for citizen access and participation, sharing of common concerns, distribution of information and propaganda, and consequent redistribution and decentralisation of administrative power.

PLAN OF THE BOOK

The book is divided into three parts. In the first part, following Ferrel Heady's insightful Foreword, an overview of development administration is provided by Dwivedi stressing decade-by-decade changes and the overall failure of development administration efforts. Next, in Chapter 2, the editors postulate two 'mega-models' of development and five 'real-world' patterns. Each pattern is associated with administrative possibilities (all five have previously been applied) and assessed in terms of its conformance to the 'ideal-typical' mega-models.

In Chapter 3, Henderson suggests an alternative to conventional public delivery of services in the 'third sector', that realm found outside the public and private sectors. Non-governmental organisations and grassroots movements offer prospective options for service delivery to poor populations.

Chapter 4, by Reeta Tremblay, is a theoretical exploration of 'inclusive administration' which emphasises the feminist critique of bureaucracy. Reconceptualisation is needed, she argues, since bureaucracy remains male-centred.

A different kind of perspective is found in Chapter 5; Jean Mercier posits a new conceptual focus on ecologists' thinking and relates this to postmodernism. Organisation theory is employed as a framework, as it is for Tremblay's chapter.

The second section of the book consists of regional studies organised by broad geographical areas but highlighting certain significant countries. Each author in this section has approached the question of bureaucracy and its alternatives from his (their) own vantage point, but all share the concern with widespread reform.

From an Australian point of view, Mark Turner and John Halligan in Chapter 6 discuss East and Southeast Asia recognising the difficulty of generalisation in this diverse group of countries. They explore bureaucratic origins, the role of the state, and 'Asian values and bureaucratic behaviour'. Confucian ideology and bureaucracy along with consensual decision-making are evaluated as a prelude to alternatives to bureaucracy such as decentralisation and the Third Sector. The latter complements Chapter 3 – A Third-Sector Alternative – and other discussions throughout the book of NGOs and grassroots movements.

Dwivedi in Chapter 7 pursues the theme of the book in its South Asia application. Governance and Administration are dealt with in historical context with administrative culture, corruption, and *Desi* style of public management explained. At the time of independence, South Asian countries had two models of development to choose from: (a) the liberal capitalist democratic model, or (b) the communist model. The emergence of the administrative state raised issues of administrative accountability and the need to empower indigenisation of administrative practice.

In the next chapter, Balogun and Mutahaba, in the African context, attempt to identify institutional arrangements which will produce a citizen-oriented, innovative bureaucracy. They indicate that the African bureaucracy needed to meet the challenges of the next century will possess characteristics totally different from the classical model. Similarly, Hilliard and Wissink, in the subsequent chapter, seek appropriate characteristics of the new, post-apartheid public service in South Africa. They, too, show the relevance of the colonial experience but posit South Africa as the current 'powerhouse of Africa'. South Africa has undertaken several large projects with other Southern African countries including giant water and electricity reticulation networks. The demise of apartheid institutions has influenced the functioning of the public service in a number of ways.

The Middle East, as discussed by Farazmand in Chapter 10, has parallel circumstances to Asia and Africa in its rich diversity and varied responses to outside rule. Farazmand explores the pre-modern origins of bureaucracy and shows the deep roots (500 BC for Iran) of present-day administration. Islamic administration has characteristic differences from the usual bureaucratic form and is best understood in cultural/evolutionary context. As an alternative, it has surprising viability.

Finally, in Chapter 11, Meacham deals with the complexity of Latin America and the Caribbean. Again, parallels are found but the distinct differences in Colonial administration, which ended more than 100 years before other areas, and the proximity to the US affect administration. Nevertheless, Spanish and (in Brazil) Portuguese influences persist in the government bureaucracy along with language and custom. Meacham explores the issue of indigenisation, indicating the few examples of governmental accommodation to needs of overlooked population groups – primarily Indian – and the long road ahead.

In the third section of the book, Future Directions,

Gerald Caiden, a participant in the United Nations' meetings of development administration experts, takes those meetings as a starting point and analyses the future of the administrative state. He charts a course into the twenty-first century.

The book as a whole, we believe, suggests several approaches which would require a re-evaluation of current policies regarding administrative reform and which affirm the relevance and importance of indigenous, non-hierarchical, sustainable and human-needs-centred administration. The usual approach to administrative change is challenged because of its heavy reliance on privatisation and its imposed Northern values.

We wish to acknowledge the forbearance and support of our family members as well as our colleagues and the press editorial staff. We are also indebted to specialists in the field for their helpful comments and suggestions. Tim Shaw, series editor, deserves a special word of thanks, as does Ms Aruna Vasudevan of Macmillan Press.

**Notes and References**

1. O.P. Dwivedi and Keith M. Henderson (eds), *Public Administration in World Perspective* (Ames, Iowa: Iowa State University Press, 1990).
2. O.P. Dwivedi, *Development Administration: from Underdevelopment to Sustainable Development* (London: Macmillan, 1994).

# List of Abbreviations

| | |
|---|---|
| ANC | African National Congress |
| ANIC | Asian Newly-Industrialising Countries |
| APEC | Asia Pacific Economic Cooperation |
| ARP | Administrative Reform Programme |
| ASEAN | Association of Southeast Asian Nations |
| C&AG | Comptroller and Auditor General of India |
| CAG | Comparative Administration Group (USA) |
| CBI | Central Bureau of Investigation (India) |
| CEBs | Christian Based Communities |
| CIA | Central Intelligence Agency |
| CIEI | Centre for the Study of Indigenous Education |
| CMD | Communist Model of Development |
| CODE-NGOs | Caucus of Development NGOs (Philippines) |
| CONAIE | Conference of Indigenous Nationalities |
| CSP | Civil Service of Pakistan |
| DIR | Directorate of Criminal Investigation |
| EAEG | East Asian Economic Group |
| EPDRF | Ethiopian Peoples Democratic Revolutionary Front |
| ESKOM | Electricity Supply Commission (South Africa) |
| EZLN | Zapatista Army for National Liberation |
| FMLN | Farabundo Marti National Liberation Front |
| GEAR | Growth, Employment and Redistribution (South Africa) |
| GNP | Gross National Product |
| HNCD | Human-Needs-Centred Development |
| HPAE | High-performing Asian Economies |
| IAS | Indian Administrative Service |

| | |
|---|---|
| IBRD | International Bank for Reconstruction and Development (World Bank) |
| ICAC | International Conference Against Corruption |
| ICS | Indian Civil Service (during the British Raj) |
| ILO | International Labour Organisation |
| IMCAR | Inter-ministerial Committee on Administrative Reform |
| IMF | International Monetary Fund |
| INCORA | Institute for Agrarian Reform |
| LCDM | Liberal Capitalist Democratic Model |
| MITI | Ministry of International Trade and Industry (Japan) |
| MPS | Ministry of Public Service |
| NATO | North Atlantic Treaty Organisation |
| NGOs | Non-Governmental Organisations |
| NIA | National Irrigation Administration (Philippines) |
| NIEO | New International Economic Order |
| OD | Organisation Development |
| ODA | Overseas Development Agency (Britain) |
| OECD | Organisation for Economic Cooperation and Development |
| OPEC | Organisation of Petroleum Exporting Countries |
| PDW | Public Works Department (India) |
| PIP | Performance Improvement Programming |
| PNDI | Paraguayan Indigenous Institute |
| PSC | Public Service Commission |
| PVOs | Private Voluntary Organisations |
| RDP | Reconstruction and Development Programme (South Africa) |
| SABC | South African Broadcasting Corporation |
| SAPs | Structural Adjustment Programmes |
| SSRC | Social Science Research Council (USA) |
| TADA | Togo Association of Development Agencies |
| TVA | Tenessessee Valley Authority (USA) |
| UN | United Nations |

| | |
|---|---|
| UNO | United Nations Organisation |
| UNDP | United Nations Development Programme |
| UNESCO | United Nations Educational, Scientific and Cultural Organisation |
| UNGASS | United Nations General Assembly Special Session (1997) |
| US | United States of America |
| USAID | United States Agency for International Development |
| VFM | Value for (public) Money |
| WHO | World Health Organisation |
| WTO | World Trade Organisation |

# Notes on the Contributors

## Editor

**O.P. Dwivedi**, Ph.D., LL.D. (hon) is a Professor in the Department of Political Science at the University of Guelph, Canada. He has been consultant/advisor to various governments such as Canada, India, Papua New Guinea and Mauritius. His international assignments include work for UNESCO, WHO, UNO and the World Bank. He has published several books and articles/chapters on development administration, environmental policy and management, public service reforms, and public service ethics. He is a former President of the Canadian Political Science Association, and the past Vice-President of the International Association of Schools and Institutes of Administration, Brussels, Belgium, and chair of the Research Committee on Technology and Development, International Political Science Association.

**Keith M. Henderson**, D.P.A., is Professor of Political Science, State University of New York, College at Buffalo, and has served as department chair and chairperson *pro tem*. He previously taught at the Graduate School of Public Administration, New York University, where he was an Associate Professor of Public Administration. He worked for the City of Los Angeles for five years. Dr Henderson has published over 40 books and articles in the field of Public Administration and has received two Fulbright Senior Lecturing awards (Iran, 1975–76; Croatia, 1998–99).

## Contributors

**M. Jide Balogun**, Ph.D., is currently Senior Regional Adviser, Public Sector Management Reform, the United

Nations Economic Commission for Africa. He has taught at the universities of Ife and Lagos, and was Director General and chief executive of the Administrative Staff College of Nigeria. He has edited the *African Journal of Public Administration and Management* since its inception in 1992.

**Gerald E. Caiden**, Ph.D., is Professor of Public Administration in the School of Public Administration at the University of Southern California. He received his B.S. in economics and Ph.D. from the University of London where he attended the London School of Economics and Political Science. Dr Caiden has taught at universities in Canada, Australia and Israel, and has published over 40 books and articles in public policy and management and comparative public administration. He is a participant in the prestigious United Nations Group of Experts in Public Administration.

**Ali Farazmand**, Ph.D., is Professor, School of Public Administration, Florida Atlantic University (Fort Lauderdale, Florida) and previously was Assistant/ Associate Professor of Political Science and Public Administration, Northern Kentucky University. He is the author of numerous books and articles and has edited the *Handbook of Bureaucracy* (New York: Marcel Dekker, 1991) and the *Handbook of Comparative and Development Public Administration* (New York: Marcel Dekker, 1991; 2nd edn 1999). He served as a public official in the Government of Iran prior to the Revolution.

**John Halligan**, Ph.D., is Professor of Public Administration and Director, Centre for Research in Public Sector Management, University of Canberra, Australia. He has published a number of books, chapters and articles on public management and reform in Australia, New Zealand, OECD countries and Southeast Asia.

**Ferrel Heady**, Ph.D., is Professor Emeritus, Public Administration and Political Science, University of New Mexico, and is former president of the University as well as its Academic Vice-President. He was formerly director of the Institute of Public Administration at the University of Michigan and has published extensively in the field of Public Administration. His standard textbook, *Public Administration: A Comparative Perspective* is in its 5th edn (New York: Marcel Dekker, 1996).

**Victor G. Hilliard** is Professor in the Department of Public Administration and Law, Port Elizabeth Technikon, South Africa. He has taught at various post-secondary institutions in South Africa since 1983. His speciality fields are human resources management and public service transformation. In 1995, he published *Performance Improvement in the Public Sector*.

**Carl E. Meacham** is Professor of Political Science, State University of New York, College at Oneonta, where he has been since 1981. He has a Ph.D. from the Rockefeller College of Public Affairs, State University of New York at Albany. He is completing a textbook on *Democracy in Latin America* and has published in the *Social Science Record*, *Policy Studies*, *Review of Asian Thought and Society* and other journals. He has served as an academic administrator in the State University of New York central administration, Albany.

**Jean Mercier**, Ph.D., is Professor of Political Science and Chair of the Department at the University of Laval, Quebec City, Canada. He has degrees from the Sorbonne in Paris, the University of Montreal (law), and a Ph.D. from the Maxwell School at Syracuse University. He has published widely including *Downstream and Upstream Ecologists* (Westport, Ct.: Praeger, 1998).

**Gelase Mutahaba**, Ph.D., is a former Professor and Head, Department of Political Studies, at the Dar-es-Salaam University. He is a past Secretary-General of the African Association for Public Administration and Management; and is currently Director, Department of Administration, at the Commonwealth Secretariat, London, UK.

**Reeta Chowdhari Tremblay**, M.A., Ph.D., is Associate Professor and Chair, Department of Political Science, Concordia University, Montreal, Canada. Her current areas of research are the secessionist movement in Kashmir, identity-based politics and citizenship and popular culture. She has published extensively on secessionist movements and public policy.

**Mark Turner**, Ph.D., is Professor, School of Administrative Studies at the University of Canberra, Australia. He has spent many years working and researching in Southeast Asia and the Pacific in the fields of public sector management and politics. His latest book is *Governance, Administration and Development: Making the State Work* (co-authored with David Hume).

**Henry F. Wissink**, Ph.D., is Professor and Head, Department of Public Administration and Law, and Dean, Faculty of Commerce and Governmental Studies, Port Elizabeth Technikon, South Africa. Previously, he taught at the University of Stellenbosch. He specialises in the field of development management and policy analysis. He is co-author of three major books.

# Part I
# Perspectives on Development Administration

# 1 Development Administration: An Overview

O.P. Dwivedi

## LINEAGE AND EVOLUTION

The concept of 'development administration' has been almost exclusively used with reference to the developing nations of Asia, the Middle East, Africa and Latin America.[1] Perhaps it was first used by Donald C. Stone, although the term was popularised by Riggs and Weidner in the 1960s. Whatever its point of origin, the conceptual genre of development administration has been distinctively Western. Two interconnected Euro-American traditions converge in it. One of these streams of administrative thought is the result of an evolving trend of scientific management that began at the turn of the century with the administrative reform movement. The second current is the somewhat newer trend towards national planning and government interventionism that emerged as a direct consequence of the Great Depression, the Second World War and postwar reconstruction. Events between the collapse of the international economic order in the 1930s and attempts to establish a newer one at Bretton Woods and San Francisco in 1944 and 1945 welded these two currents of administrative thought into a new synthesis that could be termed crisis management and reconstruction administration.

There are at least three historical perspectives that influenced the evolution and concept of development administration: the impact of the Great Depression and the New Deal philosophy, postwar challenges, and lessons from the Marshall Plan.

3

## From the Great Depression and Postwar Reconstruction

With the Great Depression, many of the political and economic assumptions of theories of scientific management came into question. In fact, what emerged was a radical reformulation of the old presuppositions about the role of the state in the form of Keynesianism. By the mid-1930s, state interventionism had become an accepted fact in the industrialised world. Massive government interventions through schemes such as the Tennessee Valley Authority (TVA) in the United States, development corporations in Europe and Latin America, and a variety of sectoral and regional programmes of economic recovery provided the necessary stimulus to refloat the troubled economies of the industrial West. In a sense, one could argue that both the New Deal and European corporatism performed a similar function: they provided a mechanism to revive the market economy. The greatest stimulus for economic recovery, however, was the way production was accelerated using technological innovations.

War efforts during the period 1939–45 established a great number of administrative, political and economic adjustments. For the most part, these were related to two developments: a drastic reformulation of economic and political thinking related to the role of the state; and the introduction of a 'new' theory that gave the government a decisive managerial role in preventing the undesirable effects of economic cycles. As an anti-cyclical function, the state assumed a leading role in procuring economic prosperity and full employment mainly through furthering industrialisation by stimulation or direct investment. The educational, scientific and research role of the state was also expanded, as well as the provision of social security and welfare functions.

The combination of this multitude of new tasks produced one central organisational trait: big government. In fact, the new vision of management also had to seek continuous mobilisation and participation of the public in such government projects. From a broad perspective, the role of the state was seen as correcting and rebuilding economic processes. Besides untangling bottlenecks and providing leadership in those areas where the private sector had proven ineffective, the public and the private sectors were supposed to join forces in mixed economic undertakings to increase employment and productivity. Thus, when independence came to the colonised nations, it was not surprising to see the same prescription given to them by the new contingent of 'experts' and international-aid people.

**Post-Second World War Challenges**

With the end of the Second World War, myriad new contextual factors would pose further challenges to the administrative state. A first priority was *European reconstruction*. The American response to the challenge was the Marshall Plan. This gigantic programme was aimed at providing a massive infusion of foreign aid, thus establishing conditions for rebuilding the devastated European economies. It was also intended to provide the stimulus for accelerated and sustained economic growth, to enable these nations to both catch up and achieve self-sustained growth. In the Marshall Plan, reconstruction and development were seen as two sides of the same coin and were conceptualised almost interchangeably.[2]

A second contextual factor emerging at the end of the war was a radical *transformation of the international system*. The age of imperialism came to an end, and a process of rapid decolonisation began. The world political structure was to shift away from a European-centred system of multipolar balance to a rigid bipolar one. The emergence of two superpowers with diametrically opposing economies and ideologies, coexisting in an uneasy climate of entangling mechanisms of collective defence, characterised the new era, one of cold war.

In the realm of international organisations, the *creation of the United Nations* was to have a fundamental impact in changing the fabric of international cooperation. True, the collective security role of the UN proved to be less effective than its framers dreamed, yet a number of functional areas of international cooperation and development gave the organisation a new direction: the promotion of change through multilateral technical aid and finance. All through the 1950s and early 1960s, the developmental role of the UN became a dominant feature of the organisation and its related programmes and agencies.

Finally – and most importantly – a Third World of new nations came into being.[3] With the exception of Latin America, the Third World was a legacy from the prewar colonial order dominated by a handful of European powers. As the process of decolonisation began, the cold war amongst other northern superpowers moved southward. Efforts by the leadership in the new nations to transform formal diplomatic sovereignty into real economic sovereignty brought them into increasing conflict with the West, whose prosperity then still depended upon the captive markets of Africa, Asia, the Middle East and Latin America. A new breed of essentially anti-colonial and anti-*laissez-faire* nationalism emerged in the former colonial territories, reinforcing Keynesian inclinations, and development became the dominant issue in the Third World.

**Lessons from the Marshall Plan**

Since the inception of the Marshall Plan, one cold-war notion had become central in Western foreign policy: prosperity was seen as an antidote to the spread of communism and other radical solutions. Both the Colombo Plan and President Truman's Point Four programme constituted the earliest Western attempts at induced development through foreign aid. On the whole, the

Marshall Plan model dominated development strategies, although the complexity of the task was clearly far beyond the possibilities of Marshall-type aid. It was also obvious from the onset that underdeveloped countries, whose economies and sociopolitical structures had evolved at the periphery of a colonial system (the major difference being cultural and indigenous technological capabilities) were not in a similar position to that of war-ravished Europe, which had never experienced protracted under-development. The latter required a reconstruction effort through the timely infusion of capital and technology to continue its prewar course. The former, by contrast, were in a completely different cultural, social, political and economic situation. In concrete terms, development aid from the West was precisely directed to maintain and modernise existing economic structures, not to redirect colonial misdevelopment.[4]

Despite this fundamental difference, the Marshall Plan became the standard model for development. The technical aid schemes and the UN first and second development decades were nothing but expressions of this accepted doctrine. Thus, development administration emerged closely tied to foreign aid and Western formulae for development planning (based on the misleading experience of Western Europe) which were supposed to have equal (and universal) applicability in the Third World.

## DEVELOPMENT ADMINISTRATION: THE CONCEPT

Development as a concept became an intellectual fixation in American social science in the early 1950s. Following Walter Rostow's *The Stages of Economic Growth: A Non-Communist Manifesto*,[5] the political development literature tried hard to search for the non-economic institutional conditions for accelerated – although orderly – economic growth. As far as the role of public administration in this process is concerned, two interrelated visions prevailed. One originated within the Committee on Comparative Politics of the Social Science Research Council (SSRC), especially within its Political Development Group. The other vision of public administration in development came from the Comparative Administration Group (CAG) of the American Society for Public Administration. While both shared many assumptions, they differed in terms of focus.

For those in political development, public administration was perceived as an institution contributing mainly to stability and *systems maintenance*. In their view, bureaucratisation was a functional condition for stability and maintenance of legitimacy in the political order (that is, political development). As for those in comparative public administration, modern administration (that is, bureaucratic administration) was essentially a mechanism for the *attainment of developmental goals*. This way, the key role of bureaucracy was seen as a processor to provide planning and an institutional infrastructure to convert inputs of objectives, capital and know-how into developmental outputs. In the words of Donald Stone:

> Development Administration is the blending of all the elements and resources (human and physical) . . . into a concerted effort to achieve agreed-upon goals. It is the continuous cycle of formulating, evaluating and implementing interrelated plans, policies, programmes, projects, activities and other measures to reach established development objectives in a scheduled time sequence.[6]

Such characterisation of development administration emphasised the formal and technical aspects of the government machinery. Developmental goals were assumed to be agreed upon by the local as well as Western elites. These goals were usually referred to as 'nation-building and socio-economic development'.[7] Swerdlow has identified two interrelated tasks in development administration: institution building and planning.[8] Other authors have outlined a number of other development-oriented activities, such as the management of change, establishing an interface between the 'inner' environment and the larger intra- and extra-societal context, and the mobilisation of physical and human energies and information and their subsequent conversion into policies and actions.

Five major themes can be identified in development administration. One is that development could only be attained by *modernisation*[9] (that is, Westernisation); that is to say, by the diffusion of Western values and technology. The second is that the predominant feature of development is *economic development*, the latter defined in terms of growth[10] (that is, the expansion of GNP per capita over a period of time). The third is that quantitative change (economic change) would produce a *critical mass* leading to qualitative changes. Sequentially, economic growth would bring about social changes that in turn would bring about political development. Structurally, an expansion of wealth in the hands of an investor elite would trickle down, bringing generalised prosperity and a higher standard of living. The fourth theme is that the process of development historically entails the movement of societies between a traditional agrarian stage of underdevelopment and that of development after the take-off stage (*industrial*). All societies are postulated to be developing or in transition between these two poles. Furthermore, all nations are said to have been at one time underdeveloped. For instance, today's industrial societies were once agrarian and feudal; by sheer accumulation or induced changes in their social structures and value systems they became developed. What is more, the paradigm postulates that once a region becomes developed, capital, technology and ideas would, in turn, bring development to other areas. The fifth main developmental underpinning of development administration is the emphasis on *harmony* – 'stable and orderly change'.[11] Development in this context is perceived not only as the attainment of change but mainly as adaptation and systems maintenance.

## DEVELOPMENT ADMINISTRATION: 1950s TO 1970s

Although from the UN viewpoint, the first development decade began from the 1960s, in reality it started in the 1950s with President Truman's Point Four programme and the Colombo Plan. This was a decade of optimism, expectations and the establishment of international aid agencies in various industrialised countries. The decade of the 1960s was an era of general prosperity and also one of pervasive intellectual optimism throughout the world. The inspiration of visionaries and the belief that modernisation and technology would surmount any obstacle to human progress were the orders of the day. It was thought that with sufficient foreign aid and a revamped administrative system, Third World countries would follow – if not overtake – the industrial and technical levels of the West.[12] There was confidence that an administrative state would triumph with the help of the new tools of development administration. Examples of reconstruction and rapid recovery in Western Europe and Japan were used to strengthen this belief. Thus, when multilateral foreign aid programmes were inaugurated in the 1950s, Western social scientists, administrators and social engineers envisioned a worldwide utopia: new societies, new frontiers, national integration and global development through technical cooperation. Several so-called 'wars' were fought with the emerging administrative hardware: the war on poverty, the war on underdevelopment, and the cold war. Administrative and military modernisation – both closely related developments – became the operational mechanisms for the preservation of post-colonial Western ascendancy over the developing areas.[13] But the expected administrative paradise did not materialise.

By the early 1970s, a rude awakening was noticed concerning the inadequacies of the developmentalist paradigm of public administration to cope with urgent problems. The crisis of development administration in this decade became one of identity and purpose with seemingly devastating effects on the entire field of public administration, in the North as well as the South. Assumptions, methodology and focus became increasingly irrelevant. In fact, after its accelerated growth of the 1960s, development administration apparently plunged into the depths of an intellectual depression.

The second decade of development had lost its impetus by the late 1960s. A spirit of frustration and despair with development administration and with development in general had set in. It appeared evident that externally-induced modernisation had failed to eradicate the basic problems of underdevelopment that it purported to solve. While some significant increases of GNP had indeed taken place, poverty, disease and hunger had either worsened or remained unaltered. The same could be said of the growing gap between the rich and poor nations, not to mention that between different social strata within nations. In many regions, incremental reformism had failed to create a more equitable socio-economic order and had proven to be an ineffective antidote to radical change. To the contrary, frustrated reformism had begun to fuel revolutions. Large on the horizon loomed the Indo-China experience. It demonstrated that over-administering was neither an efficient nor an effective insurance against revolution.

By the 1970s development could no longer be taken for granted. At the same time, the tendency towards decay had become noticeable in both the North and the South. The energy crisis, the growing economic recession in the major industrial countries, and a crisis of liberal democracy

in the early 1970s dampened most traces of early optimism. An increased contradiction between market
economies and market politics would also serve to undermine some of the once-persistent civic traditions of
Western pluralism. This contradiction was rooted in the
severe limitations of even continuous economic growth
to reduce social antagonisms. Its implications – the fiscal
crisis of the state and a manifest trend towards stagnation and political stalemate – constituted a new context
for public administration.

## DEVELOPMENT ADMINISTRATION IN THE 1980s

By the mid-point of the third development decade
(1971–81), then, the very foundations of the development
administration paradigm were severely in question. Not
only was their usefulness in the Third World itself in
doubt, but an intellectual crisis had set in among students
of development administration in the West. The gap
between the centre and the periphery was widening rather
than narrowing in both relative and absolute terms. Instead
of development and nation-building, turmoil and frag-
mentation proliferated throughout Africa, Asia, the Middle
East and Latin America. Urban crises, energy crises,
cessation of growth, unemployment and breakdowns
of public institutions and public morality had all disappointed the early optimism about the ability of First World
administrative technology to solve problems everywhere.

During the fourth development decade, the New
International Economic Order (NIEO), became an important new symbol in the development arena. Its demand
for a basic realignment of the world economy through
changes in trade, aid and technological transfer was appreciated but generally ignored by the richer donor
nations. There was in fact no global consensus concerning NIEO objectives, and some commentators felt that

it might even harm certain countries. At the same time, the NIEO represented a basic needs strategy, attempting to redirect the terms of reference of the development debate; that is, the strategy would provide the essential necessities for people, yet worry less about such traditional indicators of growth as GNP per capita. While the World Bank and the International Labour Organisation (ILO) symbolically endorsed this approach to development, the monumental change in the world system demanded by the NIEO did not occur. In the absence of a common strategy adopted by both the West and the Third World, the NIEO also went the way of earlier concepts.

Another recent factor that has broadened the scope and spectrum of Third World problems is the withering away of Eastern European and Soviet Union communist states, and the entry of at least some of them – particularly in Central Asia – into the realm of the Third World. It should be noted, however, that this is likely to be a transitional state for many of these nations. Although the Eastern bloc nations may be considered 'poor' for the time being, many will not remain so for long. Akin to the economic recovery of Western Europe after the Second World War, many nations in Eastern Europe and the former Soviet Union – except Central Asia and parts of the Balkans – may leave the rest of the Third World nations behind.

Development administration cannot be divorced from either political economy or a theory of development. Its core assumption is the identity between development and modernisation[14] – the latter understood as Westernisation. The function of development and administration was chiefly that of a midwife for Western development, creating stable and orderly change. The West would produce the external inducements thought necessary to promote such change.[15] Development-mongering became synonymous with reform-mongering. The latter was always oriented to preventing discontinuities in the mode of production, elite structure and international alignments.

The implicit goal, it now seems, was to modernise yet not to uproot the existing structures and processes, thereby keeping the poor, mono-producer and backward societies locked into a cycle of dependence and underdevelopment. Put in rather simplistic terms, the prevailing paradigm assumed that the problem, whatever its nature, remained with and at the periphery; however, the solution was always locked in the centre. In an extreme way, the prevalent attitude was not only that 'they' had the problem, but that they *were* the problem. Conversely, the West was postulated both to *have* and to *be* the solution. Traditional societies had to be saved, if not from the appeals of communism, then at least from themselves.

A developmental creed soon emerged that posited that in order to attain development, a country's administrative structure should conform to the standards of the most advanced industrial societies. The key issue, then, was the transformation of the existing traditional machinery into the new entity. This was to be accomplished through administrative development: the modernisation of the public service machinery through external inducement, transfer of technology, and training by foreign so-called experts. For this task, there was already a neat prescriptive model to be found in Western tradition. This tradition was based on the dichotomy between politics and administration; it was a system that relied on hierarchy, unity of command, political neutrality, recruitment and promotion on the merit principle, public service accountability, objectivity and ethical probity. While external sources placed a great insistence on sustaining these values in the Third World, in reality these principles were supplemented by existing traditional methods. Thus, a parallel value system gained currency; Western models were set up and existed simultaneously with the traditional economy and black market. Rarely were the principles of development administration as recommended by the experts from the West questioned; on the other hand, these were generally accepted at face value by native elites, especially where a relatively smooth transition to nationhood took place.

The post-independence political and bureaucratic leaders rapidly moved to replace colonialists.[16] Western education, as formally imparted in these countries and as continued by returning graduates from the West, was perceived as a tool both for personal advancement within the organisation and for acceptance by similarly trained professionals in the West. Thus it is not surprising to find that an administrative machinery took shape that was incapable of implementing developmental goals, particularly in dealing with poverty and scarcity. In spite of much rhetoric, the emergent administrative systems tended to be imitative and ritualistic. Practices, styles and structures of administration generally unrelated to local traditions, needs and realities succeeded in reproducing the symbolism, but not the substance, of a British, French or American administrative system. Even where a relatively large contingent of trained functionaries existed, such as in India, Pakistan, Kenya, Nigeria and Ghana, a continuation of colonial administrative culture prevailed. At the same time, a massive dose of political interference in the way of doing things stifled developmental initiative. Confronted with an ineffectual developmental bureaucracy, the Western solution was to call for even more administrative development. This was also the preferred option of the local elites. Technical solutions were more palatable than the substantive political decisions needed to bring about real socioeconomic change. Administrative reorganisations and rationalisations for the sake of abstract principles soon became the ends rather than the means of development administration.

The developing nations were disillusioned when they found that, instead of being recipients of capital *from* the West, they were forced to make net transfers of their meagre resources *to* the West. In order to service their debts, several developing nations became virtually bankrupt. Restrictive trade practices prohibited the poor from

exporting their products. The problem was further compounded when commodity prices fell to the lowest level
in fifty years, while the prices of manufactured products
kept rising. It is no wonder that starvation, destitution,
inequality and oppression have continued in most of the
developing nations. The Golden Age of the 1950s had
turned into the Age of Pessimism and Disillusion by the
1980s. Nevertheless, some rays of hope came from the
worldwide awareness displayed at the Earth Summit in
1992, which demonstrated that no one group of nations
could keep on 'progressing' while the majority remained
hungry and poor. It may sound moralistic to argue that
it is the duty of the North to help close the development gap with the South, but is there another way out?
Until now, the South has adopted a weak approach to
negotiations with the North. This awakening means that
new approaches to North–South relations are required.


DEVELOPMENT ADMINISTRATION IN THE
FIFTH DECADE: THE 1990s – DILEMMAS
BEFORE US

From anyone's standpoint, the decade of the 1990s – as
it nears its end – does not represent an improvement
over the last forty years. Administrative culture and
morality remain problematic, and improvements within
the administrative infrastructure are few and far between.
Several long-established assaults on administrative inadequacy were still to be found in the 1990s, but there is
also one newer approach. The former were in the nature of orchestrated campaigns supported by top political
leadership; the restructuring of administrative organisations including the creation of new agencies; use of control
mechanisms, increased penalties, anti-corruption boards,
and the like; various training programmes; and streamlining of procedures. In its early years, comparative public
administration and its protégé, development administra-

tion, were closely associated with these activities. The newer approach is to cut back the scope of government activities through privatisation (particularly of parastatals), deregulation, decentralisation, and similar efforts, all of which may be subsumed under the rubric 'debureaucratisation' – in other words, a reduction in the scope (or at least in the rate of growth) and the streamlining of procedures of the centralised administrative apparatus in the public sector. This is the dominant trend of the 1990s.

**Administrative Structure**

The newer approach – sanctioned by the World Bank, IMF, the US Agency for International Development (USAID), the British Overseas Development Agency (ODA) and other similar international aid agencies – appears to provide an alternate model to the panoply of problems associated with administered development through 'de-administered' development. The opportunities for improper actions are lessened by reducing the scope of government activities: no bureaucratic structure equals no bureaucratic problems. Thus the market-friendly policies championed in the United States, in Canada, or in the United Kingdom, as well as by numerous other Western European governments, are being universally applied. And since public administration is seen more as a problem than a solution, the granting of aid is made conditional upon policy changes involving a downsizing of the bureaucracy as well as the elimination of subsidies, the acceptance of devaluation, and other changes in monetary and fiscal policy. These 'structural adjustment' policies have had mixed results, with some desirable reductions but much human suffering. The first to be axed are the bloated parastatals, now to be entrusted to the private sector. At one time these were deemed administrative innovations that would circumvent the established rule-bound bureaucracy. Unfortunately, over the years, they have proved a bastion of patronage, are often terrorised by powerful unions, and are a drain on scarce resources.

## Administrative Personnel

If the downsizing of the bureaucracy continues, by the turn of the century there should be fewer public service officials proportionate to the population (compared to the 1980s), even though some systems will continue to expand. Ideally, public servants at all levels and in all areas of the world would be better trained, more professional, more aware of the world at large, more ethical, more productive and more humble. If this happens, morale would improve and public attitudes toward bureaucrats will change for the better. In that case, administered development would co-exist with private-sector entrepreneurship, and private voluntary organisations (PVOs) and non-governmental organisations (NGOs), with public officials providing an enabling environment and the necessary security, infrastructure and financial regulation (unencumbered by red tape). One downside of this scenario – the upside of which is a true 'partnership' – is that it may open up opportunities for abuse.

If the new administrative environment emphasises public–private cooperation and market-friendly strategies, those managers who remain in strictly government service would need to reorient themselves towards a more facilitative role. The potential for abuse consists in the existing informal techniques for avoiding and expediting myriad official regulations, supplemented by new rules aimed at making it easier for entrepreneurs to do business. The tendency to blame the bureaucrat for corrupt behaviour needs to be tempered by a realisation of how the whole system encourages unethical actions. Middlemen, touts, politician-protected elements, and the politicians themselves play their roles in the system. In Brazil the expediters are even unionised.[17] And nearly everywhere, public and private roles are easily mingled.

## Administrative Procedures

Much attention is given by public administration specialists in developed countries to systems approaches and management information systems. These days, systems are computerised and administrators (especially in national and provincial capitals) are computer-literate. In developing countries, the process of computerising requires detailed analysis of operations. Properly done, the introduction of computers is based on a series of studies that focus attention on legal requirements, the quality of statistics, overlap and duplication, cross-checking and cost-effectiveness. In India, a national computer network has been established that encourages uniformity and interchangeability. It links districts, states and the central government, and provides information flows through both mainframes and microprocessors.[18] Numerous other examples of intelligent use of computers may be cited, from Kenya's calculation of crop yields to India's application in railway seat reservations to Vietnam's computerisation training centres in Ho Chi Minh City.

Considerable attention by both indigenous and Western specialists has been given to computerisation, with some important cautions regarding the pitfalls as well as opportunities in their use.[19] By the twenty-first century, the remarkable developments in telecommunications should make information available worldwide through networks using fibre-optic cables, digital switches, extremely powerful computers and methodologies of artificial intelligence. Those politico/administrative systems which are able to maximise the free flow of ideas and to promote the widest possible dispersion of information will be the ones that benefit. This new era will produce a reduced role for the public sector and an expanded reliance on private enterprise. Therefore numerous controlling and licensing activities will have to be eliminated or overhauled. This calls for streamlined decision-making, fair and uncomplicated rules and enforcement mechanisms, and opportunities to appeal unfavourable decisions.

CONCLUDING OBSERVATIONS

A brief overview of some of the challenges facing development administration in the South in the next century is given below:

1. *The growing influence of religion and traditional values in politics and administration*    Religion has emerged once again as a force to be reckoned with in many Third World nations. In some cases, religious fundamentalism has a mass appeal, especially when it involves a rejection of Western-style modernisation and replacing alien norms and customs with indigenous cultural and religious values. In many instances, these traditional values are at odds with Western-style development, secular politics and cold efficiency. While the administrative machinery continues to function within professed secular values, fundamentalism gets reflected not only in the political process but also finds expression in the style of administration. These tensions and conflicts should be appreciated so that the demands of fundamentalism and the role of religion are accommodated within the needs of development administration.

2. *Political factors in managing the public sector*    Development administration, sired by the West, assumed many Western values, including the separation of politics from administration. It was thought that the management of the public sector would be done largely by administrators, ably assisted by economic plans formulated to achieve national goals. Consequently there was no place for the political dimension in the administration of development. However, as the Iran experience and similar instances proved, politics could not be kept separate from economic planning, management of resources or administration of the public sector. Either the administrative system responded to political demands, or politicians and indigenous leaders

simply bypassed the established administrative apparatus and created their own network to accomplish their objectives. This created confusion and delays which were blamed on the lack of ability of leaders and administrators. Public sector management then became a source of economic ills, administrative mismanagement and political blundering. The separation of politics from administration remained artificially embedded in the parlance of theory and practice of development administration, while political factors dominated economic, social and administrative concerns. This realisation is yet to be acknowledged by many scholars, practitioners and international aid personnel.

To reiterate, by their nature, *developmental issues are political* because they deal with the authoritative allocation of values in the context of limited and sometimes fast-diminishing resources. In developing countries, therefore, public sector management cannot remain purely within the domain of so-called value-free administration. Otherwise, irrespective of the amount of international aid, history may repeat the failed experiment of America's massive involvement in Iran. Such repetitions have already occurred elsewhere. What is immediately needed is a new style of development administration and management, that blends political, economic, administrative, cultural and religious forces to produce the desired results.

3. *As the Third World enters into the twenty-first century* The past few decades of developments in politics and administration have demonstrated two major trends: standards of conduct and probity have steadily declined among politicians; and such a massive regression is yet to engulf the bureaucracy. Despite charges of overwhelming corruption, the administrative apparatus is functioning, and statecraft has not become completely contaminated by sectarian and similar insidious forces. Although the media continue to project

a negative image of bureaucracy as being bloated, inefficient, status-conscious and authoritarian, it is not totally
cynical or bereft of idealism and dedication. The next
few years are going to be crucial for Third World
politicians and administrators as they make efforts to
lift up their people from the quagmire of poverty,
malnutrition and underprivilege.

The challenge before the leaders and administrators of the Third World is this: to achieve the
developmental objectives of basic human needs (the
provision of food, appropriate habitat, health and education), as well as social justice, removal of poverty,
and self-reliance with very limited resources. They will
have to be more self-reliant in the twenty-first century; they cannot expect the same level of aid should
the attention of the West turn towards helping Eastern Europe. They must turn to their own resources
among and between themselves much more than they
have done so far. For this they will require a cadre
of professionally trained and dedicated administrators,
as well as moral and just politicians who can stand
against the forces of corrupt politics and unscrupulous commercial and business interests. They must not
only learn the lessons of the 'debt crisis' of the 1980s
but, also, of the 'Asian crisis' of the late 1990s.

This chapter has surveyed a difficult terrain, the top-
ography of which is continually changing. In light of the
preceding analysis, one should now ask a number of
fundamental questions: Is the present theory and practice of development administration – its basic concepts,
assumptions and values – still relevant for the twenty-
first century? Should we not take into consideration
various indigenously-developed alternatives more suited
to tackling the satisfaction of people's basic needs, the
eradication of poverty and the protection of human dignity? Could those alternatives be based on human-centred
sustainable development? Answers to these questions are

provided in the essays following this chapter. One thing is clear: the current crisis of development administration is precisely a consequence of the inability to incorporate the substance of other non-Western developmental experiences into the prevailing conceptual mould. This is the focus of this book.


## Notes and References

1. This chapter is drawn in edited form from O.P. Dwivedi, *Development Administration: from Underdevelopment to Sustainable Development* (London: Macmillan Press, 1994), pp. 1–41.
2. Clyde Sanger, 'Pearson's Eulogy', *International Journal*, no. 325 (1969–70), p. 179.
3. Irving Louis Horowitz, *Three Worlds of Development. The Theory and Practice of International Stratification* (New York: Oxford University Press, 1966), pp. 3–14.
4. C.R. Hensman. *Rich Against Poor. The Reality of Aid* (Harmsworth: Penguin, 1975), chapter 3, passim.
5. Walter W. Rostow, *The Stages of Economic Growth: A Non-Communist Manifesto* (Cambridge, Mass.: Harvard University Press, 1960).
6. Donald C. Stone, 'Tasks, Precedents and Approaches to Education for Development Administration', in D.C. Stone (ed.), *Education for Development Administration* (Brussels: International Institute of Administrative Sciences, 1966), p. 41.
7. Milton D. Easman, 'The Politics of Development Administration', in J.D. Montgomery and W.J. Siffin (eds), *Approaches to Development, Politics, Administration and Change* (New York: McGraw-Hill, 1966), pp. 69–70.
8. Irving Swerdlow, *The Public Administration of Economic Development* (New York: Praeger, 1975), pp. 15–19.
9. I. Swerdlow, *Economic Development, op. cit.*, p. 345.
10. Gerald Meier (ed.), *Leading Issues in Economic Development* (New York: Oxford University Press, 1970), p. 7.
11. Susanne Bodenheimer, 'The Ideology of Developmentalism: American Political Science's Paradigm – Surrogate for Latin American Studies', *Berkeley Journal of Sociology*, vol. 15 (1970), pp. 95–137.
12. Garth N. Jones, 'Frontiersmen in Search for the "Lost

Horizon"', *Public Administration*, vol. 36, no. 1 (January–February 1976), p. 99.

13. Brian Loveman, 'The Comparative Administration Group, Development and Anti-Development', *Public Administration Review*, vol. 36, no. 6 (November–December 1976) pp. 6–20.

14. I. Swerdlow, *Economic Development, op. cit.*, p. 345.

15. See, for example, Ralph Braibanti, 'Transnational Inducement of Administrations Reform. A Survey of Scope and Critique of Issues', in Montgomery and Siffin (eds), *Approaches to Development, Politics, Administration and Change*, pp. 133–83; and Bernard Schaffer. *The Administrative Factor* (London: Frank Cass, 1973), pp. 244–5.

16. See L. Kooperman and S. Roseberg, 'The British Administrative Legacy in Kenya and Ghana', *International Review of Administrative Sciences*, vol. 43, no. 3 (1977), pp. 267–72.

17. Robin Theobald, *Corruption, Development and Underdevelopment* (New York: Macmillan, 1990), p. 157.

18. See Mukul Sanwal (ed.), *Microcomputers in Development Administration* (New York: McGraw-Hill, 1987).

19. See, for further reference, USAID, *Cutting Edge Technologies and Microcomputer Applications for Developing Countries: Report of an Ad-Hoc Panel on the Use of Microcomputers for Developing Countries* (Boulder: Westview Press, 1989); OECD, *The Internationalisation of Software and Computer Services* (Paris, 1989); Heinrich Reinesmann, *New Technologies and Management: Training the Public Service for Information Management* (Brussels: International Institute of Administrative Sciences, 1987); William J. Stover, *Information Technology in the Third World* (Boulder, Co.: Westview Press, 1984); and Mukul Sanwal, 'An Implementation Strategy for Developing Countries', *International Review of Administrative Sciences*, vol. 57, no. 2 (June 1991), pp. 220–35.

# 2 Alternative Administration: Human-Needs-Centred and Sustainable

O.P. Dwivedi and Keith M. Henderson

## THE SEARCH FOR ALTERNATIVES

In this chapter, we will sketch two 'ideal-typical' models of development that involve universalised values: human-needs-centred development and sustainable development. We will then examine several real-world development models (Liberal Capitalist Democratic; Communist; Sarvodaya; Islamic Revivalist; and Liberation Theology) in terms of their philosophy and application; finally, we will attempt to reassess and suggest possibilities for some of these existing development models through corresponding alternative models of development administration. Our ambition is to suggest a *realistic* 'unity through diversity', contingent upon the full potential of human nature – in its religious and cultural dimension – being effectively marshalled.

As discussed in Chapter 1, the administration of development – as conducted by Third World governments – with 'help' from outside – has not yielded the anticipated results. This recognition is widespread: it is not limited to academic critics, 'postmodernists' in developed and developing countries, or political opposition groups. It has called forth a variety of responses, ranging from neo-isolationist sentiments in many OECD (Organisation for Economic Cooperation) countries to the World Bank/IMF/bilateral donor consensus that emphasises political and economic conditionality for loans and grants. Even for those who do not accept this 'Washington/ London/Paris/Tokyo consensus' and its requirements for debureaucratisation and privatisation, there is agreement that the North–South interaction pattern of the 1960s, 1970s, 1980s, and even 1990s is not desirable. Some elite groups still call for 'more of the same' (that is, large doses of funds without conditions that strengthen existing institutions and reward those already in power) but their number is dwindling without widespread support. In the days when strong administration in Western-oriented polities was thought of as a bulwark against communism, it was easy for political leaders to seek funding in return for loyalty or at least neutrality. In some cases, it was easy for politicians in developing countries to play one lending nation or multilateral agent against another in a competition for fealty. Such circumstances no longer apply.

Development administration and its handmaiden, comparative public administration, is an academic field that encouraged the old pattern. It has not succeeded in breaking loose from its old moorings, although there is considerable discussion of the type of administration that might be preferable to the status quo. In most of its applications, development administration still presses for Northern, universalistic designs tied to a single, competitive world economy. Alternatives to bureaucracy in its usual Weberian guise and to debureaucratisation and privatisation need to be further explored.

Lonely voices in the development community call for realisable change from the bottom up. David Korten, for example, suggests a strategy for creating local economies that empower poor people and small communities within a network of global competition.[1] Korten and other social/political movement theorists, however, do not specify details of administrative structure, procedure or personnel. Central–local relationships, organisation of ministries or departments, the role of parastatals, linkages with grassroots groups for purposes of licensing, permitting and regulation, and the recruitment/socialisation mechanisms for whatever administrative personnel are required are not discussed.

Similar gaps exist in the environmentalist/ecologist literature and in feminist approaches to administration in developing countries. Yet these are the sources (that is, NGO/PVOs; sustainable development thinking in all its forms; and the inclusion of the other half of the world – the distaff side – in power and decision-making) from which a meaningful public administration study and practice must be drawn.

Interesting currents in the broader literature on development are beginning to move towards the inclusion of voices previously unheard. For example, a paradigm shift seems to be occurring in feminist perspectives on sustainable development as the women-in-development discourse is replaced by a women-environment-development concept. The women-in-development philosophy and literature emphasised the importance of women in the development process, but required no basic questioning of the development enterprise itself. Women would be *included*, but would not determine overall directions; more women administrators at all levels presumably would satisfy the participatory requirements, and gender *awareness* would assuage the demands of women's groups. The new paradigm – discussed in Chapter 4 – goes beyond this model to include reconceptualising 'development' to incorporate and respond to gender concerns.[2]

Similarly, an ecological reconceptualisation may help to shift the 'consensus' paradigm away from its economic roots. This approach will be discussed in Chapter 5. Along with a strong moral consciousness, administrators would think in terms of natural growth and change, eschew overly-specialised and hierarchical bureaucracies, and seek adaptive patterns of behaviour. Structurally, moral government and administration with gendered representation and rethinking would move towards participative, bottom-up organisations based on democratic management. Decentralised people-centred organisations – such as the National Irrigation Administration in the Philippines discussed in Chapter 6 – would predominate, along with 'self-help' and Third Sector organisations. Partnerships – with cooperative relations between public, private and voluntary organisations – would multiply.

Towards the end of charting a new course for development administration, two overarching models are presented, followed by five descriptive models.

## MEGA-MODELS OF DEVELOPMENT

Development models are influenced by the theorist's perception of the economic, social and political needs of a country or a region. The models change as perceptions change. For the twenty-first century, new models and theories are needed to guide administrations of countries involved in development. All models of development might be evaluated in terms of the conformity to two basic mega-models: human-needs-centred development, and sustainable development.

### Human-Needs-Centred Development (HNCD)

The theory of HNCD is based on the requirement to create new conditions of conceptualising development. These conditions, including the reality of the New World Order resulting from the collapse of communism and the widening gap between North and South, are recognised as the basis for sound analytic thinking. In fact, it has been demonstrated that present social and economic theories are incomplete and inadequate.[3] Governments, policies, development and administration should be geared towards meeting human needs. The HNCD model recognises that economic, political, social and moral factors cannot be separated.[4] Its essence has been widely discussed in United Nations conferences and in works of scholarship.

HNCD focuses on meeting basic human needs. It recognises the difficulty in answering the question, 'Who decides how the basic needs of individuals are satisfied?' Fundamental human needs are the same in all cultures; what varies is the way or the means by which the needs are satisfied. Political leaders do not change basic needs – they simply influence how those needs are met. HNCD puts people at the centre of its thinking and emphasises self-determination and participatory approaches. Its methods are flexible, depending on the country and the political situation, but its goals are the same.

In this arrangement, civil servants and the government as a whole are expected to assume greater moral responsibility for their actions. The unstructured format would improve the ability to have effective administration, and putting humans first would require that officials be accountable to the public and be at service to their needs. Individuals in the society would be recognised and each would be treated with dignity and respect; arrogance of officials would disappear along with favouritism and corruption.

However, even the best officials face difficulty in attempting to organise administration around a new development concept that changes to meet changing needs and different development methods. The usual bureaucratic processes represent inflexible adherence to rules and procedures.

**Sustainable Development**

Sustainable Development is a second alternative development model. It also has been widely discussed as a goal, with some attention to its practical implementation. This model is based on long-term thinking and conservation of nature's finite resources. In numerous countries, the existing political organisations still view the environment as a resource to be used and exploited for private gain. In the past, many development theorists ignored the impact of degradation of the environment on the future.

The key propositions of sustainable development were contained in the Bruntland Commission Report in 1987 – a UN-sponsored study showing the intimate links between economic development and the environment – and in Agenda 21 (1992), which resulted from the United Nations Conference on Environment and Development (the 'Earth Summit') held in Rio de Janeiro. These propositions recognise the potentially constructive tie between economic development and the environment, as well as the reality of environmentally inappropriate policies and actions often pursued by governments.

The sustainable development model relies on a social consciousness that recognises the need to protect the resource base while also meeting the present needs of the people. Its success is dependent upon the input of decision-makers, ecologists, economists and others, including individuals at the grassroots level. Sustainable development combines resource management with production, creation of sufficient jobs, food security, fair access to products, opportunity and equal distribution of resources between sexes and generations.

Economically, the environment is easy to view as a commodity available for personal exploitation. Sustainable development, however, changes people's perceptions about their resources. It divides resources into natural capital (non-renewable and renewable), human-made capital, and cultural capital. It recognises both the need to generate economic progress and the limitation of natural resources.

Politically, each government has an obligation to assume the responsibility of guiding its nation's progress towards sustainable development. It can reinforce principles in its legislature, executive policies and investment decisions. It can facilitate efforts by non-governmental organisations (NGOs) and grassroots movements concerned with the environment.

The 1997 United Nations General Assembly Special Session (UNGASS) reviewed the progress, after five years, on the Agenda 21 document of 1992. Delegates to the session revealed continuing wide gaps in thinking between rich and poor nations, and disappointing progress towards Earth Summit goals. Wise resource management, equitable distribution of benefits, and lessening of negative impacts from economic growth are agreed-upon goals, but the South perceives unwarranted pressure to pursue a Northern agenda, while the North refuses to bear what it perceives as an undue burden.[5] The difficult interface between environment and economic development remains, and many – in both the North and the South – are not happy about the lack of constructive improvement since 1992.

The World Bank – now an advocate of sustainable development – is more optimistic than many. The World Bank's Vice-President for Environmentally Sustainable Development reported as follows:

Although the challenges are still daunting – over 800 million people worldwide are hungry because they cannot afford to buy the food that they need, and inadequate water supply and sanitation services create health problems for millions in the world's rapidly growing megacities – we are identifying cost-effective solutions to many of these problems and are beginning to address the fundamental problems associated with empowering the poorest (who are often located in rural areas) to lift themselves out of poverty.[6]

The obligation for administrators is to translate worthy objectives into administrative action while using a people-centred outlook to treat people fairly and impartially. Decisions would also have to be prompt and equitable. However, administrators could become overwhelmed in trying to incorporate many different ideas from different groups. In many areas, spiritual/religious teachings may provide a bond between administrators and the people they serve; awareness of and sensitivity to the surrounding environment can be shared values. Certainly, moral adequacy is required on the part of administrators.

## OTHER MODELS OF DEVELOPMENT

### The Liberal Capitalist Democratic Model (LCDM)

This model – usually characterised as the Western or Northern model – uses the concepts of democracy and progress as its cornerstones. In compliance with these concepts, values such as 'life, liberty and the pursuit of happiness' are enshrined. Peace, order and good government are also prominent. Based on classical liberalism – which includes political philosophers such as Locke and Montesquieu – it emphasises individualism and the dangers of undue ambition.[7] In addition, there is stress on business and commerce. The LCDM has been in practice for about 300 years; therefore, it is easier to evaluate and discuss its actual success or lack thereof.

Countries adhering to the LCDM place emphasis upon the economy with particular concern for free enterprise, innovation and consumerism. State regulation, encouragement, subsidisation and ownership vary considerably, but a common feature is sharp differentiation of the 'haves' and 'have-nots'. Even today in the benign welfare states in Scandinavia, for example, the rich are clearly divided from the poor. Consumerism can be said to define social, political and economic status in LCDM nations, and the corporate structure has been created due to consumer demand. Spirituality has declined, even though many nations (for example, the United States and Canada) were founded on religious morality.

When examining this model and relating its attributes

to the mega-models of development, it falls short in a number of areas. Lack of recognition of the honour and dignity of each human being is one shortcoming; arrogance of those in power might be another. Among other things, the practice of the LCDM over the past centuries has resulted in the demise of some of the important non-economic, non-market-based values better expressed in other models. It is based on this model that its proponents prescribed structural adjustment programmes for developing countries, with numerous unfortunate results. In an earlier era, colonialism and imperialism derived from an admittedly non-democratic variant of this model; in the current era, the near collapse of Asian economies shows the dangers of unfettered capitalism.

**Communist Model of Development (CMD)**

This model was based on Marx's theory of a classless society. It began as a reaction against the exploitation of the worker under industrialisation, and declared capitalism and the elite bourgeois as the enemies. The ironic result is that communism has succumbed to the fate it predicted for capitalism.

Theoretically, the CMD supports the destruction of the capitalist economy and the redistribution of wealth equally. Its purpose is to restructure society, taking power and wealth from the hands of an elite few and putting it into the hands of the proletariat/working class. The idea was for the proletariat to have the power to run the country, with an ultimate 'withering away of the state', but once the model was applied, the control of power simply changed from being held by a few elite royalists and capitalists into the hands of a new elite.

November 1917 saw the rise of the Bolshevik Party in Russia, based on Marxist–Leninist principles. To increase its power, it centralised its leaders into a single-party system with state control over all enterprises and investments in the nation. The decision was made to use a 'dictatorship' to control the social development of the state and eliminate the existing class structure.[8] The Russian Communist Party became a system with monopolistic control of the state, all social organisations and the channels of communication. Communism became a militant ideology based on the total authority of the communist party; party unity and discipline were the governing principles and decisions were based on a 100 per cent vote. Disagreement meant expulsion from the party; the military ensured that no friction or dissent occurred.

A second premise was 'democratic' centralisation. All governing bodies were elected bottom-up, but the decisions were top-down. In essence, the political system was a dictatorship with nothing left to chance.

The focus on a common enemy – capitalism – led to replication of the communist model in various other countries. Following the Second World War, Russia achieved domination of the states of Central and Eastern Europe, and attempted to extend its influence in Asia, Africa, Latin America and the Middle East. A 'cold war' ensued as the West sought to contain communist expansion.

Socially, communism allows for little individual freedom; the party seeks to control all aspects of life. Originally devoted to a classless society – emphasising the needs and concerns of the proletariat – in practice, the system has been a dictatorship over the working class. Changes in the power hierarchy brought no changes in the basic power structure. Only the faces occupying the top echelons of the hierarchy changed, not the distribution of power.

Economically, the communist party's focus was on redistribution of wealth out of the hands of capitalists. Capitalism was seen as the main enemy, and its elimination was a driving force behind policies and strategies. In the communist design, private enterprise is limited; assets are state-owned and the state plans investment. A first step for the party – once it assumed power – was the nationalisation of banks and insurance companies, beginning the process of a state-owned and controlled economy. In the agricultural sector, collectivisation was the pattern. In the communist system, public officials are influenced socially, culturally, spiritually and economically by the party. If a public official follows party guidelines, he or she is acceptable to the party; justice, fair play and impartiality are superseded by party rules. Individualism as found in the West is not permitted, because party leaders rule and dictate procedures. Party ideology is all-encompassing.

In contrast to the LCDM – which is well-entrenched and expanding, although occasionally threatened by collapse of financial markets – communism has been on the wane through the 1990s. The exception to this trend lies in its modified version in places such as China. The Chinese practice is sufficiently different – embracing capitalist ideas while still acknowledging the importance of the Chinese Communist Party – to deserve separate treatment.

**Sarvodaya**

Small-scale development initiatives such as those discussed in this chapter (Sarvodaya; Liberation Theology) are important alternatives to the LCDM and the CMD. They may arise spontaneously from the bottom up and spread through political or economic success, even though their goals are spiritual. They are often controversial and their original purposes may be undermined or subverted by insurrection, cooptation or repression.

The Sarvodayan movement's original inspiration was Gandhi. Sarvodaya signifies an awakening of spirit – and therefore liberation of the individual as well as groups. The result of this personality-awakening is intended to be a dynamic, non-violent revolution that results in a transfer of political, social and economic power to all the people. Sarvodaya has been practised in Sri Lanka since the mid-1950s.

Religion plays an important role in legitimising the Sarvodayan movement, supplying its leaders with rhetoric and inspiration,[9] and the religious aspects permeate the movement at every level, encompassing goals and tactics. However, it is the broad appeal of Sarvodaya's ideals and philosophy that makes it a viable development strategy and gives it potential to be transposed to different kinds of community development and to influence government services. Although it is a bottom-up, self-reliant approach, many of its ideals are attractive to moral administrators in government agencies and to other service-to-the-public organisations. Technically, in the Sri Lankan context it is an NGO (non-governmental organisation, discussed in Chapter 3).

There are six mutually supportive components in the Sarvodayan definition of development. These are the political, economic, social, moral, cultural and spiritual. Drawing on these aspects, Sarvodaya has grown in Sri Lanka from a brief work-camp organised by science teachers for their students, to a self-help movement active throughout the country.

The social construct of the Sarvodayan model focuses on achieving equality and solidarity. In order to accomplish intangibles such as these, it was necessary to use such things as health care and education, ensuring that all citizens had access to both regardless of their social status. The economic component of the model is of integral importance, however, it cannot be taken in isolation from other aspects. The Sarvodayan movement recognises that the individual and group need parallel development. Therefore, all efforts focus on projects that will accomplish both. This aspect is called *Abhyudaya* – the lifting up of all and everyone together. It places a strong emphasis on self-reliance as the ultimate goal of development. This requires an awakening of people's spirits and enhancing of skills, and development with minimum participation from outsiders. The people's participation is the basis for integrated economic development. With this in mind, Sarvodaya focuses on participation of all ages, sexes and occupations in order to utilise both formal and non-formal groups.

Development should begin with empowerment of the least powerful groups and help them move upwards. This means that the realisation and satisfaction of all basic human needs should be met first. Sarvodaya sets out to do this by emphasising *Swadeshi* (homemade) goods, while conserving precious resources. Cooperative methods are employed, allowing for maximisation of public participation. Enabling people to make their own decisions and giving them the means to implement those decisions creates awareness. The 'people power' that this awareness generates goes hand in hand with a desirable and appropriate kind of consumer consumption.

Politically, the movement focuses on decentralised participation in decision-making. Sarvodaya is non-partisan, which allows the movement to amass the needed trust of the population. Sarvodaya rejects power politics and institutionalised structures of power; instead, it emphasises participation and public service in a political context that uses non-violent structures and processes. It is opposed to political parties as a means of achieving reforms.

The moral aspects of the Sarvodayan development definition are based on *Dharma* (virtue; right conduct) but are applicable to other religious traditions as well. The basic premise is to enhance the dignity and self-respect of each other, which assumes that killing, stealing, lying, sexual misconduct and drug abuse will be minimised and eventually eradicated at the village and higher levels. Culturally, Sarvodaya instills harmony in relationships, not only among human beings but also between humans and other living creatures. Also, there is emphasis upon artistic expression through song, poetry and even village architecture. In short, Sarvodaya fosters cultural pride which will then have a significant impact on other development factors.

Lastly, the Sarvodayan movement is entrenched in the spiritual realm. The movement hopes to move people from a life of greed, hatred and delusion into one of awareness, truth and compassion. Although it is based on the principles of one religion, it is religiously plural and draws from other belief systems as well as Hinduism.

**Liberation Theology**

The roots of Liberation theology stem not from the poor or those who work among the poor, but from Protestant and Catholic theologians. In 1962, a Liberal Protestant group called the Church and Society in Latin America (ISAL) was formed. It applied the social messages found in the Gospel to helping the common people of Latin America. It was thought that political revolution was necessary to help the public, and Marxism was one of the strategies available to bring about desired goals. In the 1963 Episcopal Conference of Latin America, liberal theologians created a working paper on the subject, modifying the one originally formulated by the ISAL. This paper raised doubts about Liberation theology based on Marxist concepts, but wholly supported its basic beliefs. More importantly, in 1968 the Latin American Catholic bishops' conference endorsed a radical Christian approach – without official permission from the Vatican – to the achievement of social and economic rights involving mobilisation of the poor to struggle for their liberation. It is from this intellectual core that Liberation theology received its impetus, upon which the concept would flourish far beyond the theological environment in which it was created.

Liberation theology has had very close ties to the left-leaning elements of the Catholic church. This association with organised religion is the most important aspect of the movement's success, and the ideas articulated by theologians were passed on to the bishops and priests within the church system. The close interaction between village or urban *favela* (very poor neighbourhood) people and their local priests enabled the concepts of Liberation theology to flourish throughout the 1970s and beyond. As further discussed in other chapters in this volume, Christian Base Communities (CEBs) were established in many Latin American countries with the class-based purpose of reacting against oppression and seeking political rights along with self-help social and economic improvement. In South Africa (see Chapter 9), Liberation theology assumed an important role in the struggle against apartheid.

One of the more noble goals contained within the movement is that God will work through 'Liberation' to establish His Kingdom of peace, justice, equality and prosperity as mentioned in the Gospel. The theory takes abstract religious concepts and turns them into practice.

Liberation theology finds itself centred primarily in Latin America because of the distinctive geo-political and cultural factors there. The role of the liberationist Catholic priests is critical, with opposition to government – seen as the source of corruption and exploitation – as a key element. The emphasis is upon the class struggle of the poor against landed gentry, power elites and political leadership. The hope is that once power is in the hands of the people, then Marxism or some other such system can be applied to the whole area to bring about equality and dignity. This goal is pursued through community-type living that emphasises the idea of working together for the collective good of all. Faith and love are practiced.

The emphasis on betterment is illustrated in a quotation from the Brazilian author Leonardo Boff: 'What liberating potential is contained in the Christian faith, a faith that promises eternal life, but also a worthy and just life on earth'.[10]

There are nine central themes in Liberation theology: (1) living and true faith includes the practice of liberation; (2) the living God sides with the oppressed against the pharaohs of the world; (3) the world is God's project in history and for eternity; (4) Jesus, the Son of God, took on oppression in order to set us free; (5) the Holy Spirit – 'Father of the Poor' – is present in the struggles of the oppressed; (6) Mary is the prophetic and liberating woman of the people; (7) the Church is the sign of liberation of the people; (8) the rights of the poor are God's rights; and (9) Liberated human potential becomes liberative.[11]

## Islamic Revivalism

Unlike Sarvodaya, Liberation theology and other movements and initiatives that form enclaves within larger political systems, Islamic revivalism is represented in entire polities. Its very different manifestations in Iran, Saudi Arabia, Afghanistan and the Sudan share a common concern with the combining of state and society and strict adherence to the Qu'ran. Often called 'Islamic Fundamentalism' in its late-twentieth-century political manifestations, 'Revivalism' better captures the intent of reviving and reasserting the essence of the 'literal word of Allah', the Qu'ran. Although particularly brutal and primitive in some of its applications (for example, in Sudan; Afghanistan), the phenomenon is widespread and appears to be growing. Islamic revivalism is unusual in its indigenous character: it is not derived from Western/ Northern ideas.

To the revivalist, Islam comprises a total belief system that provides direction for all aspects of life. Islamic revivalists use the Shari'a law, the direct rule of Allah over society. Its objective is to develop the Islamic person; and this is reflected in moral codes, education, family organisation, and in other ways. Some countries maintain full rule by the Shari'a, but others (such as Pakistan) count themselves as Islamic states. Revivalism (or 'Fundamentalism') as a movement has asserted itself in recent years in countries as varied as Algeria, Egypt, Turkey, Kuwait, Bangladesh and Malaysia. Often suppressed, these and other Moslem states are experiencing its impact. Moslems (both Shia and Sunni) believe that they have a perfect code of behaviour that is true for all times to come. The universal Islamic declaration of human rights states:

> Islam approaches life and its problems in their totality. Being a complete and perfect code of life, it holds no brief for partial reforms or compromise solutions. It starts by making man conscious of his unique position in the universe, not as a self-sufficient being but as a part, a very important part, of Allah's creation. It is only by becoming conscious of their true relationship with Allah and his creation than men and women can function successfully in this world.[12]

Socially, Islamic Revivalism attempts to combine egalitarianism, militant puritanism, and an emphasis on the individual. The state acquires the right to rule and govern by the literal interpretations of the Qu'ran, which allows it to place social and ethical constraints on the individual. Revivalists believe that there are social limits to development, as illustrated in the 'failures' of Western societies.

Economics is of integral importance to the Islamic revivalist mode of development. Again, the individual plays a key role, for he or she is viewed as the primary economic unit. Economic performance is influenced by the availability of natural and raw material resources, religious and other social institutions, and Islamic philosophy, which supports and controls the sociopolitical superstructure. Regardless of this influence, all traditional economic activities and enterprises may be privately owned and operated. Action in every field of human activity – including economics – is spiritual, and should be in harmony with the goals and values of Islam. Politically, Islamic revivalism requires that there be a judicious distribution of economic and political power among individuals. This complements the principle aim of Islamic society, which is to maximise social welfare. The word 'Islam' in Arabic means 'submission' and 'peace'. A Moslem (Muslim) is a person who submits to the will of Allah and finds peace therein.

Morally, Islamic revivalist polities – notably Saudi Arabia and Iran – are opposed to drinking, narcotics, abortion, homosexuality and premarital sex. Traditionally, Moslem society was firmly committed to and entrenched in a range of sanctions – from censorship to dismemberment – to discourage the above-mentioned behaviours and others that are perceived as manifestations of the modern world. From an outside perspective, restrictive laws in the strictly Islamic states violate certain standards as enshrined in the universal declaration of human rights, particularly the equal treatment of women. Women are deprived and barred from sharing many public places with their male counterparts. They are barred from certain careers (notably in the judiciary and public service); restricted in dress and in inheritance rights; generally treated legally as less than men (the law of Hodud and Qesas); restricted in their behaviours at public places, their testimony in court, and in the use of power.

In summary, the spiritual realm of Islamic revivalism is all-encompassing. The state, its laws, and development practices are firmly rooted in the Qu'ran. Islamic revivalism is an affirmation of religious authority as holistic and absolute, admitting neither reduction nor criticism.[13]


## CAN THERE BE ALTERNATIVE MODELS OF DEVELOPMENT ADMINISTRATION?

In the ideal world, human-needs-centred development and sustainable development would be combined and realised through development administration. This would call for, first, a recognition that such outcomes are possible and, second, alternative models of development administration to achieve those outcomes. These alternative models would be required to redress the inadequacies of both the liberal capitalist democratic and communist development models.

As we saw, communism leaves little room for the individual; it has failed economically, politically and – arguably – socially, and has no viable future without an alternative communist model such as in China. Evidence of human rights abuses in China suggest that much change is required in the techniques of administration as well as the policies of the party before there is any approximation of 'ideal-typical' models.

The liberal capitalist democratic model of development – which has existed for several hundred years – has been in competition with the communist model for the last 50 years, and has successfully survived and displaced it only in the last few. The current development administration effort emanating from the West is based on this model, and emphasises extending Western materialist values by requiring policy changes based on these values as a condition for aid in the Third and former Second Worlds. The current consensus by the World Bank, the International Monetary Fund, the US Agency for International Development, and other Western (Northern) aid agencies is that public administration must be reformed by downsizing (or 'rightsizing'), deregulating, decentralising and democratising (the 4 Ds). The last – democratising – requires a more involved citizenry that is 'served' by public officials. (There is a slight difference in the World Bank's 'governance' approach and the USAID's 'Democracy Initiative'.) For all Western donors there is increased emphasis upon the private sector in this consensus, including privatisation, removing impediments to business expansion, and – generally – using businesslike techniques to improve productivity. Materialist values emphasising individual desire for economic and physical security are paramount. Many scholars and practitioners in the Third World have recognised the 'culture-bound' character of the supposedly universal prescriptions imposed by the West. Todd J. Moss states it well:

> The thesis presented here is that the United States is primarily defined by a particular liberal philosophy and concept of modernity, and that the projection of 'democracy' abroad is not necessarily a 'natural' or universal evolution of human development.[14]

For those concerned about the dangers of excessive materialism and neo-colonialism or even neo-liberalism, and disinclined towards the communist model, what are the alternative models of development and the corresponding models of development administration? We have suggested three other types, all of which have been implemented someplace, and which emphasise spiritual or religious values. In their improved form, these three models of development better meet the test of the desirable mega-models – human-needs-centred development and sustainable development. Their viability in a conflictual world may be unlikely, however, and some of their applications – such as Islamic revivalism in the Middle East – have been problematic at best.

One encouraging sign in an otherwise depressing prospect for religious or spiritual models is the evidence that value systems are changing around the world. A World Values Survey systematically conducted in 40 societies, representing over 70 per cent of the world's population in 1990–91 (including low-income countries such as India, China, Mexico and Nigeria; newly-industrialised countries such as South Korea; and former state-socialist countries in Eastern Europe and the former Soviet Union), found a gradual shift from materialist values to post-materialist values. The latter include the desire for freedom, self-expression and the quality of life.[15] Abramson and Inglehart's account also analysed over 20 years' worth of national surveys in European countries, finding the same result. Similarly, it has been determined that urban citizens in Latin America (Argentina, Brazil, Chile and Mexico were studied) value individual freedom somewhat more than equality of income.[16] Results such as these show that the materialistic culture of the West may be less highly regarded than is commonly supposed. What are the administrative prospects for realising post-materialist values and 'spiritual' cultures?

- Sarvodaya   In order for the non-materialist Sarvodayan movement to be implemented through a development administration model, some changes will be necessary. Key components of the movement would need to be adapted to fit the broader polity (assuming acceptance and support by political leaders) and the inadequacies of its application in Sri Lanka and India corrected; it would need to return to its Gandhian roots. For example, a sense of compassion, justice, fair play and impartiality would have to be instilled by training and reorientation of civil servants, who would then allow the movement to be fulfilled. Sensitivity and responsiveness are at the heart of such movements, for these two key traits recognise the honour and dignity of all. Since Sarvodaya is based on popular participation in small village areas, it remains easily accessible to the public, while maintaining a policy conducive to responsible and accountable development. Although highly idealistic, the possibilities are impressive.

  Again, the principles of the Sarvodayan movement as applied on a limited basis in Sri Lanka (and India) can be extended elsewhere for effective administration. Although the movement employs a bottom-up approach, it may be possible to interest civil servants in its feasibility.

- Liberation Theology   As further discussed in the chapters on Latin America and Southern Africa, Liberation theology has had a checkered history in its applications. It played a key role in Latin America and – in a rather different way – in the anti-apartheid struggle in South Africa, but now appears to be on the decline.

To revitalise Liberation theology as an alternative development administration approach would require its reassessment by the Roman Catholic church and its realignment with other movements such as the feminist movement. It has received challenges to this effect from women's groups and feminist theologians. The concepts of Liberation theology are impressive, but to administer them poses many difficulties.[17]

There are several steps in implementation. The first is for the professional and pastoral workers to become involved with the day-to-day lives of the community and people. This may involve support for cultivation of crops, construction of facilities, and cooperation with other agents such as trade unions. The second element is to help the local people to articulate and conceptualise those things that constrain them. Recognition of the problems that people face and assistance with resolution of those conflicts then leads to the third stage, which is self-assessment. Self-assessment and awareness are integral to the establishment of unity. Humanistic administration is practiced along with development of trade union activity, cooperatives, and other forms of organising for the benefit of the people. Administrative dimensions of the Christian Base Communities are discussed by Meacham in his Chapter 11 on Latin America.

- Islamic Revivalism   When judged by the criterion of good and effective administration in the two 'ideal-typical' models, Islamic revivalism in its philosophical form has both advantages and disadvantages. The combination of religion and government and the quest to address the whole individual has dimensions which are akin to human-centred development and sustained development, but also admits of discrimination against women and disregard for the environment. On the positive side are protection and respect for women, and the general Islamic emphasis upon harmony of person and nature as seen, for example, in the traditional design of Islamic cities. Building in harmony with nature and utilising impressive technological skill has resulted in a superior technology for dams and viaducts which have survived for over a thousand years, domes which can withstand earthquakes, and steel metallurgy in other structures imparting impressive strength.

In application, Saudi Arabia's monarchy lacks many requisites of human-centred development and sustainable development. The contrasting and antagonistic regimes in Iran and Sudan are even more repressive in human-rights terms, and evidence an inability to relate in a tolerant manner to other nation-states. The Taliban in Afghanistan – forbidding education and outside employment for females; requiring beards for men – appears mediaeval to Western eyes.

To properly judge the Islamic revivalist development model as a prospect for Islamic countries, it is necessary to move beyond its reactionary (Saudi Arabia) and militant (Iran and Sudan) manifestations to a purer form.

Implicit in the model is the notion that civil servants will be trained in the Shari'a rather than the usual Western precepts of good administration. In the perversion of this idea in the Sudan, Moslem fundamentalist ideologues dominate the military rulers and are guided by Islamist leader Hassan al-Turabi. In countries where fundamentalists are suppressed – as with the Moslem Brotherhood in Egypt, which has existed since 1928 – some popular fundamentalist activities are sometimes tolerated (Egyptian Brotherhood members have been allowed to form alliances with other political parties, under certain circumstances). Despite the rhetoric concerning democracy and pluralism, virtually all the more militant Islamists oppose both.[18] Generally, the prospects for an idealised version of Islamic fundamentalism as a development administration model are not good because of the way it has become politicised in its applications. However, some have argued cogently for its relevance.[19]


CONCLUSION

The United Nations Development Programme has published a *Human Development Report* since 1990, and stresses 'sustainable human development'. The Programme emphasises that the purpose of development is to enlarge human choices, not just income,[20] and the *Reports* provide a global assessment of human progress and list the various country strategies to realise human well-being, heavily emphasising the importance of women. Similarly, the Worldwatch Institute issues a yearly assessment on progress toward a sustainable society.[21] In the future, as in the past, the United Nations and other monitoring bodies will enable analysts to assess the degree of constructive change within nations.

Development theories vary across countries and regions; different theories are appropriate in different areas. Islamic fundamentalism, for example, would not be suitable for non-Muslim areas. The development models that rated highest as judged by the standards in the two 'ideal-types' are not universal. Although they could be extended, they would probably always be area-specific in their application. Both Sarvodaya and Liberation theology have high ratings because of their moral and ethical codes of behaviour.

Several of the models sound good in theory, but once they were actually applied, their original purposes were twisted to meet the needs of a few people rather than serving the general good. This problem is most obvious historically in the communist model and the liberal capitalist democratic model; at the present time, it manifests most clearly in the contemporary applications of Islamic fundamentalism. Sarvodaya and Liberation theology may also be improperly used to serve the interests of particular groups.

Development administration is the essential element for realising the development models. Even with a minimised role under structural adjustment and other required economic reforms, it will remain at the core of development initiatives. Sometimes development administration does best by doing nothing except facilitating the private and non-governmental organisations that do appropriate development work. At other times it constructively engages in partnerships, and in still others it provides the total effort. In all cases, moral adequacy is required on the part of officials.

Even though each culture is different and faces different constraints, a basic code of ethics for administration is a universal necessity. Corruption and partiality are unacceptable behaviours in administration everywhere, and the problems associated with unfair treatment because of haughty civil servants must be eliminated wherever they occur. As discussed elsewhere in this volume, the tendency in many areas for civil servants to pursue self-interest strategies to the neglect of the people needs to be corrected. Unfortunately, the solutions offered by the 'Washington consensus' – downsizing and debureaucratising – do not go to the root of the problem.

The challenge for the larger players in development administration – the World Bank, IMF and bilateral government programmes – is to transform their rhetoric into reality and pursue a basic 'bottom-up' policy, thinking first of the poorest peoples and the need to sustain the environment while at the same time implementing 'development' – itself a Western concept – while also tolerating and encouraging other approaches to change. The essential need is to shift from materialist to post-materialist and spiritual standards.

50     *Alternative Administration*

## Notes and References

1.  David Korten, *When Corporations Rule the World* (West Hartford, Conn.: Kumarian Press, 1995). See also his *Getting to the 21st Century, Voluntary Action and the Global Agenda* (West Hartford, Conn.: Kumarian Press, 1990). The 1990 volume deals with NGOs, the subject of Chapter 3 of this volume.
2.  For a multicultural analysis, see the various selections in Wendy Harcourt (ed.), *Feminist Perspectives on Sustainable Development* (London and New Jersey: Zed Books, 1994).
3.  O.P. Dwivedi, *Development Administration, from Underdevelopment to Sustainable Development* (New York: St Martin's Press, 1994), pp. 4–17.
4.  For further details, see O.P. Dwivedi, 'Stewardship of Governance: Ethics and Values of the Public Service,' in O.P. Dwivedi, R.B. Jain and Dhirendra K. Vajpeyi (eds), *Governing India: Issues Concerning Public Policy, Institutions, and Administrations* (Delhi, India: B.R. Publishing Co., 1998), pp. 1–24.
5.  Richard Sandbrook, 'UNGASS has run out of steam', *International Affairs*, vol. 73, no. 4 (1997), pp. 641–54.
6.  Ismail Serageldin, 'Sustainable Development: From Theory to Practice', *Finance and Development* (December, 1996), p. 3.
7.  Pierre Manent, *An Intellectual History of Liberalism* (Princeton, N.J.: Princeton University Press, 1995).
8.  Richard Lowenthal, *Model or Ally? The Communist Powers and the Developing Countries* (New York: Oxford University Press, 1977).
9.  Joanna Macy, *Dharma and Development: Religion as a Resource in the Sarvodaya Self-help Movement* (West Hartford: Kumarian Press, 1985), p. 11.
10. Leonardo Boff and Claudius Boff, *Introducing Liberation Theology* (New York: Orbis Books, 1987), p. 42. Also see Roger Haight, *An Alternative Vision, an Interpretation of Liberation Theology* (New Jersey: Paulist Press, 1985); and Jorge Garcia Antezana (ed.), *Liberation Theology and Sociopolitical Transformation, a Reader* (Vancouver, B.C.: Simon Fraser University, Institute for the Humanities, 1992).
11. Leonardo Boff, *op. cit.*, pp. 49–61.
12. *Universal Islamic Declaration of Human Rights*, 1981, p. 9.
13. Bruce Lawrence, *Defenders of God* (San Francisco: Harper

& Row, 1989), p. 98. See also Tareq Ismael and J. Ismael, *Government and Politics in Islam* (London: Pinter, 1985); and Khalid Bin Sayeed, *Western Dominance and Political Islam, Challenge and Response* (Albany, N.Y.: State University of New York, 1995).

14. Todd Moss, 'US Policy on Democratisation in Africa: The Limits of Liberal Universalism', *The Journal of Modern African Studies*, vol. 33, no. 2 (1995), p. 189.

15. Paul Abramson and Ronald Inglehart, *Value Change in Global Perspective* (Ann Arbor: University of Michigan, 1995).

16. F.C. Turner and Carlos Elordi, 'Economic Values and the Rule of Government in Latin America.' *International Social Science Journal*, vol. 1 (1995), pp. 145–54.

17. For the Brazilian experience, see John Burdick, *Looking for God in Brazil: The Progressive Catholic Church in Urban Brazil's Religious Areas* (Berkeley: University of California, 1993); for the Peruvian experience, see Milagros Pena, *Theologies and Liberation in Peru: The Role of Ideas in Social Movements* (Philadelphia: Temple University Press, 1995).

18. Judith Miller, 'The Challenge of Radical Islam', *Foreign Affairs, Agenda 1994* (New York: Council on Foreign Relations, 1994), p. 177.

19. See, for example, Youssef Choueiri, *Islamic Fundamentalism*, revised edn (Washington, D.C.: Pinter, 1997); Dr Behrooz Kalantari, Associate Professor, Savannah State University has sympathetically interpreted Islamic Administration for the editors.

20. United Nations Development Programme, *Human Development Report* (New York: Oxford University Press), yearly.

21. Lester Brown, Project Director, *State of the World, a Worldwatch Institute Report on Progress Toward a Sustainable Society* (New York: W.W. Norton), yearly. The World Bank and other institutions, of course, also maintain comprehensive social indicators of development.

# 3 A Third-Sector Alternative: NGOs and Grassroots Initiatives

## Keith M. Henderson

## INTRODUCTION

The search for alternative modes of service delivery has taken some unexpected turns, one of which is towards non-governmental organisations and grassroots initiatives as primary providers of the basic services normally associated with government: health, education, social welfare, shelter, emergency relief, agricultural assistance, rural credit, and others. Unlike privatisation and an expanded business sector, the 'Third Sector' is a less-discussed source of ongoing services. Northern NGOs were, until recently, thought of only as short-term providers of assistance or developmental catalysts. Southern NGOs and grassroots initiatives were frequently viewed as small-scale, fragmented efforts with little ability to become institutionalised, and were commonly regarded as a nuisance – if not a potential threat – by indigenous government administrators.

Typically, NGOs, private voluntary organisations and grassroots initiatives (which we will treat together if they engage primarily in development activities, and distinguish only as Northern or Southern) have had important advocacy roles in addition to their service-provider functions. Southern NGOs in particular may play an important part in the development process alongside various small-scale development initiatives which do not (yet) have organisational form. Such initiatives are often products of grassroots movements, concerning which there is a large literature. Popular participation and innovation characterise many grassroots activities that may eventually become institutionalised as political parties or factions, unions or voluntary associations. These activities may have a profound effect upon environmental policy (as with the rubber tappers in Brazil who organised resistance towards multinationals destroying the rain forest) or gender discrimination (as with the Self-employed Women's Association in Ahmedabad, India, which acted against unscrupulous moneylenders and obtained municipal market space for women vendors).

NGOs, private voluntary organisations and grassroots movements are found in virtually all the 'developed countries', usually focusing on citizens of their respective areas. These and interest (pressure) groups, professional associations, the media, unions, philanthropic organisations, research centres, and other elements in the Third Sector are not considered in the present analysis.

The Third Sector is a vast and powerful grouping of disparate actors with overlapping concerns and roles. Its distinguishing characteristic – there are often no sharp demarcations – is as a residual grouping of organisations and 'quasi-organisations' that are neither governmental (First Sector) nor profit-making (Second Sector).

## SCOPE AND GROWTH OF NGOs

Around the globe, a proliferation of organised groups concerned with development issues has emerged with both 'Northern' and 'Southern' (indigenous) sponsorship. Building upon the record of well-known Northern-based organisations such as CARE, the International Red Cross, OXFAM, and Catholic Charities, they have extended a primary concern with temporary or emergency assistance to a broader involvement with functions usually associated with government: health clinics; schools; infrastructure construction; social security nets; micro-credit; housing construction; and numerous other activities. Those based in Northern (that is, Organisation for Economic Cooperation and Development countries) regions are complemented – and often ultimately linked – with tens of thousands of indigenous grassroots initiatives. The latter may vary from a small group of village women engaged in craft production, to a large-scale agricultural cooperative providing housing and minimal social services for hundreds of members.

Also included are some social movements themselves concerned with environmental, civil rights or other grassroots objectives, if they also provide significant services or learning opportunities for members. As with established pressure (interest) groups, service provision may mix with advocacy in a web of activities. When OXFAM, for example, engages in reclamation of salinised farmland for rice farmers in Guinea Bissau, provides milk cows to improve nutrition among returned refugees in Guatemala, or supplies revolving loan funds for self-employed poor women in India, it is inevitably making a statement concerning unmet needs and 'helping to break down the barriers that create hunger, poverty and economic injustice around the world'.[1]

Beginning in the early 1980s, non-governmental organisations increased their influence and assumed greater significance as service providers as well as advocates for the poor and instruments for achievement of 'civil society'. Simultaneously, they were recognised by Northern donors (particularly the World Bank and International Monetary Fund) as a useful conduit for international assistance, bypassing inefficient and often corrupt Third World governments.

More established first-generation organisations, after many years of quietly labouring in isolation under church, charity and assistance-organisation sponsorship, were followed by others which came to the forefront and found themselves the subject of intense interest and a voluminous literature. Two complementary factors account for the renewed concern, one of which might be labeled 'push' elements, and the other 'pull'.

The 'push' side involves efforts by NGOs themselves to pressure governments and the world community to change their agendas. Abuse and neglect of human and environmental needs was forcefully pointed out not only by isolated agents but also by the combining of hundreds of NGOs into unified voices. This was evident at the Rio 'Earth Summit' in 1992 (the United Nations Conference on Environment and Development) when – by some counts – over 20 000 NGOs were represented and acknowledged. Similarly, the Beijing UN Conference on Women (the Fourth World Conference on Women) brought together thousands of separate organisations and interests – as well as unaffiliated individual women – to express their views. Media attention focused on the way in which the NGO delegates were dispatched to an out-of-the-way location and harassed by Chinese officials, but the more significant accomplishment was the gender-consciousness demanded by the participants. As with the Rio conference, 'push' factors helped to 'reverse the agenda' (see pp. 61–2 following) to include not only additional agenda items but a reordering of priorities: environment and gender were expected to be incorporated into all development considerations. Similarly, a groundswell of grassroots sentiment brought additional attention to general and specific humanitarian and civil rights crises, ranging from genocide to famine to resettlement of refugees. Media coverage galvanised world opinion, if only on a sporadic basis, and – while it lasted – facilitated global reaction.

On the 'pull' side is the visible hand of the World Bank and International Monetary Fund, supplemented by similar action in bilateral lending agencies in the OECD countries. Massive loan and grant efforts dating back to the end of the Second World War had yielded few clearly positive outcomes, and disenchantment with developing countries. By the end of the 1970s, disillusionment had reached a high point. Domestic pressures for foreign aid reduction, the widespread belief in the private sector as more effective than the public, and other matters alluded to in Chapter 1 all conspired together to bring about a change in loan and grant policy in the direction of 'conditionality'. Recipients would have to meet Northern-imposed economic measures in connection with 'structural adjustment' lending or its equivalent. Emphasis upon proper 'governance' or adherence to 'democratic practices and institutions' would be required.[2]

As 'downsizing' and 'debureaucratisation' of government became important due to limitations on financing and the imposed policies of lenders, attention turned towards successful small-scale development initiatives and NGO-organised services as alternative models for socio-economic growth. While at first they were given less attention than the privatising of government services and economic restructuring for debt reduction, ultimately the 'push' factors – including widespread criticism of the structural adjustment loans as burdens for the poor – turned Northern lenders toward the Third Sector. The intent was not to bypass host governments but – if feasible – to develop partnerships devoted to poverty reduction. The rhetoric is impressive: visitors to the World Bank web site (www.worldbank.org) are now greeted by the following description of The World Bank Group: 'The World Bank Group is a partner in opening markets and strengthening economies. Its goal is to improve the quality of life and increase prosperity for people everywhere, especially the world's poorest'. Towards that goal, the Bank has undertaken a substantial reorganisation of its 50-plus-year-old institution.

Importantly, many Third Sector NGO activities fit the North's neo-liberal goals of improving individual rights against the state and providing for open competition in a free-enterprise environment. It is now commonplace to hear calls for cooperation and an expanded role for NGOs along with a downplaying of the state as service provider and increased use of the private sector. NGOs are frequently mentioned as a means to improve the delivery of basic services because of their relative flex-ibility, experience dealing with the poor, cost-effectiveness, and freedom from politicisation. At one extreme, they are at the forefront of an effort to remove power from multinational organisations and restore local control and benefits;[3] in an establishment vision they are part of the 'New Policy Agenda' to be incorporated into the designs of international donors.[4]

As of the late 1990s, non-governmental organisations must be considered contenders in the competition for appropriate methods of service delivery along with the private sector and the government itself. Various com-binations of service-delivery and transitional arrangements are now part of World Bank-led efforts as Third World (and former Second World/post-communist) governments are expected to adjust the size of their public sector downwards, and accommodate both privatised services and NGOs. However, a maze of uncoordinated North-ern and Southern NGOs, coupled with even more uncoordinated, unorganised small-scale indigenous ini-tiatives at the local level presents a host of problems and challenges for development administration at the near turn of the century. For many, the answer is not a World Bank/IMF-led drive for poverty-reduction partnerships (with NGOs as the subordinate partners), but indigenous alternatives reflecting local circumstances through a strengthened Third Sector.

## CONFRONTING THE STATE

The retreat or 'shrinking' of the administrative state or its complete absence leaves a vacuum into which both Northern and Southern NGOs have moved. Northern NGOs – usually somewhat less politicised and more ex-perienced – have intervened with or without the explicit approval of host governments. At one extreme, NGOs have stepped in when governments completely ceased

to function. For example, primary education was provided by NGOs in northern Sri Lanka after the civil unrest
of 1987. Similarly, the Bangladesh Rural Advancement
Committee assumed responsibility for some 35 000 schools
when the government stopped providing services.[5]

In Latin American countries during the debt crisis of
the 1980s, NGOs frequently attempted to fill the gap as
governments retrenched on social services. Avina reports
that this placed 'unbearable pressure on NGOs and other
development agencies'.[6] Even prior to the 1980s, the
Liberation theology movement had attempted to provide
basic needs for the poor through local Catholic priests.

In Togo in the early 1990s, a continuing strike by civil
servants directed at the long-term dictator, General
Gnassingbe Eyadema, increased pressure on Northern
NGOs such as Save the Children, the International
Planned Parenthood Federation, and Catholic Relief
Services. Save the Children provides small grants of money
for tuition in return for school attendance; Catholic Relief
Services gives free food and cooking oil in return for
baby weighing; and Planned Parenthood operates entirely
with female health educators, hence establishing rapport
with women in a male-dominated society. All enjoy good
reputations among workers in the field.[7]

Elsewhere in sub-Saharan Africa, as services provided
by the civil services have sharply deteriorated since the
1970s, self-help initiatives have proliferated. Building upon
long-standing traditions of mutual aid and labour-sharing,
peasant farmers, women's groups and others have created
micro-banking schemes, food-storage arrangements, barter
exchanges, family planning centres, and traditional medicine clinics.[8]

Bypassing the state poses numerous problems for NGOs
in addition to heavy workloads and adverse physical conditions. Needed support and security may be unavailable;
coordination is likely to be lacking; fragmented efforts
under uncertain conditions may be unsustainable; and –
at the same time – a dependency may be created among

the population served. In Togo, for example, village mothers' dependence upon NGO health services made future development of government clinics difficult; the mothers preferred the Northern agencies to any government substitute.

The most significant administrative challenge to state sovereignty is replacement of government services by NGO or grassroots services, often infringing on perceived prerogatives of mainstream ministries. Confrontation with state authorities also arises from advocacy of various kinds. As organisations in touch with the poor and needy recognise the inadequacy of government programmes, NGOs may step in, organising publicity or even violent protest, to counter current policies and actions. This not infrequently plays into the political process, providing witting or unwitting support for political opposition groups and movements.

The scenario in many areas is a patchwork of programmes of small scale and short duration conducted by Northern NGOs, along with indigenous (Southern) grassroots initiatives and movements lacking administrative skills and upward linkages. From the standpoint of a host government they may be problematic on a number of counts, especially as critics of the government in power. As the NGOs and grassroots movements gain strength (see the section below), they may be in competition with each other as well as with public and private providers. While few will be functioning in a location completely without government activity, many will be in the position of challenging the state's sovereignty if they expand rapidly or appear to be mobilising local populations.

Controversy may be engendered because existing power balances will be upset, but also because of skepticism about non-governmental solutions to indigenous problems. A former Ghanaian minister of finance, speaking at an international development conference in Maastricht, Holland stated, 'Experience in many places suggests that there are many who are jumping on the NGO bandwagon for reasons that have nothing to do with development as such'.[9] In some countries, the availability of funding and acceptability of NGOs have encouraged their proliferation, sometimes offering opportunities to the middle class for remunerative employment and prestige. Former ministers and high-level government officials have – on occasion – formed NGOs. In other countries, small-scale NGOs receiving external funding have been seen with suspicion as foreign agents (CIA or neighbouring nations' intelligence agencies).

'Solutions' to the dilemma of a conflictual or redundant relationship with the state lie in constructive linkages with democratic governments, or accomodations and counterstrategies until democracy is attained. Partnering, networking and coordinating are all possible and have been evidenced in many existing relationships. Linkages with host governments may be formal or informal and typically include a supervisory role on the part of the government, such as legal or financial regulation of NGO activity. A number of countries (for example Sri Lanka, Kenya, Rwanda) have introduced restrictive legislation designed to regulate NGOs; such regulation often implies distrust and deterioration of host government–NGO relations.

Effective collaboration with host governments involves at least a minimal recognition by the governments concerned (central and local) of the legitimacy of the NGO operation, and some cooperation between NGO officials and host government officials. These linkages could involve coordinating committees, consortia with single contact points, or ongoing 'fluid' links with officials. To ensure the viability of programmes – many of which might evolve into government-led efforts – it is obviously desirable to have sympathetic and supportive collaboration. At best, host governments can provide an enabling environment and encourage the work of NGOs while complementing NGO (and perhaps private sector) efforts with government programmes. At a minimum, they can avoid interference and refrain from excessive restrictions relating to permits, visas, taxes, tariffs and so on. The instability of many regimes as well as the administrative inadequacy of stable ones frequently makes NGO–host government collaboration difficult.

## 'SCALING UP' AND THE 'REVERSE AGENDA'

Recognising their limitations as fragmented, often small-scale, temporary operations, NGOs have sought to increase their power at least to the extent of counteracting immediate obstacles from host governments. The 'push' factors discussed above may take on specific, strategic dimensions as NGOs – both Northern and Southern – seek to monitor, persuade and engage with governments.

Empowerment of the NGOs to facilitate service-delivery may involve support-building for a particular cause in the international community (including media appeals), or attempts to increase their strength along religious, ethnic or geographic lines. The term in the development community for such efforts and the consequent organisational changes – particularly applicable to Southern NGOs – is 'scaling up'.

John Clark offers a variety of examples of how NGOs can 'scale up' through (1) project replication; (2) building grassroots movements; and (3) influencing policy reform. Project replication involves using successful experiences again; building grassroots movements uses NGOs' knowledge and contacts to overcome oppression of the poor; and influencing policy reform relates to both host governments and official aid agencies.[10] Uvin and Miller discuss different types or paths of 'scaling up': quantitative, functional, political and organisational.[11] The most usual definition of scaling up is in terms of an expansion of membership, influence or scope. Vertically and horizontally, NGOs and grassroots movements may combine through 'intermediaries' (some of which are also called 'grassroots support organisations') for increased impact.

Another aspect of empowerment for NGOs – related to influencing policy – is reflected in the expression 're-verse agenda'. Their commitment to gender issues, sustainable human development, a variety of environmental concerns, human rights, poverty alleviation and other matters has impacted not only United Nations bodies but also the World Bank/IMF, bilateral donors and host governments. Rather than merely carrying out the agendas of lending agents, the NGOs' own agendas have been incorporated into at least the rhetoric and often the programmes of the other agencies.

As instruments in the development of civil society, NGOs have pressured host governments on behalf of the poor and those without voice. In the view of John Clark,

> The opportunities for NGOs have never been greater, and neither have the resources at their disposal. They have the chance today not just to influence the shape of projects being executed by official agencies, but also to influence critical aspects of development policy itself.[12]

Given the wide scope and rapid growth in numbers of NGOs, the technique of 'scaling up' and the 'reverse agenda' (emphasising the NGOs' own priorities) present a timely opportunity to move beyond top-down 'projectitis' and change the development process. However, even with cooperative networks and partnerships – hard enough to achieve – and after successful 'scaling up' and impo-sition of the 'reverse agenda', there are still parochial perspectives that need to be corrected, managerial ca-pacities that need to be strengthened, and accountability and transparency that need to be increased.

## ISSUES OF AGENCY MANAGEMENT, ACCOUNTABILITY AND TRANSPARENCY

It is clear that an increased burden is being placed on NGO officials at headquarters and in the field, a burden that they are often ill-equipped to handle. Although there is an enormous variety of Northern and Southern NGOs, certain general administrative observations may, nevertheless, be made.

First, it might be noted that NGOs are different from the usual agencies discussed in public administration, business administration or management thought, and conventional wisdom may not apply. They are non-public and non-profit-making, and typically are organised around fundraising, devote considerable attention to support-building, and utilise volunteer staffs. Professional or member considerations may override administrative concerns in managing the agency; matters of record keeping, budgeting and formalised personnel actions may be given low priority when the primary humanitarian mission of the agency is the principle organisational focus. There is often a jealous guarding of perceived prerogatives that limit cooperative activity. Secondly, the management style of NGOs is often different from the usual government or business agency, sometimes reflecting amateurism and – even in established Northern NGOs – a 'charismatic but sometimes autocratic leadership; committed but untrained staff; weak monitoring, inadequate reporting, little accountability or transparency, and above all, financial confusion'.[13]

Thirdly, there are few educational programmes specifically for the administrative aspects of NGO work that might help to overcome parochial attitudes, disdain for bureaucratic processes and rules, and an ethos of participatory collegiality that eschews hierarchy. Some successful, rapidly growing organisations have sought to develop their own middle managers, notably the Aga Khan Foundation and the Bangladesh Rural Advancement

Committee. Performance contracts are sometimes used.

Specialised training may be required for both governmental and NGO personnel who are tied together in institutional networks. Milton Esman argues for the importance of governance networks and a kind of skill not usually found even among successful programme managers operating in conventional bureaucratic settings:

> Before undertaking such responsibilities, persons selected for this role would normally benefit from special training, probably in executive development workshops oriented to these tasks, in which senior persons from the voluntary and private sectors, as well as government managers, participate. Their performance evaluations and career rewards should take full account of the distinctive responsibilities of network management.[14]

Perhaps responding to such suggestions, the World Bank has undertaken training programmes jointly for Bank personnel, NGO representatives and private sector officials which include field-work at NGO sites. Of course, NGOs are envisioned as subcontractors in networks under Bank control.

Finally – and partially in contradiction to top-down training and education – is what might be labelled another kind of 'reverse agenda': the learning and understanding deriving from grassroots organisations themselves which is not in accord with conventional Northern thinking. Norman Uphoff expresses an appreciation for this in a detailed account of his experience in establishing farmer organisations among the poorest families in Sri Lanka: 'I found myself rethinking much of what I had learned as a student and as a professional social scientist'.[15]

Closely related to the problems of agency management are those revolving around accountability and transparency. Again, the enormous variety of NGO and potential NGO activity makes it difficult to generalise about these issues, but some broad observations may be made. Without formal government sponsorship – typically rejected by NGOs, which prize their independent, non-governmental character – NGOs escape the usual mechanisms of accountability and their activities are not open to public scrutiny. Lacking sovereignty, they nevertheless perform government-like functions. Their performance is judged – if at all – by their donors, and host governments intent on their own agendas.

A more desirable course of action would be to provide greater transparency for financial and operational matters, and to hold NGO personnel fully responsible for their actions and choices. The 'bottom-up' development philosophies of most Southern NGOs should facilitate popular involvement in decision-making, target-group oversight, and open record keeping, but it often does not. As Paul Streeten has pointed out, 'Participation has been used more often as a slogan than a thought-out strategy'.[16] Northern NGOs may have codes of ethics (or codes of conduct governing their rules of engagement) and often stress their depoliticising of aid and conformance with 'international humanitarian law', but they may also resist full accountability and transparency. In a few circumstances, avoidance of transparency may be necessary to protect humanitarian operations. For example, when providing services to combatants in a conflict zone, secrecy of operations may ameliorate the perception of imbalance of benefits. Usually, however, openness is desirable.

It is clear that NGOs – both Northern and Southern – need to get their own houses in order so that they may undertake more permanent roles. New thinking in the academic community – including training and education programmes – is required beyond government-focused public administration study and application. Skillful NGO agency management, accountability and transparency are essential for an expanded service-delivery role.

CONCLUSION

There are both opportunities and pitfalls in extending the service-provider role of NGOs, but the former outweigh the latter. Bypassing the state raises questions about sovereignty and the manner in which political roles are played; acceding to repressive government policies, on the other hand, compromises the potential contribution of NGOs and grassroots initiatives to development.

This chapter has focused on expansion of the service-delivery function of NGOs and the linkages with public administrators in host countries as well as strategies of 'scaling up' to expand influence and the 'reverse agenda' to impact policies of multinational lenders and others. For their part, NGOs must subscribe to appropriate co-ordination, become accountable to more than their sponsors, participate as partners in networks, and upgrade their skills. As emphasised in other chapters in this volume, NGOs are positioned to play a critical developmental role.

The extent of NGO and grassroots initiatives in service delivery will vary greatly from area to area. At this stage, they have been particularly important in South and Southeast Asia, parts of Africa, and in Latin America. For a variety of reasons they have not been prominent in the Middle East, with notable exceptions such as Palestine and some important projects in Lebanon. In the former communist countries of Central and Eastern Europe, their role in transition to free-market democracies – as yet unproven – may be critical.

NGOs and grassroots movements are properly perceived as agents for alternative development, and should pursue their service-delivery function without being coopted into the broader designs of the World Bank/IMF, or drawn into the political machinations of host governments. They should recognise their political impact, however, and pursue advocacy as a byproduct of service-delivery.

Indigenous arrangements can be developed by skilled

NGO leadership working cooperatively alongside other agents of change who have both integrity and competence. This is one alternative to First Sector administration.

## Notes and References

1. Letter from Raymond C. Offenheiser, President, Oxfam America, 10 June 1997.
2. World Bank, *World Development Report, 1997* (New York: Oxford University Press, 1997). The 1997 Report emphasises 'bringing the state back in'.
3. David Korten, *Getting to the 21st Century* (West Hartford, Conn.: Kumarian, 1991); and *When Corporations Rule the World* (West Hartford, Conn.: Kumarian, 1995).
4. World Bank, *The World Bank's Partnership with Nongovernmental Organizations* (Washington, D.C.: World Bank, 5 January 1996). This is a 44 page report.
5. L. Gordenker and T. Weiss 'Pluralizing Global Governance: Analytic Approaches and Dimensions', *Third World Quarterly*, vol. 16 (1995).
6. Jeffrey Avina, 'The Evolutionary Life Cycles of Nongovernmental Development Organizations', *Public Administration and Development*, vol. 13 (1993), p. 468.
7. Interviews by the author were conducted in Togo in December 1992 and January 1993 in the district of Ave – approximately one hour north of the capital of Lome – with the District Prefect, village headmen and volunteer workers, principally American Peace Corps volunteers. In the capital, interviews were held with the US Ambassador to Togo, the Peace Corps Director and city-based volunteer workers.
8. P. Pradervand, *Listening to Africa: Developing Africa from the Grassroots* (New York: Praeger, 1989).
9. H. French, 'Donors of Foreign Aid Have Second Thoughts', *New York Times*, 7 April 1996, E5.10.
10. John Clark, *Democratizing Development: The Role of Voluntary Organizations* (West Hartford, Conn.: Kumarian, 1991), p. 74.
11. Peter Uvin and David Miller, 'Paths to Scaling-up: Alternative Strategies for Local Nongovernmental Organizations', *Human Organization*, vol. 55, no. 3 (1996), pp. 344–53.
12. John Clark, *Democratizing Development, op. cit.*, p. 11.

13.  Mary Jennings, 'New Challenges for Northern NGOs', *Trocaire Development Review*, vol. 10 (1995), p. 24.
14.  Milton Esman, *Management Dimensions of Development* (West Hartford, Conn.: Kumarian, 1991), p. 128.
15.  Norman Uphoff, *Learning From Gal Oya: Possibilities for Participatory Development and Post-Newtonian Social Science* (Ithaca: Cornell University Press, 1992), p. 3.
16.  Paul Streeten, 'Nongovernmental Organizations and Development', *Annals of the American Academy of Political and Social Sciences*, vol. 554 (November 1997), p. 193.

# 4 Inclusive Administration and Development: Feminist Critiques of Bureaucracy

Reeta Chowdhari Tremblay

The effectiveness of development policies and the economic well-being of women have been the dual objectives underlying the gendered approaches to development in the Third World such as women in development, gender and development and empowerment. Although the United Nations Decade for Women, 1975–85 – with its themes of equality, development and peace – was largely responsible for the global spread of women's studies,[1] the emphasis on women in development is mostly attributable to a recognition of the failure of the process of economic modernisation. By the early 1970s, a general consensus prevailed among both academics and practitioners that development policies had left women marginalised socially and economically, while increasing their dependence on men. Women in development, with an emphasis on equity in the early 1970s that shifted later to an anti-poverty approach, pressed for the efficient integration of women in the development process.[2] However, Third World feminist scholars, in explaining the inadequacies of the approach of increasing women's participation in the development process, began an examination of the structural relationships between problems of women on the one hand, and the global capitalist social and economic relations and patriarchy on the other.[3] The new direction in the literature on women and development is oriented towards defining the

69

Third World women as the agents of change, rather than 'the passive recipients of policies and projects' which would be conceived from the bottom up, rather than 'imposed from above'.[4]

Feminists such as Mohanty, Sangari and Vaid established on an autonomous footing Third World explanations of constituting and reconstituting patriarchy by exploring the problematics of homogenising women in relation to different experiences of racism, class, ethnicity, historical processes, colonialism and imperialism. However, their contributions are focused either on explanations of societal practices both national and international (where political economy, religion, law and culture play the determining role), or on detailed empirical analysis (policy studies) without, unfortunately, taking into consideration the discourse and practices underlying the state and its various structures. Sangari and Vaid, in their excellent work on *Recasting Women: Essays in Colonial History*, acknowledge the role of the state in 'maintaining, modifying or aggravating patriarchal practice', yet their concern was 'to focus primarily on the regulation and reproduction of patriarchy in the different class–caste formations within civil society'.[5]

Common to both First and Third World feminist scholarship is a paucity of analyses of the state and its relationship to women's experiences. Although reference is often made to the fact of uneven representation of women in the bureaucracy, feminist academics have avoided asking questions relating to the relationships between development policies, the empowerment of women, the state as a gendered hierarchy, and the embedded masculine style and organisation of its bureaucracies. Except for studies conducted by Mckinnon, Franzway, Ferguson and Stivers, analysis of the state and its structures has been confined to two extreme interpretations: the state as a source of modernisation, therefore potentially performing a constructive role, or the state as a passive actor representing the interests of the dominant class and the male gender. What I would suggest here is that, in order to understand the ideological and historical processes underlying gender inequality and to explore the possibilities for the empowerment of women, we need to shift our focus to the study of the state. The state should be viewed as both reflecting the society (socially constructed and produced subjective identities) and at the same time constructing, modifying and maintaining gender-, class- and race-based identities through its legal and constitutional apparatus. Waylen notes:

> it is far better to see the state as a site of struggle, not lying outside of society and social processes, but having, on the one hand, a degree of autonomy from these which varies under particular circumstances, and on the other, being permeated by them.[6]

It is through such a conceptualisation of the state as evolving, dialectic and dynamic that one can begin to have some understanding of both the successes (however limited) of the feminist movement and of the persisting practices of the gendered states. This formulation of the state, furthermore, suggests a possibility for the marginalised groups to have some influence over the 'way the state acts'. While some feminist scholars such as Ferguson strongly advocate the establishment of different organisational structures which would be reflective 'of the individual and the collective that reflects the caretaking and nurturant experiences embedded in women's role', it is instead the state which, as the femocrats would argue, appears to hold the key to the empowerment of women.[7] Franzway sums up the complexity of the state's involvement in sexual politics by suggesting that

> The state is dynamic and sexual politics is dynamic; and that is perhaps the key point. The state is culturally marked as masculine and functions largely as an

institutionalisation of the power of men . . . Yet this
institutionalisation is uneven and generates paradoxical
reversals, in which the state participates in constituting antagonistic interests in sexual politics and can
become a vehicle for advancing those interests.[8]

For her, the feminist's dual role involves knowing the
mechanisms underlying the masculine embeddedness in
state structures and at the same time identifying 'the
points of opportunity and the mechanisms of change that
make successful strategies possible'.[9]

In a democratic polity, where the notions of legitimacy
and citizenship are intertwined, the state in resolving its
own identity crisis must intervene on behalf of the
marginalised sections of the society. In his recent work,
*The Language of Public Administration: Bureaucracy,
Modernity and Post-Modernity*, David Farmer argues that
in order to conceptualise bureaucracy as a legitimate part
of democracy, the field of public administration needs
to move away from metanarratives and one-dimensional
rationalism based on single truths. Instead, diversity and
openness can find their place in public administration
where contradictions and paradoxes become the guiding
forces. Indeed, it is the state's requirement for legitimacy
which pushes for a radical change in which one 'concep-
tualizes the role and nature of public administration
theory'.[10]

It is within this context that a methodology emphasising an understanding of the discourse and practices of
bureaucracy in relation to gender and development
emerges as significant. This chapter pursues three lines
of inquiry. First, in order to explore the issue of administrative inclusiveness in Third World bureaucracies, it
is necessary to understand the public administration
project as imported from the Western discourse, and its
interaction with the colonial and postcolonial context of
each state and its various fragments of civil society. The
borrowed Eurocentric concepts of state, sovereignty and

bureaucracy à la Weber allowed the postcolonial elites to introduce modern secular hierarchies into the 'archaic' traditional world, thus enabling them to construct the foundations for a just and an egalitarian order. However, as Ashis Nandy suggests, the consequence of these imports for these societies has been to enter into a second stage of colonialism where

> this colonialism colonizes mind in addition to bodies and it releases forces within the colonized societies to alter their cultural priorities once and for all. In the process, it helps generalize the concept of the modern West from a geographical and temporal entity to a psychological category. The West is now everywhere, within the West and outside; in structures and in minds.[11]

Borrowing concepts without at the same time pursuing critical discourse on their relationship to indigenous cultural and political practices has caused inevitable dichotomies where the modern, the secular, the expert, the rational and the developed triumph over the primitive, the non-secular, the layman, the irrational, the emotional and the underdeveloped. In such a restricted discourse, there is no space for a dialogue between the polarities. In their critique and reinterpretation of Weberian bureaucracy, Rudolph and Rudolph question Weber's emphasis on the West's uniqueness and on the historical importance of its cultural phenomena with their universal significance and value. They point out that

> Weber's conceptualization of bureaucracy in terms of rational-legal authority and formal rationality fails to take account of the existence and use of power within and outside of organizations and of the persistence of patrimonial features. The use of power produces conflict and pathologies. What is good for organizations is not necessarily good for their participants or for

the society: conflict and pathology – when they serve
the legitimate values and interests of participants and
actors in the organizational environment – can have
benign consequences. The persistence of patrimonial
features, rather than signaling the survival of dysfunctional atavisms, can promote administrative effectiveness
by mitigating conflict and promoting organizational
loyalty, discipline and efficiency.[12]

In a similar vein, Stanley Heginbotham interprets policy
stalemate as largely a product of the imposition of an
administrative process on the indigenous cultural Hindu
dharmic tradition which allows for no strict differentiation between the political and administrative spheres at
the village level. In his study of the local government
and policy process in India, Heginbotham emphasises that,
contrary to the Western notion of a unified authority
role that handles both the formulation and implementation of policies, the Indian dharmic view 'emphasises the
dual character of authority roles. Appropriate policies
define proper patterns of relationship . . . implementation through enforcement of rights and duties is a distinct
and essentially independent enterprise'.[13] The threat of
social sanctions ensures compliance and makes the individual rather than the authority-holder responsible for
the enforcement of norms and behaviour. Needless to
say, this contradiction between the indigenous cultural
practices and the imposed 'technical' policy process has
been partially responsible for local government's inability
to implement the national objectives of postcolonial
leadership to usher in a new just and equitable society.
  The second line of inquiry concerns the fact that not
only does the imported public administration project
introduce the universalising and homogenising concepts
of administration, but it also brings with it the patriarchal and gendered discourse underlying the state and its
structures. Consequently, this discourse legitimises the
already existing relations of feminism and patriarchy, thus

enhancing the resilience of patriarchal systems in postcolonial societies. In this gendered discourse, which is presented as non-political, neutral, technical, scientific and efficient, women are neither objects nor subjects. Not only are they not seen as agents but also they emerge as marginal to the debate. Their regulation through legal and administrative channels therefore becomes a central mechanism of social control. As Sangari and Vaid eloquently put it: 'both tradition and modernity have been, in India, carriers of patriarchal ideologies. As such neither is available to us in a value free or unproblematic sense, nor is either, as they are usually conceptualized, necessarily the solution'.[14] Indeed, it is only by dismantling the traditional–modern opposition and viewing the construction of each as a political-cultural project that one may understand the complexities of change in societies.

Third, in order to gain further insight into the dilemmas and contradictions generated by the 'imported discourse' on the gendered state and its structures, I suggest that a discussion of the embryonic Western literature on the feminist critiques of bureaucracy should form a starting point, although that literature cannot be merely replicated within the Third World context. There are three reasons for my selection of this material:

1. The contributions of the feminist scholarship on public administration, particularly bureaucracy, largely consist in their rejection of the Western paradigms of the state and its structures as universally applicable, objective and neutral. Abstracting even from the feminist dimension, the Third World and the feminist project share the common feature of a deconstructive approach to the Western bureaucratic model;

2. The existing Third World discourse on feminism is missing a crucial linkage between the state, including its administrative structures, and the empowerment of women. If it has taken so long for the state-focused feminist discourse and debate to emerge in the West,

why shouldn't the Third World, at a relatively earlier stage in its feminist project, benefit from this literature and review it in the light of its own historical, cultural and political contexts? This discourse and the indigenous responses it elicits will contribute to setting up a framework for fundamental changes in the developing societies;

3. Deconstruction and reconstruction are complementary projects. The reconstructive project, involving 'rethinking fundamental relationships of knowledge, power and community' marks a shift from 'margin to centre'. Because politics combined with distinct gendered relations has a differential impact on men and women, the project of reconstruction takes on a variety of shapes and suggests an interplay of several strategies. The following discussion on the Western feminist critiques of bureaucracy is basically meant to serve as a guideline towards thinking of political strategies so that the goals of the empowerment of women and of their inclusion in the state structures can be achieved.

## FEMINIST CRITIQUES OF BUREAUCRACY

The embryonic critiques of organisational theory – in particular bureaucracy – based on gender and sexuality have taken two forms. Within the context of comprehending the organisational culture and discourse generating gendered social and power relations, one set of studies, through their focus on gender, generally 'add in' or 'add on' to the Weberian formulations of bureaucracy. The other set of studies, following largely a Foucaldian framework, view sexuality, its 'social organization and social control' as fundamental to both gender relations in general and to organisations in particular.[15] Although since the 1960s public administration theory has been reformulated as a result of increasing concerns for social equity and representative bureaucracy, the fundamental conceptualisation of bureaucratic organisations remained unchallenged until the recent feminist and profeminist critiques. In reaction to the issues of accountability, responsibility and responsiveness, the concept of representative bureaucracy developed from the initial addition of social equity as a 'third pillar' to the two existing pillars of public administration, economy and efficiency (passive representation) to a later emphasis on participatory bureaucracy by bringing in different elements of the population (active representation). While representative bureaucracy recognized that the dichotomy between administration and politics is untenable and that public administration should respond to the requirements of a just and a democratic society, there remained a large degree of ambiguity and controversy regarding the classification of women as one of the targeted groups.

In defense of women, Harry Krantz wrote in 1976:

> although they constitute 51 percent of the total population, women – like blacks in the Union of South Africa – are a minority by all the relevant criteria. Sharing physical characteristics and usually cultural experiences because of their sex, women have been denied political, social, and economic opportunities and have been frequently socialised to accept their 'inferior' status. Because of the past and continuing overt discrimination and institutional barriers, they have been deprived of equal opportunities for public employment, where they are currently underrepresented.[16]

Consistent with the feminist challenges to mainstream political theory in the past two decades – which assert that sex and gender are central to political analysis and that institutionalised dominance is socially constructed – the gender-based public administration literature, although slow in response, has recently begun to question the premises upon which the concepts of representative and participatory bureaucracy were based, and to suggest that discrimination against women in bureaucracies cannot be addressed without an active engagement of academics in the issues of organisational discourse, organisational culture and the social construction of power and dominance. Ironically, this new discourse has already begun to face challenges from an intensifying popular distrust of the overgrown Western industrialised bureaucracies. A public administration whose legitimacy is constantly being questioned must indeed justify its existence.

In addition, the rise of the neo-conservative ideology emphasising a reduced scope and increased efficiency of government by undoing the Keynesian consensus and reclaiming political control over the bureaucracy by the elected representatives of the public, has once again opened the debate on the traditionally established politics-administration dichotomy. As Donald Savoie notes, the new managerial culture which sought to transform public administrators into managers has both inadvertently and by design curbed the bureaucracy's capacity to devise change and 'to meet the new challenges confronting the nation state'.[17] At this critical juncture of a legitimacy crisis where the neo-conservative agenda is to reestablish the so-called 'neutral' and 'objective' principles of administration, feminist critiques of organisations have acquired further relevance.

The following discussion, based on a brief description of the existing research on gender/sex and bureaucracy, will advance the following argument. The contribution of the studies based on the gender paradigm of organisations which generally add in or add on to the Weberian discourse on bureaucracies lies precisely in the fact that although they are critical of both the practices and the discourse of the liberal state (its emphasis on individualism, private–public realm separation and the neutrality and objectivity of the state), they have looked to the state as the conduit for both social and political change.

Unlike the literature concentrating primarily on the sexuality of organisations with its postmodern ambiguities and pessimism, the gender-based studies offer both an insight into the issue and a direction for change.

Although there are a large number of women employed in public-sector bureaucracies, the observations made by Grant and Tancred-Sheriff regarding the dual structures of uneven representation of women in the bureaucracies remain largely true.[18] Women are not only unevenly distributed within the state hierarchy, but the positions they occupy have marginal organisational power. In her 1994 study on the prospects for the advancement of women in the US civil service, Katherine Naff points to the perpetuation of a glass ceiling through formal and informal structural barriers and women's own perceptions of their treatment within organisations.[19] In her examination of two decades of affirmative action policies, Mary Guy concludes that women have a long way to go before they can reach parity with men, for

> the confluence of opportunity, power and proportion produces upward cycles of advantage [for men] or downward cycles of disadvantage [for women]. The cycles of high opportunity, power, and numbers make it very difficult for newcomers (such as women) to break into the managerial workforce (1993, p. 289).[20]

In her 1977 study of *Men and Women of the Corporation*, Rosemary Kanter related the powerlessness and subordinate position of women within the bureaucracy to power rather than sex differences. Consistent with liberal-feminist formulations, her hope for change rested in the fact that bureaucracies could be modified through the promotion of equal opportunities, so that women could have access to power on the same terms as men. Her 'socially constructionist' approach suggests that male homosociability not only generates power for men, but it also limits the access to organisational power of other men. Desire for sameness is a result of a bureaucratic kinship system whereby men guard access to power and privilege by selecting exclusively those who effectively fit their own image and speak the same language. Kanter observes, 'Social certainty, at least, could compensate for other sources of uncertainty in the tasks of management. It was easier to talk to those of one's kind who had shared experiences – more certain, more accurate, more predictable'.[21] While women are excluded from the organisational resources of power by virtue of the fact that they are women, their inclusion in the bureaucracy is shaped by the terms of subordination to male managers and bosses.

For example, those who are in subordinate positions tend to have low expectations and seek satisfaction in activities outside work. On the other hand, people in high career opportunities are constantly guided by both expectations and desires for upward mobility and future rewards in terms of enhanced power. For Kanter, the secretaries' relationship to their bosses as office wives is a relic of the patrimonial structures in our modern society. Rosemary Pringle's 1989 study of secretaries disagrees; she suggests that the boss–secretary relation 'need not be seen as an anomalous piece of traditionalism, or an incursion of the private sphere, but rather as a site of strategies of power in which sexuality is an important though by no means an exclusive dimension'.[22] For Kanter, the rationalisation process awaits 'the modernizing impulse of a rational basis' (when women can acquire organisational power on the same terms as men) whereby 'gender will not taint the form nor the content of the relationship'.[23] While later feminist studies, pointing to the subtle relationships between gender and power, were to question her assertions such as that power 'wipes out sex' and her 'de-gendered' reading of Weber and the Weberian bureaucratic rationality, Kanter's work was one of the very first studies to appear on the relationship between gender and bureaucracy, and her hypothesis of power resonates with the workings of a large number of bureaucratic organisations.

Since the 1980s, feminist theorising of state and bureaucracy have been largely influenced by the poststructuralist and postmodern critiques of essentialising and universalising characteristics of metanarrative theories. Interestingly, while the Weberian construction of bureaucracy looms largely in the background, Foucaldian characterisations of power, gender and knowledge have been integrated into the examination of patriarchal bureaucratic structures. Contrary to Kanter's conclusions, socially constructed institutionalised dominance, the masculine culture and practices of the bureaucratic organisation, and a systematic gendering pattern within the state in its selection of both agenda and personnel are largely responsible for the failure of the liberal state's affirmative action policies to equalise opportunities for women in state bureaucracies. As Franzway asserts, 'reform is not just a matter of changing the personnel at the top. It is a matter of unpicking a complex texture of institutional arrangements which intersect with the construction of masculinity and femininity'.[24]

Although the recent literature on gender, power and bureaucracy is quite complex, at a very simple level it lends itself to three summary statements: (a) while subscribing to the Weberian notion of modernisation and the inevitability of the bureaucratic organisations, modernisation is perceived as a gendered process; (b) organisations are sites of gendered contests which shape the organization itself both diachronically and synchronically; and (c) since the bureaucratic discourse and structure are masculine, there are some feminists such as Ferguson who find that women's interests can only be accommodated in alternative organisations of a feminist mode, while others expect to reconstruct the Weberian so-called 'rational' bureaucratic structures through their deconstruction of the patriarchal discourse.

Savage and Witz suggest that the development of

organisational hierarchy, a natural outcome of the rationalisation process associated with modernisation, took place on gendered lines. While the modern hierarchical bureaucratic organisations began to make a distinction between intellectual and mechanical labour, the latter became the domain of a relatively cheap female workforce. They note that 'development of large organizations around the turn of the 20th century was directly associated with what has been called the 'white Blouse Revolution', the employment of large number of women in routine clerical work'.[25] Similarly, Rosemary Crompton points out that the career pattern of male bureaucrats, another essential characteristic of Weber's bureaucracy, depended upon female facilitators. At work, women performed routine jobs, thus allowing a smooth career progression of men to senior positions, while at home they took the responsibility of household duties and raising children, freeing their husbands to pursue their careers with a minimum of distractions and interruptions. By barring married women from the job market, 'modern bureaucratic hierarchies both helped to construct the idea of the dependent housewife and drew upon this for their own advantage'.[26] Stivers similarly comments that 'standard organizational and professional career patterns and personnel policies depend on the existence of someone (that is, a wife) who takes care of household and child-care responsibilities'.[27]

Burrell and Hearn, who describe themselves as pro-feminist men, in their study on the sexuality of organisations present a different kind of critique of Weber's modern bureaucratic structures. Burrell views the historical modernising ('civilising') process as contributing to an ideology of organisational desexualisation, where sexuality is 'often subjugated to the demands and powers of organization'.[28] In the interests of calculative rationality and the advancement of capitalism, sexuality in the modernising project is to be controlled in order to reserve energy for productive use in the workplace, thus causing the separation of work (public) and non-work (private) time and spaces. However, as Pringle remarks, workplaces do not manage to exclude the personal or the sexual:

Far from being marginal to the workplace, sexuality is everywhere. It is alluded to in dress and self-presentation, in jokes and gossips, looks and flirtations, secret affairs and dalliances, in fantasy, and in the range of coercive behaviours that we now call sexual harassment . . . Sex at work is very much at display.[29]

One can find parallels between the gendered rationalisational process of modern bureaucracies, as discussed by the Western feminist scholarship on organisations, and the Third World critiques of the colonialist project in Asia and Africa, which assert that not only was the British empire constructed around the white male, but also that the colonial discourse was itself gendered around an imagery of the colonised invested with feminine attributes. In India, the masculine and feminine distinction corresponded to the British division of Indian society into martial and non-martial races, for example the aggressive and robust Sikhs, Pathans, Rajputs or Muslims in contrast to feeble, effeminate, helpless, supple, vapour-bathed creatures such as Bengalis. Rudolph and Rudolph have noted that the success of colonialism depended upon the internalisation of these character distinctions and the moral worthiness or unworthiness associated with them by the Indians themselves. This ideology, legitimising superior–inferior relations, generating a 'state of mind – a sense of impotence combined with the fear of moral worthiness arising from impotence – was not unique to India' and formed a part of a generalised gendered colonial discourse.[30]

Similarly, Lata Mani, in her analysis of the colonial discourse on *sati*, suggests that in prohibiting *sati* practices in India, women's concerns were in fact made marginal to the British debate. Rather, the discourse grounded on women's issues was created to respond to the regime requirements of 'an expanding colonial power in need of systematic and unambiguous modes of governance, of law, for instance out of a particular view of Indian society'.[31] Furthermore, the colonial administration introduced bureaucratic, hierarchical and centralised structures from which colonised women were almost always excluded. Generally disadvantaged within their own societies, colonised women were not only barred from formal power but also found themselves simultaneously negotiating 'the imbalances of their relations with their own men' and 'the baroque and violent array of hierarchical rules and restrictions that structured their new relations with imperial men and women'.[32]

What makes the feminist critiques of bureaucracy interesting and suggestive for students of the Third World is their deconstruction of a gender patterning within the state which, although systematic, is not a fixed ideological entity. In the complex and contradictory processes of state formation, the state presents itself as a collective patriarch and agent of patriarchy. MacKinnon's assertion, that feminism has no theory of the state for it lacks 'a theory of the substance of law, its relation to society, and the relationship between the two' notwithstanding,[33] Franzway provides useful insights into state processes and their relation to gender and power. Her discussion of the state accommodates specificity, diversity and heterogeneity whereby gender patterning, patriarchy and the state in the Third World can be analysed from the perspective of a multiplicity of differences. Her conceptualisation of the state is based on four major assumptions: the state is a social process and not merely a legal category; the state as a social force and site is the 'initiator of important dynamics' where 'interests are constituted as well balanced'; the state is internally differentiated; and there is a tactically complex interplay between the state and its environment. Relating this conceptualisation to a social theory of gender and an uneven institutionalisation of domination, Franzway maintains that the state and its practices must be understood within its historical context. The state is 'the product of specific, historically located social processes . . . What kind of state we have depends on who was mobilized in social struggle, what strategies were deployed, and who won'.[34] Moreover, the state is actively involved in the construction and modification of gendered identities and in regulating the 'relationship between them by policy and policing'.[35]

This view of the state allows one to acknowledge victories, however small, of the marginalised groups, and suggests that female bureaucrats (whose number has been increasing in Western societies) have been either coopted into the system (they have turned into surrogate men), or the areas into which women have entered 'tend to be barred from effective organizational power'.[36] In such a state – where social processes constitute and reconstitute it historically and where it prominently constructs and regulates gendered identities – bureaucracy, its essential component, does not operate in a static manner. Instead, 'the rise of bureaucratic forms of organization is historically linked to the rise of new forms of hegemonic masculinity oriented to technical knowledge and personal competitiveness, displacing aristocratic models of masculinity'.[37] In other words, the rules of the game for institutionalised domination change and gender relations within state structures take different forms and thus demand different strategies of resistance. This, for example, explains the replacement of formal restrictions on the appointment of married women to career positions or the exclusion of women from certain sectors of public services by indirect mechanisms. As formal restrictions would be perceived nowadays as discriminatory and as excluding a group of citizenry from its just claims to power, instead, according to Franzway, 'the masculinization of bureaucracy operates powerfully though subliminally'.[38] In the final analysis, the state's relationship to feminism is 'a complex patchwork of compromises and trade-offs between strategies, on both sides of the interaction'.[39]

Each deconstructionist project entails a distinct reconstructive strategy. A case in point is the sharply divergent strategies of empowerment in administrative structures proposed by Ferguson and Stivers which arise from their differing conceptualisations of the bureaucratic discourse. Following Foucault's usage of the term 'discourse' as the domain of speech and language, Ferguson points out that since bureaucratic discourses and structures – with their persistent patterns of dominance and subordinance that parallel power relations between men and women – are both alien to and oppressive towards women, the latter need to reformulate a feminist discourse on political questions and seek alternative organisational forms. For her, bureaucratisation is a dialectical process of domination and resistance which is constantly reproduced. The stability, persistence and pervasiveness of bureaucratisation are often the product of its own capacity to 'co-opt, marginalize and destroy its opposition' which is constantly produced by the multiple contradictions of the bureaucracy itself. Building on a Weberian interpretation of bureaucratic structures, Ferguson suggests that in order to understand the oligarchical and political characteristics of bureaucracies, the latter must be located within their social contexts of unequal relations between classes, races and sexes. Bureaucratic structures are the institutional avenues for a scientific rationalisation and reinforcement of unequal social relations. The older distinctions of public (government) and private (market) replaced by the emphasis on the private as 'the set of institutional practices of domestic life' and public as 'the outside world of paid labor' are intertwined to serve the ideological purposes of bureaucratic capitalism.[40]

The historical exclusion of women from the public realm leads to their marginalisation and their resistance through a submerged discourse. Women in bureaucratic organisations find themselves caught between 'the instrumentality of male-dominated modes of public action and the expressive values of female-dominated modes of action in the private realm'.[41] In order to eliminate uncertainty and ensure control, bureaucracy imposes depersonalisation and isolation of individuals by separating people from one another through the capitalist work-process (division of labour, hierarchy, delegation and diffusion of responsibility). Resistance to their alienation and domination occurs in various forms, such as sub-organisations' pursuance of their own interests, bureaucratic inertia, and subordinates' detailed knowledge about the boundaries of unacceptable behaviour. Ferguson maintains that 'bureaucracy is anti-political because it cannot recognize the legitimacy of conflict, seeing it as a temporary aberration to be dealt with through elaborated administrative techniques'.[42] The bureaucracies thus have the effect of creating both bureaucrats and their clients as the objects of administration, and they 'harm' the capacities of all the actors to interact with each other and devise alternative political strategies out of their shared experiences. In relating this discourse of dominance and resistance in bureaucracies to women's experiences, Ferguson suggests that women must confront bureaucracy within its own (feminist) discourse and seek alternative organisational forms based on the concrete life experiences of women. For her, as women experience their social worlds differently and as a society without domination is unthinkable, the only choice for women is to create the real possibility of 'an alternative vision of collective life' within feminist organisations. It is only 'by rethinking politics in light of women's experiences as caretakers and subordinates, the possibilities of collective action can be reconceptualized so as to make feminist principles central to public life'.[43]

On the other hand, Stivers' reconstructive project suggests that one needs to identify 'windows of vulnerability' through which changes can be made towards the conceptualisation of a feminist theory of public administration.

For her, the historical and the present bureaucratic practices which reflect simultaneously gender paradoxes and contradictions provide many points of entry for the feminist discourse whereby it can engage with the 'conceptual tradition' it is attempting to change. For Stivers, 'this move involves not wiping out what exists but using its elements to make something better – to expand, turn inside out, or otherwise reshape aspects of existing theory as well as to sound new themes'.[44] She is optimistic about seeking solutions and reforms to the gendered biases of administration because, as her work points out, the thinking and actions of various women have influenced the emergence of the administrative state. She also finds solace in the fact that the public administration project is, in Waldo's formulations, 'an ongoing struggle to reconcile or harmonize norms of democracy and efficiency'.[45] This would clearly imply reshaping the public administration enterprise and reconstructing it from the 'ground(s) up', where the boundaries of discipline and its practices cannot be maintained at the expense of women. Stivers points out that while the Wilsonian politics–administration dichotomy has been abandoned by contemporary theorists in light of the political character of the bureaucrats' behaviour, so far as sexual politics is concerned, it still guides a public administration theory shaped by the public-private realm dichotomy whereby the household is distinguished from governmental and business enterprises, thus conceptualising women's exclusion from the public domain and leaving women struggling about whether to 'become men' in order to participate.

Administrative discretion within the bureaucracy is justified, and it widely prevails within a gendered discourse which, for example, intertwines masculinity with the concepts of leadership and professionalism, and which suppresses the feminine virtues underlying the public services such as nurturing, caring, service and benevolence. Social services, historically based on the volunteer work of middle-class women, took on increasingly male values as they became professionalised, in order 'to control and limit a female effusion of emotion, sensibility or passion', thus obliterating women's central role in public service. As Stivers puts it:

> the original rhetoric of difference (True womanhood) that made women's benevolent work possible in the first place now had to be suppressed in favour of a rhetoric of professionalism and efficiency, large powers and the harnessing of forces. In the process, women's central place in an entire-cultural political phenomenon, the reform movement out of which self-conscious public administration emerged, was obliterated.[46]

She argues in her deconstruction of public administration concepts and of their understanding by bureaucrats that while the images of expertise, leadership and virtue which are characteristically masculine are acknowledged by the practitioners, various significant feminine elements remain ignored and unrecognised. For example, the public administrator must constantly live down and deny 'the femininity that lies beneath the image of the responsive administrator'. Moreover, the masculine image is presented as universal and neutral, thus creating actual gender-bias and discrimination against women. The masculine discourse and practices of public administration favour men over all but exceptional women.

Feminist alternatives to the embedded patriarchal bureaucratic structures thus range from Ferguson's radical construction of alternative feminist organisations to Ramsay and Parkin's neo-bureaucracy which, while maintaining certain Weberian organisational features such as limited task specialisation, would require a centre responsible for decision-making and coordination, but whose power 'would be constantly re-negotiated by the members of the organization'. In her study of feminist interventions in organisations, Iannello also favours a model of modified, consensual, non-hierarchical organisations where critical decisions with the potential to change the organisation's direction are reserved for the entire membership and where routine decisions, important to the daily operation, are delegated horizontally.[47] Australian feminist intervention in the state has taken the shape of so-called 'femocrat' strategy. The femocrats have sought to work within the existing bureaucratic structures by seeking the appointment of women to work either in 'women's affairs' or specifically created women's units within the civil service. Although the femocrats in Australia have been criticised for their co-optation into the system, their impact has certainly been evident in fundamental policy reforms and in changes to the organisational culture and processes within the bureaucracy.

## ANY LESSONS FOR INCLUSIVENESS IN ADMINISTRATION AND DEVELOPMENT?

Female participation in the public administration of developing countries is limited. In the 1980s, Latin America had the highest proportion of women in governmental bureaucracy – 20 per cent – followed by Africa with 15 per cent and Asia with 10 per cent, with an insignificant number occupying strategic higher level positions in the bureaucratic hierarchy. Not only are women represented unequally and in low numbers in the state structures, they have also been the major target of the past decade's structural adjustment policies. With state retrenchment, middle-class professional women have been deprived of state employment, while a defeminisation of the workforce, whereby men have been displacing women in lower level jobs, has also increased the burden of poor women in generating income through the informal sector. Recent data for India, for example, show that during the three year period from 1990 to 1992, the poverty ratio in the rural sector has risen from 35 per cent to 42 per cent, and that female labour and female-headed households form a major part of this hard-core group of the rural poor.

While various international developmental agencies and countries with comprehensive planning processes – such as India – have acknowledged the relationship between the empowerment of women and their participation in the grassroot state institutions such as *panchayats*, women have been the least successful in receiving the benefits of anti-poverty policies. This can be largely attributed to a bureaucracy with deeply embedded class and gender constraints and normative values. The bureaucracy, as the Western feminist critiques have shown us, does not constitute a neutral instrument to be used by the state in implementing its goal. While in the Third World a large feminist literature has begun to examine the issues of patriarchy within a social and cultural context, there is virtually no work being done to relate to women's issues the masculine discourse embedded in bureaucratic structures and processes.

The above discussion of the feminist critiques of bureaucracy clearly suggests that the western paradigms of the state and its structures cannot be perceived as either universally applicable, objective or neutral. Although the state may claim to speak on behalf of all its population and to pursue the common good, its structural and ideological grounding in patriarchy makes it extremely difficult for women to escape a socially constructed institutionalised dominance. Issues relating to women's poverty and to women's negligible representation within the bureaucracy cannot adequately be addressed without an active engagement of academics in the issues of organisational discourse, organisational culture and the social construction of power and dominance. Each society in the Third World may have to develop its own deconstruction of the gendered bureaucratic discourse and its relationship to indigenous institutionalised patriarchal structures, and construct its own strategies for the empowerment of women.

## Notes and References

1. Mariam K. Chamberlain and Florence Howe, 'Women's Studies and Developing Countries: Focus on Asia', in R.S. Gallin, A. Ferguson and J. Harper (eds), *The Women and International Development Annual*, Vol. 4 (Boulder, Col.: Westview Press, 1995).

2. E. Boserup, *Women's Role in Economic Development* (New York: St Martin's Press, 1970).

3. See Bina Agarwal, 'Rural Women and the High Yielding Variety Rice Technology in India', *Economic and Political Weekly*, vol. 19, no. 13 (1984), pp. 39–52; L. Beneria and G. Sen, 'Accumulation, Reproduction, and Women's role in Economic Development: Boserup Revisited', *Signs*, vol. 7, no. 2 (1981), pp. 279–98; and N. Kabeer, *Reversed Realities: Gender Hierarchies in Development Thought* (London: Verso, 1994).

4. Georgina Waylen, *Gender in Third World Politics* (Boulder: Lynne Rienner, 1996).

5. Kumkum Sangari and Sudesh Vaid (eds), *Recasting Women: Essays in Colonial History* (Delhi: Kali for Women, 1993), p. 1.

6. G. Waylen. *Gender in Third World Politics*, op. cit., p. 16.

7. Kathy E. Ferguson, *The Feminist Case against Bureaucracy* (Philadelphia: Temple University Press, 1984), p. x.

8. S. Franzway, D. Court and R.W. Connell, *Staking a Claim: Feminism, Bureaucracy and the State* (Cambridge: Polity Press, 1989), p. 41.

9. Ibid., p. 32.

10. David John Farmer, *The Language of Public Administration: Bureaucracy, Modernity and Post Modernity* (University of Alabama Press, 1995), p. 4.

11. Ashis Nandy, 'Colonization of the Mind', in M. Rahnema and V. Bawtree (eds), *The Post Development Reader* (London: Zed Books, 1997), p. 170.

12. Lloyd I. Rudolph and Susanne Hoeber Rudolph, 'Authority and Power in Bureaucratic and Patrimonial Administration: A Revisionist Interpretation of Weber on Bureaucracy', *World Politics*, vol. XXXI, no. 2 (January 1979), p. 196.

13. Stanley Heginbotham, *Culture in Conflict: The Four Faces of Indian Bureaucracy* (New York, Columbia University Press, 1975), p. 54.

14. K. Sangari, and S. Vaid, *Recasting Women: Essays in Colonial History*, op. cit., p. 17.

15. Gibson Burrell and Jeff Hearn, 'The Sexuality of Organization', in J. Hearn *et al.* (eds), *The Sexuality of Organization* (London: 1992).
16. Harry Krantz, *The Participatory Bureaucracy: Women and Minorities in a More Representative Public Service* (Massachusetts: Lexington Books, 1976), p. 83.
17. Donald Savoie, *Thatcher, Regan, Mulroney: In Search of a New Bureaucracy* (Toronto: University of Toronto Press, 1994), p. 344.
18. Rebecca Grant and Peta Tancred-Sheriff, 'A Feminist Perspective on State Bureaucracy' (1986), in S. Franzway, D. Court and R.W. Connell (eds), *Staking a Claim: Feminism, Bureaucracy and the State* (Cambridge: Polity Press, 1989), p. 31.
19. Katherine Naff, 'Through the Glass Ceiling: Prospects for the Advancement of Women in The Federal Civil Service', *Public Administration Review*, vol. 54, no. 6 (November/December 1994), p. 507.
20. Mary E. Guy, 'Three Steps Forward, Two Steps Backward: The Status of Women's Integration into Public Management', *Public Administration Review*, vol. 53, no. 4 (July/August 1993), pp. 285–91.
21. Rosemary M. Kanter, *Men and Women of the Corporation* (New York: Basic Books, 1977), p. 58.
22. Rosemary Pringle, 'Bureaucracy, Rationality and Sexuality: The Case of Secretaries', in J. Hearn *et al.* (eds), *The Sexuality of Organization* (London: Sage, 1992), p. 162.
23. Mike Savage and Anne Witz, 'The Gender of Organizations', in M. Savage and A. Witz (eds), *Gender and Bureaucracy* (Oxford: Blackwell, 1992), p. 17.
24. S. Franzway, D. Court, and R. W. Connell (eds), *Staking a Claim: Feminism, Bureaucracy and the State*, *op. cit.*, p. 31.
25. M. Savage and A. Witz, 'The Gender of Organizations', *op. cit.*, p. 10.
26. *Ibid.*, p. 12.
27. Camilla Stivers, *Gender Images in Public Administration, Legitimacy and the Administrative State* (Newbury Park, Cal.: Sage, 1993), p. 24.
28. G. Burrell and J. Hearn, 'The Sexuality of Organization', *op. cit.*, p. 61.
29. R. Pringle, 'Bureaucracy, Rationality and Sexuality: The Case of Secretaries', *op. cit.*, pp. 162–3.
30. Lloyd I. Rudolph and Susanne H. Rudolph, *The Modernity of Tradition: Political Development in India* (Chicago: The University of Chicago Press, 1967), p. 167.

31. Lata Mani, 'Contentious Traditions: The Debate on *Sati in Colonial India*', *Cultural Critique* (Fall 1987), p. 123.
32. Ann McClintock, *Imperial Leather: Race, Gender and Sexuality in the Colonial Context* (London: Routledge, 1995), p. 6.
33. Catherine A. MacKinnon, *Toward a Feminist Theory of the State* (Cambridge: Harvard University Press, 1989), p. 159.
34. S. Franzway, D. Court and R.W. Connell, *Staking a Claim: Feminism, Bureaucracy and the State, op. cit.*, p. 35.
35. *Ibid.*, p. 53.
36. M. Savage and A. Witz, ' The Gender of Organizations', *op. cit.*, p. 12.
37. S. Franzway, D. Court and R.W. Connell, *Staking a Claim: Feminism, Bureaucracy and the State, op. cit.*, p. 46.
38. *Ibid.*, p. 48.
39. *Ibid.*, p. 55.
40. K.E. Ferguson, *The Feminist Case Against Bureaucracy, op. cit.*, p. 8.
41. M. Savage, and A. Witz, 'The Gender of Organizations', *op. cit.*, p. 18.
42. K.E. Ferguson, *The Feminist Case Against Bureaucracy, op. cit.*, p. 20.
43. *Ibid.*, p. 212.
44. C. Stivers, *Gender Images in Public Administration, Legitimacy and the Administrative State, op. cit.*, p. 127.
45. *Ibid.*, p. 102.
46. *Ibid.*, p. 119.
47. K.P. Iannello, *Decisions Without Hierarchy: Feminist Interventions in Organization Theory and Practice* (New York and London: Routledge, 1992).

# 5 Ecological Principles, Emerging Organisational Forms and Postmodernism

Jean Mercier

## INTRODUCTION

An immediate outcome of the United Nations Conference on Environment and Development (the Earth Summit) held in Rio in 1992 was Agenda 21, an ambitious design to implement the Rio Declaration and create environmentally sound and responsible sustainable development. Enlightened leaders in all corners of the globe are seeking new ideas on the delivery of services that go beyond the usual design for strengthening government capacities and 'debureaucratizing'. Along with the Third Sector, feminist, spiritual and other new models are those whose starting point is 'ecology'. Replacing unsustainable development patterns with environmentally sound and sustainable development may require considerable rethinking, including a basic reorientation of organisational approaches and a new vocabulary emphasising ecological principles. This chapter seeks a starting point in 'ecology' and the ideas of ecologists. It postulates an approach based on ecologists' own small-scale, non-hierarchic organisations and the concept of a protoplasmic living organism. Compatible with feminist, non-governmental and spiritual approaches, this concept attempts to extend the thinking of organisational ecologists and certain postmodern management scholars in a way that is applicable to both developing and developed areas. Unlike

95

approaches that stress exchanges with the environment, the biological analogy of competition for resources and survival of the fittest, or adaptation characteristics, the approach suggested here emphasises 'ecological aesthetics' that raises ecological consciousness.

The purpose of all knowledge, Harlan Cleveland once observed,[1] is to organise things or people. Considering the increasing influence of ecological knowledge in contemporary societies, how does such knowledge affect administration, and what would an ecological organisation look like? Answers to this question would offer many dimensions. For the purposes of understanding, more specifically, the influence of ecology on the emergence of alternative patterns of administration, it is necessary to first make a survey of a few ecological principles.

The principles of ecology – with their emphasis on interdependence, adaptation and holism – are echoed in several disciplines today. The field of ecology, then, offers models, methods and a theoretical perspective that provide theoretical foundations for other fields as well.[2] The parallel between emerging administrative practices and ecological principles has been facilitated by the fact that ecological thinking has not limited itself to questions of air, water and soil. The holistic tradition of ecology has encouraged its proponents to address themselves to matters institutional, organisational and political[3] in such a way that we can now make reference to *institutional ecology*.

Indeed, some ecologists recommend certain institutional or organisational principles. Let us first look at these institutional principles; we will then look at more exclusively biological principles; and finally we will take a more detailed look at the interaction between these principles and their application in concrete cases.

Among the institutional ecological principles is diversity (there is diversity in nature, and humans should not seek to standardise their creations, be they physical or institutional); the principle of self-regulation, with its implication for decentralisation; the principle of human scale, with its implication for organisation size; the principle of finality, or the knowledge of larger, more inclusive goals, a principle that discards an excessively segmented view of reality; and the megaprinciple of 'thinking globally and acting locally' (a typical ecological paradox), which may have more implications for public policy than for organisational arrangements.

It could even be argued that there are counter-principles in ecology. Such is the case with specialisation, which is frowned upon as much in institutional life as it is in agriculture. Certainly, excessive specialisation in the form of clogs within a bureaucratic or technocratic organisation is rejected outright by ecological thinkers. In fact, bureaucracy and technocracy can even be seen as the ecologist movement's first target, at least from a European perspective.[4] Generally speaking, what has facilitated the parallels between ecological principles and administrative life is that, increasingly, administration and management have been perceived through biological as opposed to mechanical metaphors.

Many images have been steering us away from the mechanical, but their common denominator is that they drew from nature, from the living, the ecological. It is as if the mechanical mode, temporary as it was in historical terms, had severed us and our organisations from the natural processes of life itself. Luther Gulick, who has followed the evolution of management all through this century and has seen the rise and then the slow downfall of the mechanical metaphor, has recently asked the essential question: 'Should we not reconsider the description of organizations as though they were machines?' All that machines show are a 'flat, static skeleton, a collection of bones for the archaeologist. Left out are the muscles, the power system, the neural system with its sensing organs'. Gulick concluded that 'an organization of people is a social and symbiotic organism, swimming in the river of time'.[5]

PRINCIPLES OF ECOLOGY: AN INTERACTION

The first principle drawn from the observation of nature is the principle of *diversity*. One of nature's foremost characteristics is its variety, its heterogeneity. A truly living ecosystem necessarily harbors a certain variety of species of plants and animals – this is the principle of *requisite variety*. The different components of a natural milieu are intimately tied together by a natural *interconnectedness*. There is a certain degree of *complexity* in the manner in which nature's components are related to each other. However, there is a *relative autonomy* between components and also between different ecosystems, which leads to a certain degree of *self-regulation*. When self-regulation is applied to institutions, it brings about smaller organisations, which respect the idea of human scale. Of course, the principle of interconnectedness and the principle of relative autonomy seem to be, at first glance, contradictory. More precisely however, they constitute a *paradox*, another ecological principle: the natural world is full of paradoxes, and sometimes humans can use these paradoxical situations, as in the exhortation to 'think globally and act locally'.

All ecologists plead in favour of the *human scale*. Ecologists believe that many of our environmental problems come from the sheer size of our institutions and physical creations: large nation-states, multinational corporations, bureaucracies, large energy projects, multi-lane highways, mega-cities and oversized shopping malls are some of their favourite targets. Yvan Illich, a French social thinker, can be considered as an ecologists' guide on this matter. For Illich, when human institutions grow past a certain size, they turn against the very purpose for which they were created:

> Illich has identified a phenomenon he calls 'paradoxical counterproductivity', whereby institutions, once they cross a certain threshold of size and intensity, begin

to frustrate and subvert the very purposes for which they were established in the first place. Education stupefies, medicine sickens, the machine turns on its creator.[6]

The principle of human scale is intimately related to another important principle, which is that we *should avoid excessive specialisation*. In the short run, intense specialisation can bring about certain quantitative results, as in the case of agriculture, but it is rarely sustainable in the long run: 'Very often, cows that produce more milk are extremely useless for other work functions'.[7] Forest fires are more likely when a homogeneous type of tree has been planted in an area.[8] Diversity is preferable. More importantly still, monoculture hinders the natural regeneration of the soil. In the world of human institutions, excessive specialisation must also be avoided: the excessively specialised human being becomes incapable, with time, of assessing a situation within its larger context. The same holds true for institutions.

The case of Brazil is an interesting one, since it is at the same time a developed and an underdeveloped country. The example of the Brazilian North-east can indeed be taken as the ultimate example of a case which would confirm ecologists' worst fears. Here is an area which has intensely specialised its agricultural production, partly to gain much needed cash inflows to pay for its involvement in a world economy in which it is not fully equipped to compete. The highly specialised agriculture practiced in that region has greatly contributed to dislodging small independent peasants who were traditionally working the soil. In the opinion of ecologists, these displaced peasants became much more numerous still when the soil in the region began to dry up as a consequence of the excessively specialised type of agriculture being practiced (systematic elimination of trees, undue exposure of the topsoil to winds, and the use of pesticides). Unfortunately, the sad story of these dislocated peasants does not stop here.

The now landless peasants, not finding the means of survival in their native North-east, migrated to large cities such as Rio de Janeiro or São Paolo, only to find that there were no more jobs there than from where they came. They could only locate in the already densely populated *favelas*, makeshift cities within cities, that stand as monuments of uncontrolled urban growth, untreated human waste and general social decay.

In the ecologist's perspective, the environmental problems found in Brazil's large cities should in fact be traced back to a strategic choice to displace small-scale agriculture in favour of a large-scale and intensely specialised type of land exploitation. Such a choice has not only brought about unfavourable consequences from a social point of view, it has attacked human sensitivity, even the human soul: when humans are packed into a large, impersonal mega-city, of course they become aggressive and violent. All the self-regulating mechanisms of small community life disappear, and the result is a wandering, anomic, rootless individual, ready to regress into senseless behaviour at the first occasion. With bigness, it is not only all the plastic and the pollution that cannot be harmoniously integrated, it is also the human being.

Excessive specialisation, whether in terms of process or of structure – a hallmark of the previous mechanical mode – has always been sharply criticised by ecologists, especially deep ecologists. 'As a cognitive deal . . . specialization renders people incapable of appreciating the "web of life"'.[9] These authors state that it is even the 'disease of the modern character', which robs the individual of personal wholeness, competence and a sense of husbandry. The specialised individual is 'the human counterpart of an ecological monoculture'.[10] What is needed is the very opposite of abstract, disincarnated specialisation: relating, opening boundaries, taking the larger ecosystemic view. As seen by many ecologists, it is the excessively specialised outlook that resulted in the present environmental problems: as ecologist Barry Commoner observed,

an ecological system cannot be treated as separate components when all its parts are truly interdependent.
Commoner[11] then criticised J.K. Galbraith's celebration
of the new industrial state,[12] describing it as reductionist
and fragmented. But some form of organisation is still
necessary, a proposition to which even the radical social
ecologist Murray Bookchin adheres. Large bureaucratic
organisations should, however, be replaced, concludes
Bookchin, 'by small units which people could comprehend and directly manage by themselves'.[13] Whether taking
the ecological approach or not, many organisations have
followed this very same line of thinking.

## ENVIRONMENTALISTS AND ECOLOGISTS AS SOCIAL MOVEMENTS

I interviewed a number of ecologist leaders on the topic
of bureaucracy; in this section I will situate their prescriptions in the context of 'social movements'. Usually,
contemporary social movements – or, as they are sometimes referred to, 'new' social movements – are 'not preoccupied with struggle over the production and distribution
of material goods';[14] rather their interests lie in issues
which, until quite recently, have been considered moral,
private or exclusively economic, and consequently outside the realms of politics or public discussion.[15] Examples
can be found in such diverse movements as the mobilisation of consumers and users of services, feminism, sexual
liberation, pro-choice or pro-life movements, health issue
advocacy or, of course, ecologist struggles.[16]

Different terms have been used to describe these movements: social movements; new protest movements,
antipolitics, or alternative movements. In developing
countries, grassroots movements, described in this volume
in Chapters 2 and 3, are often an important element in
the evolution of civil society. Social movements everywhere often question 'the dominant images of modernity,

fundamentally challenge the dominant economic and political structures, and force public debate about how we want . . . to work and live' in the future.[17] By raising 'radical questions about the ends of personal and social life, they warn us of the crucial problems facing complex societies'.[18] Thus they address themselves to large topics, but they also address more limited questions such as administration, and that is why they can help us identify alternative administrative principles.

As social movements, these organisations appear to be the proverbial 'tip of the iceberg'. Although they might seem, at times, to represent no one but themselves, they can act as sensors, as scouts, sending us back a message about our society as well as our organisations. As we have just seen, social movements are concerned with a certain type of issue, a certain type of content, with issues that were once considered outside public discussion. Just as important is the fact that social movements can be characterised by their methods, their means and their operating modes, including, of course, their administrative modes. It is not only that they 'exercise the repertoire of existing democratic rights more extensively',[19] through nonconventional forms of political participation such as sit-ins or staged events; it is through their own internal administration that they try to make a statement. Indeed, there is an important self-reflexive aspect to social movements: 'The organizational forms of (social) movements are not just "instrumental" for their goals. They are goals in themselves . . . The form of the movement is itself a message, a symbolic challenge to the dominant codes'.[20]

Drawing upon the work of Marshall McLuhan, Melucci insists that the form of social movements is their essence – that their medium is the message: 'Their "journey" is considered at least as important as their intended destination',[21] as it 'signals the possibility of alternative experiences of time, space, and interpersonal relationships, which in turn challenge the technological rationality of the system'.[22] More specifically, social movements 'place a high value upon grass-root, informal and "hidden" forms of organization and they consequently tend to be suspicious of business organizations, trade unions and hierarchies, political parties and state bureaucracies'.[23] Their preferences go to 'temporary and *ad hoc* organizational structures',[24] where hierarchy is either avoided altogether or kept to a minimum. For certain ecologist organisations, doing away with hierarchy is profoundly ecological, since, in their view, hierarchy is a man-made concept that is unknown in nature.

Drawing from the above, several questions come to mind. First, are all these social movements (feminism, ecology, pro-life and so on) going in one unified direction, and are their alternative administration methods a set of coherent prescriptions? Or are these different movements a 'loosely connected set of issue movements that does not strive for ideological or organizational integration?'[25] Second, to what extent are these social movements tied to the relatively recent sociological notions of postmodernity and Inglehart's notion of postmaterialism?[26] Finally, to what extent are environmentalist and ecologist organisations typical of social movements? It may very well be that some of these organisations exhibit the characteristics of social movements, while others do not.

In order to answer this last question, we should draw a distinction I made between environmentalists and ecologists. Environmentalists are preoccupied with the physical state of the environment, searching for concrete remedies to improve the situation, remedies such as legislation and technological improvements. We can describe them as 'downstream', since they concentrate on the results of pollution. Others have described this type of group as 'success-oriented':[27] 'these organizations tend to be small, hierarchical and . . . appeal to practically oriented, well educated individuals . . . Greenpeace is probably the most obvious example of this kind of orientation'. The professionalisation of this type of organisation, which quite inevitably fosters 'careerism on the part of staff members, and passivity on the part of volunteers',[28] is due to a number of factors, among which the fact that second-generation environmental problems require a high level of legal and scientific expertise;[29] in the United States, the complex organisational requirements that stems from the desire to have the advantage of non-profit tax status is also a factor.[30] For all these reasons, the group which we have described as environmentalists (as opposed to 'ecologists'), who are success-oriented and who are interested in downstream-type issues, do not exhibit all of the characteristics that describe social movements, and are not really proposing a radically new set of administrative methods.

On the other hand, the groups I describe as 'ecologist' (as opposed to 'environmentalist') are more interested in 'upstream' issues, such as the root causes of environmental degradation. These exhibit to a greater extent the characteristics of social movements. First, they have a more holistic, all-encompassing approach to environmental problems, an approach that touches upon subjects that are relatively new in public debates (the ends of life, the transcendence of nature, industrialisation itself). Second, and more importantly still, they are social movements because they are 'value-oriented',[31] – they are more interested in organising according to their own principles than achieving specific and measurable goals. Thus, they often reject professional roles and the use of experts, develop different organisational structures, avoid hierarchy and sometimes rely on charismatic leadership.[32] In other words, there is a definitely 'self-reflexive/the medium is the message' quality about ecological groups that squarely puts them within the social-movement domain. They are therefore more interesting to our search for alternative administration.

I referred earlier to Alberto Melucci's idea that for social movements, 'the medium was the message', meaning that in their organisation's day-to-day functioning, members try to apply the principles which, in their view, should be applied by other organisations and society at large. In the case of ecologists, this often means applying the principles of ecology in their own organisational life. In general, according to Offe, 'the process by which multitudes of individuals become collective actors (in social movements) is highly informal, ad hoc, discontinuous, context sensitive and egalitarian'.[33]

In contrast to traditional forms of political organizations, they do not employ the organizational principle of differentiation in either the horizontal (insider versus outsider) or the vertical (leader versus rank and file members) dimension. On the contrary, they seem to have a strong reliance on systhesis.[34]

More specifically, the principle of non-hierarchic organisation is very dear to many ecologists. That principle is intimately related to the all-important ecologist principle of diversity, since one way to respect – and indeed, encourage – diversity is to refrain from stifling it by censure or by hierarchic authority.

But how enduring are these organisational and administrative values, even among ecologists themselves? Is there not the possibility that ecologists, just like the Dutch ecologists,

> after a period of experimentation with all forms of democratization . . . begin to question the effectiveness of their sometimes 'overly democratized' organizations . . . As a result, the search for greater efficiency and a certain degree of hierarchy and centralization can become acceptable.[35]

The principle of non-hierarchy and its corollary principle, the respect for diversity, although they are valuable, seem to be more easily applicable when nothing constraining has to be concretely produced. There may be a greater possibility for discussion in non-hierarchic organisations than in hierarchic ones, but once a course of action has been specified, hierarchy appears. For example, even if Earth First! is considered officially to be a non-hierarchical organisation, there are in reality leadership roles within that group, and leaders do lead the team into action.[36]

But what of the *belief* in the non-hierarchy principle? Can it have administrative consequences, even though it is not *applied* as extensively as ecologists would like it to be? Christa Daryl Slaton has closely followed the functioning of a Green organisation in Hawaii. Like many green organisations, this one firmly believes in the respect for diversity and its corollary, the principle of non-hierarchic organisation. In practical application this group had no official titles, nor official responsibilities. Still, the work had to be done:

> While the Greens do not establish hierarchical structures that produce dichotomies between leaders and followers, their decentralized, postpatriarchal organizational designs and/or operations still frequently rely heavily on the strong commitment and intense energy of those who are willing to devote an inordinate amount of time organizing and keeping the group together.[37]

When those active members, 'who had been strong advocates for a more formal, albeit organic, organization and who had been ones to take on the tedious day-to-day tasks . . . left Hawaii within a few weeks of each other . . . the Movement stopped in its tracks'.[38]

This disparity between ecologist theory and ecologist practice may not be typical of only North American ecologist groups. Much the same situation has been described for ecologist groups in France, where quite a large group can come to depend on a couple of active volunteers; when they leave, the whole edifice collapses,[39] without those volunteers ever having official recognition for the many hours of work they have contributed. Similarly, in developing countries the departure of key members of non-hierarchic grassroots organisations may precipitate their decline.

And yet, through all the efforts at negating hierarchy's presence, it still shows its (presumably) ugly face, only in a more insidious manner. There are cliques[40] and tensions between university and non-university Greens.[41] Unofficial hierarchy may be worse than official hierarchy in the sense that hidden hierarchy is not as accountable as official hierarchy. It may very well be situations such as these which prompted Feher and Heller to conclude that while the goal of many social movements is the promotion of democracy, 'modern movements . . . are non-democratic in their internal practices'.[42]

Feher and Heller conclude that the chances of many social movements becoming realistic alternatives to existing political organisations are rather slim. In the case of many ecologist organisations the details of administration have been looked upon as something beneath them, something that could be dispensed with. However, as Slaton observed, 'if a movement cannot agree on an organizational structure that clearly defines roles, responsibilities, decision making processes, goals, and policies, it is not likely to survive, much less attract broader support'.[43] Somewhat paradoxically, 'administrative problems stem from an insufficiently bureaucratic (or hierarchic) organization'. Often, the ecologist, upstream-oriented organisations are caught in a bind: either they have little influence and keep their organisational principles, or they compromise their organisational principles and influence the outside world.

## ENVIRONMENTALIST AND ECOLOGIST ORGANIZATIONS

Looking at ecologist organisations as social movements, as organisations that try to challenge society's values by doing things differently in their day-to-day operations, is only one way of understanding them. Another way is to look at them as organisations.

Let us bypass, for the moment, the organisational literature that deals with mainstream organisations, such as corporations and government units and go directly to descriptions of the administrative characteristics of 'Third Sector' volunteer organisations. Among this specific but quite large literature, let us concentrate on those descriptions that might apply to environmentalist and ecologist organisations. We will first look at whether they correspond to Douglas and Wildavsky's descriptions of sectarian organizations (or 'sects'); then we will look at Mintzberg's 'missionary' organisations; finally, we will look at Tixier's theory of *fonctionnement collectif* (the collective model of organisation).

Mary Douglas and Aaron Wildavsky have stated that there are essentially three types of organisations in society at large. There are hierarchies, mainly in governments, but also within private corporations. Then there are markets, somewhat less stable, whose situation is more contingent upon the give and take of offer and demand. Finally, the authors looked at the development, in the midst of our modern and technologically sophisticated world, of a third type of organisation, the *sects*, whose members want to opt out of mainstream society and situate themselves at its periphery. How do ecologist organisations compare with Douglas and Wildavsky's sects?

What are, then, the characteristics of sects? The first element is that sect members see themselves as being at odds with mainstream society. The world outside the sect is seen as an impure entity, with which no compromise is possible.[44] Barriers must be put in place so as to protect its members from the outside world. As an alternative to the outside world, sects elaborate an all-inclusive and utopian vision of future life,[45] where the inevitable conflicts of day-to-day living in society are usually ignored. The other component of the philosophy of the sects is more complicated: it concerns the sects' attitudes toward leadership and leaders. Douglas and Wildavsky point to the fact that, in their official discourse, sects prefer equality to leadership.[46]

For reasons which probably go well beyond administrative principles and reach deep into the human psyche, groups that act like sects have an ambivalent and contradictory attitude towards leaders. They officially like to declare that leaders are not needed, since the strong convictions of its members suffice to keep the group coordinated without there being the need for an authority to keep them in line. Still, the lack of an official leader creates a vacuum, and it is from this vacuum that an unofficial leadership emerges, with powers that go well beyond those that an official, accountable leader would enjoy. This may explain why a sect-like organisation tends to 'lose direction by attacking its leaders'.[47]

We can also look at ecologist and environmentalist groups as 'missionary' organisations, according to the definition by Henry Mintzberg. The missionary organisation is dominated by its central ideology, its central mission, which becomes pervasive in all its activities. To become a member of a missionary organisation, one must believe in its essential precepts. Are environmentalist and ecologist organisations missionary organisations?

If we first consider structure, we are tempted to answer in the affirmative. Indeed, Mintzberg, sometimes referring to another author interested in the subject, Niv, describes missionary organisations as being confronted with a dilemma. The missionary organisation usually stays small 'because personal contact among the members is crucial in retaining a sense of cohesiveness and identification with the ideology'.[48] But if the goal is to change the world – and a missionary's goal often is – how is this momentous task realised with a miniature organisation? If the tasks are limited, as is the case for small local *environmental* concerns, then the dilemma does not even arise, since a small organisation will be sufficient.

And so the dilemma is more intense for *ecological*, larger concerns. As Mintzberg observes, there is an answer to the dilemma: the missionary organisation can have both the advantages of large size and of small by regrouping small, autonomous organisations into a larger federation, 'splitting like amoebae into similar smaller units when they have grown too large'.[49] And, 'if each enclave succeeds in changing its immediate environment, together they can change the world'. In terms of structure, ecologist – and sometimes also environmentalist – organisations resemble Henry Mintzberg's descriptions of missionary organisations.

Let us now look at another model of alternative administration, a model that is somewhat closer to standard organisations. It is a model described by Pierre-Eric Tixier in France. Tixier has referred to his organisational model as the *fonctionnement collectif* model, which might be translated as the 'collective decision-making process' model or 'the collective model'. To understand it fully, we must first refer to classic sociologist author Max Weber's description of standard bureaucracy. Bureaucracy's essential characteristics can be summed up as follows: specialisation, hierarchy, continuity, neutrality, objectivity and emotional non-involvement. Interestingly enough, Weber compared bureaucracy to 'machines', specifying that bureaucracy was to administration what machines were to material production. Tixier sees a new type of organ-isation emerging, one that would be a historic reversal of the bureaucratic model described in Weber's classic observations. In contrast to other organisation theorists who posit non-Weberian ideal-types based on teams, matrixes, contingency, transaction cost economics and so on, Tixier includes the emotional commitment of organisational members in his model.

To begin with, Tixier's *fonctionnement collectif* organisations are essentially found outside of society's mainstream organisations: they are to be found in alternative education schools, in nurseries or in associations.[50] They also can be found as small enclaves within larger mainstream organisations.[51] Their mode of operation is different from what Weber had described for the organisations of his time – the early part of this century. The specialisation Weber describes is not as pervasive in Tixier's model: organisational members have a quite homogeneous level of education and training[52] and that level is usually quite high. The homogeneity is one that is more based on comparable levels of expertise and the recognition of complementarity[53] than on an artificial standardisation within fixed and rigid categories. Most members participate in the decision-making process,[54] and the decision itself is usually the result of a consensus, and is not merely handed down by a hierarchic superior, as in Weber's model. The legitimacy of one's authority does not come from his position in the official hierarchy (of which there is little in any case), but from his authentic expertise and his capacity to really draw support from his colleagues.[55]

A very important departure from Weber's description is the fact that Tixier's *fonctionnement collectif* organisations do not rule out emotional involvement. Now *that* is a big change from the classic bureaucratic organisation, since one of the latter's most important characteristics is that it operates in an emotional vacuum, or, as Weber described, *sine ire et studio* (without anger or passion). Members of Tixier's organisations are emotionally involved; they participate in organisational life with all of their being;[56] participation encompasses love, affection, anger and passion, and all the rest. The advantages of working in such an environment have a qualitative, emotional aspect to them.

Tixier admits he does not really know why this type of organisation is appearing at this time. Typical left-wing French ideology would tend to understand these innovative organisations as a particular application of the long-standing principles of *autogestion*, a movement which has called for democratic, participative and equalitarian organisations for several decades. Tixier rules out the possibility that these new organisational methods would simply come from a sudden and unexpected conversion to the principles of *autogestion*.[57] Is their presence due to some sociological factor – a new way of rewarding personnel in an economic downturn, where financial rewards are more difficult to come by – or a response to new qualitative needs searching to express themselves among new generations of workers?[58] Are these new forms of organisation a real alternative to Weber's bureaucratic structure or to Frederick Taylor's scientific management, or are they merely restricted to organisations in their infancy, which will later adopt more traditional methods to assure their survival, or limited to organisations which are, and will undoubtedly remain, marginal components of the larger society?[59] Will they remain, in certain cases, small enclaves within larger bureaucratic organisations?[60] Tixier opens the door to other explanations when he mentions that these innovative organisations could be the result of something that has changed in the organisations' context.[61]

There are parallels to be drawn with ecologist *fonctionnement collectif* and environmentalist organisations. As with Tixier's organisations, ecologist and environmentalist groups will typically be small, egalitarian (at least in principle), be situated at the margin of mainstream social activities, severely limit their bureaucratic procedures, and have members who will sometimes invest their whole selves in their work.

In our search for alternative administration, our question now becomes this: what are the common alternative administrative patterns suggested by Douglas and Wildavsky's sects, by Mintzberg's missionary organisations, and by Tixier's *fonctionnement collectif*? Unlike most mainstream organisations, they are often spared the *details of administration*. This characteristic explains why this emerging form of organisation is found at the periphery or outside of the area of organisations producing physical goods, and why they can also exist within large bureaucratic organisations, as long as, in this latter case, they are spared from 'the details of administration'. There is some overlap here between what these authors describe and the notion of *service*-oriented organisations. Ecologist and environmentalist groups are service-oriented: they do not produce physical goods for an outside market. This characterisation is certainly true for Douglas and Wildavsky's sects and partly true for Mintzberg's missionary organisations. Interestingly enough, Tixier's examples (schools, nurseries, associations) are exclusively taken from the services sector. In fact, the patterns found here correspond to one of Mintzberg's five original *mainstream organisation* configurations, *adhocracy*. Indeed, adhocracy is usually small, is composed of participants whose role will be determined by their expertise and personal qualities, not by their official rank; adhocracy does away with the usual bureaucratic methods, does not have the continuity that bureaucracy has, and, most important, is spared from the details of administration, because they are created to conceptually solve a specific problem which is then entrusted to a regular administrative unit for implementation.

We are now in a position to draw some conclusions about ecologist and environmentalist organisations as organisations: what ecologist and environmentalist organisations share with many other organisations of our time, and what explains most of their structural characteristics, is that they are service-oriented organisations. Are these organisations marginal, since they do not seem to produce much of what is physically necessary for society to survive? Of course, as an ever-greater proportion of the employed are engaged in the services sector, new organisational structures will inevitably appear and, indeed, already have. In this sense, ecologist and environmentalist service-oriented organisations are very much representative of their time, and not at all in opposition to it. In fact, ecologist and environmentalist organisations may only exhibit, in an extreme form, patterns which will eventually characterise a great number of our organisations, even those which are considered very 'mainstream'. In actual fact, as far back as 1961, British organisational theorists Tom Burns and G.M. Stalker[62] described an emerging type of management which they called 'organic'. That type of management had structural characteristics similar to those that we described earlier: a looser structure, more egalitarian relationships, leadership based on knowledge and not on hierarchic rank, and an emotional commitment that ventured well beyond what Weber had described for classic bureaucracy. And so, as far back as the early 1960s, organisation theorists had already begun to identify management structures that today's ecologist leaders go out of their way to recommend.

There is an important theoretical point to be made, here. We can use *mainstream organisational theory* concepts in order to understand emerging, alternative modes of administration. Indeed, as we have suggested earlier, emerging organisational forms share many characteristics with, for example, Mintzberg's adhocracy, and with Burns and Stalker's organic structure. They may also share some of J.D. Thompson's[63] 'mutual adjustment' forms of coordination. It is not the purpose of this chapter to review extensively traditional organisation theory concepts that would help us understand some of the characteristics of emerging and alternative forms of administration. However, in my view, this could quite easily be accomplished.


## THE AESTHETICS OF ECOLOGY AND POSTMODERNISM

In my study of ecologists and their contribution to alternative administration, I was struck by the fact that some ecologist propositions had, apparently, nothing to do with the quality of the air, the water or the soil.

Indeed, after studying ecologists, after reading their work and after listening to them, I am left with some propositions that have little to do with the environment *per se*. For example, what does diversity as such have to do with the quality of air, water and soil, and why do Deep Ecologists prefer small dams to one larger dam (equivalent in energy), even though the larger dam may be, in fact, less polluting than the addition of smaller ones? Why do ecologists of the social movement, 'in contrast to traditional forms of political organisations . . . not employ the organisation principle of differentiation in either the horizontal (insider versus outsider) or the vertical (leader versus rank-and-file members) dimension'?[64] And why do they have such great reservations about hierarchy? How is the negation or disappearance of hierarchy related to the environment?

What exactly holds ecologists, as a group, together? One way to answer this is to use the idea that Jamison, Eyerman and Cramer have called the environmental 'knowledge interests'.[65] The 'knowledge interests' are 'those dimensions on the cognitive plane where environmentalism (and ecologism) forms its collective identity . . . these knowledge interests are a new way of seeing, of conceptualising . . . as well as defining "harmony" and "balance"'.[66]

Drawing from Jamison, Eyerman and Cramer, and from their notion of environmental knowledge interests, we want to go one step further and state that what ecologists share, above all and apart from questions of the physical environment, is an *ecologist aesthetic*. I will try to identify some of its components: the aesthetics of ecology encompasses the cognitive dimensions of ecology that favour some arrangements, forms, processes (and other elements) while ruling out some others; for example, the aesthetics of ecology favour small scale over large scale, the diverse over the standardised, and the holistic over the specialised.

In another publication,[67] I have gone to some length

to identify precisely the essential components of the 'ecologist aesthetic' and 'knowledge interests'. It may be sufficient here to summarise some main elements:

1.  a bias in favour of diversity, of the particularities of a specific element, which is at the same time a bias against uniformity and standardisation;
2.  a bias in favour of the earthy and the sensuous, which is at the same time a bias against the disincarnate and the abstract;
3.  finally, a bias for fusion and 'connection', which is at the same time a bias against separation and differentiation.

It would be outside the purpose of this chapter to draw extensive parallels between these components of ecologist thought and other intellectual currents, but let me state nevertheless that these aesthetic components have much in common with what has been called postmodernism.

I need to give a brief introduction to postmodernism. What first developed as a protest against 'modern architecture, art, literary criticism and philosophy, and all language, science and technology was inevitably extended to such fields as organisation study and even public administration'.[68] Postmodernism questioned the very possibility of objective representation, inquiry, or service-provision – and as a mode of thought and a movement, impacted feminist thinking (see Chapter 4) and anti-Western discourse. From the standpoint of 'ecologist aesthetics', we recognise in postmodernism a movement in which its adepts are more concerned with the cultural patterns that may lead us to pollution than with the environment *per se*.[69] Postmodernism is very much about forms, and less about content, which makes it similar to Deep Ecology, which is also concerned with forms. Postmodernism is about the 'contamination of the aesthetic and the non-aesthetic'[70] and the 'philosophical, historical, and political issues raised by the question of form or the problem of beauty, rather than form and beauty as narrow aesthetic questions'.[71]

In architecture, for example, the movement criticised modern architecture's indiscriminate practices around the world, its attempt to impose a uniform model of architecture without regard for the particular traditions and environment in which a given project was planned. Modern architecture emphasised mass, volume and straight lines along with mechanical forms and an overdose of technology. In its search for the new at all costs, modern architectural design disregarded an area's natural equilibrium and thus created environments without collective values. In so doing, modern architecture was much like 'the inflated claims of Esperanto . . . [with its project of an] a-historical, logical language spoken in every major city'.[72] In place of modern architecture, postmodernism proposed to learn modesty and to adapt to particular circumstances, local character and local history by recovering certain aspects of tradition and acquiring a sense of place, much in the same vein as the Deep Ecologists recommend when they speak of bioregions, for example. Through an understanding of certain aspects of postmodernism, it is easier to comprehend ecologists' vehement opposition to the development of suburbs, to the construction of multilane highways, and to the destruction of historic parts of urban areas, most of which, at first glance, have no immediate or substantial relation to the quality of the air, the water or the soil. In developing countries, the postmodern perspective gives encouragement to opposition toward Western mind-sets, hierarchical administrative systems, and patriarchal decision-making processes.

To summarise, ecologists can be considered as part of contemporary social movements which are very much preoccupied with the aesthetic dimension of life. Their insistence on small organisations, non-specialisation and unstructured forms, and their search for alternative experiences of time and space can be interpreted as being political, but these elements can also be considered as part of an aesthetic: just like postmodernists, they are searching for diversity, non-standardisation and fusion.

By considering the ecologist movement as at least partly an aesthetic movement, it is possible to answer a question that has been raised regarding the nature of social movements: are social movements in general (not only ecologist moments) part of one large unified movement (as Frenchman Alain Touraine claims[73]), or are they only a set of separate, loosely connected organisations? If we consider them tied together, above all, by aesthetic (and somewhat unconscious) values, then it does not really matter whether they are tied together in a large organised movement. They are bound by something stronger than politics; they are bound by a cognitive reference to forms and arrangements which then find their way into organisations and political processes. They are united by what is technically called an 'intersubjective element' – that is, a subjective, apolitical sentiment that is shared by several individuals, and thus loses its idiosyncratic character.

The aesthetic I have been referring to in this chapter and which is present among Deep Ecologists, postmodernists and some other groups, I will call 'the aesthetic of the protoplasm'. In protoplasm, elements are intimately tied together – the components of the cell are joined by a viscous and dense liquid. The metaphor of the protoplasm entails not seeing our environment as something different from us, something 'out there', and thus would lead to less pollution.

According to several ecologists, we should extend ourselves into 'protoplasmic relationships': people should indeed be concretely and intimately joined in a common endeavour. We should look upon developing countries, for example, as 'being in the same boat as us', not as parts of the world from which we are separate. Maffesoli has argued that aesthetics 'irrigate' in a fundamental way the 'spirit of the times', the *ambiance* which bathes all situations, both important and not, of our daily lives.[74]

The aesthetic of the protoplasm, which is an important component of the aesthetics of ecology, can be summed up by a preference for the particular, the intimate and the close at hand, and a bias in favour of holistic but immediate relationships, uninhibited by abstract and larger forms of rationality.

If indeed our ecological consciousness is a function of an emerging aesthetic, the aesthetics of the protoplasm, and if this aesthetic is rooted in our cognitive system inscribed in the manner in which we perceive and arrange the world, we should be able to locate it in almost all facets of our lives: in the renewed importance of rootedness, localism and the revival of the tribal feeling; in the rediscovery of organic food and natural medicine; and even in business trends and in government administration. If aesthetics are anything at all, they are everywhere.

## ECOLOGIST AESTHETICS AND DEVELOPMENT

We have seen earlier that postmodernists are against the ideas of uniformity and standardisation, preferring instead the ideas of diversity and variety. In the same spirit, they question that there is a uniform and standardised model of development. If there is not a unique model of development, originating in the Western industrialised countries, it follows that the Western industrialised countries' role in development should not necessarily apply to others what may have worked for them. As O.P. Dwivedi has correctly observed, we must 'realise that the technological package which is being transfered . . . was developed, in the first place, for a specific climatic and consumption pattern of the North, where conditions are different'.[75]

This latter pattern-change leads to another one. Indeed,

if conditions are different in developing countries, the Western industrialised nations cannot assume the role of 'head-office', directing operations from an abstract point, removed from the situation at hand.

The third pattern of change has to do with planning itself. It is changing in the relationship between developing nations and Western industrialised countries because, to a large extent, planning itself has changed in recent years. To sum up these changes, we can say that planning has taken on biological (or organic) characteristics, as opposed to mechanical ones. When an organisation is viewed as a living entity immersed in an equally alive environment, the methods used to coordinate its activities undergo some degree of transformation. Whatever the specific labels, planning has moved away from a single-forecast solution to a more flexible and pragmatic approach – 'one that assigns sufficient value to the possible need to change plans'.[76] At the same time, strategic planning is viewed as embracing a broader set of both internal and external stakeholders in the process.

These developments, which all point to a more flexible approach to planning, have rendered planning more akin to a biological process[77] in which systems are partly autonomous and outcomes cannot be forecasted in every detail, such as was thought to be possible under the rule of traditional organisations. Thus, again, the biological metaphor replaces the mechanical one and sets the stage for parallels with ecology. But the biological metaphor is not the only reason to draw a parallel with ecology, because the respect for the complexity (and not mere complication) of life[78] and the diversity implied in feedback-planning points to a strong link with ecological matters. Indeed, deep ecologists have always viewed 'bureaucratic centralism ... [as] remote, objectifying, and manipulative, if not too structurally rigid'.[79]

It is with this latter parallel that we come to the end of the comparison between recent changes, both theoretical and practical, in administrative process and ecological thought. The point to emphasise is that organisational processes are increasingly seen and indeed practiced as life-like elements, opening up numerous parallels with ecological principles, such as diversity, thinking globally or holistically, and being aware of large goals (the principle of finality).

## CONCLUSION

In comparing ecologist principles and organisations with emerging patterns of alternative administration, I come to the conclusion that there are several common characteristics. My goal here was to draw these parallels, not to speculate on the origins and underlying causes of the common patterns.[80]

Even while we recognise the common patterns between ecology and alternative administration, some reservations must be made. First, ecologist and environmentalist organisations do not espouse, to the same extent, all the patterns of alternative administration. There are, especially among environmentalist organisations (as opposed to ecologist ones), 'success-oriented' groups who exhibit more traditional administration patterns such as specialisation and hierarchy. Moreover, the groups that exhibit more traditional characteristics are also those that produce a more tangible output. This suggests that alternative administrative principles cannot be applied everywhere, anytime.

My first reservation brings me to our second one. Indeed, some of the alternative administrative principles seem to be related to emerging aesthetic patterns, and we have tied these patterns to postmodernism. Especially in ecologist organisations that can be considered 'social movements', there is a need to experiment with new forms, with alternative notions of time and space. The motivation being partly aesthetic, the result is not always efficient, operational or even practicable.

My third reservation has to do with the presumed 'new-ness' of these emerging organisational principles. One could argue that they are not really new. Indeed, many of the emerging administrative patterns can be understood through traditional organisation theory. They can be understood through Burns and Stalker's concept of 'organic' management, Mintzberg's concept of 'adhocracy', and J.D. Thompson's concept of coordination through feedback. In addition, the decline of head offices and of 'one way planning' can be linked to a predictable decline of the 'technostructure', one of Mintzberg's five administrative components.

My fourth reservation has to do with the universality of these emerging alternative administrative patterns. It is clear that they are inapplicable to many types of organisations. For example, hierarchy is often necessary in public administration because of the necessity of accountability. Also, many emerging administrative patterns require high levels of professionalisation and training for a great proportion of the personnel, and these requirements almost rule out their applicability to the least-developed countries.

Many emerging patterns of management will prove to be enduring; some others, only an involuntary consequence of new aesthetics. Only time will tell whether a specific characteristic is of the first kind, or of the second.

## Notes and References

1. Harlan Cleveland, 'The Twilight of Hierarchy: Speculations on the Global Information Society', *Public Administration Review*, vol. 45 (1985), pp. 186–95.
2. J. Pfeffer, *Organizations and Organizational Theory* (Marshfield, Mass.: Pitman, 1982).
3. L.P. Hinchman and S.K. Hinchman, 'Deep Ecology and the Revival of Natural Right', *Western Political Quarterly*, vol. 42 (1989), pp. 201–8.
4. G. Sainteny, *Les verts* (Paris: Presses Universitaires de France, 1991).

5.  Luther Gulick, 'Time and Public Administration', *Public Administration Review*, vol. 47 (1987), p. 118.
6.  David Caley, interviewer and writer of *The Age of Ecology, Part I: Ideas* (Ottawa: The Canadian Broadcasting Corporation, 1990), p. 9 (transcripts).
7.  Vandana Shiva in David Caley, *op. cit.*, p. 24.
8.  Serres quoted in Jean-Marc Drouin, *Réinventer la nature – L'écologie et son histoire* (Paris: Desclée de Brouwer, 1991), p. 16.
9.  L.P. Hinchman and S.K. Hinchman, *op. cit.*, p. 215.
10. *Ibid.*, p. 216.
11. John Kenneth Galbraith, *The New Industrial State* (Boston: Houghton Mifflin, 1967).
12. Barry Commoner, *L'encerclement: problèmes de survie en milieu terrestre* (Paris: Seuil, 1972) (translation of *The Closing Circle: Nature, Man and Technology*, New York: Knopf, 1971).
13. Murray Bookchin, *Toward an Ecological Society* (Montréal: Black Rose Books, 1980), p. 92.
14. John Keane and Paul Mier in the Preface of Alberto Melucci, *Nomads of the Present – Social Movements and Individual Needs in Contemporary Society* (Philadelphia: Temple University Press, 1989), p. 5.
15. Claus Offe, 'Challenging the Boundaries of Institutional Politics: Social Movements Since the 1960s', in Charles S. Maier (ed.), *Changing Boundaries of the Political – Essays on the Evolving Balance Between the State and Society, Public and Private in Europe* (Cambridge: Cambridge University Press, 1987), p. 63.
16. *Ibid.*, p. 68.
17. A. Melucci, *op. cit.*, p. 203.
18. *Ibid.*, p. 12.
19. C. Offe, *op. cit.*, p. 63.
20. A. Melucci, *op. cit.*, p. 60.
21. *Ibid.*, p. 205.
22. *Ibid.*, p. 60.
23. *Ibid.*, p. 1.
24. *Ibid.*, p. 60.
25. C. Offe, *op. cit.*, p. 94.
26. Ronald Inglehart, *The Silent Revolution: Changing Values and Political Styles Among Western Publics* (Princeton: Princeton University Press, 1977).
27. Andrew Jamison, Ron Eyerman and Jacqueline Cramer, *New Environmental Consciousness: Environmental Movements in Sweden, Denmark and the Netherlands* (Edinburgh: Edinburgh University Press, 1990), p. 8.

28. Riley E. Dunlap and Angela G. Mertig, *American Environmentalism – the U.S. Environmental Movement, 1970–1990* (Philadelphia, Washington and London: Taylor & Francis, 1992), p. 23.
29. *Ibid.*, p. 21.
30. *Ibid.*, p. 22.
31. A. Jamison, R. Eyerman and J. Cramer, *op. cit.*, p. 8.
32. *Ibid.*
33. C. Offe, *op. cit.*, p. 70.
34. *Ibid.*, p. 71
35. A. Jamison, R. Eyerman and J. Cramer, *op. cit.*, p. 171.
36. Manussos Marangudakis, 'Emerging Ideologies in the Environmental Movement', unpublished MA thesis, Department of Sociology, McGill University, Montréal, 1991, p. 89.
37. Christa Daryl Slaton, *The Politics of Symbolic Consistency: Being Green While Organizing Greens*, paper presented at the Annual Meeting of the American Political Science Association, Atlanta, 1989, p. 30.
38. *Ibid.*, pp. 29–30.
39. Daniel Le Conte des Floris and Thierry Grillet, 'Les natures du vert', in *Environnement: une grande cause, mais moi d'abord* (Paris: Édition Autrement, 1986), p. 198.
40. C.D. Slaton, *op. cit.*, p. 25.
41. *Ibid.*, p. 10.
42. F.B. Feher and R. Heller, *Social Movements* (Toronto: University of Toronto Press, 1999), p. 43.
43. C.D. Slaton, *op. cit.*, p. 30.
44. Mary Douglas and Aaron Wildavsky, *Risk and Culture: An Essay on the Selection of Technical and Environmental Dangers* (Berkeley: University of California Press, 1982), p. 137.
45. *Ibid.*, p. 136.
46. *Ibid.*, p. 133.
47. *Ibid.*, p. 137.
48. Henry Mintzberg, *Power in and Around Organizations* (Englewood Cliffs, N.J.: Prentice Hall, 1983), p. 378.
49. *Ibid.*
50. Pierre-Éric Tixier, 'Démocratie directe et organisation: Pour une théorie du fonctionnement collectif', *L'année sociologique*, vol. 33 (1983), p. 21.
51. *Ibid.*, p. 32.
52. *Ibid.*
53. *Ibid.*, p. 27.
54. *Ibid.*, p. 22.

55. *Ibid.*, p. 25.
56. *Ibid.*, p. 26.
57. *Ibid.*, p. 34.
58. *Ibid.*, p. 35.
59. *Ibid.*, p. 22.
60. *Ibid.*, p. 34.
61. *Ibid.*
62. Tom Burns and G.M. Stalker, *The Management of Innovation* (London: Tavistock Publications, 1961).
63. J.D. Thompson, *Organizations in Action: Social Science Base of Administrative Theory* (New York: McGraw-Hill, 1967).
64. C. Offe, *op. cit.* pp. 70–1.
65. A. Jamison, R. Eyerman and J. Cramer, *op. cit.*
66. *Ibid.*, p. 5.
67. Jean Mercier, *Downstream and Upstream Ecologists* (Westport: Praeger 1977).
68. David Farmer, *The Language of Public Administration, Bureaucracy, Modernity, and Post-modernity* (Alabama: University of Alabama Press, 1995); Charles Fox and Hugh Miller, *Postmodern Public Administration: Toward Discourse* (Thousand Oaks, Cal.: Sage, 1994).
69. Postmodernism should be distinguished from postmodernity. The latter term is more of a description, the former is a movement. Modernity is a historical fact, just as postmodernity can be seen as a description of an historical period; but with postmodernism we are referring to a movement, to a set of ideas.
70. David Carroll, *Paraesthetics. Foucault, Lyotard, Derrida* (New York and London: Methuen, 1987), p. xv.
71. *Ibid.*, p. xiv.
72. Richard Kearny, *The Wake of Imagination: Toward a Postmodern Culture* (Minneapolis: University of Minnesota Press, 1988), p. 349.
73. Alain Touraine, *Anti-Nuclear Protest: The Opposition to Nuclear Energy in France* (Cambridge: Cambridge University Press, 1983).
74. Michel Maffesoli, 'Socialité et naturalité ou l'écologisation du social', *Cahiers de l'imaginaire*, vol. 3 (1989), p. 10.
75. O.P. Dwivedi, 'Institutional Issues in Environmental Protection: A Third World Perspective', in Paul Painchaud (ed.), *Le partage des responsabilités publiques en environnement* (Sainte-Foy (QC): Les Éditions la Liberté, 1997), p. 151.
76. A.R. Haynes, 'What about the Future?', *Business Quarterly*, vol. 53 (1989), p. 56.

77.   H. Cleveland, *op. cit.*, p. 188.
78.   Laurent Dobuzinskis, *The Deep Structure of 'Deep Ecology' and its Political Implications*, paper presented at the Annual Meeting of the American Political Science Association, Atlanta, 1989.
79.   L.P. Hinchman and S.K. Hinchman, *op. cit.*, p. 216.
80.   This latter task has been done elsewhere (Mercier, *op. cit.*).

# Part II
# Regional Studies

# 6 Bureaucracy and the Alternatives in East and Southeast Asia

Mark Turner and John Halligan

## INTRODUCTION: IMAGINING ASIA

East and Southeast Asia are essentially terms of geographical convenience used to delineate a disparate group of countries that demonstrate enormous ethnic, cultural, linguistic and political diversity. Once they could be identified, perhaps with others, under the vague notion of the Far East. In the 1950s, the term 'Southeast Asia' was normally used to mean 'the non-European, non-Middle East, non-socialist, non-Soviet and non-Japanese part of the Eurasian continent'.[1] Even Taiwan, Hong Kong and South Korea were often judged to lie within Southeast Asia because they were poor and underdeveloped. China was simply seen as China, a self-perception that still dominates in China today. Attempts to forge regional identity have been largely a process of post-Second World War cooperation especially associated with economic growth and manifested in organisations such as the Association of Southeast Asian Nations (ASEAN) and Asia Pacific Economic Cooperation (APEC). The difficulties encountered by Malaysia's prime minister, Mahathir Mohamad, in attempting to establish the East Asian Economic Group (EAEG), later recast as the East Asian Economic Caucus (EAEC), reveal continuing ambiguities about regional membership and what it actually means to the participants. The situation is further confused by other metaphors used until the economic setbacks of the late 1990s such as High-performing Asian Economies

(HPAEs), Asian Newly-Industrialising Countries (ANICs), or simply Asian 'tiger' economies which cut across the geographical delineation of East and Southeast Asia.

The active process of imagining[2] an East Asian or Southeast Asian cultural or political community has always proved difficult for the potential members of that community because of their diversity and caution in forging bilateral and multilateral relationships. In this chapter, we will adopt the term 'East Asia' to cover the countries of China, Japan, South Korea, North Korea and Taiwan. 'Southeast Asia' is comprised of Burma, Thailand, Vietnam, Cambodia, Laos, Indonesia, Malaysia, Singapore, Brunei and the Philippines, most of which now belong to ASEAN. It is obvious that such a diverse range of countries defies generalisation. Thus, in our discussions of bureaucracy and the alternatives in East and Southeast Asia, it is difficult if not impossible to make generalisations that will apply to all countries. Where generalisations occur in the chapter, we acknowledge that there will always be exceptions.

The chapter is divided into two sections. The first examines the nature of bureaucracy in East and Southeast Asia, stressing its longevity and variation from both the Weberian ideal type and the Western experience. The second section looks at the alternatives to bureaucracy in the region, focusing on the transformation of bureaucratic agencies into people-centred organisations, the role of non-governmental organisations (NGOs), and the practice of decentralisation. The Philippines provides a disproportionate number of the examples both because it has a record of greater experimentation and experience than most other countries, and because one of the authors has long experience in Philippine research.

# BUREAUCRACY IN EAST AND SOUTHEAST ASIA

## Bureaucratic Origins

Bureaucracy has been and continues to be a favoured organisational form in East and Southeast Asia. Despite its popularity and ubiquity, its origins are diverse, its longevity varies considerably between countries, and there are differences in its operation across the region. China has one of the world's oldest and most continuous bureaucratic histories. Weber notes that by the time of Confucius's death in 479 BC, the Chinese army 'already had the characteristics of a disciplined bureaucracy'.[3] Gladden[4] traces Chinese bureaucracy back to more recent origins in the Qin dynasty (221–206 BC), and notes the opening of official service to 'the talents' through the introduction of merit entry and examinations under the Han Dynasty (206 BC–AD 220). Following from Eisenstadt, Heady[5] describes China as a 'centralised bureaucratic empire' whose great achievement was as 'the one steadying factor that contributed more than anything else to the remarkable staying power of the Chinese civilisation'.[6]

In Japan, the 'centralised feudalism' of the Tokugawa shogunate, which commenced in 1603, 'developed a civil bureaucracy which had basic patrimonial characteristics'.[7] Recruitment was made according to a system of stratified families, while within the bureaucracy there was considerable emphasis on status distinctions in the hierarchy. The humiliation inflicted by Commodore Perry's unwelcome arrival in 1853 contributed to the ascendancy of a modernising oligarchy and a bureaucracy the higher officers of which became very powerful and were recruited on ascriptive lines through competitive examination to serve the Emperor.

Before the arrival of the European imperialists, there were rudimentary patrimonial bureaucracies in the Hindu-influenced Southeast Asian kingdoms and empires based on irrigated rice production (for example, the central Javanese kingdom of Mataram and the Khmer kingdom of Angkor). Similar structures emerged under Chinese Confucian influence in the northern parts of contemporary Vietnam. The tribal peoples and harbour principalities were non-bureaucratic in character. The first centuries of Western intrusion did not bring about profound structural change in Southeast Asian societies.[8] With the considerable capitalist expansion of Southeast Asian economies starting in the nineteenth century came the progressively deeper penetration of bureaucratic administration into the predominantly rural countries of the region. Even in Thailand, which escaped colonisation, the threat of Western domination led to a policy of modernisation in the nineteenth century that required a bureaucracy modelled along European lines. But in Thailand, as in the colonised states, many patrimonial traits were preserved, for as Furnivall[9] has pointed out, a completely Westernised system of administration was simply impossible to organise and too costly.

In all cases the modern bureaucracies were established not as providers of services to the indigenous populations but as integral components of imperialism with the dual objectives of assisting imperial economic exploitation and maintaining order. The case of Thailand merely emphasises the fact that not only the imperialists realised the necessity of having more efficient administration. Only in the later colonial years were there belated efforts to utilise bureaucracies to extend the benefits of 'development' to native populations.

The postcolonial years following the Second World War were notable in all East and Southeast Asian countries for the massive expansion of their bureaucracies as the state assumed ever more functions and attempted with varying degrees of success to exercise increased control over wider areas of social life. For example, at the end of Dutch rule in Indonesia there were approximately

50 000 civil servants.[10] Shortly after independence in 1950, the number had swelled to 303 500, and by 1970 there were around 525 000 public servants. In 1980 the civil service had ballooned to over 2 million persons, eventually reaching 4 million or 21.8 public servants per thousand population in 1993.

The important finding of this brief and selective historical survey is that the region's bureaucracies are not simply Western transplants. There are diverse origins even within colonialism, and the Weberian ideal type is not to be found. Hybrids abound with elements of precolonial bureaucracies mixed with colonial forms, overlaid with postcolonial features. A universal language of public sector management has been adopted and formal structures can show remarkable similarity between countries but actual practice may often vary considerably.

## State and Bureaucracy

While the formal structures and declared operational principles of bureaucracies in East and Southeast Asia often resemble the model of bureaucratic organisation developed by Weber, in practice these bureaucracies deviate considerably from this ideal type. In part, this is due to the nature of the state in East and Southeast Asia and to the relationships that link politicians, bureaucrats and people. Such patterns are not in conformity with either the Weberian model or Western experience.

Firstly, many of the region's bureaucracies are characterised by bureaupathologies or dysfunctions, practices that hinder the accomplishment of formal organisational goals. They are expressed in 'excessive aloofness, ritualistic attachment to routines and procedures, resistance to change, and petty insistence upon the rights of authority and status'.[11] There may have been a constant procession of administrative reforms but they have often been fragmentary and unsuccessful if they threaten radical change. There are obvious exceptions to this generalisation (for example, Singapore), and the level of bureaupathology can vary considerably between countries.

A second observation is that the political regimes of East and Southeast Asia have often been authoritarian or combinations of both democratic and authoritarian features. However, the bureaucracy may be integrated into the state in a variety of ways.[12] In certain circumstances (for example, Thailand), the bureaucracy may become so powerful as to create a bureaucratic polity – a bureaucracy-for-itself. In others (for example, Korea under Park Chung Hee or the Philippines under Marcos), the executive can reign supreme over the bureaucracy. Also, a powerful bourgeoisie can determine the policy regime of the state and so determine the orientation and operation of the bureaucracy. There is no single East or Southeast Asian way in which the bureaucracy is integrated into the state, although in no case is the state–bureaucracy relationship a precise replica of that found in Western democracies.

A third feature of Asian state and societies is the practice of patronage. Neher[13] maintains that 'Throughout Asia, "exchange bonds" determine power, status, authority relations, and the citizen's role in society'. Such dyadic reciprocal patron–client ties permeate state institutions and society, sometimes linking the two. They can be found in a multitude of situations: between political leaders and bureaucrats; superimposed over formal bureaucratic structures; and linking citizens or business people to bureaucrats. While capitalist modernisation has diminished the importance of patron–client ties, the values embodied in them continue to be important. Neher notes that 'even in China and Vietnam where communist governments forced fundamental changes in the relations between landlords and peasants, the traditional notion of reciprocity remains an important part of political culture'.[14] Whole countries can be dominated by networks of patronage in which patrimonial leaders dispense favours to their trusted clients in order to ensure their continued loyalty.

Finally, there is the long-standing observation that 'there is in Asia less mental resistance to State intervention than in the West, for Asia has a long history of effective and helpful State action'.[15] However, we are in an era in which the dominant global ideology expects the state to play a supporting role to market forces in the quest for development and sustained growth. Undoubtedly, the governments of East and Southeast Asia have adopted the neo-liberal rhetoric but the early evidence clearly demonstrates that the huge economic gains they have made have in large part been due to state intervention. The state is popularly viewed as having major responsibility for socioeconomic development and is more than willing to adopt this role. Success in this venture became a 'political placebo in postcolonial Southeast Asia',[16] with regime legitimacy often relying on performance rather than on democratic ideals. It also ensures the maintenance of large bureaucracies to manage the considerable business of the state.

It has been claimed of East and Southeast Asia that there is a set of core Asian values that marks out the region from the rest of the world (especially the West) and determines behavioural patterns. As bureaucracies are not surrounded by *cordons sanitaire* designed to remove non-rational, non-Weberian values, it can be assumed that distinctive Asian values are brought into bureaucracies and exercise an influence over the ways in which they operate. A common managerial perspective is that the traditions of Confucianism, Buddhism, Islam and Hinduism have transmitted a legacy of behaviour, attitudes and beliefs that result in certain 'enduring characteristics of Asian social organisation and group behaviour which are present across the region'.[17] Typical values are identified as group rather than individual reference: conflict avoidance; the importance of 'face'; respect for authority and seniority; paternalism; respect for academic credentials; undervaluation of the professional role of women; belief in cosmology and superstition; and the importance of family support.[18]

'East Asians do not believe in the extreme form of individualism practiced in the West' wrote Tommy Koh, Singapore's Ambassador-at-Large.[19] Such modern reassertions of 'Asian values' by political leaders have become increasingly common and can be seen as a response to the efforts of the West to impose their values especially in the fields of politics and human rights.[20] Many feel that yet another neo-colonial assault has been launched on Asia with Western powers trying to reassert their hegemony in the face of Eastern economic success and relative autonomy. This would perhaps confirm Huntington's finding that 'the values that are most important in the West are least important worldwide'.[21] But is it gross oversimplification to talk of a set of distinctive 'Asian values'? Is it possible to identify common 'Asian values' from cultural influences which include Confucianism, Buddhism, Islam, Hinduism and even Christianity? Even taking Confucianism on its own, it has been used to explain both the retarded development of China and the dynamic development of Korea. To some, 'Asian values' are simply an ideological smokescreen to mask authoritarianism and conservatism.[22] Bureaucracies are seen to collaborate in promoting such values as they maintain the desired status quo.

While there is obviously not a single cultural system in East and Southeast Asia that influences bureaucratic behaviour, it may still be possible to identify some significant shared values. For example, the value of equilibrium or moderation appears to cross religious boundaries.[23] The idea of duties as distinct from rights is firmly embedded in many Asian societies, while the notion of responsibilities to community and/or family is widely held. Belief in frugality, hard work, saving and sacrifice are widespread; they are not the Protestant ethic imported from Europe but are historically rooted in Asian culture.

The critical question is whether Asian values – one set or many sets – make a difference to bureaucratic behaviour. The answer must be yes. These values reinforce government intervention and control in any activity. They support the idea of consensual rather than confrontational decision-making in bureaucracy (although this can also be interpreted as a justification of hierarchy). Asian values also include the importance of personal networks and personal ties, thus emphasising informal structures and processes in bureaucracy. They emphasise the concern with formality that pervades Asian bureaucracies. But values are never the sole determinants of behaviour, and to explain bureaucratic performance solely in terms of values is a foolish venture. Values are simply one component of the broad environment in which bureaucracies operate, their singular influence being impossible to disaggregate. In East and Southeast Asia values have certainly contributed to the evolution of particular bureaucratic structures and behaviours, and while some may be widely spread, others are specific to particular countries.

**Confucian Ideology and Bureaucracy**

Confucianism has been identified with distinctive components of Asian culture, and in recent years some authors have noted its contribution to the economic success of Japan, Taiwan, Korea and Singapore. Here the concern is with its impact on bureaucratic organisation in Asia with particular reference to China, the source of Confucianism, and Korea, arguably the most committed Confucian state.

Confucius (551–479 BC), a Chinese philosopher and adviser to leaders, drew on fundamental precepts about human nature, correct conduct and social relationships. Confucianism emphasised hierarchy in the political and social realms and the force of moral principles. Also important was the need to comprehend and conform to the correct conduct appropriate for each type of relationship. Bureaucratic systems operating under

Confucianism favoured the generalist who was knowledgeable of Confucian principles. Confucianism has been deemed to be a philosophy, sometimes a religion, and generally a set of social mores. In reviewing its historical role in relation to Asian governments it is often depicted as an ideology, and generally a highly conservative one.[24] After its rise to prominence in China, Confucian teachings spread to Japan, Korea and other East Asian countries. The role and forms of Confucianism in these countries has varied widely and this diversity is evident today.

During the Chinese imperial system, which lasted until the communist succession in the 1920s, the official state ideology was Confucianism. Among the features that continued to be important were the role of moral principles as a basis for action, the role of the generalist, and the leader. Traditionally, Chinese government was identified with moral standards and behaviour prescribed for officials. The practice of ritualism was one means of demonstrating moral behaviour. The traditional examination system was based on the Confucian classics and designed to test whether candidates had absorbed the literature and whether their thinking was 'conducive to virtue'. As such, examinations reflected morality more than merit, and they were not designed to test administrative skills.[25]

The Chinese system lacked elements of the Weberiantype bureaucracy, such as functional differentiation and division of labour. The absence of specialisation was partly a product of the low demand historically for technical expertise, but importantly the lack of instrumental focus in Chinese culture. Similarly, the study of administration involved philosophical analysis of how bureaucracy should be organised in order to achieve moral values. Consequently, 'the Weberian ideal of administrative rationality had no root in ancient China . . . [and] public administration in China cannot be based on the legacies of ancient administrative studies'.[26]

While the Chinese communists rejected both the models from traditional China and from the West, the embedded cultural legacies of Confucianism nevertheless continued to have a significant impact on the establishment of government. The Chinese communists sought to develop a bureaucracy that was not Weberian but 'a moral administration with an emphasis on ethics rather than administrative efficiency'. The weaknesses of this type of system included the lack of administrative competence and skills, specialisation and public responsiveness, and the excessive emphasis on formalities.[27] The Chinese, according to Pye, have felt

> uncomfortable, dissatisfied, and threatened whenever their politics has not been characterised by a dominant hierarchy and a single ideology . . . It is significant that the imperial bureaucracy and the Communist Party in procedural practices, and both Confucianism and Maoism in ideological content, have explicitly stressed the problems of authority and order.[28]

Under the Chinese Communist Party's system of government, rule by powerful leaders was favoured over the rule of law.

The centrality accorded to the moral authority of the ruler and officials under Confucianism, meant that administrative law was unimportant for the implementation of policy. Because the law lacked an external basis to the bureaucracy, it was subordinate to morality and a system of administrative law did not evolve. One consequence was the subjective basis for the selection of staff. The weakness of administrative law also affected bureaucratic rationalisation. The underdevelopment of administrative law has been seen as a major reason for bureaucratic problems in modern China, although significant advances have been made over the last decade, and the challenge now is to implement the new laws.[29]

During Korea's Chosôn dynasty (1392–1910), Confucianism

was adopted as the state's official ideology, early bureaucracy being based on Chinese models. Korea provides one of the earliest cases in world history in which 'a non-religious ideology was consciously employed as an instrument of dynastic policy'.[30] At the time of contact with the West in the late nineteenth century, Korea's governmental system could still be regarded as a Confucian state comprised of the bureaucracy and monarchy.[31] Although the centrality of Confucianism lasted until the end of the Chosôn dynasty, in the early twentieth century there was continuity in official support for the ideology. Confucianism was promoted by the Japanese during the colonial era (1910–45), and by subsequent military regimes that understood that the principles could support their interests. South Korea has been depicted as the most Confucian nation in both East Asia and the world.[32]

Confucianism is deeply embedded in Korean culture and affects all aspects of society. Confucian values and norms influence personal, family and institutional relationships covering economics, politics, and in particular governance. One core Confucian value is reverence for the political and social order, the main loyalties being to the family, ruler and state.[33] The continuing influence of Confucianism on Korean political culture and administrative system is widely accepted. Although the political culture continues to reflect the 'historical residues' of Buddhism and Taoism, and more recently Western principles, it is the Confucian influence that has received the most critical attention.[34]

The Korean political culture (following Ro's summary of Gregory Henderson's vortex theory[35]) consisted of three elements: centralisation and the lack of local power bases; form predominating over content (that is, access to status, rank and prestige has taken precedence over substantive questions, such as legislating and economic management); the preference of authority over leadership; and 'bureaucratism over individual responsibility'. The bureaucratic organisation, following Confucian principles about the importance of moral rules and the avoidance of specialisation, provided for generalists who worked in different positions. Western liberal pluralistic ideals have influenced the political elite, but not the core values of the political culture. Following Korean independence in 1945, Western pluralism had a major impact on the framework of government, but its influence was otherwise limited. The elite political culture remained authoritarian, and policy-making was centralised, bureaucratic and elitist.[36]

This Confucian cultural context continues to influence bureaucracy and the system of governance. The 'historical stamp' of Korea's political culture is 'characterised by bureaucratic elitism and political-administrative centralism'.[37] There is 'a cultural undercurrent which sanctions hierarchical organizational structures in society'.[38] In turn, a bureaucracy that was a combination of authoritarian and elitist led to the interventionist role of governments, while the subservience of business to the government allowed for a strong state. The reliance on the centralised administrative elites encouraged bureaucratisation of politics which constrained the development of democratic pluralism.[39]

There is now greater specialisation in Korea and considerable discussion about different approaches including the New Public Management. Confucianism continues to be adapted and reinterpreted in Korea, while in China the Communist Party recently declared a return to the values embodied in Confucian principles. Confucianism has been predicted as having a future in East Asia.[40]

**Consensual Decision-making**

Japan acquired an enviable reputation for its rapid economic growth, leading to international attention to its approach to management and governance. Specific areas of interest have included the use of total quality management and the approach to state intervention, and in particular the formidable reputation of MITI, the Ministry of International Trade and Industry. Many of Japan's management characteristics span the public and private sectors because they share a common origin in traditional Japanese culture and practice. Some of the commonalities with respect to decision-making style and careerism are regarded as idiosyncratic or unique to administrative culture in Japan. But there have also been significant differences. The public bureaucracy – in some respects resembling the traditional system of Western countries – did not focus on goals and cost-cutting. These have been suggested as among the reasons why quality circles – the standard management tool for business – have not been adopted by either central or local governments.[41]

The civil service has been a hierarchical system that has been dominated by a small elite of generalists who were recruited through a highly competitive examination system. Although illustrating features of a Weberian model, traditional values such as the emphasis on seniority and hierarchy have been derived from Confucianism. Japan has been depicted as 'a vertical society' in which hierarchical relationships reflect status and position, and Confucianism influences social organisation. A characteristic of Japanese management is the strong group orientation by which individual interests are secondary to collective behaviour.[42]

Consensual decision-making is well-established in private and public-sector organisations. In developing consensus the *ringisho* and *nemawashi* are key elements. The *ringisho* is a formal document, a policy proposal, that is drafted by a relatively junior official and then circulated within the agency. *Ringisei* refers to the circulation of this document up the agency hierarchy for approval. The second component, *nemawashi*, is the process of consultation with all officials relevant to a decision. *Nemawashi* lays the groundwork through extensive negotiation undertaken prior to drafting a policy proposal.[43]

The *ringi* system has strengths and weaknesses. It produces a high level of participation in decision-making. In leading to consensus among the participating officials concerned, a decision is reached that all can support; and because a long time has been spent in drafting the proposal, implementation is unlikely to be resisted. However, the system may encourage inefficiency because of the very length of this process. Decision-making may be particularly slow when *nemawashi* occurs on an interagency basis. The *ringi* system may not result in innovative policies because incremental change is favoured. Also, responsibility is diffused among many participants and senior officials may not identify with it.[44]

There are indications that the *ringi* system has been changing and is not as rigid as before. Subordinates, once depicted as playing influential roles, have been recognised as reflecting their superiors' preferences, particularly on major policies. The system is recognised as applying to minor and routine policies that account for most decisions.[45]

The Japanese bureaucracy has remained more powerful and more immune to change than most OECD countries' systems. However, crises of performance of the civil service specifically, and the country economically, have led to mounting pressures for administrative reform.[46] It will be interesting to see the extent to which traditional Japanese modes of behaviour such as *ringisei* and *nemawashi* survive.


## ALTERNATIVES TO BUREAUCRACY

### Creating People-centred Organisations

For many years in Southeast and East Asia governments have proclaimed their commitment to the process of debureaucratisation. Policies such as cutting red tape, speeding up procedures and developing a client focus have been commonplace. However, the results of such initiatives have not matched the rhetoric. The model of mechanistic bureaucracy, with all of its attendant dysfunctions, has maintained preeminence in practice. The elements of mechanistic bureaucracy are deeply embedded in the structures, processes and cultures of large public-sector organisations and are highly resistant to significant change.

The case of the National Irrigation Administration (NIA) in the Philippines is a dramatic demonstration that 'it is possible to convert a conventional, technically-oriented bureaucratized public development agency into a more people-centred strategic organisation'.[47] The NIA is a large state agency which, in the mid-1980s, employed 30 000 staff and oversaw the operations of 508 000 hectares of national irrigation schemes and 615 000 hectares of community irrigation schemes.

When, in 1974, the NIA was ordered to take responsibility for communal irrigation schemes, 'the NIA viewed its work primarily as the construction of physical facilities and paid minimal attention to forming irrigator associations'.[48] Its configuration was that of a classical bureaucratic organisation focusing on standardised procedures performed by distinct functional units, each claiming exclusive responsibility for discrete portions of the process. The engineer-dominated NIA was able to create and impose standard specifications with standard costs, times and budgets ruled by accountability within the organisation. The assumption inherent in the NIA was that effective and efficient performance would inevitably derive from the application of a 'one best way' standardised approach. Where problems occurred they could be attributed to external factors such as contractors, the farmers and other government agencies. The closed system of the NIA remained blameless and the superiority of its 'scientific' approach was unchallenged.

All of this was overturned in the capacity-building programme adopted by the NIA under presidential instruction during Marcos' martial-law era. The objective of involving and strengthening irrigator associations resulted in the adoption of a 'learning process approach' as conceptualised by David Korten,[49] in which villagers and officials come together to create a small-scale experiment that is closely monitored and modified according to this knowledge. The participants eschew blueprints and embrace the idea of learning from errors, redesigning organisational structures and processes according to them. The pilot project is eventually extended over a wider area when suitable effectiveness is achieved.

The 'learning process' initiated by the NIA in the mid-1970s and expanded in the 1980s involved farmers 'from the very conception of a construction project, and once the project was completed, to support the capacities to manage it'.[50] While the NIA experience was highly successful in terms of participatory development and also seems to have generated improved system performance,[51] there are questions about sustainability and replicability. The 'learning process' runs the risk of becoming another standardised process, especially as communal organisers came to form a large specialised group within the NIA. Success may breed an organisational preference to bureaucratise procedures and promote an NIA-preferred irrigation association structure and processes, rather than let the farmers decide what they think is most appropriate.

The NIA experience does not seem to have been emulated by other large government organisations in the Philippines. They have remained aloof from such radical participatory approaches, preferring to maintain mechanistic bureaucratic configurations in which the exclusive, formally-acquired and specialist knowledge of 'normal professionalism' holds sway.[52] This contributes to the maintenance of pronounced power differentials between poor clients and dominant bureaucrats accountable only to their organisational superiors.

**The Third Sector**

Until the late 1970s the universally prescribed strategy for socioeconomic development was for the state to lead and consequently grow in size as it assumed ever more functions. A 'counter-revolution' in the 1980s led to the ideological victory of market-based development and advocacy for 'rolling back' the state. But vast numbers of organisations have grown which are 'neither prince [state] nor merchant [market]'.[53] An 'associational revolution'[54] has occurred whereby associations of individuals with common purposes have been formed within civil society. One component part of this 'third sector' is made up of organisations which in one way or another are oriented to the pursuit of development: for example, as relief and welfare agencies, technical innovation organisations, public service contractors, popular development agencies, grassroots development organisations, and advocacy groups and networks.[55]

Non-governmental organisations (NGOs) are seen to hold a range of characteristics which makes them superior to the state in certain developmental circumstances – especially in addressing poverty. 'These include flexibility, responsiveness, the capacity to experiment and learn from experience, linking processes to outcomes and the NGO ability to enlist the energies and commitment of intended beneficiaries'.[56] However, NGO activity often involves 'empowerment' or making incursions into the activities traditionally claimed by the state.

These NGOs are found in developing countries across the globe but in East and Southeast Asia, with the exception of the Philippines, their development has been slow. Authoritarian, semi-democratic, or one-party regimes have been antagonistic or highly mistrustful of them, fearing that their activities could challenge the state's preeminence. Bureaucracies are suspicious of NGO involvement in developing activities. Officials can be concerned about NGOs' performance, and about NGO workers, now receiving better pay and conditions, questioning bureaucratic authority. The legacy of the centralised state, big bureaucracy and poorly-developed civil society provides difficult conditions for nurturing NGOs.

There are encouraging signs that tend to be positively but by no means exclusively correlated with democratisation. Northern NGOs have been active in the former centrally-planned economies in Indochina. In Cambodia, their contribution has been essential for service provision in a country which has severe financial and human resource shortages. Indigenous NGOs are typically fragile and lack the resources and organisational strength of international NGOs. In Laos, financial assistance from international NGOs has increased from US $950 000 in 1987 to over US $16 million in 1997, with 53 international NGOs operating in 1997 compared to 13 in 1985.[57] Although the Constitution makes provisions for indigenous NGOs, the absence of any regulations means that they do not have official recognition and hence do not yet officially exist. In Indonesia, welfare organisations date back to the beginning of the twentieth century but by the 1960s the first developmental organisations began to emerge in agriculture, health and community development, with others in human rights, legal aid, the environment and consumer protection following in the 1970s and 1980s.[58] While the sector has grown and networks have been established, NGOs are still relatively small in scale and must negotiate a difficult authoritarian political environment. Although the central government has recognised the role that NGOs can play in national development, state relationships with NGOs depend heavily on the outlook of local government where distrust and antagonism can be prevalent.

In Thailand, the prevalence of the bureaucratic polity for much of the twentieth century held back the development of civil society, including the NGO sector apart from traditional welfare organisations. However, in the 1980s, 'popular local movements' were created around such issues as forest protection, marine resource preservation and land rights. Sixty per cent of today's developmental NGOs originated later than 1984 and may have been encouraged by the opportunities offered by increased democratic space, but surprisingly they had little formal relation with the urban democracy movement.[59] Some Thai NGOs are still apparently controlled by autocratic leaders and others may retain a confrontationist orientation, but there is a general impression that NGOs are increasing in numbers, professionalism and influence as the democratic space and civil society expand.[60]

The Philippines provides a contrast with other developing East and Southeast Asian countries as it has a vigorous and large indigenous NGO sector comprised of an estimated 20 000 NGOs. These can be divided into three major groups: people's organisations (POs), which are grassroots, membership-based organisations operating in support of collective welfare goals; civic and professional organisations, generally lacking grassroots membership; and development NGOs, which are intermediate agencies providing services to POs and encouraging their formation and development.[61] There are also umbrella organisations which keep NGOs and POs in touch with each other and facilitate discussion on matters of common concern. Notable among these is the Caucus of Development NGO Networks (CODE-NGO), which by 1993 encompassed over 3500 NGO networks. CODE-NGO also provided a means for strengthening relationships with the state and with foreign aid donors and partners.

Philippine NGOs are typically small, with only three having more than 200 staff.[62] Most commonly, NGOs operate as developmental and advocacy organisations on a local base. They are engaged in an extraordinarily wide variety of activities and have diverse ideologies and approaches to development. Different organisations and support such as elite philanthropy, Christian churches, official development assistance, and the underground Left explain the heterogeneity of the NGO sector and the difficulty of reaching common policy platforms and coordinated actions. The concerted campaign to oust the authoritarian President Marcos is perhaps the only example of cooperation between NGOs from all political sides. Under President Aquino, NGOs were officially awarded a role in national development as one expression of the 'people power' that brought Aquino to power, and the number of NGOs mushroomed. The 1987 Constitution even declares that 'the state shall encourage non-governmental organisations, community-based or sectoral organisations to promote the welfare of the nation' (Article II, section 23), while the Local Government Code of 1992 requires NGO involvement in local-level planning and development bodies. Donors have channelled increased official development assistance (ODA) into NGO activities in the belief that NGOs are efficient and effective providers of services. Bureaucracy has increasingly cooperated with NGOs which have gained access to state officials and undertaken tasks for and with a variety of agencies. But even in the Philippines, NGOs are not the 'magic bullet' to ensure equitable and sustained development.[63] The state is still a far more important actor in the provision of services, while the NGO community is heavily dependent on ODA and other foreign assistance. Indeed, some NGO leaders worry about whether they are being co-opted by the state[64] or are simply being used as the implementors of donor policy.[65] If this is so, then the empowerment goal of NGOs is being usurped by the achievement of short-term project goals. There is even the allegation that NGOs are merely an expression of a certain middle-class view of development, and that middle-class leaders dominate the NGO sector.[66]

**Decentralisation**

Decentralisation has been utilised across the world as an antidote to large centralised bureaucracies. 'Rolling the state downward' is the current global trend, encouraged by democratisation and arguments extolling the technical efficiency of decentralised governance. Even in

East and Southeast Asia, a heartland of large centralised bureaucracy, reportedly 'there have been dramatic
steps . . . of dispersing or decentralising the highly centralised power structure'.[67] However, with the notable
exception of the Philippines, the process of decentralisation in the region has been cautious and incremental.
In China, the debate has been phrased in terms of the
'adjustment of powers', the most recent stage being 'characterised by the centralisation of financial powers and
decentralisation of service delivery powers'.[68] Japan, whose
system of local government was externally imposed and
is already fairly decentralised in Asian terms, established
a Committee for the Promotion of Decentralisation in
1995. In South Korea, the politics of decentralisation have
eventually achieved 'combined' local elections where both
councillors and chiefs (mayors and governors) of local
governments are elected. However, there still appears
to be a considerable distance to go, especially for the
determination of 'to what extent local government should
be self-governed' rather than centrally-controlled.[69]

In some cases a rhetoric of decentralisation is not
matched by practice. For example, Indonesia's system
of central–local relations is formally guided by three
principles which stress decentralisation. In reality, the
central state dominates, a result of both the widespread
belief that development is a national responsibility and
the government's determination to maintain the unity
of a large state which sprawls across a massive archi-
pelago and now has a population approaching 200
million.[70] Finance, policy-making, and the issuance of rules
and regulations are the concerns of agencies in the capital,
while sub-national governments are allocated significant
roles in service provision. Personnel from the central-
line agencies dominate the regions and are accountable
upwards to their headquarters in Jakarta. Such power
arrangements encourage a culture of risk-aversion at the
regional and local levels, a situation compounded with
capacity problems at the local level.

At least one country, Laos, is currently engaged in a process of recentralisation.[71] Under socialism, political centralisation proved to be impossible to enforce and in reality there was a large amount of sub-national autonomy. The centre was only loosely connected to sub-national units, a situation which was exacerbated when the government decided to begin economic reform with the New Economic Mechanism. Provincial governments became responsible for planning and managing all local resources, even tax administration, while central ministries had no authority over technical services or personnel at the sub-national level. Inter-provincial and inter-district inequalities widened, regulatory frameworks were absent, administration was typically inefficient, and service provision was often poor or non-existent. The Fifth Party Congress of 1991 decided that the highly decentralised state was to be reconfigured into a 'unitary deconcentrated state'. Since then, a stream of decrees has seen the reassertion of central government authority, with the imposition of fiscal centralisation, the restoration of line ministry control, the establishment of an office to determine all government personnel matters, and the abolition of local people's councils.

In the Philippines the reverse has been happening. Under the Local Government Code of 1991, the traditionally centralised system of central–local relations was radically altered.[72] Services in health, agriculture, public works, social welfare and environmental and natural resources were devolved to local levels. Additional licensing and regulatory functions were given to local governments, and the amount of funding from central government to local governments was dramatically increased. And NGOs and the private sector were to participate in local governance in a system which already had popularly elected assemblies at the levels of province and city, municipality and *barangay* (local community).

Implementation has faced a range of problems. National legislators watered down the original Code and the public servants transferred from central agencies to local authorities provided active opposition to the changes. The new funding arrangements have created winners and losers among the different types of local government units. The accreditation and involvement of NGOs has varied between local government units while there are concerns that decentralisation might hand out greater power to entrenched local elites. Despite these problems, the Local Government Code has met with widespread approval in the Philippines, including the vital backing of the President. The annual appraisals indicate that 'real gains have been made in promoting local autonomy and enabling local governments to run more of their own affairs in cooperation with NGOs and the private sector'.[73]

The lesson of this excursion into central-local relations is to note that there is considerable diversity between the countries of the region. Decentralisation is certainly the language of current central–local discourses, but the pace of that reform is often slow or the realities may not match the rhetoric. In certain circumstances, in order to improve services it has even been judged necessary to recentralise.

CONCLUSION

East and Southeast Asia is a region of big centralised bureaucracy. The state is not something which people and their leaders seem anxious to 'roll back'. Bureaucracy is viewed as performing necessary functions and having the obligation to do so. The definition of what are 'necessary' functions and determinations about how big bureaucracy should be do not coincide with Western perceptions. Similarly, while the formal structural features of East and Southeast Asian bureaucracies often resemble the mechanistic models of Weberian origin, the practice is more complicated. They are integrated into the state and society in ways which are at variance with

Western experience. Also, they are set in cultural contexts where the values which influence human behaviour can be in contrast to – even opposition to – contemporary Western practice.

But there are examples of alternatives to bureaucracy in East and Southeast Asia. The Philippines has been most experimental in this regard. In this chapter we have seen how a mechanistic bureaucracy, the NIA, was turned into a people-centred organisation, how NGOs have flourished in the post-Marcos democratic space, and how radical decentralisation initiatives can be introduced into traditionally centralised settings. There are other examples of administrative reforms from the region, not covered in this short presentation, which also show glimpses of departure from bureaucratic rigidity. East and Southeast Asia has a history of reform and cautious experimentation. Whether the pace of such reform and experimentation quickens in the context of the current economic crisis sweeping the region, or whether there is a retreat into the traditionally safe stronghold of centralised bureaucracy, remains to be seen.

**Notes and References**

1. P. Kornhonen, 'Monopolizing Asia: The Politics of a Metaphor', *The Pacific Review*, vol. 10 no. 3 (1997), p. 357.
2. B. Anderson, *Imagined Communities: Reflections on the Origin and Spread of Nationalism*, revised edition (London: Verso, 1991).
3. H.H. Gerth and C.W. Mills (eds), *From Max Weber: Essays on Sociology* (London: Routledge & Kegan Paul, 1948).
4. E.N. Gladden, *A History of Public Administration*, vol. 2 (London: Frank Cass, 1972).
5. S.N. Eisenstadt, *The Political Systems of Empires* (New York: Free Press of Glencoe, 1972); F. Heady, *Public Administration: A Comparative Perspective*, 3rd edn (New York: Marcel Dekker, 1984).
6. E.N. Gladden as quoted in *ibid.*, p. 145.

154     *Bureaucracy and Alternatives in Asia*

7.   *Ibid.*, p. 222.
8.   W.F. Wertheim, *Comparative Essays on Asia and the West* (Amsterdam: VU University Press, 1993).
9.   J.S. Furnivall, *Colonial Policy and Practice: A Comparative Study of Burma and Netherlands India* (New York: New York University Press, 1956).
10.  R. Rohdewohld, *Public Administration in Indonesia* (Melbourne: Montech, 1995).
11.  R.C. Chandler and J.C. Plano, *The Public Administration Dictionary*, 2nd edn (Santa Barbara: Clio Press), p. 121.
12.  L.V. Cariño, *Bureaucracy for Democracy: The Dynamics of Executive–Bureaucracy Interaction During Governmental Transitions* (Quezon City: College of Public Administration, University of the Philippines, 1992).
13.  C.D. Neher, 'Asian Style Democracy', *Asian Survey*, vol. 34, no. 11 (1994), pp. 949–61.
14.  *Ibid.*, p. 951.
15.  Maurice Zinken (1953) as quoted in W.F. Wertheim, 'The State and the Dialectics of Emancipation', *Development and Change*, vol. 23, no. 3 (1992), p. 257.
16.  M.R.V. Vatikiotis, *Political Change in Southeast Asia: Trimming the Banyan Tree* (London: Routledge, 1996).
17.  P. Lasserre and H. Schütte, *Strategies for Asia Pacific* (South Melbourne: Macmillan, 1995), p. 270.
18.  A danger of the culture-personality approach is that it can lead to an unsophisticated normative determinism with data that are selective and impressionistic, and that may result in the 'replication of uniformity'. For an excellent critique of this approach, see R. Lawless, *An Evaluation of Philippine Culture-Personality Research* (Quezon City: University of the Philippines Press, 1969).
19.  M. Chew, 'Human Rights in Singapore: Perceptions and Problems', *Asian Survey*, vol. 34, no. 11 (1994), p. 935.
20.  D.K. Mauzy, 'The Human Rights and "Asian Values" Debate in Southeast Asia: Trying to Clarify the Key Issues', *The Pacific Review*, vol. 10, no. 2 (1997), pp. 210–36; M.R.V. Vatikiotis, *op. cit.*
21.  S.P. Huntington, 'The Clash of Civilizations', *Foreign Affairs*, vol. 72, no. 3 (1993), pp. 22–49.
22.  For example, G. Rodan and K. Hewison, 'The Clash of Cultures or Convergence of "Political Ideology"', in R. Robison (ed.), *Pathways to Asia: The Politics of Engagement* (St Leonards, NSW: Allen & Unwin, 1996), pp. 29–55.
23.  D.K. Mauzy, *op. cit.*

24. K. Lieberthal, *Governing China: From Revolution through Reform* (New York: W.W. Norton, 1995), pp. 29–55.

25. S.K. Ma, *Administrative Reform in Post-Mao China: Efficiency or Ethics* (Lanham: University Press of America, 1996), pp. 23–24.

26. C.F. Zhang, 'Public Administration in China', in M.K. Mills and S.S. Nagel (eds), *Public Administration in China* (New York: Greenwood Press, 1993), pp. 6, 8; S.K. Ma, *op. cit.*, p. 13.

27. *Ibid.*, pp. 23–24 and 33–35.

28. L.W. Pye, *The Spirit of Chinese Politics: A Psychocultural Study of the Authority Crisis in Political Development* (MIT Press, 1968), p. 16; K. Lieberthal, *op. cit.*; S.K. Ma, *op. cit.*, pp. 22–3.

29. C.F. Zhang, *op. cit.*, pp. 8, 12; G. Hintzen, 'Drilling the State: An Introduction to Administrative Law in the PRC', in D. Lisheng (ed.), *Administrative Reform in the People's Republic of China since 1978* (Leiden: International Institute for Asian Studies, 1994), pp. 8–26.

30. C. Ro, *Public Administration and the Korean Transformation: Concepts, Policies, and Value Conflicts* (West Hartford: Kumarian Press, 1993), p. 8.

31. B.W. Kim and P.S. Kim, *Korean Public Administration: Managing the Uneven Development* (Elizabeth, N.J. and Seoul: Hollym, 1997), p. 51; W.K. Young, 'The Legacy of Confucian Culture and South Korean Politics and Economics: An Interpretation', in S-Y. Choi (ed.), *Democracy in Korea: Its Ideals and Realities* (Seoul: Korean Political Science Association, 1997), p. 122.

32. K.S. Kim, 'From Neo-mercantilism to Globalism: The Changing Role of the State and South Korea's Economic Prowess', in M.T. Berger and D.A. Borer (eds), *The Rise of East Asia: Critical Visions of the Pacific Century* (London: Routledge, 1997), pp. 100–1; E. Friedman, 'Introduction', in E. Friedman, *The Politics of Democratization: Generalizing East Asian Experiences* (Boulder: Westview Press, 1994), p. 9.

33. K.S. Kim, 1997, *op. cit.*, p. 100; B.W. Kim and P.S. Kim, *op. cit.*, p. 51; W.K. Young, *op. cit.*, p. 114.

34. C. Ro, *op. cit.;* B.W. Kim, 'Public bureaucracy in Korea', in A. Farazmand (ed.), *Handbook of Bureaucracy* (New York: Marcel Dekker, 1994), p. 591; B.W. Kim and P.S. Kim, *op. cit.;* W.K. Young, *op. cit.*

35. C. Ro, *op. cit.*, pp. 13–14.

36. B.W. Kim, 1994, *op. cit.*, p. 591.

37. W.K. Young, *op. cit.*, p. 112.
38. K.S. Kim, 1997, *op. cit.*, p. 101.
39. B.W. Kim, 1994, *op. cit.*, p. 595.
40. M.T. Berger, 'The triumph of the East? The East Asian Miracle and post-Cold War capitalism', in M.T. Berger and D.A. Borer, *op. cit.*, p. 271; J. Cotton, 'Korea in Comparative Perspective', in J. Cotton (ed.), *Politics and Policy in the New Korean State: From Roh Tae-woo to Kim Young-sam* (Sydney: Longman, 1995), p. 239; W.K. Young, *op. cit.*, p. 113.
41. W.G. Ouchi, *Theory Z: How American Business Can Meet the Japanese Challenge* (New York: Avon, 1981); C. Johnson, *Japan: Who Governs? The Rise of the Developmental State* (New York: W.W. Norton & Co. 1995); J.S. Jun and H. Muto, 'The Hidden Dimension of Japanese Administration: Culture and its Impact', *Public Administration Reviews*, vol. 55, no. 2 (1995), p. 127.
42. *Ibid.*, pp. 126–7; J. Elliot, 'Japan: The Prospects for Public Sector Change', *Australian Journal of Public Administration* vol. 55, no. 4 (1996), pp. 46, 49; P.S. Kim, *Japan's Civil Service System: Its Structure, Personnel and Politics* (New York: Greenwood Press, 1988).
43. B. C. Koh, *Japan's Administrative Elite* (Berkeley: University of California Press, 1989), pp. 194 and 256; J.S. Jun and H. Muto, *op. cit.*, pp. 131.
44. B.C. Koh, *op. cit.*, pp. 195–7; J.S. Jun and H. Muto, *op. cit.*, pp. 131–3.
45. Y.H. Park, *Bureaucrats and Ministers in Contemporary Japanese Government* (Berkeley: Institute of East Asian Studies, University of California, 1986), p. 21; B.C. Koh, *op. cit.*, pp. 196–7.
46. J. Elliot *op. cit.*
47. D.C. Korten, 'From Bureaucratic to Strategic Orientation', in F.F. Korten and R.Y. Siy (eds), *Transforming a Bureaucracy: The Experience of the Philippine National Irrigation Administration* (Quezon City: Ateneo de Manila Press, 1989), p. 140.
48. B.U. Bagadion and F.F. Korten, 'Developing Irrigators' Organizations: A Learning Process Approach', in M.M. Cernea (ed.), *Putting People First: Sociological Variables in Rural Development* (Washington D.C.: Oxford University Press, 1985), p. 55.
49. D.C. Korten, 'Community Organization and Rural Development: A Learning Process Approach', *Public Administration Review*, vol. 40, no. 5 (1980), pp. 480–511.

50. F.F. Korten and R.Y. Siy, 'Summary and Conclusion', in F.F. Korten and R.Y. Siy (eds), *Transforming a Bureaucracy: The Experience of the Philippine National Irrigation Administration* (Quezon City: Ateneo de Manila Press, 1989), p. 145.
51. R.P. de los Reyes and S.M.G. Jopillo, *An Evaluation of the Philippine Participatory Communal Irrigation Program* (Quezon City: Institute of Philippine Culture, 1986).
52. Chambers describes 'normal professionalism' as 'the thinking, values, methods and behaviour found in a profession or discipline', which represents the knowledge, attitudes and interests of those who are not poor and disadvantaged. R. Chambers, *Challenging the Professions: Frontiers for Rural Development* (London: IT Publishers, 1993), p. 3. See also R. Chambers, *Rural Development: Putting the Last First* (London: Longman, 1983).
53. M. Nerfin, 'Neither Prince nor Merchant: An Introduction to the Third Sector', *IFDA Dossier*, vol. 56 (1996), pp. 3–29.
54. L. Salamon, 'The Global Associational Revolution: The Rise of the Third Sector on the World Scene', *Institute for Policy Studies Occasional Paper*, 15 (Baltimore: Johns Hopkins University, 1993).
55. J. Clark, *Democratising Development: The Role of Voluntary Organisations* (London: Earthscan, 1991).
56. M. Turner and D. Hulme, *Governance, Administration and Development: Making the State Work* (London and West Hartford: Macmillan & Kumarian, 1997), p. 207.
57. P. Keuleers, 'Central–Local Relations in the Lao People's Democratic Republic: Historic Overview, Current Situation and Trends', paper presented at the workshop, 'Central–Local Relations: Asia–Pacific Experiences', University of Canberra, 21 March 1997.
58. J. Farrington and D.J. Lewis (eds), *Non-governmental Organizations and the State in Asia: Rethinking Roles in Sustainable Development* (London: Routledge, 1993).
59. *Ibid.*
60. R. Mawer, 'Mice Among the Tigers: Adding Value in NGO–Government Relations in Southeast Asia', in M. Edwards and D. Hulme (eds), *NGOs States and Donors: Too Close for Comfort?* (London: Macmillan, 1997), p. 244.
61. G. Clarke, 'Participation and Protest: Non-governmental Organisations and Philippine Politics', unpublished PhD thesis, University of London, 1995; A.G. Miclat-Teves and D.J. Lewis, 'NGO–Government Interaction in the

Philippines: Overview', in J. Farrington and D.H. Lewis (eds), *NGO–Governmental Organisations and the State in Asia: Rethinking Roles in Sustainable Development* (London: Routledge, 1993), pp. 227–39.

62.    G. Clarke, *op. cit.*

63.    M. Edwards and D. Hulme (eds), *NGO Performance and Accountability: Beyond the Magic Bullet* (London: Macmillan, 1995).

64.    A.G. Miclat-Teves and D.J. Lewis, *op. cit.* and A.B. Brillantes, 'NGOs as Alternative Delivery Systems: The Philippine Experience', in R.B. Ocampo and O.M. Alfonso (eds), *Alternative Delivery Systems for Public Services* (Quezon City: ADIPA, 1995).

65.    M. Edwards and D. Hulme, *op. cit.*

66.    A. Gregorio-Medel, 'Development Work is Middle Class Oriented as much as it is Poverty Oriented', in *Philippine Politics and Society* (Ateneo Center for Social Policy and Public Affairs, Ateneo de Manila, Quezon City, 1993), pp. 58–93.

67.    S. Kurosawa, T. Fujiwara and M.A. Reforma, 'Preface', in S. Kurosawa, T. Fujiwara and M.A. Reforma (eds), *New Trends in Public Administration for the Asia–Pacific Region: Decentralization* (Ministry of Home Affairs, Tokyo: EROPA, 1996), p. vii.

68.    J. Xiaonan, 'The Reform of the Economic System and the Adjustment of Powers Between the Central and Local Governments in China', in S. Kurosawa, T. Fujiwara and M.A. Reforma (eds), *op. cit.*, p. 26.

69.    C. Chang-Hyun, 'The Politics of Decentralization: The Case of Korea from 1991 to 1995', in S. Kurosawa, T. Fujiwara and M.A. Reforma (eds), *op. cit.*, p. 62.

70.    M. Turner, 'Central–Local Relations in the Asia-Pacific: Convergence or Divergence', in M. Minogue, C. Polidano and D. Hulme (eds), *Public Sector Management for the 21st Century* (London: Routledge, 1999).

71.    *Ibid.*

72.    M. Turner, 'Central–Local Relations in the Philippines: From Centralism to Localism', paper presented at the workshop 'Central–Local Relations: Asia–Pacific Experiences', University of Canberra, 21 March 1997. There is a wealth of literature emerging on the Philippine experiment in decentralisation, including P.D. Tapales, 'Philippines', in P.L. McCarney (ed.), *The Changing Nature of Local Government in Developing Countries* (Toronto: Centre for Urban and Community Studies, 1996); P.E.

Legaspi (ed.), *Decentralization, Autonomy and the Local Government Code: The Challenge of Implementation*, Vol. 1 (Quezon City: Local Government Center, University of the Philippines, 1992).

73.  M. Turner, 1999, *op. cit.*

# 7 Governance and Administration in South Asia
O.P. Dwivedi

## HISTORICAL PERSPECTIVE

Mapping the political and administrative history of South Asia since independence over a period of fifty years is indeed a difficult exercise. At the time of independence, the divided old British India was faced overnight with the movement of millions of refugees, perhaps the largest exodus of people at any one time anywhere on the earth. This posed the problem not only of relief and rehabilitation, but also of welding the various communities divided by language, culture, religion, caste and creed into the working cohesion of two single yet separate unions. There was an immediate confrontation between them in October 1947 that only added to the perennial problems of economic disaster, inflation and food shortage. Each one of the problems not only had implications for politics and policy, but also for administration. This indeed was a monumental task for the two nations. These problems put the inherited and emergent administrative structure and governing process to a severe test.[1] Over the years, there have been changes in administrative institutions, structures, styles and cultures in post-independence India and Pakistan, the two major countries of the region; however, administrative development has been an uneven process which can be best understood only in the context of the totality of this region's politico-administrative environment.

In this chapter the author discusses the nature of the

colonial legacy of the law-and-order administration, the emergence of the administrative state which assumed the responsibility for development plans and social change, the growth of governmental activities and efforts towards administrative reforms, the administrative culture and *desi* (indigenous) style of administration, and the issue of public accountability in the face of widespread corruption. I conclude with a discussion of ways to enhance the capacity for good governance by strengthening the institutions of legislative and judicial oversight, creating a clean electoral process, and exhorting for a moral government. While the essay may appear to draw more from India, the analysis applies equally to other South Asian nations, as they share the same administrative culture and style. However, generalisations used in this chapter should be considered useful only as a first approach to the situation.

**The Colonial Legacy**

At independence, the South Asian countries inherited from the British a monolithic, highly-stratified, and strictly hierarchical administrative structure. The line of command ran unimpeded from the Viceroy and Governor-General in New Delhi to the farthest village head. The administrative system – evolved during the time of Warren Hastings and Lord Cornwallis – had four distinguishing features: (a) the district as the basic unit of administration, with the District Collector or Deputy Commissioner acting as the alter-ego of the vice-regal authority, controlling, directing and coordinating all administrative activity in his district; (b) centralisation of authority, as the recognised principle of administration both territorially and functionally, with centralisation of decision-making in almost all policy areas; (c) a single dominating civil service, with the Indian Civil Service (ICS) an elite generalist service, occupying the top policy and management position in the country; and (d) a system of elaborate rules and regulations designed by the British to control their large number of Indian subordinates, dispersed far away from the administrative capitals of the provincial and central governments.

Such a system of administration suited the British. It maintained and preserved the broad structure of society in India, particularly the large proportion of the rural society, as it then existed. It did not concern itself with any radical developmental or socioeconomic changes; and its impact on the larger proportion of Indian citizens was minimal.

**The Aftermath of Independence**

The attainment of independence gave an opportunity for political leaders to usher in momentous changes. A number of revolutions were tried. First, a political revolution, resulting in transition from a colonial system of government to a full-fledged parliamentary democracy with a federal structure of government (in India and Pakistan) and commitment towards a welfare state. Second, an economic revolution, caused by transforming a semi-subsistence economy into a modern industrialising community to solve the problems of poverty, unemployment and want. Third, a social revolution, changing the caste-ridden stratified society into a progressive community oriented towards social justice. Finally, a technological revolution, to let in the light of modern science and technology on the traditional ways of a conservative people. To usher in these revolutions, various strategies and development models were adopted by the South Asian leadership. These were: (a) political integration (especially in India and Pakistan); (b) the framing of a new Republican Constitution; (c) the adoption of adult franchise; (d) a system of rule of law and independent judiciary; (e) the economic policy based on the Five Year Plans, with emphasis on agro-industrial growth; (f) the policy of equal opportunity and protective discrimination for providing social justice to backward groups; and (g) a number of changes in policy development with necessary administrative reforms. To accomplish these strategies, the South Asian nations initially had two models of development to choose from.

**Models of Development Used**

The two models of development available at the time of independence were: (a) the liberal capitalist democratic model (LCDM), or the Western model, and (b) the communist model.[2] South Asian countries had some exposure to the LCDM during the British Raj; however, their experience in running government and administration was very limited in such areas as democratic governance, universal adult franchise, individual rights and freedom, market-based economy and social capital. However, leaders of these countries were in a hurry to achieve a similar level of economic prosperity, and neglected to worry about the strengthening of institutions and democratic process. Despite their familiarity with the LCDM, it was realised by these leaders that it took more than 300 years for the West to reach its present level of political maturity and economic progress.

However, developing nations did not wish to wait that long; they were in a hurry to achieve the same level of economic progress as their colonial masters. The communist model appeared to provide them a similar level of economic progress within a shorter time span, but the political ideology of the communist model was not preferred by many of the developing countries' leaders. In India, Prime Minister Jawahar Lal Nehru, greatly attracted by Fabian socialism, ushered in a new era of economic planning by slowly bringing major elements of the economy under the direct control of the state. In addition to many developing nations, other South Asian countries followed Nehru's example. But instead of achieving economic prosperity, poverty increased in India. As

## 164    *Governance and Administration in South Asia*

*Table* 7.1    Selected indicators about South Asian countries

| Indicators | India | Pakistan | Bangladesh | Sri Lanka | Nepal |
|---|---|---|---|---|---|
| Population (millions) | 929.4 | 129.9 | 119.8 | 18.1 | 21.5 |
| Surface (sq km) | 3 288 000 | 796 000 | 144 000 | 66 000 | 141 000 |
| % of urban population 1994 (1980) | 27 (23) | 35 (28) | 18 (11) | 22 (22) | 14 (7) |
| Adult illiteracy (%) | 48 | 62 | 62 | 10 | 73 |
| Life expectancy | 62 | 60 | 58 | 72 | 55 |
| Public access to safe water (%) (1994–95) | 63 | 60 | 83 | 57 | 48 |
| Public access to sanitation (%) (1994–95) | 29 | 30 | 30 | 66 | 6 |
| GNP per capita ($) | 340 | 460 | 240 | 700 | 200 |
| Energy use per capita in kg for 1994 (1980) | 248 (137) | 254 (142) | 64 (32) | 97 (96) | 28 (12) |

*Source*: The World Bank, *World Development Report, 1997* (Washington D.C.: The World Bank, 1997), pp. 214–32.

economic controls were applied, the economy became increasingly stifled, and the nation became poorer. Not only India, but also other South Asian countries found themselves in the same position. At the time of independence, the South Asian nations were economically healthier than East Asian countries (excluding Japan); even by the 1960s, the 'countries of South Asia and East Asia were at approximately the same level of per capita [income] ... In the last three decades, however, per capita income in East Asia has increased about four times as fast as in South Asia'.[3] Tables 7.1 and 7.2 illustrate the current profile of the South Asian nations. Mahbub ul Haq, writing about the state of human development in South Asia, has made the following remarks:

The extent of human deprivation in South Asia is co-lossal. The sheer magnitude of human distress numbs the mind; over 500 million people living in absolute poverty; 260 million people lacking access to even rudimentary health facilities; 337 million people without

*Table* 7.2 Ranking of South Asian countries, selected indices

| Index/ranking (# of countries surveyed) | India | Pakistan | Bangladesh | Sri Lanka | Nepal |
|---|---|---|---|---|---|
| Human development index (174) | 135 | 134 | 143 | 89 | 151 |
| Economic freedom index (103) | 62 | 51 | 66 | 57 | 85 |
| Human rights index (120) | 60% | 32% | 43% | 54% | — (poor) |
| GNP per capita ranking (133) | 107 | 99 | 121 | 86 | 125 |
| State religion (religious freedom) | Secular | Islamic state | Islamic state | Buddhist | Hindu |
| Level of corruption index (54) | 46 | 53 | 51 | — | — |

*Source*: For human development index, see UNDP, *Human Development Report* (New York, Oxford University Press, 1996), pp. 135–7; for economic freedom index, see, James Gwartney, Robert Lawson and Walter Block, *Economic Freedom of the World, 1975–95* (Vancouver, BC, Canada: Fraser Institute, 1995), p. xx; for human rights index, see, Charles Humana, *World Human Rights Guide* (New York: The Economist, Facts on File Inc., 1986), pp. xiv and xv; for GNP per capita ranking, see *World Development Report 1997* (Washington D.C.: The World Bank, 1997), p. 214; and the corruption index is based on a report by Transparency International, *Ranking 1996* (Berlin: Transparency International an Gottingen University, 1996) (out of 54 countries surveyed, Pakistan was ranked second from the bottom).

safe drinking water; 830 million people with no access to basic sanitation; 396 million adults unable to read or write.[4]

It is amazing that this region, which started from a better position at independence with respect to its economic and human development status, became by the 1990s one of the poorest regions on earth, even below sub-Saharan Africa (in 1993, South Asian per capita income was $309 US compared to $555 in sub-Saharan Africa).[5] Among the many factors that contributed to this state of deprivation, the politico-economy planning system used by these countries must primarily be blamed. Of course, these countries did not become communist, but the communist ideology did sway sufficiently their planning process and their understanding of market and society. Greed and power-plays dominated their vision. They might have continued in their thinking had it not been the demise of communism in East Europe in the late 1980s that sent shock waves through many political leaders of developing nations. In countries like India, where communist parties had made successful inroads in governance, it took time for local communist parties to adjust their course and to lean towards either the LCDM or a variety of it. How long it will take the South Asian nations to move from their present level of deprivation it is too early to say.

In addition to these two major models of development, two indigenous models of development emerged in the region. In Sri Lanka (and to some extent in India), the *Sarvodayan movement*, inspired by Mahatma Gandhi, was operationalised by A.T. Aryaratne. The movement was aimed at integrating low-caste families into the mainstream of national life by creating some income-generating and welfare activities for the poor. The programme, called Sarvodaya Shramadana Movement, is based on the participation of people by instilling in them confidence to build their life and surroundings through their own efforts: *Shramdana* means donating labour for lifting up the workers themselves and their community. The movement signifies an awakening of spirit, and therefore liberation of the individual as well as the group. Personality-awakening is a dynamic, non-violent revolution that results in a transfer of political, social and economic power to all people.

Another experiment in Sri Lanka, based on a concept similar to *Sarvodaya*, has been the Sarvodaya Women's Movement. Since 1987, it has prompted a literacy programme, home gardening, dress-making and sewing, carpentry and so on.[6] The movement does not separate individuals from the group; instead it is based on the upliftment of everyone together. Moral, cultural and spiritual dimensions are as important as the political, economic and social. Despite civil strife in Sri Lanka, this movement among poor women is continuing. The Sarvodayan concept is one of the best examples of civil society initiatives based on Hindu and Buddhist heritage. The other indigenous model of development tried in South Asia is Islamic revivalism, originating from Iran. It is based on literal interpretations and application of the precepts mentioned in the Qu'ran. Although not as fundamentalist as Iran, Saudi Arabia and Sudan, Pakistan and Bangladesh have declared their countries as Islamic Republics. The Revivalist movement attempts to combine egalitarianism and militant purism with an affirmation of religious authority as holistic and absolute.[7] Table 7.2 identifies the state religions of the major South Asian nations.

## THE EMERGENCE OF THE ADMINISTRATIVE STATE

In order to fulfil the objectives of a welfare state and promote rapid economic growth, India led the South Asian countries by adapting Five-year Plans as a major instrument of its economic policy, itself based on the principle of 'mixed economy'. Attempts to formulate and implement development plans were accompanied by a vast expansion of various administrative institutions and agencies, as well as by a phenomenal growth of government employees to serve varied developmental programmes.

Of course, the adoption of planned economic development inevitably led to an increase in the size of the bureaucracy. The planning system placed heavier responsibilities on the district, a traditional unit of administration in South Asia. However, the British-devised administrative system could not carry on, and eventually suffered from (a) the rigid adherence to, and inflexible dependence upon rules; (b) a focus on top-down decision-making with a lack of delegation of authority, and a generalised rigidity that prevented the organisation from adapting readily to the changing demands placed upon it; and (c) a lack of trust and reluctance on the part of the senior echelon to delegate authority, and the structuring of human reactions in rigid hierarchical terms, a tendency encouraged by the caste system and by the tradition of deference toward authority.[8] It was no surprise that in a few years time, the administrative system adopted 'ad hocism', both in the governing and administrative sectors, resulting in low levels of efficiency, integrity and public trust.

The political leaders of the South Asian nations tried to govern too much, when compared to the Britishers who governed too little, and did not concern themselves enough with changes in the social and the economic order. Perhaps it was inevitable – partly because the political leaders were in a great hurry to reach a level of industrialisation akin to the West, and partly because they had a great deal to make up relative to other nations of the world. Nevertheless, this seeming haste resulted in a snowballing influence on the political culture and administrative process, especially its efficiency, effectiveness and standard of conduct. South Asian governments became more intensively involved in regulating, planning, stimulating and even undertaking directly economic and commercial activities in many significant areas. In the case of India, socialism as a state ideology accelerated the public demand on the government apparatus, which in turn gave more authority to government to penetrate various aspects of citizens' life. Over time, citizens found themselves dependent upon the activities and the initiative of the government in all spheres of their lives, and seeking government employment became the major occupation of the people.[9]

**Growth of Governmental Activities**

The expansion of government activities has brought in its wake an inevitable increase in bureaucracy and public employment at all levels of government. Government employment has expanded not only because of the radi-

*Table* 7.3   India: growth of all government-sector employment (selected years, 000s)

| Year | Central government | State governments | Public enterprises (central govt.) | Public enterprises (state govts) | Local governments | Total government employees |
|---|---|---|---|---|---|---|
| 1960–61 | 2 090 | 3 014 | 773 | — | 1 173 | 7 050 |
| 1970–71 | 2 771 | 4 152 | 1 928 | — | 1 878 | 10 729 |
| 1980–81 | 3 195 | 5 676 | 2 739 | 1 837 | 2 037 | 15 484 |
| 1987–88 | 3 376 | 6 796 | 3 454 | 2 492 | 2 207 | 18 325 |

*Source*: Based on *India, Statistical Abstract 1990*, Ministry of Planning, Department of Statistics, New Delhi, March 1992, p. 309.

cal changes taking place in the nature and number of government functions, but also because of the fact that, in a country like India, the creation of posts in lower echelons of administration has often been used to placate the demands of the backward communities.

**The Dimensions of Public Service Growth**

It is difficult to establish a direct correlation between government employment and public-sector spending; however, it is quite fair to assume that many new programmes that the newly independent states had to undertake did add to the increasing size of governmental bureaucracy. In Bangladesh, for example, the size of government effectively doubled in the 20 years after independence: there were formerly 21 ministers to manage 109 departments and directorates, but by 1992 this number had grown to 35 ministers and 221 departments. At the same time, the number of government employees increased from about 450 000 to almost 1 million.[10] Similarly, in India the universe of total government employment (including state governments, local governments and public enterprises) has more than doubled in about 27 years (see Table 7.3). And to take another example of a South Asian country, in Sri Lanka the number of government employees swelled from about 222 940 in 1958 to 399 840 in 1980; but if one considers the entire universe of all kinds of government employees (including those working for local governments and public enterprises), this number in 1980 was 1 199 825 in a population of 15 million.[11] The situation in Pakistan is similar to that which we find in other South Asian countries.

This expansion of government bureaucracy has been accompanied by a proliferation in rules and regulations. The expanding sphere of government places the administrative machinery in a monopolistic position and enhances the opportunities for greater administrative power and discretion. During the first two decades of the post-independence period in India, about 1600 laws (including 21 constitutional amendments, more than 100 regulations, 100 President's decrees and 150 ordinances) were enacted. In addition, an average of about 5000 new rules were being issued every year.[12] Executive regulations, together with increased bureaucratic discretion, have provided opportunities and incentives for corruption, since regulations governing access to goods and services can be exploited by civil servants to extract 'service charges' from the needful. In all the South Asian countries, government departments such as the Public Works (popularly called PWD) became infamous for systematising corruption. Especially at the provincial and municipal levels, South Asian governments became uncontrolled and unaccountable centres of power.

## THE EMERGING ADMINISTRATIVE CULTURE: *DESI*-STYLE ADMINISTRATION AND CORRUPTION

The first ten years of independence in India and Pakistan represented a period of remarkably smooth change and adaptation from the British Raj to a democratic parliamentary system. There were no visible cracks in the system; rather it developed the necessary resilience and the capacity to both mend, mould and build itself. But within the next ten years of development, cracks were to manifest in Pakistan. In 1958, General Ayub Khan took over the government; in India, although there was no such drastic shift in governance, a new era of politics developed during the Indira Gandhi regime. In a short space of time, a new generation of politicians emerged for whom the old liberal democratic traditions and morality were a mere hindrance which could be sacrificed for political expediency, status and private gain. What Pakistan faced with respect to the weakening of democratic governance and effective administration in the 1950s and 1960s, India was also to face in the 1970s and 1980s. The emergence of a new breed of politicians brought in its wake an erosion of many of the fundamental values of the governing system that had been consolidated during the earlier years of independence. Whether this happened because of a personal struggle among political leaders to consolidate and preserve their power-base, or whether it was a reflection of changing economic times is a matter for speculation; but the net consequences of this uncertainty was that the policy-making administrative apparatus became disoriented and seems to have been replaced by a 'shotgun' approach to government and administration. Finally, political interference, influence peddling and muscle-flexing government employees' unions made even the most legitimate means of accountability meaningless in the administrative parlance.[13]

There have been a number of visible changes in the administrative system and style since British rule. The 'district' – the fundamental unit of administration – underwent a metamorphosis in terms of the importance, position and stature of its chief executive. The importance of both the district and district officer was reduced due to the fragmented expansion of governmental activities on the one hand, and to the growth of 'mafia' politics on the other. Much of a district officer's time was simply wasted on listening, persuading and arguing with a host of political leaders – including some antisocial elements – while the regular official work remained unattended. During elections, district officers were expected to exhibit soft corners for the political party in power, and after elections they expected to reap some reward. Young district officers, many of them ambitious, wanted to complete their tours of duty in the district as early and smoothly as they could, and then looked forward to the day they were to be posted to senior positions in the state capital, away from the rough and tumble of district politics. The result of this has been that district and local administration suffered both at the delivery point and at upper levels.

Along with the decline in performance of the district level of administration, there has been a simultaneous decline in the strength and morale of the government service in general. Although in India the IAS (Indian Administrative Service) – and to some extent the CSP (Civil Service of Pakistan, and its successor) – maintained its dominant position, its power and prestige suffered. Constant political interference, caste politics, money, prejudices and related matters affected the performance and morale of governmental bureaucracy in South Asia. The morality of politicians, businessmen and some bureaucrats seems to have declined to the point that there is virtually no aspect of public life today which is free of corruption or 'black (untaxed) money'. People in authority seems to have acquired dual personalities; their private actions ill-match their public pronouncements.[14] Thus, the climate for corrupt practices is ripe.

Until very recently, government control over the granting of industrial licenses and its heavy-handed regulation of all industrial activities in favour of monopolistic state enterprises earned it the nickname 'licence, permit, quota raj', which has opened opportunities for corruption, bribery and affluence through ill-gotten wealth. The policy of industrial controls and licensing was earlier considered necessary for fulfilling the objectives of planning and for ensuring that scarce resources were allocated to priority projects. The system which one economist calls 'command capitalism' was originally intended to make India self-reliant, egalitarian and labour-intensive. Although some measure of self-reliance was achieved at the cost of the other two objectives, it has led to the emergence of a parallel black market economy and to corruption which – far from promoting rational allocation of resources – has only led to the growth of the luxury sector. It has been estimated that 'black' or untaxed money amounts to at least 20 per cent of gross domestic product, with perhaps another 15 per cent generated by smuggling. Particularly since the 1980s, corruption became the way of life. This contributed to the emergence of an administrative culture whose workings can be summarised in the following manner:

> The officers' excessive dependence upon notations entered by the assistants and clerks on every file, the outdated administrative procedures and formalism, the excessive delay in forwarding an application and the infinite time taken to pass the final order, the uncertainty in the application of rules or regulations, the methods of flattery and the encouragement of subservience for obtaining service from administrators, and the lubrication required in the form of payment to powerful or bureaucratic functionaries to get the work done, have all become a part of the administrative culture of India.[15]

This insidious subculture does not encourage a citizen even to attempt and seek what is legally due to him; instead of facing the ordeal, such a citizen employs the services of 'agents' to lobby and get the work done, for which a fee is paid. It appears that the administrative system is unable to show concern for the common people, their time and difficulties, or the inconvenience of coming to the office again and again. Furthermore, the lower echelon of employees seems to have become insensitive and unresponsive towards their duties, although they do not hesitate to impose on clients the importance of their office.

The public believes that corruption and unethical activities among officials (both politicians and appointed government servants) is inevitable and incurable. Their pessimism is justified because they know that the custodians of government administration are under the unholy grip of corruption, and nothing moves smoothly without the help of influence, connections or bribery. Although the public is overburdened with the amount of corruption prevailing in politics and administration, it continues to suffer.

**Corruption as the Way of Life**

It is an irony of history that the empire builders of Europe, who started their business in Asian and African nations with naked corruption, ended up handing over a relatively clean administration to the leaders of those independent colonies. Of course, the British rule was not free from corruption, but compared to the present situation in South Asia, the corruption of the British Raj pales into insignificance. Another irony is that although the leaders of those newly-independent nations started off with very high standards of probity and accountability, they are now deep in the cesspool of corruption.[16] The major difference between corruption in industrialised nations and the developing world is that in the West, an office does not sanctify the office-holder. The office of US President could not protect Richard Nixon, and he was forced to resign; on the other hand, the office of President or the Prime Minister of several developing nations protects its holders against prosecution and being held accountable while in power.

The three major causes of corruption are (a) delays in government decisions; (b) the concentration of regulatory and discretionary power in the hands of a few government officials; and (c) cumbersome procedures in dealing with public needs. We already know that where there is a concentration of power and discretion, there is always the possibility of abuse, more so when power and discretion have to be exercised in the context of scarcity of resources, a high demand exceeding services, and control and pressure to spend public money. India's Santhanam committee on corruption, appointed by Lal Bahadur Shastri in June 1962, reporting in 1964, noted:

> The people of India rightly expected that, when the governance of the country passed into the hands of the disciples of the Father of the nation who were in their own individual capacities known for high character and ability, Governments in India, at the Centre and the States would set up and achieve a standard of integrity, second to none in the world, both in political and administrative aspects. It has to be frankly admitted that this hope has not been realized . . .[17]

The Santhanam committee acknowledged that there were two major contributory factors for the growth of corruption: (a) government unwillingness to deal drastically with corrupt and inefficient public servants, and (b) an iron-clad protection given to public servants under Article 311 of the Constitution, whereby permission to prosecute an accused public official must come from the authority that appointed him in the first place. Thus, if a public servant belonging to an All India Service received a letter of initial appointment in the name of the President of India, permission to prosecute him must be secured from the same authority. But securing permission is so cumbersome, and delays are so drawn out, that cases are not pursued. Elected members of parliament and legislative assemblies are given the same protection. For example, in the case of corruption charges in 1997 against the Bihar State Chief Minister Laloo Prasad Yadav, it took several months and the interference of the Prime Minister before the Governor could permit the Central Bureau of Investigation to lay charges of corruption in a court.

Another facet of government activity that breeds corruption is the development work based on international aid projects. For example, in India the federal and state governments together allocate about 500 000 million rupees for poverty alleviation and rural development; and it is alleged that not more than 10–15 per cent gets used for that purpose, while the rest disappears among contractors, officials and politicians.[18] If this is true, an enormous amount of public resources gets channelled into corruption, resulting in a loss of credibility largely due to rampant corruption, criminality, and blatant selfishness in politics and administration. Thus it is no surprise that the ordinary people of these countries have lost their faith in the ability of the present group of politicians and political parties to deliver good governance. Despite the fact that in India and Pakistan all kinds of political parties have received opportunities to form governments, none of them have escaped blame after being in power for some time. The public is looking for an alternative to provide them with an honest, decent, credible and moral government.

For an alternative or plan to become successful, the first requisite is that the public's confidence and trust will have to be restored. This will require grassroots action to shake up public apathy and helplessness, and to build instead self-confidence and the courage to fight corruption and criminality. To start with, the first phase of this fight will have to be at the local (including the municipal) government level. At this level, the public will have to know first how much has been collected in taxes and where the money gets spent. At this level of governance it will not be too difficult to monitor corruption. Once some success is gained at the local government level, such an organisation can then direct its attention to the next higher level. A good organisational set-up will be needed to keep up the struggle for government transparency and accountability. Cooptation and cooperation of honest officers and political leaders will have to be cultivated, and should be welcomed in whatever manner it comes.

Some transparency in government organisations will have to be established in various countries. For example, the organisation Transparency International has included both India and Pakistan in its ranking of corrupt nations (see Table 7.2). In 1996, the three South Asian countries, India, Pakistan and Bangladesh, were ranked 46, 53 and 51 respectively among the 54 countries surveyed. Despite public cynicism and apathy, what is needed is a mass movement against corruption and bad government, something akin to the independence struggle. (In February 1997, while visiting New Delhi, I noticed the slogan *Sau me assi beyimaan, fir bhi apanaa desh mahaan* printed on the backside of an auto-riksha. It says that though 80 per cent of the political leaders are dishonest or corrupt, nevertheless, my country is great.) Of course, this second movement will be against their own corrupt leaders and government officials, instead of the colonial powers.

Regarding corruption, specifically in Pakistan, Nasir Islam writes:

> Corruption in Pakistan is so pervasive that it cannot be viewed merely as a structural issue ... Pakistani society and culture reveal an inherent contradiction in their attitude towards corruption. Although there is vehement criticism of corruption in public and at the collective level, in private, individuals are ready to make deals with the decision makers.[19]

Despite widespread corruption, there are still public servants that are not corrupt, although they no longer influence the overall character and culture of their group; the tone for corruption and unethical behaviour is set by the others. This core of exceptionally hard-working, dedicated and conscientious persons in the bureaucracy is overwhelmingly outnumbered by those who are complacent, obsessed with status and rank, and addicted to habits of personal luxury and indolence.

## ISSUES OF ADMINISTRATIVE ACCOUNTABILITY

There are four major issues related to administrative accountability: the status of government officials; security of service; de-criminalising politics; and enforcing accountability.

### The Lofty Status of Government Officials

Government bureaucracy in South Asia suffers from certain strange paradoxes, for example extreme impersonality combines with a ready susceptibility to personal pressures and interventions. A public servant may be theoretically preoccupied with correctness and propriety, but in practice he may behave with irregularity and impropriety. Similarly, his pursuit of absolute justice and uniformity in civil service rules, regulations and procedures often leads to glaring anomalies and injustices. It is a curious reflection on attitudes and thinking that Indian public services are willing to tolerate such contradictions between theory and practice.

Public servants in South Asia also have excessive self-importance, indifference towards the feeling or the convenience of individuals, and an obsession with the binding and inflexible authority of departmental decisions, precedents, arrangements or forms, regardless of how badly or with what injustice they may work in individual cases. One example of self-importance is when an officer signs a letter. He or she will invariably signify his title as 'Deputy, Joint/Additional/or Secretary to the Government of India', as if the government of India is under his command. Additionally, the public services have developed a mania for regulations and formal procedures, a preoccupation with activities of particular units of administration, and an inability to consider the government as a whole. The public servant also fails to recognise the relationship between the governors and the governed as an essential part of the democratic process.

**Security of Service**

Bureaucracy in South Asia has followed the Weberian spirit of hierarchy and span of control so religiously that mutual trust does not exist, either in interorganisational relations or in interpersonal relations in administration. Instead 'mutual suspicion' is its prime tenet, leading to authoritarianism among superiors which then destroys any team spirit within the organisation. When confronted with a difficult decision, the bureaucracy seldom makes any attempt to tackle the problem with initiative and imagination, and instead passes the problem to another department or makes a series of unnecessary references to subordinates to gain time. Also, non-performance or lower productivity has never been grounds for disciplinary action. The result is a psychology of evasion wherever possible.

**De-criminalising Politics**

The Indian Election Commissioner G.V.G. Krishnamurthy announced in August 1997 that during the 1996 General Election, 40 MPs and about 700 MLAs – out of the total of 4027 elected – were facing criminal charges and trials; out of 13 952 candidates for the federal level, about 1500 candidates had criminal records and were also facing charges of dacoity, rape, theft and extortion.[20] Under the existing election laws, unless a person has been successfully prosecuted and convicted, he or she cannot be prohibited from contesting the election. But when such a person gets elected, they are able to influence the prosecuting authorities to delay the process or even withdraw cases pending against them.

Criminalisation of politics – especially the entry of criminals into politics and other sensitive areas of national life – has brought the political system under the sway of gangsters and bad characters. The challenge before the Election Commission is to force candidates to state, at the time of filing their nomination papers, whether they were ever jailed, for what offence and for what period. If a candidate gives false information, then he should be prosecuted and punished, and if elected his election should be annulled. Criminals must not be allowed to rule the nation.

**Enforcing Accountability**

Apart from the traditional constitutional institution of the Comptroller and Auditor General of India (C & A G) and its counterparts in other South Asian nations, which conducts audits of accounts of the government of India and reports on the maladministration of funds or un-authorised or inappropriate expenditure, the two other institutions involved in such a process are the Central Bureau of Investigation (CBI), established under a Government of India resolution in April 1973, and the Central Vigilance Commission established on the rec-ommendation of the Santhanam committee report on corruption in Indian administration of 1964. While the CBI was to be concerned with the investigation of hoard-ing, blackmarketing and profiteering in essential commodities, as well as the collection of intelligence relating to certain specific types of crimes, the Central Vigilance Commission was to investigate public complaints against administrative action or inaction. But both of these institutions have been weakened, perhaps the Vigilance commission more so than CBI.

Enforcing accountability can be realistic only when an offending officer or group of officers can be identified clearly, and quickly prosecuted and punished in all cases of proven malfeasance and abuse of authority for greed and gain. However, it must be noted that efficiency and ethics in administration cannot be improved without first reforming the political system. The prevailing political atmosphere, the falling standards of public life, and the loss of moral values amongst political leaders have bred a corresponding insensitivity, demoralisation and unresponsiveness amongst public officials.

## THE NEED TO ENHANCE GOOD GOVERNANCE AND ADMINISTRATION

The above analysis of the style and culture of administrations of South Asia may seem to be pessimistic. However, it is not intended to undermine the achievements and performance of the governments and administrations of these nations. Despite corruption in government and politics, their administrative systems are functioning as fine machines that have proven themselves capable of sometimes excellent performance in the spheres of policymaking and implementation. As stated by the World Bank:

> The situation is different in South Asia, where in many countries state inefficiency and corruption have co-existed with a relatively competent and efficient civil service, albeit one whose quality has suffered a noticeable decline.[21]

That coexistence of corruption and inefficiency with a competent civil service whose quality of service is continually declining is also eating away the public trust in effective governance. Bureaucratic delays, ambiguous laws, rampant corruption, and a very slow redressal judicial mechanism have all effectively accelerated the common person's misery and distress. The will to fight back is minimal, and the desire to surrender and go with the tide is greater. For a common person, there is nothing but a perpetual ordeal, and it is accepted silently.

At the same time, while a majority have taken corruption and bureaucratic harassment as a way of life, the work of nations continues. The *mantra* for survival seems to be to pay or suffer; because citizens have realised, based on their bitter experience, that without the ability to pull strings in the corridors of power, nothing will get done. Of course people complain; asking them to list their grievances is like taking the lid off Pandora's box. From erratic electric power and water supply to ill-maintained roads and street lights, illegal encroachments, open drains and practically useless sewage disposal facilities, to the tardy public transport, the list continues. At the same time, for those who can pay, everything is available. Convinced that the political and administrative system can never get better, many people have become too tired to even ask questions. Is there any hope for them in the future? In there no end in sight for their misery? The South Asian nations therefore have many challenges to face, three of which are discussed below.

**Reducing Corruption**

The World Bank, in its *World Development Report 1997*, has suggested the following strategy to reduce corruption:

(a) creating a rule-based bureaucracy with pay structure that rewards civil servants for honest efforts;
(b) a merit-based recruitment and promotion system to shield the civil service from political patronage;
(c) credible financial controls to prevent the arbitrary use of public resources;
(d) to reduce the opportunities for officials to act corruptly, by cutting back on their discretionary authority; and
(e) enhancing accountability by strengthening mechanisms of monitoring and punishment – using not only criminal law but also oversight by formal institutions and ordinary citizens.[22]

The World Bank also believes that 'any reform that increases the competitiveness of the economy will reduce incentives for corrupt behaviour'; however, this assertion is based on the experience of the United States and may not apply in the case of developing countries, because when a country is forced to '*contract for services with a private company, possibly a foreign firm with no close ties to the country*',[23] it may be seen as an official invitation for a multinational corporation to overcrowd and intervene in the tight domestic market, and to take away jobs from the locals.

**Good Governance**

As mentioned earlier, the public believes that corruption in public service is a way of life. In fact, malpractice pervades practically every sphere of South Asia's national life – from corruption among police officers, to educational institutions, in municipal bodies, in health services including government hospitals, and in government departments. With the perceived decline in ethics and morality in public life, citizens' trust and confidence in political leaders has waned. Bureaucracy is seen as being ready-at-hand to accomplish the wishes of the politicians in power, so therefore it is not surprising to find that the public displays a cynical view about any claim made by a political leader that his/her party will bring about moral administration. It is here that the stewardship of governance becomes an important issue.

The concept of stewardship of governance provides us with a system of action and implementation. The term is based on the ideal of service to others, particularly to the community at large, a concept that rises above individualism and hedonism to create an environment of public duty among government officials. At the same time, self-sacrifice does not necessarily mean that government servants must take a vow to remain poor; rather, it means that officials must adhere to the principle of serving others by setting a high standard of moral conduct and by considering their jobs to be vocations. This is possible by strengthening the strongest asset in human beings – that is, the inner satisfaction one gets through helping others. The objective is to create an atmosphere that motivates officials to respond to the challenges of government by adhering to the notion of duty and service to the community, as well as taking responsibility for the welfare of others. From this author's perspective, confidence and trust in the democratic system can be safeguarded only when the governing process demonstrates a higher moral tone.

## The Need to Empower Indigenisation of Administrative Practices

At present, the administrative system of developing nations is facing three major challenges: (a) internationalisation, (b) globalisation and (c) indigenisation.[24]

*Internationalisation*
This may mean dependence and continued reliance on the theory and methodology of Western-style public administration with the same emphasis on transplanting and replicating ideas and institutions of the West. This style of administration continues to be hierarchical, bureaucratic and centrally-managed. The internationalisation of public administration requires that Western values and practices prevail everywhere, with standards of performance based on the indicators developed by the West, a downsized and streamlined government, commerce and business not exasperated by over-regulation and red-rape, and the World Trade Organisation acting as a clearance house for the smooth running of the dominant commercial interests of the West.

*Globalisation*
With instant communication through the internet, fax and jet travel to distance corners of the world, fast move-

ment of people and services is now a reality. Technology and education is becoming more uniform; English has become the *lingua franca* of the world; economically, the world is much more dominated now than ever before with multinational corporations, forcing developing countries to open up their markets in the name of trade liberalisation; and Western (read American) administrative values (such as efficiency, accountability and professionalism) have become the watch-words. McDonald's, Kentucky Fried Chicken, Pizza Hut, Levi Jeans, Elvis Presley, Michael Jackson and Hollywood films dominate the world cultural scene. In essence, globalisation has become an Americanisation of world culture. Development administration could not remain immune from the onslaught of Americanisation of its practice.

*Indigenisation*
Seen as the opposite of internationalisation, indigenisation refers to a culture managing its own affairs by using an indigenised system, remaining unsusceptible to Western imperatives. In the field of public administration, there has been a view that dependence on localised customs and traditions generally distorts effective and efficient administration, and any administrative innovations are seen as peculiarities and undesirable ingredients, ill-serving the country. When this happens – as the argument goes – it leads to underemployment and overstaffing; corruption and patrimonial ties; protects arrogant officials; supports unproductive public enterprises; and produces an overall inadequacy of governance. Thus, it is no surprise that Western advisors recommend government restructuring, public service reforms, campaigns against corruption, and extensive training and education for public servants so that they become a mirror image of what is seen in Washington DC, London, Paris, Bonn and Ottawa.

For developing nations, there is no choice but to accept such a bitter medicine. The result is a hodge-podge of updated colonial or neocolonial administrative practices superimposed on ineffective bureaucracies being pulled in different directions: to internationalise or to indigenise. Is it absolutely necessary to have only one uniform administrative system suggested by the West? Is it not possible to strengthen 'unity in diversity', that is, to promote a *convergence* of the two styles, internationalisation and indigenisation, in such a manner that self-reliance, respect for diversity, and bottom-up initiatives replace reliance on outside consultants, conformity to Western thinking, and top-down initiatives coming from the World Bank, IMF, WTO, and the like. The world of the twenty-first century may be ready for the American style of fast food chains, denim blue jeans and Michael Jackson, *but certainly not for the Western notion of 'one size fits all' in the field of governance and administration.* Of course, the developing world will have to set its house in order by controlling corruption, discontinuing unproductive public enterprises, and reforming the inefficient administrative system. South Asian countries have a lot to change, and so does the West.

## SUMMARY

Despite severe economic and various political problems facing South Asian nations over the years, these countries have sustained the workings of the democratic process through some politically-conscious people. They have been able to achieve a relatively strong industrial base; there has been an absolute growth in terms of literacy, education, and scientific and technical knowledge; there has also been relative prosperity; and the bureaucracy has responded well in times of crisis, particularly when given clearly defined objectives and unambiguous priorities. All these give a ray of hope for further improvements in the style, management and operations of governance and administration. However, bureaucracy tends to be seen as an agency of employment for the region's unemployed youth; thus it is prone to overstaffing and slow action, rather than designed to produce results or be accountable for its decisions. We already know that an oversized administration tends to promote lethargy, inefficiency and corruption. That is why the government administration of the post-liberalisation era in South Asia will have to be result-oriented, service-driven, accountable and responsive.

Responsive governance and administration requires an integrated approach that draws upon several sub-systems and approaches. Such an integrated system is based on:

- a governing system that encourages civil society and public participation in decision-making;
- an economic system that emphasises self-reliance and the use of indigenous know-how, as well as the use of scientific/technical data for sustainable development;
- a social system that stresses strengthening social capital, *sarvodaya*, community and development;
- an administrative system that is responsive, ethical and accountable.

Finally, people holding public office will have to behave in a manner that enhances their capability to protect and defend humanity in an ethical way, without allowing the land, its natural resources and social capital to be impoverished. Having been entrusted with the stewardship of governance, they are accountable for any infraction in the effective management of the machinery of government.

For South Asians, as for the rest of humanity, the turn of the century is a reminder that the dreams of a heaven on earth (promised during the struggle for independence) have not materialised; that the concept of a perfect society advanced by some political leaders and scholars in the West was nothing but an idea:

The idea that opportunities were unlimited and the future unbounded, that the entire world would benefit from open-ended economic progress, and that science and technology would triumph and eradicate poverty and disease proved to be an illusion. Instead we have a profound sense of lost opportunity: the opportunity to create a perfect world, the opportunity to have lasting peace on earth and the opportunity for worldwide *sarvodaya* (upliftment of all people together).[25]

Instead, India, Pakistan, Bangladesh, Sri Lanka and Nepal are as impoverished as they were 50 years ago. It seems that somehow they have mislaid their future.

**Notes and References**

1.    For a historical perspective, see, O.P. Dwivedi and R.B. Jain, *India's Administrative State* (New Delhi: Gitanjali Publishing House, 1985); and O.P. Dwivedi, R.B. Jain and B.D. Dua, 'Imperial Legacy, Bureaucracy, and Administrative Changes: India 1947–1987', *Public Administration and Development*, vol. 9 (1989), pp. 253–69.
2.    For a discussion on various models of development, see O.P. Dwivedi and Keith M. Henderson, 'Development Alternatives: Alternative Administration', *Indian Journal of Public Administration*, vol. 42, no. 1 (January–March 1996), pp. 16–31.
3.    Mahbub ul Haq, *Human Development in South Asia 1997* (Karachi, Pakistan: Oxford University Press, 1997), p. 3.
4.    *Ibid.*, p. 8.
5.    *Ibid.*
6.    *Ibid.*, p. 103.
7.    Bruce Lawrence, *Defenders of God* (San Francisco, Cal.: Harper & Row, 1989), p. 98.
8.    Richard P. Taub, *Bureaucrats Under Stress* (Berkeley, Cal.: University of California Press, 1969), p. 161.
9.    O.P. Dwivedi and R.B. Jain, *India's Administrative State* (New Delhi: Gitanjali Publishing House, 1985), pp. 16–17.
10.    The World Bank, *The World Development Report* (Washington D.C.: The World Bank, 1997), p. 86.

11. B.S. Wijeweera, 'Policy Developments and Administrative Changes in Sri Lanka: 1948–1987', *Public Administration and Development*, vol. 9, no. 3 (June–August 1987), p. 297.
12. R.C.S. Sarkar, 'Role of Government Departments in the Legislative Process', *Journal of Constitutional and Parliamentary Studies*, vol. 2 (1968), p. 1.
13. O.P. Dwivedi and R.B. Jain, 'Bureaucratic Morality in India', *International Political Science Review*, vol. 9, no. 3 (1988), pp. 205–14.
14. O.P. Dwivedi and R.B. Jain, *India's Administrative State*, *op. cit.*, pp. 122–3.
15. R.B. Jain and O.P. Dwivedi, 'Administrative Culture and Bureaucratic Values in India', *Indian Journal of Public Administration*, vol. 36, no. 3 (July–September 1990), p. 444.
16. Jai Narain, 'Political Corruption: Reversal of Gandhian Legacy', *The Tribune* (Chandigarh), 30 November 1996.
17. India, *Report of the Committee on Prevention of Corruption*. K. Santhanam, chair (New Delhi: Ministry of Home affairs, 1964), p. 13.
18. Mukut Shah, 'Good Governance: Time for Another Freedom Struggle', *The Tribune* (Chandigarh), 21 April 1997.
19. Nasir Islam, 'Colonial Legacy, Administrative Reform and Politics: Pakistan 1947–1987', *Public Administration and Development*, vol. 9, no. 3 (July–September 1989), p. 282.
20. 'De-criminalising Polity', Editorial, *The Tribune* (Chandigarh), 22 August 1997, p. 8.
21. *World Development Report* (1997), *op. cit.*, p. 165 (emphasis in the text).
22. *Ibid.*, p. 105.
23. *Ibid.*, p. 106 (emphasis in the text).
24. For further details, see Keith M. Henderson, 'Internationalization and Indigenization', in A. Farazmand (ed.), *Handbook of Comparative and Development Administration* (New York: Marcel Dekkar, 1999).
25. O.P. Dwivedi, *India's Environmental Policies, Programmes and Stewardship* (London: Macmillan, 1997), p. 224.

# 8 Redynamising the African Civil Service for the Twenty-first Century: Prospects for a Non-bureaucratic Structure

M. Jide Balogun and
Gelase Mutahaba

## INTRODUCTION

Even with all the attention so far given to classical bureaucratic theory, its contribution to our knowledge of how societies organise themselves for the attainment of specific objectives still promises to remain a hotly debated theme up to the beginning of the next century and possibly beyond. The reasons for the continuing interest in the subject are clear. First, the bureaucracy is, for better or for worse, one dominant (if not the only) instrumentality for achieving socioeconomic ends. Secondly, and because of its dominant role, the many shortfalls in its performance have proven extremely costly and have triggered a frantic search for alternatives, particularly in the developing countries of Africa. Thirdly, previous attempts at identifying and controlling bureaucratic 'dysfunctions' have by and large proceeded on the assumption that the bureaucracy is an independent variable – one which influences and yet remains immune to the influence of other factors.

This chapter[1] represents a departure from the gener-

190

ally deterministic view of classic bureaucratic theory. It joins an emerging but growing school of thought that traces the impact of entrepreneurial behaviour on the performance of bureaucratic organisations. The underlying thesis is that while change and uncertainty in the external environment dictate the need for the deployment of entrepreneurial skills within organisations, the conditions prevailing at any point in time within each organisation may impede the risk-taking and innovative thrusts needed to steer an enterprise away from trouble to prosperity. The question then is how to identify those institutional arrangements that liberate entrepreneurial energies in an otherwise lethargic, change-resisting, rule-bound, goal-displacing and failure-bound bureaucracy.

## PARADIGMS OF BUREAUCRATIC BEHAVIOUR

**Definition of Terms**

That the bureaucracy plays a dominant, even if not always development-oriented, role in the life of human beings is beyond doubt. It has facilitated the development of science and technology in some societies, while sustaining genocidal and despotic actions in others. A modified form of the classic model of bureaucracy would certainly claim substantial credit for the welfare gains recorded in the developed economies of Western Europe and North America in the twentieth century, while the same model or a variant thereof could be implicated in the production and deployment of weapons of mass destruction.

Bureaucracy is therefore a different animal to different people. However, if we are to have a fair and accurate picture of its role in development and to identify conditions making for bureaucratic success or failure at any particular time and place, we have to remove semantic obstacles to understanding and define the key terms. Germane to our present concern are at least four concepts, *viz*: bureaucracy, entrepreneurship, buccaneering, and corruption or misdirection of authority. Each of these concepts in its different sense reflects current concerns about the workings of the civil service and the directions future reform efforts should follow.

**Bureau and Bureaucracy**

In its generic sense, a bureaucracy is 'government by un-elected, career officials'. The term was popularised by Max Weber, who associated it with the exercise of 'legal-rational' – as different from 'traditional' or 'charismatic' authority. The legal-rational order is preferred by Weber for the simple reason that it proves more 'rational' and more 'efficient' than any other system of administration – traditional or charismatic.

As presented by Weber, a 'bureau' or bureaucracy organised along 'legal-rational' lines has the following attributes, among others:[2]

1. *Rationality*: actions are directed towards the solution of specific problems and the attainment of predetermined objectives. What is rational is, therefore, relative to the objective in view.
2. *Politics–administration dichotomy*: in an ideal bureaucracy, the politicians determine *what* is to be done, while the career officials concern themselves with *how* to achieve the objectives.
3. *Legality*: since the actions taken within a bureaucracy are goal-directed rather than spontaneous, there can be no room for arbitrary conduct. Bureaucratic actions are thus guided by enabling laws, administrative rules and regulations.
4. *Continuity*: the legal instrument establishing a bureau frequently confers on the bureau the status of 'a body perpetual with an eternal seal'.
5. *Specialisation*: the bureaucracy's preoccupation with the accomplishment of specific objectives is behind

the emphasis most frequently placed on the qualifications and expertise possessed by prospective employees. The merit system is at once a reaction to the negative effects of patronage or nepotism, and a feature distinguishing a bureaucracy from primordial systems.

6. *Hierarchical conformation*: holding the bureaucracy together and ensuring conformity with its legal-rational edicts is an organisational device termed 'hierarchy' – a mechanism for keeping each job under the control and supervision of a higher one.

7. *Accountability*: as a further attempt at promoting unity of purpose and direction and maintaining discipline, a bureau establishes mechanisms for holding individuals accountable for the authority conferred on his or her office.

8. *Specified sphere of competence*: in a classic bureaucratic order, jobs are not only expected to make specialised contributions to the attainment of corporate objectives, but are to operate within predetermined limits. Under the *ultra-vires* principle, a traffic cop is limited to the performance of traffic duties, and would have exceeded his or her authority if he or she deems it his or her responsibility to verify hawkers' licences, or demand proof of payment of custom duties on petty traders' wares.

9. *Precedents and record-keeping*: if a bureau is to operate in a legal-rational – and therefore predictable – way, it needs a memory: an institutional memory. This it provides for by maintaining an elaborate record-keeping system.

Taken together, these well-known Weberian attributes project a bureaucracy as a value-neutral, tight-knit, mechanistic and predictable institution established to accomplish predetermined objectives. Does it then mean that the bureaucracy, as a programmed and 'fully automated' system – if ever developed in the African context – is also self-propelling, self-regulating and self-correcting? A response to this question is deferred to a later part of this chapter.

### Entrepreneurship

Regardless of whether or not homoeostatic features are built into the classical bureaucratic model, it is clear that its performance as an entrepreneurial agent has to date been far from impressive. Like their private sector counterparts, public entrepreneurs take risks (political, emotional and financial), and they assemble teams of managers to implement their innovative ideas and maximise their gains. Unlike the orthodox bureaucrat who cherishes anonymity, the public entrepreneur has a name that can be recalled, a face that can be identified, and a telephone number that can be dialled by 'customers'.[3]

In Weber's analysis, of course, charisma is that quality of leadership that appeals to non-rational motives. It is precisely because of its 'irrational' tendency that he excluded it from his legal-rational model. However, the new concern with entrepreneurship in the public sector is beginning to highlight the relevance of charisma not only to politics, but to the implementation of innovative policies.[4] In fact, Kouzmin and Cutting go as far as to argue that the three rationalities identified by Weber (traditional, charismatic and legal-rational) are, in various combinations, critical to the success of innovative policies and essential to the maintenance of organisational equilibrium in a period of rapid change.[5]

While charisma is important to our understanding of public sector entrepreneurship, it should be noted that the reference in this analysis is not to that type of charisma often associated with arbitrary behaviour. If the 'profits' accruing from public sector entrepreneurial behaviour are to be maximised, it is necessary to temper the 'irrational' impulses of charisma with information – particularly information on markets and market opportunities, competitors' plans and strategies, internal production strengths and weaknesses, and the potential for management and technological innovation. Indeed, the failure of the classical bureaucratic organisations to 'discover' opportunities for entrepreneurial profit and to allocate resources accordingly emanates from the contempt with which these organisations treat data and information.

**Buccaneering**

Perhaps a better understanding of entrepreneurship will be provided by describing what it is not. Buccaneering is, for instance, a pattern of behaviour that shares with entrepreneurship the desire for 'profit maximization', but which, unlike the latter, inverts the means–ends relationship for the sake of maximising profits.

Buccaneering parts ways with genuine entrepreneurship at the *value-added* point. While the latter translates market opportunities into a search for perfection and productivity gains, the former is content to corner the market and pocket the profits. Thus, the buccaneer-official ensures that he or she is fully informed about the location of power in an otherwise fuzzy organisational setting. He or she conforms to the stereotype of the ultimate cynic who hankers after authority and, on attaining it, thinks that he or she is now licensed to act 'unrestrained by concerns with the rights of others, constitutional checks and balances, or even prudence'.[6]

How long the buccaneer-official remains successful depends on whether the organisational environment continues to value his or her *'bureau-political'* skills over genuine *professional contributions.*

**Corruption or Misdirection of Authority**

Like other forms of ethical violations, buccaneering inevitably results in the distortion of internal rules and procedures. It can even be described as a localised form of corruption – one that takes place *within* the organisation, as against other forms involving the external clients of the organisation.

The subject of corruption or rent-seeking in the African context has received enough attention lately to obviate any further detailed analysis. As a pattern of behaviour with unique 'entrepreneurial' and buccaneering attributes, its relevance to this paper lies in highlighting another bureaucratic 'ideal-type'. The corrupt official is one who, with his or her own set of rules, operates entirely outside the 'legal-rational' system. To the corrupt official, the job is another source of private income or prebend – one that opens up opportunities to utilise public resources for private gain.[7]

**Bureaucracy and Development: Working Hypotheses**

With all these characters (legal-rational, entrepreneurial, buccaneering, and corrupt officials) jostling for positions or influence within the bureaucracy, what are the chances that the bureaucracy will acquit itself creditably as an agent of African development? There are at least two ways of viewing the developmental role of the bureaucracy. First, it may be assumed that the legal-rational momentum of classic bureaucracy is strong enough to overcome the dysfunctional effects and thus propel the bureaucratising systems to growth and development. Second, the classic bureaucracy may be seen as containing the seed of its own destruction – that by its very nature, the Weberian bureaucracy is incapable of pioneering change or bringing about substantial development. The succeeding paragraphs set out to test these two conflicting hypotheses.

Caiden's J-Curve theory depicts bureaucratisation as beginning with 'a burst of energy'.[8] The acceleration of productivity continues during the growth stage; however, by the time the bureaucracy reaches maturity, age will begin to tell on its performance. At this bureaupathological stage, the originally positive attributes (rationality, legality, hierarchy, specialisation and so on) will become inverted, with serious consequences for productivity. For example, hierarchy will not stop at holding the organisation together but will, with age, begin to stifle creativity and individual initiative. Rules will also start to take on a life of their own as they are mechanically enforced by officials who have no clue as to the circumstances under which the rules were enacted in the first place, or the purpose they were meant to serve.

Even the 'merit system' will not be spared by the aging process. In addition to the possibility of specialisation turning incumbents of positions into alienated robots, the pattern of recruitment will also reflect the *status quo* bias of those doing the recruiting.[9] The lack of homoeostatic features in the classic bureaucratic model impedes the developmental capability of the bureaucracy and points to the need for an entrepreneurial leadership class to fill the void. But, as Adedeji observes, leadership may be a 'captive' of the environment.[10]

It has also been argued that when the hierarchical orientation of the classic bureaucracy is combined with the generally static and conformist values of traditional society, entrepreneurial leadership will tend to find itself greatly handicapped. This is another way of saying the developmental role of both the bureaucracy and of its entrepreneurial leadership class is a function of the prevailing environmental conditions.

There is, however, no conclusive empirical evidence in support of this fatalistic view. One lesson brought out in the next section is that while some public service bureaucracies in Africa have succumbed to environmental influences, others have responded positively to leadership and entrepreneurial initiatives. In any case, systems that give up on the need for change – and the possibilities of change – are doomed to extinction. The economies that are most likely to prosper in the next century will be those in which 'informed', information-led, and quickly adapting organisations take and implement the critical allocative decisions.

## THE BUREAUCRACY IN AFRICAN PUBLIC SERVICES: A SURVEY OF EXPERIENCES

In external appearance, if not always in substance, the African public service is bureaucratic. Whether the reference is to the civil service, or to public enterprises, local government units, institutes of higher learning and research agencies, the formal attributes of the bureaucracy are discernible: legality, departmentation by purpose, hierarchy, specialisation (grouping of activities into specialised compartments and recruitment based on academic/professional qualifications), accountability, specified sphere of competence, continuity, record-keeping and precedents, and so on. However, to say that the bureaucracy is the organisational model adopted in the African public service is not to say that the bureaucratisation experiences of the public services are uniform. In fact, a notable feature of the administrative experience of African countries is the difference in the stages reached in developing and operating legal-rational bureaucratic systems.

### Bureaucracies at the Traditional Stage: A Case Study of Ethiopia

One thing is clear: chronological age appears to be irrelevant to the evolution of public bureaucracies in Africa. In fact, if we go by their 'dates of birth', only two bureaucracies will qualify as 'elders' (Ethiopia and Liberia), and the 'toddlers' will include Botswana, Namibia and South Africa. However, in terms of structural complexity and the goal-attainment capacity of institutions, the 'elder bureaucracies' of Ethiopia and Liberia are at the primeval stage, and are way behind the newly-emerging bureaucracies of Botswana, South Africa and Namibia.

Incidentally, the Liberian bureaucracy is just beginning to pick up the pieces after being set adrift by years of civil war.

With specific reference to Ethiopia, Asmeron advances the thesis that the origin of a bureaucracy and the purpose it was required to serve at the time of birth are crucial in determining the evolution of the bureaucracy over a period; because according to Asmeron, the Ethiopian public service began as an extension of the Imperial household, and it soon developed into a patrimonial system.[11] Emperor Menelik – a modernist by imperial standards – laid the foundation of the centralised and patrimonial bureaucracy. He appointed his relatives, trusted courtiers and powerful generals to key offices. Complete loyalty to the Emperor was a major condition for survival in the imperial court and for progress within the bureaucracy.[12]

Although the 1974 revolution got rid of the monarchy, the succeeding socialist regime inherited and probably reinforced the patrimonial bureaucratic system. Deference to authority, hierarchy and inflexible application of bureaucratic rules conspired against innovative impulses in the bureaucracy, and dampened the tall industrialisation ambitions of the then-revolutionary government. Routine administrative decisions continued to be based on personalities rather than on precedence or systematic guidelines. Buccaneering and corrupt activities appeared to be alien to the bureaucracy, but so was entrepreneurial behaviour. Caution, meticulous observance of rules and preoccupation with survival were among the recipes of success mastered by the average civil servant in Mengistu's Ethiopia.

When the Marxist-oriented Derg regime was itself replaced in 1991 by the EPDRF (Ethiopian Peoples Democratic Revolutionary Front), the issue of how to reorient the bureaucracy in the direction of change featured prominently on the new Administration's agenda. The government's concern was understandable. It had wide-ranging plans for the modernisation of its sociopolitical and economic institutions, but the bureaucracy that it had to rely on was still years behind in human and institutional capacity as well as in operational procedures. Getting an import cleared through customs often required scaling many obstacle courses, collecting multiple signatures at different layers of authority, and waiting interminable periods for the final approval.

In November 1994, the government invited the UN Economic Commission for Africa to collaborate in the design and implementation of various schemes of administrative reform. One of the projects focused on the rationalisation of the procedure adopted in delivering services to clients. According to the project synopsis, the situation to be rectified was one in which requests from members of the public remained unattended by civil servants, unless and until the applicants appeared in person at the scene of administrative action. The cumbersome procedures adopted in processing the various categories of applications also needed to be critically reviewed.

The agencies requiring members of the public to appear in person to follow up their requests and applications (or to wait until long and complicated processes were exhausted) include those responsible for:

1. *Product/service-delivery*: emergency relief, water pipe connections and maintenance, electricity connections and reconnections, telephone cable repairs and maintenance, maintenance of government-owned housing units, and so on.
2. *Regulatory and related activities*: vehicle licensing, issuance and renewal of driving licences, passport issuance/control, business registration, immigration and exit clearance formalities, and so on.
3. *Revenue/bills collection*: merchandise valuation and customs clearance, settlement of electricity, water and telephone bills, payment of rent on government housing units.

The project's strategic objective was to evolve a new system of public administration which would place a higher premium on the quantity, quality and promptness of service than on informal relationships and face-to-face contact.

The procedure rationalisation project in Ethiopia was one of many embarked upon as part of the effort to raise the public service to the level desired by the government. It was to be undertaken simultaneously with other reform measures – notably, the restructuring of central government institutions, privatisation of state enterprises (together with the management of the retrenchment 'fall-out'), the establishment and strengthening of regional administrations, financial management reform, design and installation of new service delivery systems, establishment of mechanisms for the enhancement of ethics and accountability at all levels, and the design of a comprehensive training programme.

The priority nonetheless lies in redynamising the bureaucracy to support the government's liberalisation programme. The success of the reform hinges, among other things, on the extent to which:

1. ongoing governance reform measures succeed in empowering the citizen sufficiently to begin to demand and exercise his/her right to quality service from public institutions;
2. institutional mechanisms coupling the exercise of authority with individual responsibility are installed and operated;
3. individual employees are 'empowered' to render quality service to members of the public (this entails substantial delegation of authority and a departure from the predominantly hierarchical and centralised system currently in place);
4. the notion of administration as a *cooperative* action is institutionalised (it was not uncommon, particularly, under the Derg regime, for subordinates to challenge

their superiors' interpretation of bureaucratic rules, or to interpose ideological variables which managers would rather leave out of administrative and technical decisions);

5. the idea that no system is perfect is accepted, and that the logic, sequence and cost-effectiveness of motions need to be constantly reviewed and improved;
6. a system is developed enabling information to be quickly retrieved, processed and transmitted to decision points and service counters;
7. a fault-reporting and client evaluation procedure is introduced across the board;
8. the quality of supervision is improved through formal and informal on-the-job training; and
9. the public service is seen as an institution encouraging 'opportunity discovery', creativity and innovativeness.

**Bureaucracies with Colonial Legacies**

Unlike the Ethiopian public service with traditional, monarchic roots, the majority of the public administration systems in sub-Saharan Africa (for example Ghana, Guinea, Mali, Nigeria, Cote d'Ivoire, Sierra Leone, Tanzania, Kenya, Uganda, Malawi, Zambia, Cameroon, Gabon) were inherited by modern political and administrative elites from the former colonial regimes. While the nomenclature adopted in describing organisation units differed from one country to another, and after we make allowances for the differences between anglophone and francophone countries, it is still possible to recognise the basic features of the classical bureaucratic model in the structure of the public services established on the attainment of independence. Ministries and departments were organised functionally (by broad areas of activity) and hierarchically (by classes and/or grades). Red-tapism waxed strong, driven by a complex set of rules and procedures. Heaps of documents were kept in archives. Professionalism co-existed with ethnic calculus and political considerations as criteria for recruitment into the public service. As 'permanent' legal entities, the public services conferred 'security of tenure' on career employees. In a number of cases, the status and role of the bureaucracy were minutely described in enabling laws or 'entrenched' in constitutions.

In the early years of independence, the public service was almost invariably looked upon by policy-makers as *the* basic instrument of modernisation. Hence the huge amount of resources invested in the expansion of public service institutions, staffing and staff training.[13] However, conflict soon arose between the political heads of departments and the senior cadres of the career public service. The former tended to distrust the 'politically neutral' advice offered by the latter, and the career officials, in turn, frequently mounted a rearguard action to 'insulate' administration from politics. In a number of countries (particularly those with 'one-party' constitutions) the politicians held sway as laws were enacted systematically, bringing the career service under direct political influence and control.

Where the bureaucracy was able to stave off systematic politicisation, elements within it engaged in activities that were inconsistent with the 'legal-rational' intentions of Max Weber. New institutions were established and additional posts created with little regard for productivity, but with dire fiscal – and subsequently, macroeconomic – consequences. Rules were deliberately elongated and 'hardened' to widen 'opportunities' for buccaneering and ethical violations. 'Modern' budgeting and personnel techniques were installed, with little impact on service delivery. Ambitious development plans were released but the bureaucracy lacked either the motivation or the capacity and resources to implement them.

A few case examples will show how the public service bureaucracy passed up opportunities to join intelligence-based organisations' march to progress. In one country, an agency responsible for the propagation of innovative management techniques is itself organised and run along pure bureaucratic lines. The agency's experts operate within a tight hierarchical structure, and are subject to the constraints imposed by civil service rules and procedure. The agency's records and archives services are still at the pre-independence stage, with no immediate plans for computerisation.

A ministry responsible for trade development in country X maintains a highly-centralised trade registration system requiring those intending to establish business enterprises to complete a series of forms (supported with 'tax clearance certificates') and to travel long distances to submit their applications and to answer 'routine' questions. The complex procedure has opened up 'opportunities' for process expediters, not only in the trade ministry but also in the tax-clearance issuing offices. A few officials of the trade ministry believe that their jobs could be made more interesting if the ministry were plugged into the global trade information network. As of the time of writing, there appeared to be no plans to supplement the basic (and grossly inefficient) postal and telephone services with fax and e-mail connections or internet access. Trade-related papers continued to be shuffled around desks, while global opportunities were passing the country by.

The mission statement of another ministry in country Y requires it to 'promote the development of science and technology'. It was on this basis that a parastatal body approached the ministry officials for information on where to find organisations or individuals that could be contracted to produce and supply communications devices conforming to certain specifications. The reply promptly came from the science and technology ministry: communications technology was still at a 'rudimentary' stage in that country. Perhaps the parastatal would like to contact the ministry of planning with a view to exploring external technical assistance sources. It later turned out that within local universities and institutes of technology were researchers who were working on exactly the same project which was of interest to the parastatal, but who were handicapped by lack of finance. Apparently the information system in the ministry of technology was still years behind developments in 'information technology' and in the local science and technology community.

**Civil Service Reform and Bureaucratisation**

To be sure, efforts have been made to revitalise the slow-moving bureaucracies. In a number of countries, high-powered administrative reform commissions were inaugurated partly to refocus civil servants' loyalty,[14] and partly to halt the precipitate decline of the inherited administrative systems.[15] Examples of the public service review commissions established in the late 1960s and the early 1970s are those headed by Ndegwa and Waruhiu (Kenya), Mills-Odoi (Ghana), Udoji (Nigeria) and Wamalwa (Swaziland). An assessment of the impact of the review bodies reveals that whatever fundamental change might have ensued from their recommendations was in fact 'nullified by political indifference and by bureaucratic chess moves'.[16] Civil servants hastily implemented measures relating to salary increases, but parried those with far-reaching implications for ethics, accountability and service delivery. The politicians for their own part could not see the political relevance or 'pay-off' of administrative reform. Terms such as 'cost-consciousness', 'productivity' and 'delegation' and 'decentralisation' might read well in the reports of reform commissions, but they do not address the direct and immediate concern of rulers – how to capture and retain power.

In any case, the administrative reform commissions failed to accomplish in an indigenous manner the structural adjustment programmes (SAPs) imposed by the World Bank. SAPs proceeded to clip the wings of the powerful and overgrown but largely unproductive bureaucracies, and sought to empower the hitherto neglected socioeconomic institutions – notably the formal and the informal private sector, as well as non-governmental organisations. The specific measures taken in pursuit of this de-bureaucratisation and balancing objective – as also discussed in other chapters in this volume – include: reduction in the size (if not always the cost) of government, privatisation of state-owned enterprises, gradual dismantling or virtual elimination of price controls and price subsidies, devaluation of currency, and trade liberalisation.

**Opportunity-discovering Bureaucracies**

Containing the fall-outs from SAPs and spearheading change has been a major preoccupation of the public services in recent years. Indeed, the magnitude of the problems which came in the wake of the cost-cutting measures (retrenchment and redundancy, morale and motivation, productivity, customer-service and other related problems) introduced a sense of urgency into civil service reform and made the otherwise conservative institution receptive to change.

Not content with leaving their fate in the hands of external policy advisers, a number of civil services are beginning to respond positively to internal leadership and entrepreneurial initiatives. Apart from Ethiopia, whose experience has been discussed above, the countries in which far-reaching bureaucratic reforms are currently being implemented include Ghana, Uganda and Tanzania.

Ghana's effort at redynamising the bureaucracy was an off-shoot of the government's strategic thrusts.[17] On the inauguration of Ghana Vision 2020, a civil service reform programme was designed, comprising the following elements:

- resuscitation and/or adaptation of the basic ethos of public service (professionalism, loyalty, dedication, accountability and transparency);

- restructuring and streamlining of central government agencies (to ensure that they are very well-focused, customer-oriented, as well as cost- and time-conscious);
- review of personnel policy and practices (with an emphasis on introduction of new performance appraisal systems, up-dating of personnel rules and administrative instructions, and launching of an integrated Payroll and Personnel Database project);
- rationalisation of pay and grading structures, and the introduction of performance- and productivity-related pay;
- labour redeployment and redundancy management; and
- improvement of records and information management systems.

The centrepiece of Uganda's reform programme is the establishment of institutional arrangements fostering a positive customer orientation in service delivery agencies.[18] In pursuance of this objective, substantial powers were delegated and resources were transferred to lower-level institutions. Human and institutional capacity-building projects were also launched to inculcate client-oriented attitudes in service-delivery agencies and their staff. Above all, watchdog institutions were established to handle public grievances against bureaucratic abuses or ineptitude.

In Tanzania, the government set up a Civil Service Reform Committee (with a full-time secretariat) to coordinate measures such as:

- organisation and efficiency reviews;
- personnel control and management;
- pay reform (and the introduction of performance-related pay);
- redeployment of retrenched personnel and redundancy management; and
- decentralisation.[19]

In addition, the Tanzanian government established a Presidential Commission of Inquiry (the Warioba Commission of Inquiry Against Corruption, 1997) which brought out cases of bribery and abuse of office in agencies responsible for education, health, trade, employment, lands, energy and minerals, as well as works and communications. The Commission identified two types of corrupt public official – those 'who receive bribes as a means of supplementing their meagre incomes . . .', and 'high-level officials and public servants whose involvement in corrupt practices [is as a] result of excessive greed for the accumulation of wealth'.[20]

**Bureaucratic Best Practices**

After all that has been said about the African public services, reference to bureaucratic 'best practices' will undoubtedly sound hollow. However, the civil services mentioned in the preceding paragraphs possessed some redeeming features at one time or another. The Uganda civil service, for instance, was at independence a paragon of efficiency, probity and dedication before it succumbed to the negative influence of despotic rule and institution decay. When political instability degenerated into a full-scale civil war in Nigeria, it was the bureaucracy that stepped in to provide much-needed continuity. After the civil war, an entrepreneurial class within the same bureaucracy supervised the implementation of the reconstruction, rehabilitation and development programmes initiated by the Gowon regime. With the knowledge of hindsight, one may now conclude that it was their innovativeness, their growing influence, and their constant departure from the bureaucratic norms of 'anonymity' that drew public attention to them and made them objects of envy and calumny.

Besides the civil services whose evolution was interrupted by external and internal factors, there are those which have maintained a steady pace of growth over the years. Examples are the Botswana and the Mauritian civil services. In the case of the former, stable but development-oriented political leadership has served as a key factor in administrative development. By contrast, the civil service of Mauritius has, despite changes of government, managed to preserve the inherited ethos of loyalty, professionalism and political impartiality. The successful implementation of the structural adjustment programme initiated by the government of Mauritius in the early 1980s also depended to a large extent on the innovative and entrepreneurial push within the career civil service.

A public service to watch is that of South Africa, discussed in the next chapter. While struggling with the legacies of apartheid, and without forgetting the growing incidence of corruption in the dying days of apartheid, the bureaucracy exhibits features which other civil services will need to study more closely.

## TOWARDS A SERVICE AND CHANGE-ORIENTED BUREAUCRACY

The underlying objective of the classical bureaucratic model is rationality. Unlike institutions established to uphold tradition and block change, a legal-rational bureaucracy is most frequently created to achieve specific, change-oriented objectives. Yet there is something about the bureaucracy that calls into question its receptivity to change.

If the bureaucratic model is contrasted with the market model favoured by economists, one begins to see the limitations to the former's rational thrusts. In a free market, rational behaviour emerges as a result of the frequent interplay of supply and demand forces. This is not always the case in a bureaucracy. The 'goods' and services produced by the bureaucracy – that is, the public bureaucracy – were, until recently, rarely based on 'demand'. In other words, until the policy of structural adjustment transferred resources from the public to the private sector, the former tended to operate independently of the 'demand' forces in the external environment.

At the time the bureaucracy was insulated from its environment, rationality tended to be defined in narrow, bureaucratic terms – that is, in terms of how the organisational bits and pieces fitted together to make for a 'unity of direction'. However, instead of fostering a sense of common purpose, the inward-oriented view of rationality produced subcultures with conflicting rationalities. So it is that in a typical bureaucratic organisation, it is possible to find individuals who are oriented towards traditional, conformist values, as against those impatient with the *status quo*. Shuttling back and forth – between the static and the dynamic poles – are the buccaneers and the crooked officials with flexible loyalties.

The mechanical analogy used in an earlier section provides a clue as to how to proceed in converting the bureaucracy into an engine of growth and development. As is already well-known, the gear shift plays an important part in the movement of mechanical systems. Depending on whether the forward or reverse gear is engaged, it is possible to determine the *direction* and *speed* of motion. As conceived by Weber, every part of the bureaucracy is expected to contribute to the system's forward thrusts – rationality, the politics-administration dichotomy, legality, continuity, specialisation, hierarchy, accountability, the specified sphere of competence, precedents and record-keeping. However, we know from experience that when the human factor is introduced, the forward gear might be shifted to 'neutral' as a prelude to movement in the reverse direction.

Bureaucracy tends to move in the reverse direction where the external stimuli to action are lacking. As long as the bureaucracy sets its own objectives and draws up its own implementation plans, it will tend to be pulled in the directions dictated by dominant groups or forces. Thus a bureaucracy controlled by the law-and-order, policing types will perceive rationality in legal and legalistic terms, and will spend a disproportionate amount of time verifying minor administrative details, pursuing 'law breakers' and frustrating genuine agents of change. A bureaucracy harbouring too many buccaneers will be busy turning out fake progress reports and promoting undeserving causes and candidates. One in which corruption is a way of life is by definition a place where individual members use their offices for private gain.

To transform inward-looking and possibly self-serving bureaucracies into agents of change and of public service, it is essential that each and every bureaucratic attribute be redefined with the clients/customers/consumers in view. The erstwhile disconnection of 'demand' from 'supply' is precisely what enabled public bureaucracies to survive for so long without entrepreneurial effort or concern for the productive combination of resources. Under the proposed dispensation, the bureaucracy will be anything but distant and 'bureaucratic'. Specifically, the new institution will, in its structure and operational methods:

1. *Focus on the citizen*: rather than be completely diverted by rules, procedures and protocol, the bureaucracy will regard the citizen-consumer as the 'king' whose tastes and demands will form the basis of rational behaviour.
2. *Take risks and cope with uncertainty*: besides advising on choices among policies and programmes that show promise of responding to tastes and demands, officials will constantly explore innovative *means* of realising policy objectives and mobilising needed resources. Experimenting with new service delivery modalities, and operational procedures are critical to the success of the citizen-oriented bureaucracy.
3. *See problems from broader sociopolitical angles*: rather than being uncomfortable in the circles of politicians, the new bureaucracy will forge partnerships with external bodies whose support is critical to the realisation of objectives.
4. *Maintain the highest professional standards in the management of human, material, financial and information*

*resources*: to meet increasingly complex challenges, excellence, the constant search for perfection, and value-for-money should underlie management practices.

5. *Respect the rule of law but not hide behind legalism*: the difference between respect for the rule of law and legalism lies in the *'ultra vires'* doctrine incorporated in the former, and the latter's tendency towards inflexible application of rules that otherwise allow a measure of discretion.

6. *Renew its mandate in line with changing priorities*: an agency or a unit within it will no longer be a 'body perpetual with an eternal seal', but one whose survival hinges on its continued relevance and effectiveness.

7. *Promote internal vitality through cross-breeding and competitive selection*: to counter the negative effects of careerism and organisational incest, recruitment policies and practices need to create room for new entrants – enterprising 'immigrants' – who might otherwise be repelled by the xenophobic attitudes of 'settlers' and long-timers.

8. *Substitute management accountability for routine hierarchical control*: instead of hierarchy for its own sake or for the sake of oiling the internal patronage machine, superior–subordinate relationships will now be based on the accomplishment of specific tasks and the delivery of specific services.

9. *Integrate the needs of individuals and informal groups with formal organisational designs*: in recognition of the conflicting aspirations of individuals and groups within organisations, it is essential that interest-aggregation and conflict-resolution mechanisms be built into the 'new bureaucracy' right from the beginning; the issue of 'internal democracy' – particularly, of how to promote high degrees of transparency, accountability and responsiveness of decisions affecting the careers and well-being of staff – also needs to be addressed.

10. *Operate with homoeostatic control*: the new bureaucracy will not only pay significant attention to data collection, storage, retrieval and transmission, but will aspire to higher levels of rationality by ensuring that decisions (having implications for steps 1–9 above) are based on knowledge and up-to-date information. This is what defines the 'new bureaucracy' as an 'intelligent' and learning organisation.

## TOWARDS A NON-BUREAUCRATIC BUREAUCRACY: A SUMMATION

The African bureaucracy that will meet the challenges of the twenty-first century will be one that is citizen-oriented rather than self-serving; innovative rather than rule-bound; capable of forging constructive partnerships with outside groups rather than being insular; professionally competent rather than being patronage- or corruption-ridden; operating within the limits set by law rather than resorting to legalisms; constantly subjecting programmes to relevance and effectiveness tests rather than being complacent; renewing itself by welcoming outsiders into its ranks rather than degenerating through in-breeding; and using hierarchical control as a means of strengthening management accountability rather than as a device for stifling initiative and creativity. Above all, it will enlist information in the service of policy and programme implementation. It will be a truly purposive, results-oriented, time- and cost-conscious institution, rather than one constantly slowed down by hierarchy, protocol and cynical interpretation and application of rules. As discussed in other chapters in this volume, it will be basically human-needs-centred and sustainable, as well as indigenous.

Is there anything on the horizon that suggests the imminent arrival of this dream bureaucracy in Africa? If we go by the three perspectives discussed in this chapter, it will take quite a while to reconstruct what is essentially a law-and-order institution into a customer-oriented body. The bureaucracies with traditional roots appear to be too slow to respond to the momentous changes taking place within and around them. Those inherited from the colonial regimes, by contrast, seem to be running faster than they were originally designed to do, and have mostly confused the creation of 'modern' structures with substantive change. Even the so-called 'best practices' are still grappling with miscellaneous human and institutional capacity problems, and are years behind in terms of the stated attributes of the citizen-focused and service-rendering bureaucracy.

Indeed, bringing the 'new bureaucracy' into being depends largely on one precondition – that is, reordering the governance arrangements in such a way that the attention of public institutions begins to shift from juggling with internal structures to serving the citizen and meeting the latter's demands. The key, as stated in an earlier part of this chapter, lies in leadership – notably, purposeful, citizen-oriented and entrepreneurial leadership. Where a leadership class is committed to turning the bureaucracy into a genuine instrument of public service, measures will be instituted along the lines suggested in the preceding paragraphs. In contrast, where political power is conceived as an avenue to riches and fame, the bureaucracy will remain essentially an instrument for rent extraction – the usual democratic pretences notwithstanding.

## Notes and References

1.  The views expressed in this chapter are the authors' and should not be attributed to the official position of either the United Nations or the Commonwealth Secretariat. Neither of the two organisations should be held liable for residual errors. It should be noted that this chapter is an abbreviated version of a paper presented at the 19th Roundtable of the African Association for Public

Administration and Management, held in Gaborone, Botswana, 27 November–2 December 1997.

2. Max Weber, *The Protestant Ethic and the Spirit of Capitalism* (London: Unwin University Books, 1930).

3. O.P. Dwivedi, 'Public Service Reforms in Canada for the Twenty-first Century', *Indian Journal of Public Administration*, vol. XXIX (January–March 1993), p. 53.

4. M. Schneider, Paul Teske and Michael Mintrom, *Public Entrepreneurs* (Princeton, N.J.: Princeton University Press, 1995).

5. A. Kouzmin and Bruce Cutting, 'Beyond Weber, We Can See Clearly Now: Explaining the Dynamics of Governance in the Maturing Westminster System', paper presented at the Roundtable of the International Institute of Administrative Sciences, Quebec City, 14–17 July 1997, pp. 2–4.

6. L.E. Harrison. *Who Prospers? How Cultural Values Shape Economic and Political Success* (New York: Basic Books, 1992).

7. Barbara Darling, 'Sustainable Development, Good Governance and Public Sector Management Reform', paper presented at the Roundtable of the International Institute of Administrative Sciences, Quebec City, 14–17 July 1997; R. Joseph, 'The Dismal Tunnel: From Prebendal State to Rogue State in Nigeria', paper presented at the University of Wisconsin's Conference on *Dilemmas of Democracy in Nigeria*, 10–12 November 1995; M.J. Balogun, 'Enduring Clientelism, Governance Reform and Leadership Capacity: a Review of the Democratization Process in Nigeria', *Journal of Contemporary African Studies*, vol. 15, no. 2, 1997; Jibrin Ibrahim, 'The Military and the Programme of Transition to Democratic Rule', in J. Ibrahim (ed.), *Expanding Democratic Space in Nigeria* (CODESRIA, Dakar, 1997); and Jacqueline Coolidge and Susan Rose-Ackerman, *High-Level Rent-Seeking and Corruption in African Regimes* (Washington D.C.: The World Bank, Policy Research Working Paper 1780, 1997).

8. See, G.E. Caiden., 'Excessive Bureaucratization: The J-Curve Theory of Bureaucracy and Max Weber Through the Looking Glass', in Ali Farazmand (ed.), *Handbook of Bureaucracy* (New York: Marcel Dekker, 1994).

9. *Ibid.*

10. A. Adedeji. '"L" and "M" Factors in the African Development Equation', *African Journal of Public*

Administration and Management, vol. I, no. 1 (January 1992).

11. H.K. Asmeron, 'Bureaucracy and Neo-Patrimonialism in Ethiopia: Implications for the Rise and Fall of the Mengistu Socialist Regime (1974–1991)', *African Journal of Public Administration and Management*, vol. II, no. 2 (July 1993), pp. 2–5.

12. *Ibid.*, p. 4.

13. Gelase Mutahaba, R. Baguma and M. Halfani, *Vitalizing African Public Administration for Recovery and Development* (West Hartford, Conn.: Kumarian Press, 1993).

14. W.N. Wamalwa and M.J. Balogun, 'Public Service Review Commissions and Administrative Reform: A Comparative Assessment', *African Journal of Public Administration and Management*, vol. 1, no. 1 (January 1992).

15. A. Adedeji, 'Formulating Administrative Reform Strategies in Africa', *Quarterly Journal of Administration* (Ife), vol. 6, no. 3 (April 1972).

16. W.N. Wamalwa and M.J. Balogun (1992), *op cit.*

17. Robert Dodoo, 'The Core Elements of Civil Service Reform', *African Journal of Public Administration and Management*, vols 5–7, No. 2 (July 1996).

18. G.E. Kyarimpa, 'Customer Service as an Element of the Ugandan Civil Service Reform Programme', *African Journal of Public Administration and Management*, vols 5–7, No. 2 (July 1996).

19. D.A. Ntukamazina, 'Core Elements of Civil Service Reform: Focus on Tanzania', *African Journal of Public Administration and Management*, vols 5–7, no. 2 (July 1996).

20. Warioba Commission of Inquiry Against Corruption (established by the President of Tanzania), in *Partnership*, World Bank/EDI, vol. 2 issue 1 (Spring/Summer 1997).

# 9 Alternative Administration: A Southern African Perspective

Victor G. Hilliard and
Henry F. Wissink

## INTRODUCTION: THE AFRICAN SET-UP

Before 1870, European interest in Africa was confined to coastal towns that were important for sea trade: Cape Town, South Africa, for example became a victualling station for passing ships on their way to the East. But by 1914 nearly all of Africa had been colonised. Africa was, so to speak, carved up by various nations, with France and Britain holding the greatest portion of the African continent. Germany, Italy, Portugal and Belgium also held some territories. Most of today's borders come from the lines drawn by Europeans at the 1884 conference held in Berlin. No native Africans were invited to attend this conference, and therefore it is not surprising that no African group accepted colonisation without resistance.

South Africa was mostly colonised by the British, the Dutch and the French, but over the years a rather cosmopolitan group of people settled in South Africa. The British influence on South Africa's public administration was profound; even to this day vestiges of the British system of government can be found in South Africa, particularly at the local government level, and especially in KwaZulu-Natal.

Although the public sector occupies a prominent position in the economy of African countries, most of these countries nowadays experience some sort of crisis in their public administration: a lack of managerial training in the fields of human and resource management, work scheduling, office layout, work simplification, productivity improvement, and a host of other difficulties.[1] In short, there is a lack of capacity in most African countries; and it would seem that 'crash' training programmes have not been particularly helpful.[2]

The crises in African public services are particularly reflected in the inability of African countries to adequately shoulder such functions as production, transportation and marketing of agricultural and industrial products; whether these functions should be performed by the state or whether they should be privatised is perpetually in dispute. The crisis even exists where clearly there are specific functions demarcated to the state, such as law and order, the provision and maintenance of development infrastructures, and the provision of social services. The crisis is also mirrored in the shrinking resource base with declining revenue reserves.[3] These crises are no less prevalent in South Africa.

Before colonialism, African governance systems usually lacked the attributes of the modern state. Colonialism normally supplanted or suppressed the various traditional administrative organisation(s), and with them the administrative cultural values. In most parts of Africa, the traditional administrative organisations were done away with and replaced by bureaucratic organisations styled after the system in the mother country, whether that was Britain, Belgium, France or Portugal. These administrative systems were imposed by the conquerors on the colonised African countries. In the civilising mission of the colonial masters, it is said that the colonialists mainly concerned themselves with pacifying the natives for the purposes of exploiting their natural resources. As such, little investment was put into the development of complicated administrative infrastructures; the administrative systems consisted of skeletal organisations, only large enough for the purposes of extracting revenues and ensuring orderly governance.[4] South Africa was also a colony of Britain, and therefore adopted many of Britain's administrative practices. Some of these vestiges are even present to this day, although the 1994 constitutional dispensation helped to make a radical departure from South Africa's colonial past and from the Westminster type of government.

The events in Africa in recent times can roughly be divided into the colonial and the postcolonial periods. During the colonial era, most African countries saw widespread decentralisation of their tiers of government right to the lowest level(s). These efforts were largely seen by the colonialists as an attempt to devolve democracy to the lowest levels of government – to bring government to the masses.[5] Although South Africa is long past the colonial era and has already entered the post-apartheid period, it nonetheless still possesses many vestiges of the colonial system that were present up until 26 April 1994. It may now be found that South Africa could adopt the same direction as the rest of post-independence Africa, stripping away any colonial features and centralising power within a small group of elites at the apex of the hierarchy. Even the local government systems in post-independence Africa became centralised because local authorities could not function independently, and the councillors were unaccountable to the electorate; in fact, the autonomy of the lower tiers of government were progressively whittled away.[6] This tendency is also apparent in present-day South Africa, where the powers of the nine provinces and the over 800 local authorities, although prescribed constitutionally, have still not been devolved adequately to the local levels. The powers of the lower tiers could also be eroded further, as occurred in the rest of Africa, because there is a lack of financial independence. Many of the new local authorities are currently experiencing financial difficulties. It is therefore possible that centralisation in South Africa could occur on a large scale – as was the practice in the rest of Africa – because of the financial impotence of the lower tiers of government. Objectives such as efficient and effective government and administration may as a consequence not be achieved under such difficult constraints.[7]

## THE SOUTH AFRICAN CONTEXT

### South Africa as Powerhouse of Africa

Although South Africa has been dogged by a racist past and some heinous crimes were committed under the apartheid regime, this country nevertheless has still made much headway in the economic and industrial spheres. Some highlights are mentioned below.

- *Science and technology*  Despite its apartheid past, South Africa was and still is a technologically and socially advanced nation. South Africa produces some of the best medical and other specialists in the world. It also has some excellent social scientists. The first human heart transplant was performed in South Africa in 1967. South Africa is also well-known for its industrial development: its diamond and gold mines have generated considerable income and jobs for the country.
- *Joint water schemes*  South Africa has undertaken several large projects with other countries. For instance, the Lesotho Highlands Water Scheme situated on the Katse River in the Maluti Mountain range of Lesotho is one of the biggest water schemes in Africa.[8] The Scheme will act as feeder to the Gauteng (Transvaal) area of South Africa, and will be a boon to water-depleted South Africa after the sluice gates are opened (in 1998).[9] South Africa, as proof of its engineering prowess, has also undertaken dam construction in collaboration with Zimbabwe (for example the Kariba Dam) and in Mozambique (for example the Cabora Bassa scheme). Furthermore, the Orange-Fish Water

Tunnel is 83 kilometres in length and is the longest irrigation tunnel in the world.

• *Electricity generation* South Africa also has one of the largest electricity reticulation networks in Africa, and the Electricity Supply Commission (ESKOM) is the largest generator of electricity in Africa. It produces 97 per cent of all electricity used in South Africa and 60 per cent of all electrical power used in Africa. South Africa also has a nuclear power station at Koeberg near Cape Town, which is the one and only nuclear power station in Southern Africa.[10]

• *Demise of apartheid institutions* In 1994 South Africa became a democracy. This event not only affected South African society in a general sense, but it also influenced the functioning of the public service in particular. The public service began to undergo a radical transformation from a rule-driven apartheid institution to a democratic, people-driven institution. The restructuring of the public service is a matter that is dealt with in detail in this chapter. Since 1994, restructuring has been tackled rather hastily; therefore it has not been all that successful. In fact, voluntary severance packages were granted to the so-called 'old guard', but in the end it was found that the best talents were beginning to leave the public service. Some of the top public functionaries have now conceded that over-hasty transformation may have resulted in the wrong people leaving the public service, and that the public service is still saddled with its dead wood.

• *Developmental initiatives* Suffice it to mention that the new government started out with many good intentions such as the *Masakhane* project (translated as 'let's build together' or sometimes 'let's build one another') to get people to pay for their essential service; the Reconstruction and Development Programme (RDP); and more recently Growth, Employment and Redistribution (GEAR).[11] These programmes have not been as successful as the government would have liked them to be, because there has generally been a culture of dependency over the years. With the new government and the global emphasis on privatisation, the mindset of the people has had to change, and the dependency culture has had to be shaken off. Once the government gains the unwavering support of the population and can muster the necessary human resources to tackle anew the proposed projects, South Africa will once again become a leading-edge nation on the African continent.

● *Advent of democracy in South Africa*   In 1994 South Africa became a fully-fledged democracy under the able leadership and statesmanship of President Nelson Rolihlahla Mandela. Not only has the transition to democracy had a marked effect on South African society in general, but the public service, which prior to 1994 was managed in an authoritarian style with the express purpose of promoting and propping up the apartheid ideology, has also undergone a metamorphosis. Since the April 1994 general election there has been an about-turn in managerial style. Indeed, the 'new' public service has had to reexamine its *modus operandi* to ensure that service delivery is no longer aimed at specific racial groups and categories or pockets of persons, but that the public service caters to the needs of all of South Africa's 45 million inhabitants on a non-racial basis.

This chapter will give a brief historical overview of those forces which from 1795 to 1990 influenced South Africa's constitutional development and which gave rise to the structural and organisational problems of the public service. These are the so-called 'before' events. We will also examine the problems of the public service prior to 1994. Thereafter the chapter will deal with the challenges facing the public service 'after' the 1994 general election.

## EVENTS BEFORE THE RELEASE OF MANDELA IN 1990

This section will briefly sketch the events preceding the release of Nelson Mandela from prison, eventually bringing about the 'miraculous' birth of a 'new' South Africa. To obtain a balanced perspective on matters, it is crucial that the pressure for change in the public service is viewed from various perspectives.

### Historical Perspective

For years South Africa was isolated from the international community as a result of its apartheid policy which became firmly embedded when the National Party came to power in 1948. In fact, South Africa was so unpopular because of its legislated racism that it was regarded by the international community as the polecat of the world. The anti-apartheid activists, who branded apartheid as a crime against humanity and as a heresy, asked the international community to assist in bringing the apartheid regime to a downfall. This led to various punitive measures against the country, including trade and academic boycotts.

So much external pressure was brought to bear on South Africa over the years that at the beginning of 1990 the State President, F.W. de Klerk, released Nelson Mandela after 27 years of imprisonment, and began negotiations with the ANC (African National Congress) and some other previously banned organisations. De Klerk's bold step paved the way for the drafting of a new constitutional dispensation for South Africa.

### Socio-economic Perspective

South African society was traumatised, socially and economically, by the apartheid system. The various racial groups, who were living apart in racially segregated group areas, had little contact with one another. The infrastructure of the country was 'socially engineered' to ensure that the whites remained isolated – in fact forcibly segregated – from the blacks. This expensive and bizarre separatist policy was said to have been part and parcel of the racially superior attitude which the white minority government had adopted, and which helped the National Party to remain in power for 46 years. The separatist policy could also have been linked to the fervent desire to attain full-blooded nationhood, instead of South Africa being regarded as an 'appendage' of Britain.

In the last throes of Nationalist rule there was little economic growth; in fact, there was a negative growth-rate. This negative trend was reversed with the ANC's ascendance to power.

According to Morphew,[12] German nationalism – national socialism (colloquially termed Nazism) – had a significant influence on South African constitutional history and some of the emerging ideologies of the time. The ideology of national socialism surfaced after the return to South Africa of several young Afrikaner academics, including Dr N. Diedericks (State President of South Africa from 1975–78 and head of the *Reddingsdaadbond*, an organisation established for 'saving' the Brothers, and used to promote Afrikaner business); Dr P. Meyer (Head of the South African Broadcasting Corporation (SABC) for 20 years until 1980, and chairperson of the *Broederbond* – the Brotherhood – from 1958–72, which was a secretive Afrikaner organisation (used primarily to promote the interests of Afrikaners); and Dr H.F. Verwoerd (Prime Minister from 1958–66 and coincidentally also a former Minister of Native Affairs from 1950–58). Verwoerd was the arch-architect of most of the apartheid legislation that began to be promulgated in 1951. He was also instrumental in ensuring that South Africa became a Republic, and succeeded in getting South Africa 'ousted' from the British Commonwealth. All three persons had obtained their doctorates in Europe.

These men had brought with them at that stage the

latest thinking from Europe: that is, nationalism and the struggle for nationhood.[13] Nationalism became a fervent ideology in South Africa; it implied love for what is one's own: one's nation, one's citizenship and one's very own South Africa.[14] The three aforementioned men involved the universities, the state and some of the churches in the 'struggle' for a racially segregated South Africa. It was particularly Verwoerd who tried to restrict the flow of black Africans into the urban areas, and who wanted influx control regulations enforced.[15] Verwoerd's intention was to prevent South Africa from being inhabited and run by blacks.[16] Of course, one of the numerous negative consequences of apartheid was that black Africans never gained a proper foothold in South Africa's white urban areas, because home ownership was initially prohibited and later discouraged in these areas, as it was contended that black Africans had to settle in their own homelands (Bantustans) or specifically demarcated territories.

**Religio-cultural Perspective**

For years, the black South African worker felt exploited by the 'greedy' capitalists, who owned most of the large conglomerates and corporations. In reaction to these conditions, some members of particularly the black racial groups favoured the ideology of liberation theology as a mechanism or vehicle of freeing themselves from the oppressive apartheid regime.

Liberation theology came to South Africa in 1971,[17] and rests on a number of assumptions, the most significant being that liberation from oppression (as in South Africa) is not just part of the Gospel; it *is* the Gospel.[18] Liberation theologians often allude to the Old Testament as an example of how God liberated the oppressed Jewish nation from Egyptian bondage through orchestrating the exodus. In the New Testament, Jesus Christ is once again viewed as a liberator who inaugurates a 'new' exodus. The liberation theologians contended that in South Africa's case, God had chosen sides and that He was favourably disposed toward the oppressed (in South Africa's case mostly blacks). God, they said, had turned against the white oppressors. The Kairos Document, as an outflow of the liberation movement, was an example of a prophetic call to action which urged all Christians and the Church to side with the oppressed.[19]

Unfortunately, liberation theology over-emphasised horizontal conflicts, postulating that the evils in society were the result of man's alienation from his fellow man, and a result of the oppressive structures created by man, that is the apartheid structures. The vertical relationship between God and man was not as important as the horizontal relationship(s) between men. Personal sins became secondary while *structural* sins became primary. The way to rectify social injustices, such as apartheid in South Africa, was to destroy the evil structures, such as racial segregation. The end thus justified the means, even if this entailed taking up the armed struggle and destroying innocent civilians in the process. The premise of these arguments, however, was flawed because evil does not reside in forms of government or man-made structures, but in man himself.[20]

From the South African liberation struggle arose the notion that corporate identity and the mobilisation of the masses or proletariat was more important than individual identity. In terms of Marxist thinking this ideology largely corresponded with the emancipation of the working classes from the domination of the elite, that is the bourgeoisie, or the capitalists in the case of South Africa.[21] The ultimate aim of communism was to ensure the downfall of the privileged classes (in South Africa's case the destruction of all vestiges of elitism and colonialism, and of course white minority rule). These aims could be achieved through revolutionary or other means. This revolutionary philosophy was reinforced by the underlying principles of liberation theology.[22]

Undoubtedly the liberation theology movement made the poor the locus of the Church. It was said that the Church grows out of the people, as opposed to the traditional stance of the Christian church that the acceptance of Christ as Saviour of mankind is unconditional and is not determined by one's socioeconomic status – that God does not discriminate against or favour one simply on the basis of whether one is rich or poor.

Liberation theologians were able to influence South African constitutional changes considerably, even though their point of departure and arguments may have been theologically flawed and largely based on Marxist thinking. Fortunately for South Africa, Marxist thinking has dwindled in prominence in many parts of the world today.

**Politico-constitutional Perspective**

South Africa has gone through various stages in its constitutional history and political development. Some of the more prominent events that have occurred, and which appear to have had an indelible impact on the constitutional progress of this country, are outlined below in chronological sequence:

1. 1795–1803: The first British occupation of the Cape (Cape of Good Hope). It was during this period that the British brought their expertise in public administration to South Africa. However, their administration was largely autocratic and did not afford many rights to the individual. This was resented by the Afrikaner.[23]
2. 1803–1806: The Batavian period at the Cape. The Dutch system of government, especially at the local government level, was introduced in Cape Town; however, the Dutch system of governance did not have sufficient time to take root in South Africa.[24]
3. 1806–1910: The second British occupation of the Cape. The British tried to impose the English language upon

the Boers or Afrikaans-speaking South Africans. This resulted in the awakening of a strong Afrikaner spirit, particularly in respect of their language and culture.[25] The struggle by the Afrikaner to retain their cultural identity, language, religion and traditions still continues to this day, and certain rights, such as the equality of languages, were negotiated and thus entrenched in section 31(1)(a) of the 1996 Constitution Act.

4. 1910: The Union of South Africa was established by an act of the British parliament which united the four independent British colonies, namely the Cape of Good Hope, Natal, Orange Free State and Transvaal into a single unitary state.[26] The Union of South Africa largely followed the British Westminster parliamentary system and was ruled by a white minority government. All black African affairs, after Union, were vested in the Governor-General-in-Council, who was regarded as the Paramount Chief of all black tribes.[27] Black affairs were largely centralised and the unitary form of government helped to reinforce the control over blacks.[28] Only a small number of black males were permitted to register as voters after Union.[29] With the promulgation of the *Black Labour Regulation Act*, 1911 (Act 15 of 1911), pass laws were implemented throughout the country, except in the Cape Province where blacks had freedom of movement.[30] These pass laws severely restricted the movement of black Africans, and many other restrictions were also placed on the movements of blacks, such as curfews.

In 1910, a Department of Black Affairs was established and took over the black affairs of the former four colonies. The *Black Land Act*, 1913 (Act 27 of 1913), kept black Africans out of white areas and confined them to scheduled areas, sometimes called native reserves. The *Development Trust and Land Act*, 1936 (Act 18 of 1936), extended the scheduled areas for black Africans even further.

From 1951 the Nationalist government began in earnest to give effect to its separate development policy and the so-called right to self-determination of the ten black ethnic groups in South Africa.[31]

5. 1912: The South African Native National Congress was founded; this later became the African National Congress (ANC) in 1923.

6. 1918: Nelson Mandela was born.

7. 1931: In terms of The Balfour Declaration of November 1926, South Africa became independent from the British Parliament by virtue of the Statute of Westminster, which took effect in 1931.

8. 1936: Black Africans were removed from the general (common) voters' role and placed on a separate voters' roll under the terms of the *Representation of Blacks Act*, 1936 (Act 12 of 1936). This action was a source of enduring dissatisfaction to all disenfranchised blacks, who only regained universal franchise under the 1993 Constitution Act.

9. 1948: The National Party came to power and started implementing its ideology of separate development, sometimes also called apartheid. From this date onwards, the National Party passed a spate of legislative measures to regulate the relations between the four racial groups (that is, whites, coloureds, Indians and blacks) in South Africa. One such piece of legislation was the *Group Areas Act*, 1950 (Act 41 of 1950), and all the subsequent amendments, until it was repealed in 1991.

The National Party, under the leadership of theologian Dr D.F. Malan from 1948–54, feared that racial integration would inevitably result in biological integration. Many of the South African whites at that stage were not only racists at heart, but were also purists, and therefore the politicians used the desire to preserve an untainted white race as a ploy to win the 1948 election, especially by propagating a black-menace mentality among white South Africans.[32]

The idea of creating separate homelands or Bantustans for the ten (black) ethnic groups in South Africa also saw its heyday under the leadership of H.F. Verwoerd from 1958–66.[33] The piece of legislation that gave effect to the Bantustans was the *Promotion of Black Self-Government Act*, 1959 (Act 46 of 1959). Six of the Bantustans remained self-governing territories: Gazankulu, KaNgwane, KwaNdebele, KwaZulu, Lebowa and QwaQwa, while four of them (the so-called TBVC or 'independent' states, that is Transkei, Bophuthatswana, Venda and Ciskei) opted for independence; however, this so-called independence was not recognised in terms of international law.[34] From 1994, these TBVC states were reincorporated into South Africa, but with much bureaucratic difficulty and considerable upheaval to the public servants who had served under the previous dispensation.

The main idea behind the separation of the various races was that black Africans had to stick to their own scheduled areas, and were not supposed to become part of 'white' South Africa. This separatist system became an enduring bone of contention to black Africans who were seen as aliens in their own country, especially when they were caught in areas outside the homelands.[35] The creation of the black homelands also led to the establishment of extensive administrative machinery (bloated bureaucracies) to run the various Bantustans. This resulted in an administrative nightmare and proved to be both costly and socially divisive.

10. 1960: African National Congress (ANC) banned.
11. 1961: The *South Africa Act*, 1909 was repealed by the *Republic of South Africa Constitution Act*, 1961 (Act 32 of 1961). South Africa was no longer the Union of South Africa, but a Republic. In 1961 South Africa left – or rather was forced to leave – the Commonwealth of Nations, and was only accepted back

into the fold in 1994 when it became a democracy
and its racist policies were repealed.

12. 1962: Nelson Mandela was tried in the Rivonia trial
for conspiracy to commit sabotage and was sentenced
to life imprisonment on Robben Island.

13. 1983: The 1961 Constitution Act was repealed by
the *Republic of South Africa Constitution Act*, 1983
(Act 110 of 1983), which introduced a tricameral parliamentary system with chambers for whites (House
of Assembly), coloureds (House of Representatives)
and Indians (House of Delegates). The 1983 Constitution Act, however, once again excluded black
Africans from participating in government; black
affairs, such as black local authorities, were regarded
as 'general affairs', and were under the control of
the central government, while the affairs of whites,
coloureds and Indians were regarded as 'own affairs'.[36]

14. 1990: Nelson Mandela was unconditionally released
from prison and the ban on many of the so-called
'illegal' organisations was lifted. Negotiations commenced in earnest in 1991 for a new constitutional
dispensation for South Africa.

15. 1993: The interim *Constitution of the Republic of South
Africa*, 1993 (Act 200 of 1993), was passed. The 1993
Constitution made provision for a non-racial, democratic South Africa and included a Bill of Rights which
prescribed minimum human rights for all South Africans irrespective of race, gender, religion or language.
The main intention was to prevent the recurrence
of any sort of discrimination as had occurred in South
Africa's historical past. The four provinces were replaced
with nine provinces, sometimes also called regions.

16. 27 April 1994: Up until 1994, full franchise rights
were not granted to black Africans, although persons of mixed racial origin (so-called coloureds) and
Indians could participate on a limited scale in the
constitutional and law-making processes. The first real
democratic elections in South Africa were conducted

in April 1994, when all citizens over the age of 18 years who met certain prescribed criteria could vote in the general elections, without any reference to race, gender, creed, religion and so on. On 10 May 1994, Nelson Mandela was installed as President of the Republic of South Africa.

17. 1996: The 'permanent' *Constitution of the Republic of South Africa*, 1996 (Act 108 of 1996), was passed. This was an improved and expanded version of the 1993 Constitution Act.

## PROBLEMS OF THE PUBLIC SERVICE BEFORE THE 1994 GENERAL ELECTION

Generally speaking the public service, prior to the general election, was characterised by the following traits:

1. *Top-down, non-consultative, authoritarian managerial style*   The previous public service focused on regulation and control and functioned largely as a closed bureaucratic system.[37] Much emphasis was placed on formal structures, drawn along racial and gender lines, to implement the apartheid policy.[38] The public service was rule-driven, so to speak. It was unresponsive to citizens' needs and utilised outdated Weberian management practices.[39] Because a preoccupation with Weberian bureaucratic structures and hierarchical status alienates supervisor from worker, this officious leadership style stifled creativity and initiative under the 'old' dispensation. Today, therefore, it is contended that the 'new' public service must focus on developmental bureaucracy; that is, efforts should be made to ensure the optimal development of all of South Africa's human resources. It should abandon those features which could result in inflexibility and which could retard the response time of the public service to changing circumstances.

The main difficulty with the 'old' public service was that there was a lack of inclusiveness, openness and participation. It possessed its own unique flavour of secretiveness. It is essential, therefore, that the 'new' public service adopt a bottom-up approach to management, so that those at the very lowest levels of the hierarchy are kept informed of developments and are included in the decision-making processes. Therefore, the 1993 and 1996 Constitution Acts now make provision for the organisational restructuring of the public service to establish a unified, decentralised public service with adequate public access and for the devolvement of power to the grassroots levels, instead of concentrating power and centres of control at the apex of the hierarchy.[40]

2. *Lack of an overall, coherent training policy*  Training under the apartheid government was ideologically restricted and fragmented. It is therefore necessary to depart from the traditional modes of uncoordinated training efforts by first assessing the actual needs of staff and then honing training to meet these specific requirements.[41] Training should be undertaken in consultation with all the stakeholders and other interest groups to ensure that training initiatives meet predetermined training objectives appropriate for a 'trans- formed' public service.

3. *Fragmented, racially-divided and unrepresentative public service*  The 'old' public service was rife with racial and ethnic divisions; it was also fragmented and suffered from racial as well as gender imbalances which were historically caused by apartheid.[42] Indeed, the racial distribution of the 'old' public service was severely skewed and was dominated by white males in the upper echelons, from Directors to Directors-General. In 1992, 95 per cent of public servants were white, 4.5 per cent were coloureds and Asians, and 0.6 per cent were black African in the South African central public service and the provinces.[43]

The public service prior to 1994 suffered from a severe identity and legitimacy crisis. Although only a minority of public officials were elderly, white, Afrikaner males, this group occupied virtually all the major management positions.[44]

4. *Admirably equipped to implement apartheid ideology* The 'old' public service faithfully implemented the National Party's apartheid policies; however, due to continuous resistance and international pressure, it was soon realised that this policy was unacceptable to the majority of South Africans.[45] Much of the work in the former Bantustans was done by seconded white officials, causing a skills shortage among the blacks and giving blacks few opportunities to develop managerial skills and technical know-how, thereby reinforcing a dependency culture and leaving blacks reliant upon whites for expertise. Some of the black public servants at that stage who had indeed advanced to higher positions, it is claimed, did so through patronage and sycophantic behaviour to their political masters; they were not equipped to handle a democratic order, but only had the prowess to implement ideologically-founded policies.[46]

5. *Pedantic paternalism and inefficient, unilaterally-imposed service delivery systems* The previous public service was paternalistic toward blacks and unilaterally decided on their behalf what was best for them. This alienated the black majority from the Nationalist government and led to frequent rent boycotts and the non-payment of services. Funds were siphoned off from the black areas to the white residential areas because white areas contained all the major commercial and industrial activity, which provided from half to almost three-quarters of all revenue for white local government activities.[47]

The erstwhile black local authorities were imposed upon the Africans by the *Black Local Authorities Act, 1982* (Act 102 of 1982), and under the terms of all the previous legislated structures such as the Community Councils and the Urban Black Councils. These were actually pseudo-democratic institutions used to delay the process of including blacks in the governing of the country.

If South Africa adopts a consultative stance towards service delivery, it will not only improve the quality of its services but it will also be able to provide services which the inhabitants really need, instead of foisting such services on inhabitants as occurred in the past. In other words, service provision should become consumer-focused and should address actual, not imaginary or unnecessary, consumer needs.

## CHALLENGES FACING THE PUBLIC SERVICE IN THE POST-1994 PHASE

Some of the challenges facing the public service in the post-apartheid era are outlined below:

### A Bottom-up, Participatory, Democratic Managerial Style

Because the 'new' public service is inadequately equipped at this stage for participatory planning and collective recommendations for new policies from all its stakeholders, the planning and recommendatory processes could be enhanced by undertaking strategic management.[48] Furthermore, the need for a democratised administration cannot be underestimated. It facilitates participatory work practices at every level of the institution. Some of the techniques used in democratisation are: the shifting of power to elected officials, the loosening of bureaucratic rigidities through the establishment of diverse task teams, and the utilisation of participatory management. Organisational democracy ranges from non-authoritarian leadership styles to worker self-management. Broadly, three types of participation can be identified in the workplace: pseudo-participation, partial participation and full participation. The last-mentioned is the ideal and refers to situations where collective decisions are reached by a group of equal decision-makers.[49]

The 'new' public service must encourage its public servants to move forward and embrace a democratic professional role that will incorporate some of the current culture with a new democratic and development-oriented ethos. South Africa must ensure that its public institutions become effective, representative and democratic delivery agents.[50]

In the 'old' public service, control was emphasised over innovative management. The former public service was characterised by a secretive ethos; it was therefore difficult to assess its precise nature. Events since February 1990 altered matters significantly, and public servants have begun to reconsider the future and *modus operandi* of the existing public service.[51]

New approaches to the practice of public administration are needed in the new South Africa. This is necessary to ensure that public services improve the quality of life of all inhabitants without discriminating against anyone, and that the public service becomes responsive to the needs of the people. The inhabitants must 'buy into' the service delivery programmes so that these can be properly legitimised and so that payment for services will be promoted and even enforced.

### Extensive *ad hoc* Training and Retraining Programmes

It is essential that (re)training and (re)orientation courses be conducted for both serving and newly-appointed officials involved in the transition process, and that training and development functions are sustained to keep the public service poised to meet the challenges and changing needs of the public. Training courses should be devised and presented by the best qualified people and institutions in order to ensure maximum success.[52]

## A Unified, Non-racial, Gender Representative Personnel Profile

The main purpose of a new approach to public administration is to ensure a just, equitable and non-racial society with equal access for all people to societal resources, including access to essential, rudimentary public services. The public service has had to be de-racialised; however, the problem of racial inequality is so entrenched in South African society that people have to be empowered in all spheres of the economy, especially in those spheres where they have been previously excluded.[53] Therefore, there has to be broad social reform to rectify unequal power relations; the public service has to be revamped to rectify the traditional relationships of domination and subordination.[54]

## Towards Service Excellence, Adding Value, and Meritocracy

The 'new' public service should focus its full attention and energy on superlative service delivery. Service excellence should become the norm instead of the exception; this could effect a savings for the taxpayer, because people will be far more willing to pay for services for which they have asked and with which they are satisfied. The 'old' public service concentrated largely on implementing the apartheid policies that resulted in the quadruplification of services, waste and frequent service breakdowns, particularly in the black local government areas; lack of accountability and disrespect for the governmental authorities was the norm. If quality goods and services are the ultimate aim, then merit should be used as criterion for the appointment of personnel, or, at the very least, merit should be married to affirmative action.

If unqualified persons are appointed to positions for the mere sake of adding colour and not adding value to an institution, then the end result could be a deterioration in the quality of public services.

## A Rightsized and Streamlined Public Service

The public service should be restructured and transformed to ensure that it attains the ideal size to function efficiently and effectively. It must not become bloated. There were complaints about the previous government's ever-expanding public service, which occurred because of the quadruplification of services and the extraordinary complexity created by the apartheid system.[55] However, it would appear that the public service is once again becoming overgrown. In fact, since 1994 when the new government came to power and until December 1996, the South African public service expanded in size from 1.88 million to 1.91 million employees.[56] The attempts by the government to discard dead wood through voluntary severance packages have also backfired because all the best public servants were leaving and going into private business.[57] Therefore, many of the downsizing techniques now need to be rethought.

## Rooting out Corruption

A new code of conduct was recently promulgated for South African public servants in terms of *Government Notice* R.825. Although this code of conduct looks similar to previous codes of conduct, and even bears certain resemblances to universal codes of conduct, its release under the new democratic dispensation is indeed a further step in the right direction to ensuring a 'corruption free' public service. Notwithstanding the good intentions of all codes of conduct, however, even more should be done to curb the unethical behaviour of public servants: otherwise South Africa's fledgling democracy will degenerate into a kleptocracy where people simply take what they want when they see the gap to do so.

The misconduct of public servants is always a contentious matter and, if unearthed, usually receives prominent mass-media coverage. The reason for this is that public servants who do not stick to the rules of the game are not only an incumbrance to their employer, but are also burdensome to taxpayers at whose behest every public functionary holds office. The public in general rely on – indeed, expect – public servants to perform their duties honestly, openly and transparently. However, when public servants start to regard a public office as being lucrative, then the public has every right to be aggrieved.

It is therefore laudable that codes of conduct exist to keep public servants honest, thereby (hopefully) deterring them from succumbing to temptation and unlawfully enriching themselves and members of their families. One must nonetheless bear in mind that a code of conduct merely serves as a guideline to direct the behaviour of public functionaries and cannot be seen as a guarantee of impeccable behaviour. In fact, a code of conduct is only one of many methods of ensuring that public servants stick to the sort of behaviour expected from a functionary who has been placed in a position of trust.

Some of the other methods of ensuring the proper conduct of public servants are:

- Prescribing, adopting and enforcing correct channels of communication and procedures, thus thwarting officials from circumventing and/or undermining the system;
- Prohibiting family members or relatives from working in the same department or even the same institution, thereby preventing collusion and connivance;
- Paying reasonable levels of remuneration to public servants to reduce the risk of their committing theft, although it should be stressed that dishonesty occurs across the socioeconomic spectrum;

- Applying strict sanctions or penalties against those who flagrantly disregard codes of conduct;
- Introducing disciplinary steps to ensure that public functionaries are punished for wrongdoing, thereby serving as examples to others contemplating similar deeds;
- Conducting regular inspections and utilising proper reporting systems to ensure that misdeeds are not over-looked due to insufficient or inadequate control measures being in place;
- Making provisions for extensive internal auditing, that is using *a priori* auditing (auditing that takes place during the implementation of transactions) to prevent fraud before or while it is occurring; and
- Dismissing habitual offenders so that the public service does not harbour undesirables in its ranks who may repeat the same misdeeds time and again.

Although the above-mentioned comments may seem hy-percritical of the 'deficiencies' of codes of conduct, such codes nevertheless remain indispensable documents to achieving a 'clean' public service.


CONCLUSION

The development of the South African public service was integrally bound up with the apartheid system; one cannot be understood without considering the other. And every facet of South African society is intertwined, so that the development of the organisational structures of the South African public service cannot be seen in iso-lation from the rest of society. The post-apartheid approach must be to ensure a just, equitable and non-racial society and to reach out to other Southern African countries through technological projects.

## Notes and References

1. M.J. Balogun and G. Mutahaba (eds), *Enhancing Policy Management Capacity in Africa* (Westford, Conn.: Kumarian Press, 1992), p. 131.
2. *Ibid.*, pp. 131–2.
3. G. Mutahaba, R. Baguma and M. Halfani, *Vitalizing Public Administration for Recovery and Development* (Westford, Conn.: Kumarian Press, 1993), p. 5.
4. *Ibid.*, p. 5.
5. P. Mawhood (ed.), *Local Government in the Third World* (New York: John Wiley & Sons, 1983), p. 27.
6. *Ibid.*, p. 34.
7. V.G. Hilliard and H.F. Wissink, 'The Rationalisation of the Public Service in a Post-Apartheid South Africa', *Administratio Publica*, vol. 7, no. 1 (June 1996) (University of Stellenbosch), p. 77.
8. *The Star*, 25 October 1996.
9. *The Sowetan*, 23 October 1995.
10. *The Illustrated FactoPedia* (Cape Town: Human & Rousseau, 1996), p. 435.
11. See *Boardroom* (Journal of the Southern African Institute of Chartered Secretaries and Administrators) Vol. 2 (Johannesburg: Fox Publishing, 1996), pp. 14–15.
12. D. Morphew, *South Africa. The Powers Behind* (Cape Town: Struik, 1989), p. 69.
13. *Ibid.*, p. 70.
14. K.A. Heard, *General Elections in South Africa, 1943–1973* (London: Oxford University Press, 1974), p. 50.
15. *Ibid.*, p. 74.
16. T.R.H. Davenport and K.S. Hunt, *The Right to the Land* (Claremont: David Philip, 1974), p. 49.
17. R. Gibellini, *The Liberation Theology Debate* (London: SCM Press, 1987), p. 66.
18. D. Morphew, 1989, *op. cit.*, p. 155.
19. M. Cassidy, *The Passing Summer. A South African Pilgrimage in the Politics of Love* (London: Hodder & Stoughton, 1989), p. 32.
20. B. Laurie, *Dominion News*, June 1989, p. 11.
21. M. Rubel, *Marx. Life and Works* (London: Macmillan, 1980), p. 69.
22. *Ibid.*, p. 23.
23. D. Marais, *South Africa: Constitutional Development. A Multi-Disciplinary Approach*, revd edn (Halfway House: Southern Book Publishers, 1991), pp. 36–7.

24. *Ibid.*, pp. 44–5.
25. *Ibid.*, pp. 70–1.
26. *Ibid.*, p. 189.
27. *Ibid.*, p. 237.
28. D. Adlem in D.J. van Vuuren, N.E. Wiehahn, J.A. Lombard and N.J. Rhoodie (eds), *South Africa. A Plural Society in Transition* (Durban: Butterworths, 1985), p. 69.
29. J.J.N. Cloete, *Democracy: Prospects for South Africa* (Pretoria: J.L. van Schaik, 1993), p. 154.
30. V.G. Hilliard, 'Acceptable Black Local Authorities for the Algoa Regional Services Council Area', unpublished thesis (Port Elizabeth: Vista University, 1991), pp. 75–6.
31. J.J.N. Cloete, 1993, *op. cit.*, p. 160.
32. See, V.G. Hilliard, 1991, *op. cit.*, p. 35.
33. See, D. Marais, 1991, *op. cit.*, pp. 242–3.
34. P.S. Botes, P.A. Brynard, D.J. Fourie and N.L. Roux, *Public Administration and Management. A Guide to Central, Regional and Municipal Administration and Management* (Pretoria: Haum, 1992), p. 8.
35. See, D. Marais, 1991, *op. cit.*, pp. 240–1.
36. J.J.N. Cloete, 1993, *op. cit.*, p. 156.
37. S. Cloete and J. Mokgoro (eds), *Policies for Public Service Transformation* (Kenwyn: Juta & Co., 1995), p. 194.
38. See A. McLennan in P. Fitzgerald, A. McLennan and B. Munslow (eds), *Managing Sustainable Development in South Africa* (Cape Town: Oxford University Press, 1995), p. 102.
39. P. Fitzgerald in P. Fitzgerald *et al*, 1995, *op. cit.*, p. 17.
40. *Ibid.*, p. 17.
41. S. Cloete in S. Cloete and J. Mokgoro, *op. cit.*, p. 196.
42. P. Fitzgerald in P. Fitzgerald *et al*, *op. cit.*, p. 17.
43. J. Mokgoro in S. Cloete and J. Mokgoro, *op. cit.*, p. 65.
44. S. Cloete in S. Cloete and J. Mokgoro, *op. cit.*, pp. 193–4.
45. *Ibid.*, p. 193.
46. J. Mokgoro in S. Cloete and J. Mokgoro, *op. cit.*, p. 57.
47. Fitzgerald in P. Fitzgerald *et al*, *op. cit.*, pp. 19–20.
48. S. Cloete in S. Cloete and J. Mokgoro, *op. cit.*, p. 197.
49. A. McLennan in P. Fitzgerald *et al*, *op. cit.*, p. 124.
50. *Ibid.*, pp. 133–4.
51. *Ibid.*, p. 132.
52. S. Cloete in S. Cloete and J. Mokgoro, p. 198.
53. R. Wooldridge and R. Cranko in P. Fitzgerald *et al*, *op. cit.*, p. 330.

54. *Ibid.*, p. 331.
55. A. McLennan in P. Fitzgerald *et al, op. cit.*, p. 103.
56. *Sunday Times*, 4 May 1997.
57. *Sunday Times*, 6 April 1997.

# 10 Bureaucracy and the Alternatives in the Middle East
## Ali Farazmand

## INTRODUCTION

The Middle East is the birthplace of bureaucracy in history. It is also the birthplace of the earliest civilisation, administration, religion, culture and market institutions. Located between the East and the West, the Middle East as a region is not only one of the oldest, if not the oldest, centres of civilisation in the world, it is also one of the richest areas of the modern world. Despite rich resources and old traditions, however, most parts of the Middle East are beset by symptoms of underdevelopment, economic poverty, enduring crises leading to political instability, continuous foreign interventions, and a general lack of progress in terms of democratic institutions.

Administration and civilisation have flourished throughout the long history of the Middle East, and bureaucracy has remained the most dominant institution of governance in the entire region. However, alternatives to bureaucracy have also been strong and flourishing in various parts of the region. Old as it is, the Middle East represents major diversity in all aspects of human life, including religion, governance and administration, and culture. Ranging from Iran in the East to North Africa in the West, there are great variations among the nations in the region, with variations within each country. Despite these variations and the turmoil that has characterised much of the region's long history, bureaucracy has survived all political changes in the Middle East.[1]

This chapter focuses on bureaucracy and public administration in the Middle/Near East. It does not deal with other traditions and institutions of the region.

## HISTORICAL CONTEXT

Bureaucracy has developed in the Middle East with great variations in different nations, and alternatives to bureaucratic systems also vary from nation to nation. The political and administrative history of the region dates back to over ten millennia, and its bureaucratic tradition is as old as civilisation. The first two written alphabets in human history – the Sumerian (present Iraq) and Elamite (early Iran) – developed around 2500 BC, and served the bureaucracy and public administration in Babylonia and the Elamite and Persian empires for almost three millennia.[2]

The bureaucratic tradition has been shaped by the political, social, cultural and economic conditions of the region throughout its long history. Some of these traditions have changed, others have been eliminated, and others have resiliently survived and conditioned the administrative and political systems. This has happened in spite of the modernisation movement that has originated from the West through colonial and neocolonial imperialistic penetration. This trend has produced significant backlash, resistance, and even recurrent revolts and revolutions against foreign interference. Examples include several revolts as well as the 1978–79 revolution in Iran, the Nasser movement in Egypt, the Bäth Party movements in Iraq and Syria, the Libyan and Algerian revolutions, the Yemeni and other movements directed against the colonial, neocolonial and imperialist powers, and their domestic agents.[3]

Among the nations of this historical region, Iran, Turkey, Iraq, Syria, Palestine and Israel, Lebanon, Egypt, Morocco and Arabia constitute the core of the ancient civilisations. Of these, Egypt, Babylon (Iraq), Syria and Iran present the most powerful and oldest traditions of administration and bureaucracy. For example, old Assyria was a major bureaucratic empire until its conquest and annexation in 612 BC by the Iranian Meads, who already had Asia under control, and who then subdued the early Iranian Elamite empire in 600 BC. The Meads then set out to conquer Babylonia, but fell in 559 BC to the rising Persians (their Aryan cousins) under Cyrus the Great, who then also conquered Babylonia and Egypt. Cyrus the Great established the first world-state Achaemenid empire, which stretched from India and north China in the east to Africa and south Europe in the west, with the exception of Athens and Sparta.

Persians were destined to change the political history of the world. They were the first to conceive of the concept of State and to turn it into a reality. All the great powers of that time – such as Babylon, Egypt and Assyria – had developed bureaucratic traditions, but none was comparable to the Persian world-state empire with a gigantic personnel – numbering eight million – and legendary bureaucracy that was both efficient and effective.[4] The combined dimensions and principles of management, strategies of centralisation and decentralisation, a universal and liberal philosophy of 'tolerant governance' towards subject peoples, swift justice administration, effective and efficient communication and road systems, sound financial/taxation management, emphasis on education and the merit system, professionalisation of bureaucracy by training as well as experience, and freedom of religion, language and culture gave the Empire many characteristics of an efficient and democratic system of administration unknown previously.[5] The Persian's two setbacks with the Greeks on the military front were more than offset by their occupation of Athens and by the Persian Gold, which was instrumental in changing and influencing Greek politicians, as well as by the famous King's Peace which the Greeks had to accept.[6]

While the West was in the Middle Age of darkness and decline, Middle Eastern civilisation under Islam enlightened the world and contributed to world civilisation in all aspects of philosophy, sciences, government and public administration. From the tenth to the fifteenth centuries, a number of giant philosophers rose in the Islamic world, mostly in Iran, but also in Egypt, Tunisia, Iraq and elsewhere in the Middle East. Great philosophers and political and administrative thinkers included Ibn Moghaffa (the last Prime Minister of the Sasanid Persian Empire), Rozbeh, (who was converted to Islam by force and who translated to Arabic many treatises, including the famous books of Adabs, *Akhlagh* or *Ethics in Government*, and *Mirrors to Princes*, on governance and administration), Mavardi, Ghazzali, Farabi, Ibn Sina (Avicenna), Nizam-ul-Mulk, Beerouni and Sohrevardi (all from Iran); and Ibn Rushd, Ibn Khaldoon and Ibn Tamyia (from the Arab world). These men made great contributions to world knowledge in politics, governance, administration and organisation theory, as well as to medicine, law, astronomy, science, theology and other areas. Their names appear alongside Socrates, Plato, Aristotle and other great thinkers of the Western Renaissance.[7] While Farabi is known as the Second Teacher after Aristotle, Ibn Sina's 'medical encyclopedia, *Qanun*, remained the textbook for centuries in Europe'.[8]

Bureaucracy and public administration expanded on a mass scale in Persia (Iran) and the Ottoman empire, which also ruled many parts of the Arab world and East Europe. After the fall of the Ottoman empire, the British and French colonial and the American neocolonial rule and interventions have inflicted heavy burdens of dependency and instability on the region.[9] Despite this dependency and Western interventions, the ancient bureaucratic legacies and the medieval Islamic administrative traditions have survived, and their manifestations are evidenced in many aspects of administrative behaviour throughout the region.[10]

Today, the administrative legacies of ancient Egypt, Assyria, Babylon and Iran/Persia are found in the structure, culture and behaviour of bureaucratic systems throughout the region. Even in Israel, the modernising Western concepts and practices of administration and bureaucracy are pushed to the background by the deeply rooted informal and cultural values and institutions that date back to ancient Jewish traditions.[11] This observation is also true of Iran and Turkey, where the modernisation programmes of the West have produced major clashes of culture, values and civilisation.

Political independence has meant little for most of the Middle Eastern nations, for they have remained plagued by a multitude of political, economic, social, military and administrative dependencies on the West. The United States has taken over the hegemonic position that Britain enjoyed until the Second World War. With the exception of Iran, Israel and Turkey, all governments of the Middle East have been subjected to direct colonial rule. And colonial and imperialist influences in the politics and administration of Middle East governments are deep.[12] This dependency is perpetuated by Western foreign aid which has further strengthened the aggressive and unpopular nature of the bureaucratic states – military and civilian – in the region.[13] For example, American aid to Egypt, totalling $20 billion between 1975–88, 'illustrates both the political sensitivity of foreign aid and the unequal impact it has on administrative as opposed to political institutions'.[14] Egyptian intellectuals have continually argued that the United States Agency for International Development 'gathers information for the purpose of manipulating Egyptian politics, engages directly in Egyptian domestic policy-making, and . . . provides cover for intelligence agents'.[15] Direct American intervention in the region has also been a frequent occurrence since the Second World War. A clear example of this is the CIA operatives under Kermit Roosevelt who led the successful military *coup d'etat* in Iran in August 1953.

This action overthrew the popular nationalist government of Iran under Prime Minister Mohammad Mosaddegh and imposed the absolute dictatorship of the Shah on the Iranian people for the next 25 years.[16] Direct military intervention by the US against Lebanon, Syria, Iran and Libya also occurred during the Reagan administration.[17]

Corruption, red tape, bureaucratism, nepotism and other aspects of insensitive bureaucratic culture have characterised modern bureaucracy in the Middle East, producing a fatal duality in their administrative and political systems. In the absence of strong political and other free-floating institutions in society, the bureaucracy – both military and civilian – has emerged as the only major institution of governance and administration.[18] This has also been due to constant foreign intervention and the fear of political leaders – both the popular revolutionary and unpopular – to lose control. The latter has been for controlling the population and for suppressing popular oppositions, whereas the former has aimed at preventing or minimising foreign interference and intervention.[19] Bureaucratisation of Middle East nations was a political phenomenon that took place during the 1950s and 1960s in an effort towards political system-maintenance and regime-enhancement, and much of this process was directed and assisted by the United States and other Western powers.[20] Therefore, except for post-revolutionary Iran, bureaucracy not only administers laws: it usually fashions them.

Middle East nations are governed by different political systems. Although only four major languages – Persian, Turkish, Arabic and Hebrew – are spoken in the region, there is great diversity in ethnic, cultural and administrative systems. Most governments are considered satellites of the United States, European powers and the former Soviet Union, including the Shah's regime in Iran which was considered the 'America's Shah'.[21] Today, post-revolutionary Iran, Syria and Libya seem to have established a pattern of independence in world politics by paying heavy prices economically and politically,[22] and Israel may be considered by some as an integral part of the United States militarily, with a political system featuring key differences with its Arab neighbours. However, the very differences that exist among the various nations of the Middle East

> should not obscure the similarities, such as the heritage of Islam, the presence of foreign influences, the concentration of power and leadership in the hands of the upper and upper-middle classes, and the rise of new elites that link them.[23]

**The Bureaucracy**

Bureaucracy has survived all political changes in the Middle East for several thousands of years. It was established as the early civilisations flourished in Egypt on the Nile, Iran in the East, and Mesopotamia around the major rivers pouring into the Persian Gulf. However, unlike Egypt and Mesopotamia, which developed around major waterways, Iranian civilisation developed in highland valleys as well as in the lowland area around the waterways in Susa, therefore refuting Wittfogel's much pronounced theory of 'hydraulic society'.[24] The growth and development of bureaucracy took on an accelerated pace under the Egyptian monarchical dynasties, with major public work projects; in Assyria and Babylon in their peaceful times; and, most extensively, under the Persian world-state Achaemenid empire, which had the first and largest administrative state in history (559–330 BC). Persian bureaucracy was the most elaborate, professional, extensive and far-reaching; there was no place in the known ancient world that could escape Persian bureaucracy and its impacts. This was true even in the defiant Greek city state of Athens, where Persian gold and bureaucrats as well as diplomats effectively influenced and impacted political and administrative life.

Everywhere the armies of the great king went, there the Achaemenid bureaucracy was planted with all concomitants of administration – military, financial, and judicial – and communication with other provinces and [satrapies] insured by the official language.[25]

The Persian bureaucracy has gained a well-earned reputation in history for being both efficient and effective, and for producing 'excellent administrators'.[26]

While Egyptian bureaucracy lost its independent identity during the Persian era in the sixth century BC, the Persians continued their own tradition as well as those of earlier ones that they inherited, supplemented, supplanted and perfected. Therefore, Persian bureaucracy and its legacies continued through the Parthian and Sasanian empires in Persia, until the fall of the empire to the invading Arabs who established the Islamic rule in 651 AD; although, even then, they adopted the Persian systems of governance, administration and bureaucracy, the only change being the imposition of the Arabic language on the conquered peoples. Following the Islamic empire, the Ottomans as well as the Persians continued the Persian bureaucratic traditions of administration and culture up to 1920, when both systems began transformations in governance, administration and politics. Similarly, impacts of Persian bureaucracy penetrated the Byzantium and Roman administrative systems, who then passed on the borrowed principles and ideas to Western public administration up to modern times.[27]

**Characteristics of the Bureaucracy**

Today, the Middle Eastern bureaucracy and administrative system may be characterised by a number of features found in different nations, with some distinctions differentiating the areas. First, the countries with long histories – such as Iran, Egypt, Iraq, Morocco, Syria and Turkey – seem to have an established tradition of bureaucratic administration that is both traditional and modernised. The traditional values and structures are proudly entrenched in their ancient backgrounds, while in modern times structural reconfiguration and value orientations towards Western concepts of rationality and a dehumanising bureaucratic culture have occurred, together with a fatality that this rational modernity has produced many superficial elements of administration purported to replace the traditional systems of values and structure. The latter has produced a bureaucratic culture that is both alien and repressive to the common people. The bureaucratic system employs an elite highly integrated with the interests of Western capitalism, values, attitudes and structure.

This problem is less pronounced in small countries with a short history, such as Kuwait, Oman and other Gulf states – including Saudi Arabia – where there is no historical bureaucratic system in place and the traditional bureaucracy is dominated by the royal families, and also where Western attitudes are deeply entrenched.[28] Countries like Iraq Syria and Libya have broken this circle, although Iraq and Syria seem to be trapped in a monolithic system of politics, with a bureaucratic elite dominating the civilian and military bureaucracies. Only post-revolutionary Iran has produced a good degree of pluralism, with a number of political and civil institutions that check the bureaucracy effectively.[29]

There is a great deal of overlap and integration between political and bureaucratic elites, and the military elite is also an integral part of the strategic alliance in governance and administration in which Western dominance are evidenced. This pattern has worked both positively and negatively in many of these nations, but it does not allow independent systems of checks and balances to monitor bureaucratic behaviour and performance. Therefore, the bureaucratic elites have little or no incentive to become accountable to citizens. In effect, they become agents of foreign-led modernisation projects, in which foreigners benefit most by keeping these nations both dependent and backward. This bureaucratic–military elite is instrumental in insuring the global hegemony and economic exploitation of local nations by multinational corporations protected by Western powers. The result is a lack of bureaucratic responsiveness to the populace.

Also significant is the lack of bureaucratic representation and the suppression of ethnic expression in the region. Much of this ethnic discontent has been fueled by outsiders, and this has exacerbated the bureaucratic lack of representation of minorities. Similarly, women, while constituting a major part of the workforce in some countries like Iran, Turkey and Egypt, have been underrepresented in higher positions of bureaucratic and administrative systems. Their situation varies from country to country. In Saudi Arabia and many of the Arab countries, their contribution to and participation in public administration is much more limited than in Iran, Turkey and Israel, where progress has been significant.

Corruption is another problem in the administration and politics of all political systems, and the Middle East has its share. Generally, corruption is a chronic problem at the political appointees level, but it also appears in various forms in the career bureaucracy, ranging from petty stealing of office supplies to embezzlement and misappropriation of funds. Attempts to combat corruption have been tried, and many have failed due to foreign involvement, domestic political instability, corruption at the political leadership level, and financial motives such as low salary and high inflation rates. The biggest share of corruption is found at the bureaucratic elite level, where dealings with large contractors – domestic and international – are conducted frequently. Corruption was both pervasive and accepted at the highest level of the military, civilian and court systems under the Shah.[30] Corruption also runs high in the Arab countries of Egypt, Saudi Arabia, Jordan, Morocco, Oman, Kuwait, Iraq and elsewhere, where Jreisat reports 'huge bribes to senior officials or members of the ruling dynasties'.[31] Government contracts produce legendary profits for the bureaucratic, military and political elites. Corruption is 'institutionalized, partly as a safety valve for the badly paid bureaucracy'.[32] Similar observations are reported in Turkey, where the military elite dominates Turkish politics, administration and bureaucracy, with profitable contracts with the NATO powers.

Enduring crises in the political and economics systems of the region have also paralysed the administrative capacity of bureaucracies. Political instability, aggravated by foreign interference and interventions, has caused problems for the bureaucracy. Often political leaders attempt to deal with political crises by curbing individual rights and freedom as well as by tightening control and dominating the bureaucracy. This has been intended to prevent coups and counter-coups, and to promote the stability and safety of the system.[33]

There is the general tendency of implementation to lag behind policy-making at the top. Rhetorical statements are too frequent, while administrative implementation is far behind or nonexistent in many situations. Implementation is also slow due to a lack of funding, poor skills and inadequate resources and administrative capacity, despite the over-population of the bureaucracy. Understaffing in required areas of expertise is an endemic problem; for example, in Egypt, the Nasserist tradition persists for provision of employment to all Egyptian college graduates.[34] The understaffing of skilled personnel and overstaffing of unskilled workers is a common problem in almost all developing countries, including the Middle East nations of Saudi Arabia, Sudan, Iraq, Jordan, Tunisia, Morocco and Egypt.[35]

Reforming the administrative system has been a recurrent event in most of the countries in the region, with various degrees of success and failure. Most of the reforms have been from above, and political and administrative elites have often enforced them as they felt necessary for political, economic and social purposes. This is a worldwide phenomenon, and the Middle East is no exception.[36] In pre-revolutionary Iran, administrative reform meant bureaucratisation of society for system-maintenance and regime-enhancement.[37] Similar observations can be made of Turkey and almost all Arab nations, especially Iraq, Egypt, Saudi Arabia, Jordan and Turkey. Israel may be a little different, where reforms have focused mostly on military, security and national capacity-building to counter the rest of the countries in the region. The recent administrative reforms have of course been launched in compliance with the prescriptions of the World Bank and IMF, requiring structural adjustments, pubic–private sector reconfiguration, privatisation and downsizing the public workforce. Critics have argued that much of these foreign-imposed privatisations and structural adjustments have benefitted the international capital and the Western governments rather than helping the governments and peoples in the region.[38] Exceptions are Iran and Libya, where privatisation has been considered with caution and without the pressures of the IMF or World Bank, which have pushed it as an ideology to promote international capital among developing nations.[39]

'A ruler dominated bureaucracy' seems to play a major administrative and political role in many countries, including especially Saudi Arabia, Jordan, Egypt and small Gulf states, where regime and public-service goals are mixed and confused.[40] Almost all governments tend to control their bureaucracies to serve the interests of the ruling elites and regimes in power. This is also true in the Middle East. The only exception may be post-revolutionary Iran, and to some extent Israel. Bureaucracy in these countries tends to balance politics and public service. Israel is too preoccupied with the constant quest and obsession for military and security superiority over the region, while Iran's Islamic Republic is committed to the demands of the poor and lower class, as well as to its reassertion as a major power in world politics.[41]

Informal organisations and family networks play major roles in the formal structure of bureaucracy in the Middle East. In fact, informality is a dominant feature of Middle

Eastern culture. Technical organisational rationality and bureaucratic structure are often ignored, overlooked and abridged by an informal system of communication, information-processing, and decision-making. Getting something done through informal processes is much easier and faster than through the formal structure of the bureaucracy. This has had both positive and negative consequences for the administrative systems in the region. Positively, it produces results and keeps rigid rules ineffective; negatively, it tends to destroy organisational rationality and delivers a fatal blow to the bureaucratic elites who tend to stick to rules and procedures. It also exposes corruption and blows the whistle on repressive, corrupt and unaccountable elites.

Bureaucracy in the Middle East is also a place where members of the intelligentsia find employment. Since most of the bureaucrats come from the educated middle and lower-middle classes, the system tends to house many intellectuals and individuals who are critical of the regime in power. The role of bureaucracy in various revolutions, including the Iranian revolution, must be noted.[42] Similar observations may be made in Egypt, Sudan, Iraq, Turkey and elsewhere.

**Bureaucracy in Transition**

A central feature of Middle Eastern bureaucracies is their transitional character, and the direction of change and transition varies from country to country. Until the 1970s, it was generally perceived that – as the main rational institution of administration and governance – bureaucracy was changing and developing toward the Weberian concept of rationality found to some extent in the West. The dominant exporters of this rational bureaucratic model were the United States, Britain, Germany and France. This gradual change has gone through several transitional stages since the 1980s, but it has taken different directions in different parts of the region.

One major development has been the anti-bureaucratic sentiment expressed strongly by citizens and political and business elites. Generally, there has been a constant clash between the bureaucratic culture associated with un- popular authoritarian and repressive regimes prone to establish firm control over citizens' rights and freedom on the one hand, and the popular culture of the people, suspicious of the state bureaucracy and desirous of freedom, on the other hand.[43] International corporations and major superpowers tended to perpetuate this problem by assisting unpopular regimes with more repressive instruments in both military security and civilian admin- istration. Examples include Iran under the Shah, Iraq, Egypt before and after Nasser, Algeria, Turkey and the rest of the region. In the postcolonial, imperialistic era, bureaucracy in most countries of the region has been identified by their peoples as an institutional instrument of repression, exploitation and control by both external powers and their local regimes.[44] Today, much of this antibureaucratic, pro-business movement has been gen- erated from the United States and Britain under the conservative governments of Reagan and Thatcher, and is still continuing at a global level.

Another major development in the region has been the ideological trend of privatisation as a public policy to reduce government size and expenditures, to promote corporatisation and commercialisation of public services, and to promote private enterprise systems around the world. Beginning in the early 1980s, this global policy has been promoted by local business elites as well as the military and political elites under the global pressures of the IMF, the World Bank and the Western powers.[45] With the exception of Iran, Libya and Syria, almost all governments of the region have been following a major privatisation policy, despite the lack of governmental regulatory schemes and the dangerously ill-equipped private sector as an alternative to public administration. This policy only benefits local and international business elites.[46] It has been carried out in most places 'under pressure/temptation from globalised capitalism and from its international institutions'.[47]

Increasing professionalisation of bureaucracy and of public administration is another manifestation of the transitional changes that are taking place in major parts of the region. Although merit system development is slow in the region, professionalisation and appreciation for professional administration is growing, as all nations of the region are in need of expertise for national development. This trend is strong in Iran, Turkey, Israel, Libya, and to some extent in Egypt and Iraq. Saudi Arabia has been trying to develop a viable indigenous administrative personnel to replace the three million foreign employees and workers. Bureaucratic professionalisation is especially interesting in Iran, which went through a massive bureaucratisation process during the 1960s and 1970s under the Shah to increase control, system maintenance and regime enhancement. After the Revolution in 1978–79, the bureaucracy experienced two stages of transition: debureaucratisation along with the radicalisation of society until 1983, followed by the process of institutionalisation of governmental organisations and of the partial rebureaucratisation of revolutionary foundations and organisations since 1983.[48]

In the 1990s, antibureaucratic feeling has grown in Iran, which now has the largest public sector in the region. The need for professional experts is also recognised, and the government has been attempting to attract Iranians back from abroad while at the same time working, with a good record of success, to indigenise Iran's administrative capacity, particularly through Islamicisation of the whole administrative system.[49] However, the antibureaucratic sentiment in Iran is generated mainly by the popular culture as well as by some leading government elites, whose genuine efforts have been aimed at improving life for the common/working-class people. The process of bureaucratisation also took its course in the Arab world and in Turkey,[50] and the bureaucrats were considered, during the decades preceding 1980, as 'agents of change' in Egypt and elsewhere;[51] but antibureaucratic sentiments and privatisation ideologies are widespread in the entire Middle East, including Egypt.[52]

Still another development has been the noticeable impact the Iranian Revolution of 1978–79 and the Islamic Republic have had on the minds of the people and the governments of the region. The bureaucracy in the Middle East has often harboured many members and sympathisers of the revolutionary intelligentsia who have contributed to the radicalisation of society and democratisation of the administrative systems. This is a gradual, important and qualitative change that has contributed to the transitional development of bureaucracy in the region.[53]

**Alternatives to Bureaucracy**

Alternatives to bureaucracy and bureaucratic administration have always been major subjects of discussion in academic and practical circles around the world. In the Middle East, several of these alternatives have arisen, but none of these can replace bureaucracy as the main institution of governance.[54] Attempts to abolish bureaucracy – even by the most radical revolutionaries of this century – have failed.[55]

One alternative to bureaucracy and bureaucratic administration in the Middle East is its unique culture. This culture is strongly rooted in the glory of the early civilisations outlined at the outset of this chapter. The past is a formidable stronghold against the pressures of current countercultures, whether bureaucratic or the dehumanising rational capitalism of the West. Domination of the region by Western powers is seen by Middle Easterners as a temporary, short-lived phenomenon. Their outlook is far broader and reaches beyond horizons, far from the shortsightedness of the Westerners interested in hegemony and control of the region and their peoples and resources under any pretext. This feeling of pride in the past is certainly very strong among Iranians as well as among Egyptians and some others in the region. Generations are taught ancient history, its glory, and advancements in civilisation and administration. Culture forms the fabric of society and glues together the parts or elements that otherwise function separately. The culture of the Middle East is anti-bureaucratic, especially in terms of Western forms of bureaucracy which is seen as an institutional arm of foreign domination, exploitation and interferences in the domestic affairs of the region. This cultural trend is promoted through family ties, communitarian relationships, Islam, and social circles found in many parts of the region.[56]

Social circles and informal networks constitute a particularly significant alternative to bureaucracy in public administration. In Iran social circles – *dowrehs* – are informal gatherings of relatives, friends, associates and those with other forms of relational ties. They are informal, with powerful formal impacts and influences on public policy-making and administration. This is a unique structure of social organisation that has flourished among Iranians for thousands of years.[57] Social circles can be open and inclusive, but they can also be very closed and exclusive, especially when politics and administration are involved. They are much more than cliques, and certainly more than simple informal gatherings. Many significant decisions in politics, administration, culture and professions are made during these informal circle meetings, which rotate among members' houses. *Dowrehs* cut many obstacles of bureaucracy in policy-implementation as well as policy development and decision-making.[58]

Informal relations also serve as an effective mechanism of administration. It is much easier to get things done through informal connections, relationships, networking and friendship. Through informal relations, one can accomplish in a few hours what would take a year of bureaucratic processing. In fact, without the assistance of informal mechanisms, it is generally futile to attempt to accomplish tasks bureaucratically. Informal systems of communication and administration have proven to be effective alternatives to bureaucracy throughout the region. This system was highly pronounced through the first stage of the 1978–79 revolution, when popular, grassroots organisations rose spontaneously through the work of people of all professions and backgrounds. These informal organisations replaced bureaucracy and took over its tasks of public-service delivery and implementation of developmental projects.[59] This informal system of administration is also found in other parts of the region, including Israel.[60]

Cooperative systems in agriculture, business and certain industrial sectors are another alternative to bureaucratic administration. Cooperatives are considered to be a major sector to be developed for promotion of self-help and economic justice in the post-revolutionary Iranian Constitution. Despite some progress in this direction, co-operatives have not developed in the region as a whole, partly due to their democratic and independent tendencies that run counter to the region's centralising authoritarian administrative systems.

Still another alternative to bureaucracy is to be found in the tradition of 'team' and 'self-help' in production and administrative service delivery. Team structure and cooperative, community-based administration were alive and active in Iran until 1960, when the Shah's massive bureaucratisation led to their virtual extinction. However, teams, cooperatives and families have appeared in the post-revolutionary administration as major alternatives to bureaucracy.[61]

Another key alternative to bureaucracy in the Middle East is the indigenous system of administration and organisation, a legacy of the ancient and Islamic periods. Significant aspects of the ancient traditions of public administration have survived for millennia. It serves not only the formal administrative system, but it also brings the popular culture closer to the bureaucratic culture mentioned earlier. Modern, Westernised bureaucracy – modeled after the Weberian ideal-type – has been exported by Westerners to make local bureaucracies more conducive to capitalist development, but this increasing rationalisation of bureaucracy has resulted to a great extent in the dehumanisation of organisation and administration. Thus the bureaucratic culture of rational administration has come into conflict with the traditional, indigenous systems of administration which contain a high degree of personalism, informalism and humanism. The personal touch is still alive and people are proud of it. In fact, it is a positive aspect of Middle Eastern civilisation that has survived the massive pressures of the rational and dehumanising bureaucratic and business cultures of the West.[62] Commercialisation, commoditisation, and marketisation of public service and administration have been resisted by many peoples in the region, especially by the intelligentsia and conscious elites who understand the danger of degrading human beings to commodities and valuing everything on a monetary basis in the market system.[63] This is especially counter to the religious values that are shared by devout peoples in the region, both Islamic and Jewish.

Finally, therefore, religion has played a key alternative to bureaucracy. Mosques and temples have always been major organisations through which many functions of public-service delivery and development projects have been carried out, and certainly they have done a remarkable job in crisis and emergency situations. Islamic values are contrary to bureaucratic cultures in many ways, and Iran's Islamic system of administration is considered by some experts as an alternative administrative system, especially for the Islamic world.

As an alternative to bureaucracy, Islamic administration is based on a totally different set of administrative, political, social and human values, attitudes and structure. It is a holistic system of governance, administration and organisation. Islamic administrators internalise many values that are primarily aimed at serving the Islamic community, God and Islam. In this way of thinking, not only piety is a central character in administrative behaviour, but also equity, fairness and justice. Efficiency is not lost in the organisational process; in fact, waste and corruption are considered among the major punishable sins. Organisationally, bureaucracy is only one of the institutional arrangements for administration of public affairs. Other institutions mentioned above also constitute the major organisational structures of administration in the Islamic *ummat* or community.[64]

The post-revolutionary Iranian public administration functions have been carried out by (a) the formal bureaucracy – with both its ancient and modern features– which has gone through significant changes in structure, process and attitude; (b) revolutionary organisations with antibureaucratic characteristics; (c) non-governmental organisations; (d) the religious institutions located in mosques, Islamic centres and societies, and Zoroastarian institutions; and (e) informal networks and organisations, including teams, cooperative systems and family organisations. Of these organisational and administrative arrangements, Islamicisation of the administrative system has been successful and has produced unique features as an alternative model of administration for development, especially in Islamic countries.[65]

**Notes and References**

1. D. Rustow, 'The Military in Middle Eastern Society', in S.N. Fisher (ed.), *The Military in the Middle East: Problems in Society and Government* (Columbus, Ohio: Ohio State University Press, 1963).
2. *The Cambridge Ancient History* (CAH), Vol. I, Part II, Vol. VI (1971, 1953) (Cambridge, UK: Cambridge University Press); R. Ghirshman, *Iran: From the Earliest Times to the Islamic Conquest* (New York: Penguin, 1954).

3.   M.E.L. Mallowan, *Early Mesopotamia and Iran* (London: Thames & Hudson, 1965).
4.   CAH, *op.cit.*; A. Olmstead, *History of the Persian Empire: The Achaemenid Period* (Chicago: University of Chicago Press, 1948); Richard Frye, *The Heritage of Persia* (New York: The World Publishing Co., 1963); A. Farazmand, 'Administration of the Persian Achaemenid World-State Empire: Implications for Modern Public Administration', *International Journal of Public Administration*, vol. 21, no. 1(1998), pp. 25–87.
5.   Richard Frye, *The Golden Age of Persia* (New York: Harper & Row, 1975).
6.   R. Ghirshman, *op. cit.*; J.M. Cook, *The Persian Empire* (New York: Schoken Books, 1983); R. Frye, *op. cit.*; A. Farazmand, 'Bureaucracy and Revolution: The Case of Iran', in Ali Farazmand (ed.), *Handbook of Comparative and Development Public Administration* (New York: Marcel Dekker, 1991b), pp. 755–68).
7.   E.I.J. Rosenthal, *Political Thought in Medieval Islam: An Introductory Outline* (Cambridge: Cambridge University Press, 1962).
8.   *Ibid.*, p. 282.
9.   James Bill and Robert Springborg, *Politics in the Middle East*, 4th edn (Glenview, Ill.: Scott Foresman, 1990).
10.  *Ibid.*
11.  David Nachmias and David Rosenbloom, *Bureaucratic Culture* (New York: St Martin's Press, 1978).
12.  Edward Said, *Culture and Imperialism* (New York: Alfred A. Knopf, 1993).
13.  Fred Riggs, 'Bureaucrats and Political Development: A Paradoxical View', in Joseph LaPalombara, (ed.), *Bureaucracy and Political Development* (Princeton, N.J.: Princeton University Press, 1963).
14.  J. Bill and R. Springborg, *op. cit.*, p. 234; Marvin Weinbaum, *Egypt and the Politics of U.S. Aid* (Boulder, Col.: Westview Press, 1986).
15.  *Ibid.*
16.  Kermit Roosevelt, *Countercoup: The Struggle for the Control of Iran* (New York: McGraw Hill, 1979); Ali Farazmand, *The State, Bureaucracy, and Revolution in Modern Iran: Agrarian Reform and Regime Politics* (New York: Praeger, 1989).
17.  J. Bill and R. Springborg, *op. cit.*, p. 233.
18.  F. Riggs (1963), *op. cit.*
19.  Jamil Jreisat, *Politics Without Process: Administering*

*Development in the Arab World* (Boulder, Col.: Rienner, 1997); A. Farazmand (1989), *op. cit.*; J. Bill and R. Springborg, *op. cit.*

20.  A. Farazmand (1989), *op. cit.*; Ali Farazmand, 'Bureaucracy and Revolution: The Case of Iran', in Ali Farazmand (ed.), *Handbook of Comparative and Development Public Administration* (New York: Marcel Dekker, 1991b), pp. 755–68.

21.  Richard Cottam, 'Goodbye to America's Shah', *Foreign Policy*, vol. 34 (1979b).

22.  Fred Halliday, *Dictatorship and Development*, 2nd edn (New York: Penguin, 1979); R. Cottam (1979b), *op. cit.*

23.  David Long and Bernard Reich, 'Introduction', in David Long and Bernard Reich (eds), *The Government and Politics of the Middle East and North Africa*, 2nd edn (Boulder, Col.: Westview Press, 1986), p. 2.

24.  Karl Wittfogel, *Oriental Despotism: A Comparative Study of Total Power* (New Haven, Conn.: Yale University Press, 1957).

25.  R. Frye (1963), *op. cit.*, p. 97.

26.  *Ibid.*, p. 53; J.M. Cook, *op. cit.*; Ali Farazmand, 'State Tradition and Public Administration in Iran in Ancient and Contemporary Perspectives', *Handbook of Comparative and Development Public Administration* (New York: Marcel Dekker, 1991a), pp. 255–75; Herodotus, *Aubrey de Selincourt*, trans. with an introduction by A.R. Burn, *The Histories* (New York: Penguin 1948, 1972).

27.  A. Farazmand (1998), *op. cit.*; R. Frye (1963), *op. cit.*

28.  Fuad Khuri, 'The Study of Civil–Military Relations in Modernising Societies in the Middle East: A Critical Assessment', in Roman Kolkowicz and Andrezki Korbonski (eds), *Soldiers, Peasants, and Bureaucrats: Civil–Military Relations in Communist and Modernising Societies* (London: George Allen & Unwin, 1982); Nazih Ayubi, 'Political Correlates of Privatization Programs in the Middle East', *Arab Studies Quarterly*, vol. 14 nos. 2, 3 (Spring/Summer 1989), p. 33; J. Bill and R. Springborg, *op. cit.*

29.  A. Farazmand (1989), *op. cit.*; Ali Farazmand, 'Religion and Politics in Contemporary Iran: Shi'a Radicalism, Revolution, and National Character', *International Journal on Group Rights*, vol. 3, no. 3 (1996a), pp. 227–57; Ali Farazmand, 'Introduction: The Comparative State of Public Enterprise Management', in Ali Farazmand (ed.), *Public Enterprise Management: International Case Studies*

(Westport, Conn.: Greenwood Press, 1996b), pp. 1–27; Ali Farazmand, 'Professionalism, Bureaucracy, and Modern Governance: A Comparative Analysis', in Ali Farazmand (ed.), *Modern Systems of Government: Exploring the Role of Bureaucrats and Politicians* (Thousand Oaks, Cal.: Sage, 1997), pp. 48–73.

30.  Marvin Zonis, *The Political Elite of Iran* (Princeton, N.J.: Princeton University Press, 1971); A. Farazmand (1989), *op. cit.*

31.  J. Jreisat (1997), *op. cit.*, pp. 97, 61, 228.

32.  N. Ayubi, *op. cit.*, pp. 97, 61, 228; Joseph Jabbra, 'Bureaucracy and Development in the Arab World', *Journal of Asian and African Studies*, vol. 24, nos 1, 2 (January/April 1989), p. 60; J. Bill and R. Springborg, *op. cit.*

33.  J. Jreisat (1997), *op. cit.*

34.  J. Bill and R. Springborg, *op. cit.*

35.  N. Ayubi, *op. cit.*

36.  G. Peter, 'Government Reorganisation: A Theoretical Analysis', in Ali Farazmand (ed.), *Handbook of Bureaucracy* (New York: Marcel Dekker, 1994), pp. 165–82.

37.  A. Farazmand (1989) *op. cit.*; A. Farazmand, 'Bureaucracy, Bureaucratization, and Debureaucratization in Ancient and Modern Iran', in Ali Farazmand (ed.), *Handbook of Bureaucracy* (New York: Marcel Dekker, 1994), pp. 675–86.

38.  B. Rich, *Mortgaging the Earth: The World Bank, Environmental Improvement, and the Crisis of Development* (Boston, Mass.: Beacon Press, 1994); R. Kuttner, *The End of Laissez-Faire: National Purpose and the Global Economy After the Cold War* (New York: Alfred A. Knopf, 1991).

39.  A. Farazmand (1996b), *op. cit.*

40.  M. Fainsod, in Ferrel Heady (ed.), *Public Administration: A Comparative Perspective* (New York: Marcel Dekker, 1996), p. 312.

41.  A. Farazmand (1996a), *op. cit.*; Fred Halliday, 'Introduction: Iran and the World: Reassertion and its Cost', in Anoushirvan Ehteshami and Manshour Varasteh (eds), *Iran and the International Community* (London and New York: Routledge, 1991), pp. 1–6.

42.  A. Farazmand (1989), *op. cit.*; A. Farazmand (1994), *op. cit.*

43.  A. Farazmand (1989), *op. cit.*

44.  *Ibid.*; Albert Hourani, *A History of the Arab Peoples*

Ali Farazmand 267

(Cambridge: The Belknap Press of Harvard University Press, 1991).
45. Michael Todaro, *Economic Development in the Third World*, 4th edn (New York: Longman, 1989); R. Kuttner, *op. cit.*; A. Farazmand (1996b), *op. cit.*
46. John G. Merriam, 'Privatization and Debureaucratization: A Comparative Analysis of Bureaucratic Alternatives', in Ali Farazmand (ed.), *Handbook of Bureaucracy* (New York: Marcel Dekker, 1994), pp. 319–30; Robert Cunningham and Yaser Adnan, 'Public Enterprise Management in Jordan: Small Steps Toward Privatization', in Ali Farazmand (ed.), *Public Enterprise Management: International Case Studies* (Westport, Conn.: Greenwood Press, 1996), pp. 189–210; Ruben Mendez, *International Public Finance: A New Perspective on Global Relations* (New York: Oxford University Press, 1992).
47. N. Ayubi, *op. cit.*
48. A. Farazmand (1994), *op. cit.*
49. *Ibid.*
50. Jamil Jreisat, 'Bureaucratization of the Arab World: Incompatible Influences', in Ali Farazmand (ed.), *Handbook of Comparative and Development Public Administration* (New York: Marcel Dekker, 1991), pp. 665–76; Metin Heper, 'Bureaucracy in the Ottoman–Turkish Polity', in Ali Farazmand (ed.), *Handbook of Comparative and Development Public Administration* (New York: Marcel Dekker, 1991), pp. 659–74.
51. J.G. Merriam, *op. cit.*
52. *Ibid.*
53. A. Farazmand (1996), *op. cit.*; Richard Cottam, *Nationalism in Iran* (Pittsburgh: University of Pittsburgh Press, 1979); F. Halliday 1979 *op. cit.*
54. A. Farazmand (1997), *op. cit.*; Ferrel Heady, *Public Administration: A Comparative Perspective* (New York: Marcel Dekker, 1988); Fred Riggs, 'Bureaucratic Links Between Administration and Politics', in Ali Farazmand (ed.), *Handbook of Comparative and Development Public Administration* (New York: Marcel Dekker, 1991), pp. 485–510.
55. A. Farazmand (1989), *op. cit.*; A. Farazmand (1994), *op. cit.*; V. Illich Lenin, *State and Revolution* (New York: International Publishers, 1971).
56. A. Farazmand (1989), *op. cit.*; James Bill, *The Politics of Iran: Groups, Classes, and Modernization* (Columbus, Ohio: Charles Merril Press, 1972); M. Zonis, *op. cit.*

57. Ali Farazmand, 'Bureaucratic Politics under the Shah: Development or System Maintenance; a Study of Administrative Theory and Behavior', PhD dissertation in Public Administration, the Maxwell School of Syracuse University, Syracuse, New York, 1982; J. Bill, *op. cit.*
58. M. Zonis, *op. cit.*
59. Ali Farazmand, 'The Impacts of the Revolution of 1978–89 on the Iranian Bureaucracy and Civil Service', *International Journal of Public Administration*, vol. 12 no. 4 (1987); A. Farazmand (1989), *op. cit.*; A. Farazmand (1994), *op. cit.*
60. D. Nachmias and D. Rosenbloom, *op. cit.*; Ali Farazmand, 'Bureaucracy and Revolution: The Case of Iran', in Ali Farazmand (ed.), *Handbook of Comparative and Development Public Administration* (New York: Marcel Dekker, 1991b), pp. 755–68.
61. A. Farazmand (1989), *op. cit.*; A. Farazmand (1996a), *op. cit.*
62. N. Ayubi, *op. cit.*
63. A. Farazmand (1996a), *op. cit.*
64. *Ibid.*
65. A. Farazmand (1996b), *op. cit.*

# 11 Development Administration and its Alternatives in Latin America and the Caribbean: Reforms and Redirection
Carl E. Meacham

## INTRODUCTION

As Latin America and the Caribbean move towards the twenty-first century, reforms are being consolidated, governments stabilised and new directions charted. Military governments have given way to elected governments. With a few exceptions, however, such as the Commonwealth Caribbean, Panama, Haiti and Costa Rica, the armed forces continue to share power with elected governments in arrangements that have been aptly referred to by Brian Loveman as 'protected democracies'.[1]

The Commonwealth Caribbean – new to self-government in the 1960s and 1970s – had escaped the onus of militarism by having the British agree to handle their defense; then, with U.S. urging, it had created lightly armed military units that pose little danger to elected governments.

In Latin America and the Caribbean sub-region – emerging from the economic stagnation of the 1980s – the private sector's economic performance has improved. Non-governmental organisations continue to play a key role, and governments have adopted some of the

269

neo-liberal reforms associated with economic advancement. On the other hand, extreme poverty persists, crowded and polluted urban centres are home to 70 per cent of Latin America's population, and biodiversity remains threatened.

This chapter focuses on reform activities in Latin American and Caribbean nations between the early 1980s and mid-1997. Examples of reforms and programmes are offered that take into account the regions' Western orientation and their attempts to internationalise as well as efforts at indigenisation.

## PUBLIC ADMINISTRATION IN THE EVOLVING DEMOCRACIES IN THE WESTERN HEMISPHERE: POST-1980

The transitions to democracies in Latin America signalled the requirement for substantive administrative reform. Congressional and state gubernatorial elections in Brazil in 1982 were akin to an opening volley in a war for democracy. Raul Alfonsin took office as the civilian-elected President of Argentina in December 1983. Tancredo Neves won the Brazilian presidency in 1985, followed by the election of a national government in 1986. Patricio Alywin was elected Chile's president in 1989. Violeta Barrios de Chamorro became Nicaragua's president in 1990.

The political changes were not nearly as dramatic in the Caribbean. One of the most significant events was the US invasion of Grenada in 1983, the Reagan Administration's putative attempt to oust Cuban communists and help establish democracy in Grenada. Under Fidel Castro, Cuba remained communist. With US guidance and assistance, Haiti held the first democratic election in its 200-year history in 1990. Despite gaining independence in 1981 and conducting democratic elections, the poor and small island of Antigua remained under the control of the infamous Vere Bird clan. Bird was its first prime minister in 1981. Lester Bird, his son, is the current prime minister.

In general, the new governments have maintained the existing bureaucracies, traditional ministries, corporations and state agencies. New ministerial offices have also been created. Haiti established a Ministry of Women's Rights in the early 1990s. Ministries of Family and Youth joined the more traditional cabinet offices in Venezuela in the mid-1990s. A Ministry of Culture and Sport was established in Guatemala in the early 1990s. Several retired military officers with allegedly difficult-to-find expertises in the civilian populations have been appointed to head state corporations and agencies. To mitigate military influence, Honduran democrats, however, disbanded the military's corrupt Public Security Force. A civilian Directorate of Criminal Investigation (DIC) was created in 1996, and placed under another new agency, the Public Ministry. With US intervention, Haiti and Panama replaced their military organisations with police organisations in the early 1990s. Mexico created a new anti-drug agency, the Special Prosecutor's Office – expected to be less corrupt than its predecessor – in late April 1997.

In public-service management, changes such as increasing the number of women ministers have also occurred. This increase has not constituted a significant numerical change since military governments frequently named one or two token women to their cabinets. The current difference is the ministries women lead. They typically have headed ministries of justice, health or education. In late 1997, Maria Emma Mejia became Colombia's Minister of Foreign Relations. In mid-1997, Maria Bernardoni de Govea became the first female to be appointed the Venezuelan Minister of Labour. As Nicaragua's President, Mrs Chamorro designated herself Minister of Defense. However, while women representatives at all levels of government has increased, few women are public managers. This will change as women increase their participation in electoral politics. El Salvador, for example, represents the future: over 10 per cent of its 262 mayors are women; and 9 of the 84 Legislative Assembly members are females. Indeed, the nation's most important leftist party, the Farabundo Marti National Liberation Front (FMLN), has 'adopted a rule that one-third of all its candidates for office must be women',[2]

For other under-represented groups, the situation has been barely altered. Indigenous persons occupy a few top posts in Bolivia and Ecuador; African-Latino public managers and ministers are rare, except in the Dominican Republic and Cuba. In black-governed Caribbean states, except Haiti, there is a sprinkling of white ministers and public managers. Peru, the only Latin American country with a Japanese-descendant President, has a few Japanese–Peruvian Ministers and senior administrators. However, in Brazil where the region's largest number of persons of Japanese origin reside, and where they are one of the wealthiest groups in the country, none is in the Brazilian cabinet. Nepotism throughout both regions also remains a concern of the most ardent reformers. In sum, the centuries-old status quo remains in the public service even as Latin American and Caribbean nations consolidate democratic practices and procedures. Elite males of European ancestry still control policy-making and policy-implementation positions. In the Caribbean, the racial and ethnic make-up in the government is more diverse, with blacks and persons of mixed races dominant. Not surprisingly, then, the absence of indigenous people in top posts in Latin American states has generated debate about autonomy.

Many of them poor, indigenous persons have sought autonomy – and not simply administrative reform – as the most effective way of addressing their legitimate grievances. Since the early 1960s, the Shining Path in Peru has 'occupied' several impoverished indigenous communities, isolating them from the political mainstream. While the Peruvian government has not granted autonomy to these communities, they are *de facto* autonomous. The

Zapatista Army for National Liberation (EZLN) seized villages in the southern Mexican state of Chiapas on 1 January 1994. Angered over the Mexican government's neglect of Chiapas' problems and a radical change in the nation's agrarian reform law that undermined collective ownership of property by indigenous communities, the EZLN led an armed revolt that involved largely poor indiginees. Autonomy has been demanded for these communities.

On the other hand, the Chilean and Brazilian poor have challenged their governments with other alternatives. In Chile in 1972, progressive Catholic clergymen – many of them foreign priests – championed adherence to Liberation theology. Briefly, Liberation theology advocates political activism in eliminating capitalism, which is viewed as anathema to the teachings of Christ. Proponents believe that their views are consistent with those of Christ, who, if he were alive, would join them in attacking capitalism. Liberation theologians urged affiliation with Salvadore Allende's Socialist government in 1970. This placed them at odds with the Chilean Catholic hierarchy which, while it supported democracy and believed Allende's government had a constitutional right to exist, vehemently opposed priests serving in any government or taking partisan political stands. Catholic church leaders considered clergy participation in partisan politics a dangerous violation of the principle of separation of church and state. Associating with any government compromised the church's ability to make independent decisions. Liberation theologians in Chile were isolated by church leaders who eventually barred the teaching of the philosophy in the church.

Catholic priests out of the mainstream in Brazil, however, had a different reception from many Brazilian Catholics. In the mid-1970s, poor urban citizens, mostly rural-born women, joined *comunidades eclesiais de base* – Christian Based Communities (CEBs) – organisations through which they could express and demonstrate their political concerns. In the 1982 elections, the CEBs actively supported the leftist *Partidos dos Trabalhadores* (PT), the Workers' Party. They asked politicians to endorse social justice and democracy by including the poor in the decision-making process. They particularly urged them to develop and implement programmes that addressed the poor's needs – jobs, housing and food. In addition, they advised politicians to devise policies that did not disproportinately continue to favour the small, wealthy elite. While the poor's activism has yet to result in definitive, permanent changes for them, the CEBs offer another model for reform. Chapter 2 in this volume has also explored the Latin American alternative of Liberation theology; and Chapter 3 has mentioned the CEBs in the context of its discussion of non-governmental organisations.

To be sure, managing political conflict and controlling political dissent are priorities in Latin America and the Caribbean. Colombia recently created a state commission, granting it the authority to censor television programmes. Argentinian and Chilean officials have purposefully undermined the freedom of press. These tactics do not bode well for advancing substantive reforms and respecting the legitimate concerns of citizens in civil societies. Simultaneously, as some Western reformers bemoan the violation of individual rights in the regions, one must be reminded that a Bill of Rights is considered by some Latin Americans to be a US innovation. Changes are regional in nature and reflect the societies' traditional characteristics, including the most authoritarian holdovers of the colonial Iberian culture. Some of the more recent significant attempts at administrative indigenisation and reform are highlighted below.

## INDIGENOUS POLICIES

One indigenist anthropologist, Gonzalo Aguirre Beltran, has described indigenous policies in Latin American nations as segregation, incorporation and integration.[3]

Each policy, he has argued, has been devised to eradicate indigenous people as diverse, distinct ethnic groups or to subsume them under the notion of national unity. Neither policy has worked. The number of indigenous people in the region, many desiring alternative policies, has contributed to the failure of policies that they have had little or no input in formulating. Approximately 50 million indigenous people live in Latin America. In Bolivia and Guatemala, 70 per cent of the populations are made up of indigenous people; in Peru and Ecuador they represent over 40 per cent of the residents; they are 5–20 per cent of the populations in Belize, Honduras, Mexico and Chile. In Brazil, Panama and Nicaragua they are small, vocal minorities who occupy ore-rich territories that are sought for development by multinationals. Influenced by the possibilities of earning large profits from external investments, many states have begun to focus on indigenous-driven problems, albeit in some cases superficially. Other changes have occurred for political reasons.

Bolivian Vice-President Victor Cardenas Conde, for example, an Aymara, has helped to shape policies designed to integrate indigenous cultures and languages into mainstream Bolivian education. Even with Cardenas' involvement, the most significant indigenous achievement has been the incorporation of bilingualism into government documents and intra-government communications. In other areas, disinterest in indigenous-related concerns, bureaucratic morass, political infighting and a lack of funds have slowed reforms. The Ministry of Economic Development, the parent agency of the National Secretariat for Agriculture and the Ministry of Human Development – which administers small-scale peasant producers' programmes – have frustrated the implementation of indigenist-related policies. Resistance occurs despite legislative directives to the contrary.

Colombians, on the other hand, have been more accommodating to their indigenous population. Concentrated primarily in the Amazon, Orinoquia, the Pacific coast, the Sierra Nevada de Santa Marta and Perija mountains, the Guajira Peninsula and the Andean Zone, they number about 800 000, representing 81 distinct groups who speak about 64 different languages. They inhabit 27 of the 32 administrative-political divisions. Although their presence is obvious throughout Colombia, they are such a minute part of the population that yielding to their policy requests does not threaten the status quo.

Colombia's most recent Constitution (1991) provided for strengthening indigenous rights. Indeed, several indigenous people served in the Constituent Assembly which drafted the document. The Constitution declared 'indigenous territories to be inalienable, imprescriptible, and unseizable'.[4] These areas were elevated to Territorial Entities: autonomous and governed by their chosen authorities, they administer their own renewable resources and taxes and receive a portion of the national taxes. Indian languages are now legally recognised.

Administrative changes followed the political reforms. An Office of Indigenous Affairs was established in the Ministry of Government, and national director of the Office supervises offices in the departments' indigenous-populated areas. In addition, independent Secretariats of Indigenous Affairs were created within the various departments. At the end of 1995, five Secretariats existed in the 32 political-administrative divisions. Administratively a step below a Deputy Minister, the Secretariat is responsible for facilitating the 'treatment of indigenous problems by the regional offices'.[5]

Other relevant state agencies include an Office of Ethno-Education in the Ministry of Education. The National Rehabilitation Planning Office, Indigenous Section, promotes development projects to weaken guerrilla influence, and a Secretariat for Indigenous Human Rights is in the National Human Rights Commission. Finally, the Institute for Agrarian Reform (INCORA), whose board of directors includes indigenous people, promotes and supervises land reform. In the main, the administrative infrastructure is in place to implement reform. Unfortunately, the structure has been created

> with no connection whatsoever to the Indians' own organisations and representatives. . . . [but it] displays to national and international public opinion [an example of reform] without resolving the problems the structure was built to address.[6]

Quite different from Colombia – at least, in theory – Paraguay has embarked on reform which in some instances legitimises decades-old customs. About 100 000 Paraguayans, or 4 per cent of the population, identify themselves as indigenous people. Residing primarily in the eastern and western regions, they are members of 17 distinct ethnic groups, many belonging to the Guarani language group. Since Guarani is spoken by most Paraguayans, it provides a pivotal basis for national unification. It became an official national language along with Spanish only in 1992, when the most recent Constitution was ratified. Drafted by the Constituent Assembly, with delegates representing a broad spectrum of the population – including indigenous people – making Guarani a national language was a recognition of an ethnic reality. Indigenous participation in the Assembly represented political reform, to be sure, and this participation influenced the creation and strengthening of administrative structures necessary to implement bureacratic reforms.

A 1981 statute provided for the establishment of the Paraguayan Indigenous Institute (INDI). The 1992 Constitution enhanced its powers by allowing it to 'determine indigenous policy and programmes [by proposing] the rules that should govern the civil registry, military service, and education in relation to the indigenous people'.[7] INDI was also granted the authority to title land under its control. The Ministry of Public Health's Rural Health Department provides medical care to Indians, a policy only put in place in 1985. Additionally, the Institute of Rural Development proposes land to be expropriated for the National Indigenous Communities. As the sole administrator of Protected Areas, the Agriculture Ministry controls the distribution of land to Indians. Sufficient funds, however, have not been made available to fully implement any indigenous-friendly programmes.

In Ecuador, political commitment and indigenous activism have been translated into limited reform. As Ecuador's indigenous people make up about 40 per cent of the population, political leaders have publicly rushed to advocate relevant reforms. Just as quickly, they have undermined their sincerity by reneging on promises made to pacify powerful indigenous political organisations. However, in Ecuador the connotation of indigeneity has changed over the last two decades, primarily because emergent indigenous organisations have presented a positive image of their members. An increasing number of Ecuadorians now identify themselves as indigenous. Much of this credit is attributed to the politically active and influential organisation, the Conference of Indigenous Nationalities of Ecuador (CONAIE). Although it was formed in 1980 as an umbrella group for most indigenous groups, the influence of the indigenous movement reached a political and administrative milestone in 1979.

In that year, following years of military rule, the first popularly elected President, Jaime Roldos, delivered his acceptance speech in Quechua, a primary indigenous language. In legitimising the language, Roldos enhanced his reform efforts. He initiated an accord between the Ministry of Education and the Center for the Study of Indigenous Education (CIEI) at the Catholic University, allowing for the systematic study of bilingual education at the national level, leading to the recognition of Quechua as a national language. Bilingualism thus became the potential cornerstone of major indigenous political and administrative reform. A significant consequence of the Catholic University accord provided for the education of a generation of indigenous intellectuals, many of whom would later occupy important positions in the bureaucracy. For example, Luis Monteluisa became the first director of bilingual education and other changes followed.

A National Office of Indigenous Affairs was created in the Ministry of Social Welfare, replacing the lower level Campesino Office in the Ministry of Agriculture. Indigenous leaders disliked that Office because it limited their access to the President and gave lukewarm support to their agenda. Roldos' unexpected death near to the end of his four-year term ended assertive indigenous political and administrative reform at the presidential level. Sixto Duran Ballen (1992–96) tried to dismantle the bilingual education programme at the Catholic University, although he was foiled by strong political opposition. Other presidents also proposed far-reaching change, although these were not followed through.

Indigenous advocacy for establishing a plurinational state – that indigenous groups should be treated as separate nations in the super state of Ecuador – also contributed to the dimunition of political support for reform. Moreover, indigenous division on this issue has given economic elites reason to oppose substantive changes. However, in Panama, Nicaragua and Mexico, conflicts between the governments and indigenous people have been resolved partially by agreements to grant autonomy to some indigenous groups. Similar groups in Chile have seized land and organised a political party as initial steps in pursuing self-determination.

In Mexico, the quest for autonomy has become a very public undertaking, reflecting the most radical type of indigenous reform in the region. On 1 January 1994, in the southern Mexican state of Chiapas, Indians – members of the EZLN – rose in rebellion against the government. The ostensible reason for the revolt was the modification of the agrarian reform programme which allowed land formerly held by a member in a community, the *ejido*, to be sold outside of the community. It repealed a

70-year-old law which had allowed the elected management committee of the *ejido* to assign the abandoned property to a person, usually within the community. The law was intended to protect poor, rural communities economically and culturally by preventing land purchases by absentee landlords who would create and perpetuate an even poorer group of landless labourers. Implemented in 1991–92, reforms based on the new law were intended to make the farms more efficient by encouraging individual ownership and eliminating the *ejido* management committees' abusive powers. Indigenous people, however, interpreted them as the state's attempt to destroy them.

Discussions and negotiations between the Mexican government and EZLN led to a 40-page agreement, signed on 16 February 1996. The agreement 'defined protection of Indian culture and civil rights and awarded Mexico's 56 distinct indigenous nations a degree of administrative autonomy from federal and state strictures'.[8] About 700 majority-indigenous municipalities dot the Mexican countryside. However, Mexican President Ernesto Zedillo has not honoured the agreement, exacerbating tensions between the EZLN and government. Clearly, administrative autonomy is not acceptable to President Zedillo or the Mexican government.

In other Latin American states – such as Guatemala and Bolivia – other recourses have been sought. The primary alternative is involvement in the political system, and this route would facilitate substantive long-term administrative reform. Indeed, in states where granting autonomy is not an option, viable indigenous-friendly reform is unlikely – short of changes in the make-up of political representation. In other areas, the prognosis is not as pessimistic.


MERIT REFORM


Concerted efforts to reform the civil service systems in Latin America including Cuba and the Dominican Re-

public began in the late 1950s, and in the Caribbean
with the initiation of self-government in the 1970s and
1980s. Assistance from a number of external organisations, however, has paid little attention to various cultural
peculiarities and national idiosyncrasies. Nepotism is a
basis, for example, for the appointment of relatives to
high posts. As loyalty is a litmus test for officials in Latin
American countries, strong family-oriented leaders believe family members are the most loyal. While US
sensibilities abhor sex discrimination in employment, Latin
American and Caribbean leaders have not completely
accepted the notion of sexual equality. Their bureaucratic
systems also tend to be more formalistic than their counterparts in the US and Western Europe. Implementing merit
systems akin to those in Great Britain or the US would
not just constitute reform, but revolution. In essence,

> Changes in recruitment and promotion that would
> convert a personalistic, patronage-based system into a
> merit-based system threaten existing employees and
> reduce the patronage resources controlled by political
> activists. Consequently, civil servants' unions, politicians,
> and party activists have often opposed such changes
> (reforms).[9]

In spite of this powerful opposition, reforms have begun to take place slowly. Most have been aimed at
redrawing political/administrative boundaries; emphasising
accountability; improving efficiency; reducing corruption;
changing values and attitudes about the importance of
non-partisanship for government employees; and taking
advantage of technological opportunities. Some of the
reforms have been innovative, but within the Western
political/public administration context. None appears to
constitute indigene-oriented changes, except to consider
language variations, hiring of indigenees, women and a
variety of ethnic group representatives, and respect for
particular tribal decision-making processes. In Costa Rica,
for example, changes began in 1949 when its new

Constitution provided for the merit appointment of civil servants. By 1985, 75 per cent of the employees in the executive branch were covered by the civil service law.

While on paper Costa Rica appears to have incorporated the merit system into its public management system, the reality there and in most countries in the region may be different. In general, most of the government jobs throughout the regions are assigned on the basis of political party affiliation, social class, ethnic group, nepotism or family connections. Political leaders responsible for selecting personnel for positions in bureaucratic agencies tend to ignore persons who have scored high on civil service examinations if they do not fit a particular mould as indicated above. In instances where merit is used in selecting personnel, external influences and pressures – for example, from the US government or an international monetary organisation – have come into play. New conditions now being contemplated in negotiations between Argentina and the IMF regarding Argentina's request for an IMF line of credit could include a merit-system component. There may be a precedent for this arrangement in the Caribbean.

Confronted with daunting financial problems in the early 1980s, Jamaica sought assistance from the World Bank. While the Bank did not specifically demand merit reform as a condition for help, Jamaica's economic plight could not be addressed if its public management system remained unchanged. As part of its Structural Adjustment Loan Programme in 1982, the Bank urged Jamaica to initiate an Administrative Reform Programme (ARP) to facilitate economic reform. This problem was exacerbated by the migration of professionals from Jamaica at an alarming rate, making it difficult for the government to hire the best talent. A major objective was to reduce the number of public employees, thereby diminishing the state's role in the economy. Between 1972 and 1982, the number of public employees rose from 80 000 to 180 000, staffing about 230 statutory bodies and over 200 public enterprises. Privatising many of the public enterprises was an obvious answer for Bank advisers to address the economic problem. Collateral steps were taken to reform the entire public service.

The duplication of responsibilities was reduced between the Ministry of Public Service (MPS) and the Public Service Commission (PSC). In part, this was accomplished by the establishment of management councils in each ministry and department to assume many of the functions of the MPS and PSC.[10] Additionally, the Jamaican government set up an Inter-Ministerial Committee on Administrative Reform (IMCAR) in 1984 to recommend changes. Chaired by the Prime Minister, the IMCAR was made up mostly of senior government ministers and Permanent Secretaries of the MPS and PSC. Subsequently, the Prime Minister established the ARP Secretariat, with two Executive Directors, both of whom sat on the IMCAR. The Secretariat reported to the IMCAR and relied primarily on professional support and advice on specific subjects from foreign consultants.

Focusing on improving the human resources management components of the MPS and PSC, the Secretariat initially delegated a number of functions to line ministries. A computerised personnel data system was developed in the PSC. Moreover, organisational development (OD) and performance improvement programming (PIP), 'a system designed to monitor the performance of individuals, and to encourage improved performance' was introduced.[11] Two significant changes had occurred by 1986. First, the number of public-sector employees, excluding those in public corporations, had decreased from 180 000 in 1982 to less than 45 000. Privatisation had occurred as well, absorbing thousands of employees who had been on the public payroll. Second, salaries had increased for professional, managerial and technical civil servants.

Additionally, Jamaica has initiated measures to remedy other problems such as inadequate training of personnel and the absence of physical resources. Borrowing from the United Kingdom, the government designated 'executive agencies', granting them:

> considerable autonomy in budgeting and personnel management, performance contracts with managers specifying expected performance level . . . and 'framework documents' that set forth performance targets that, together with annual reports, are in the public domain.[12]

Finally, in 1993 Jamaica created a cabinet-level office in the Prime Minister's Office to coordinate policy-making, planning, and to facilitate the implementation of public policy.

Other nations in the English-speaking Caribbean, however, have not been as assertive as Jamaica in implementing human-resource management reforms. For example, in Trinidad and Tobago senior civil servants attempted to block the implementation of a pilot Human Resource Information System, and a related performance evaluation and classifications system. Interested in preserving the status quo, they did not want to share information about how promotion and salary decisions were made. As public employment accounted for 20 per cent of total employment, the government also manipulated employment decisions for political reasons. Trinidad and Tobago only began to implement public-sector reform in 1991, when a cabinet level minister was appointed and given a mandate to accomplish this objective.

As Trinidad and Tobago resisted change, Montserrat and Anguilla experimented with a new personnel approach. Called *Team Management*, with shades of Management-by-Objective, both began using the technique – which combines the principles of team work and collective management – in the late 1980s. Responsibilities are devolved to senior and junior public servants on the basis of expertise. Higher civil servants agree to relinquish some of their powers in order to ease the accomplishment of common goals. Junior civil servants are treated as equals by their supervisors to encourage open discussions on how to develop the best ways to implement policies. Grudgingly respected at the Permanent Secretary's level, the technique is recognised by many public personnel experts as a way of building consensus and efficiently running a small public service. However, fully implementing the team-management approach in Monserrat and Anguilla has been frustrated by a variety of factors.

That Monserrat is not an independent nation is one factor. However, as a British colony it has wide latitude in devising and implementing laws designed to enhance the delivery of public services. A few of the six Permanent Secretaries have given lip service to the team-management approach, while others have attempted to incorporate it into their decision-making systems. Implementing the approach has been stymied, however, by players who have tried to organise themselves by ignoring the leadership of the crucial Permanent Secretary.[13] This has led to frustration and morale problems, additional inhibitors to accepting the approach.

In Anguilla, on the other hand, the team administration philosophy has been generally accepted by the Permanent Secretaries. Some view consultative management as 'essential to effective micro-government'.[14] They believe that in a small state, teamwork and team management are necessary to facilitate training and other personnel goals. What has set Anguillans apart from their Monserratian counterparts is their understanding of how their scarce resources limit their ability to implement the best programmes, and how their willingness to use the team approach in solving problems. Monserrat's Chief Minister was an advocate of the approach, setting an example for other top officials. Anguillans had also developed 'a strong sense of community bred of living in harsh circumstances with comparatively undiluted African collective traditions'.[15]

Even as Caribbean and Latin American nations have become more willing to try different approaches and techniques to reform their public services, they have been reluctant to alter the services gender make-up. All are driven by machismo and class concerns. A few upper-middle and upper-class women hold cabinet positions, but elsewhere in the public sector, 'More than a third (36.7 per cent) of the women . . . are from lower middle and lower class backgrounds'.[16] Concentrated in the lower levels of the bureaucracies, most do not expect to achieve higher positions.

Costa Rica may be an exception to this rule, however. A country with a long democratic tradition, Costa Rica ratified laws granting equal pay and equal employment to women in the 1980s. In electoral politics, women have also benefited: about 12 per cent of the national deputies were females in 1986. Successes in politics have contributed to raising female expectations about acquiring public management positions. A 1995 survey of the attitudes of Costa Rican women in upper-level bureaucratic positions confirms this assertion.[17] Indeed, Costa Rican female public managers maintained that they had the same opportunities to fail or succeed as did men. They reported little direct experience with sexual harassment, and believed they were primarily stymied in advancing to even higher positions because of the wrong political party affiliation. However, only three women were Cabinet ministers in 1996; the Ambassador to the United Nations and the Second Vice-President were also women. Still, Costa Rica has an enviable human resources system. Others countries, like Ecuador, are moving slowly to correct inequities.

Debate over civil service reform began in Ecuador in 1924, but little real progress took place for several years. With assistance from the United Nations, an Administrative Career Law based on merit principles was formulated in 1948. The Law was enacted in 1952, but was repealed by President Jose Velasco Ibarra 'on the grounds that it violated his constitutional right to appoint and remove public employees'.[18] When the transition to democracy began in 1979, interest was rekindled in public service reform. Although personalism continued to drive decision-making and the appointment of public managers, the advent of electoral politics and coalition political parties gave impetus to civil service reform.

In 1982, job tenure was granted to 10 per cent of the Ecuadorean civil service's 26 000 employees. Position classifications were instituted. The number of competitive examinations doubled between 1980 and 1983, although the number was less than under the military government. As one means of improving and evaluating employee performance, some public agencies like the National Finance Corporation, the Central Bank and the National Pre-Investment Fund have experimented with a Management-by-Objective system.

Despite these gains, reform suffered a setback between 1979 and 1984. In these years, the number of politically-appointed jobs eclipsed merit-based positions. Agency administrators encouraged the appointments because they complained that the merit system caused long delays in creating positions and placing staff in newly-created positions. Clearly, this was a manifestation of the prevailing view of the merit principle: when convenient, it will be subverted for political and administrative expediency. Nevertheless, resorting to old methods is directly related to the nascent tradition of participatory government and *personalistic-driven* political systems. Ecuador and other Latin American countries have been shaped in part by the Iberian cultural tradition that does not frown on extensive use of the spoils system. However, in financial matters evidence suggests that reforms are consistent with those likely to be made by democratic governments.

## BUDGETARY AND FINANCIAL REFORMS

Specific budgetary and financial reforms have varied widely throughout Latin America and the Caribbean. One of the major goals has been to decentralise powerful planning ministries and to eschew the use of econometric models that are irrelevent in problem-solving. Increasingly, budget reforms have stressed decentralised expenditures, public accountability and transparency in coverage and classification.

In 1989, Argentina 'initiated a comprehensive public sector reform through budget systems development'.[19] Later, in 1991, Argentina reduced the power of its central bank to create money as well as eliminating its power to liquidate failed financial institutions. The Argentines have sought fiscal accountability and an improvement in expenditure planning. They have also strengthened their financial system by doing something that many interpret as revolutionary: the government has begun to pursue tax evaders. For the first time in its history, the country has a law establishing a prison term for those found guilty of tax fraud.

In pension reform, Colombia has instituted a system 'based on competition between a new privately managed, fully funded pillar and a reformed pay-as-you-go component'.[20] And Chile is one of the most successful nations at pension reform. Experts throughout the region and in the US are examining Chile's pension fund system, and considering adopting some of its aspects. Under this Defined Contribution System, mandatory deductions – averaging about 13 per cent of wages – are taken from each worker's salary and deposited in individual, privately-managed accounts. The assets are invested in stocks and bonds. A minimum pension is guaranteed by the government to those who do not 'accumulate sufficient savings to cover subsistence after retirement'.[21] The accounts are managed by about 20 private mutual fund groups known as *Administradora de Fondos Pensiones* (AFPs).

The system is not without flaws, however. For example, some AFPs, allegedly to keep their clients happy, engage in wasteful activities like unnecessary advertising. Also the government guarantees everyone a minimum pension, even those with low wages who hide income, and the programme may be over-regulated by the government, creating a bureaucratic mess. To maintain accountability, the government requires AFPs to report their activities monthly. Others believe the number of AFPs should be reduced to increase returns on investments. While the Chilean pension system obviously has flaws, Argentina, Mexico and Peru have nevertheless modelled their systems after it.

## CONCLUSIONS

Even as reform takes place in the Caribbean and Latin America, constraints on change remain. Democracy has not persuaded them to accept many changes that would accelerate the movement of the poor, indigenous people, and women into the political and economic mainstreams. Pressures from external organisations, foreign governments, international monetary organisations and multinationals have played tremendous roles in encouraging change. At the same time, democrats in the respective nations have demanded the initiation of substantive administrative and political reforms. Some democratic activists hold elected offices and are able to effect change from the inside. Still, resistance persists, and it is manifested in several ways.

Political leaders are more concerned about economic progress and modernisation than reform, and erstwhile hostile political parties easily develop political alliances to advance political agendas. However, the alliances are rarely stable and permanent, and when they fracture, planned good deeds end. Attempts to effect reforms are undermined and sometimes gutted by the failure of political leaders to appropriate sufficient funds to implement policies they have agreed to earlier. Public managers are for the most part underpaid, and as a result they are susceptible to bribes and open to better offers from the private sector. Elites fear reform will too rapidly change the socioeconomic status quo. They do not imagine sharing power with people they have long considered inferior.

Nonetheless, in terms of administrative reform alternatives, innovative approaches have been introduced in a variety of areas. These are manifestations of efforts to make the political systems in these regions work for all citizens, and administrative models are available that are peculiar to the regions. Additional experiences in participatory government are bound to result in the effective implementation of more substantive reforms, and participants now entering the political systems are not likely to allow a few elites to continue to dominate. There are movements for autonomy in several countries, and efforts to respond to citizens' legitimate demands in others.

### Notes and References

1.  See Brian Loveman, '"Protected Democracies" and Military Guardianship: Political Transitions in Latin America, 1978–1993', *Journal of InterAmerican Studies and World Affairs*, vol. 36 (Summer 1994), pp. 105–67.
2.  Tommie Sue Montgomery, 'Constructing Democracy in El Salvador', *Current History*, vol. 96, no. 608 (February 1997), p. 66.
3.  Hector Diaz-Polanco, 'Indian Communities and the Quincentenary', trans. John F. Uggen, *Latin American Perspectives*, vol. 19 (Summer 1992), p. 14.
4.  Philip J. O'Brien, 'Participation and Sustainable Development in Colombia', *Revista Europea de Estudios Latinamericanos y del Caribe*, vol. 59 (December 1995), p. 25.
5.  Jesus Avirama and Rayda Marquez, 'The Indigenous Movement in Colombia', in Donna Lee Van Cott (ed.), *Indigenous Peoples and Democracy in Latin America* (New York: St Martin's Press, 1995), p. 94.

6. *Ibid*, p. 95.

7. Esther Prieto, 'Indigenous Peoples in Paraguay', in Donna Lee Van Cott (ed.), *Indigenous Peoples and Democracy in Latin America* (New York: St Martin's Press, 1995), pp. 243–44.

8. John Ross, 'In Chiapas: Death of a Dialogue', *Latinamerica Press*, vol. 29, no. 9 (13 March 1997), pp. 1, 8.

9. Barbara Geddes, *Politician's Dilemma: Building State Capacity in Latin America* (Berkeley: University of California Press, 1994), p. 24.

10. Richard Kitchen, 'Administrative Reform in Jamaica: A Component of Structural Adjustment', *Public Administration and Development*, vol. 9 (September–October 1989), p. 344.

11. *Ibid*, p. 348.

12. Malcolm D. Rowat, 'Public Sector Reform in the Latin American and Caribbean Region – Issues and Contrasts', *Public Administration and Development*, vol. 16 (October 1996), p. 408.

13. John E. Kersell, 'Team Management and Development in Monserrat and Anguilla', *Public Administration and Development*, vol. 10 (January–March 1990), p. 83.

14. *Ibid*, p. 87.

15. *Ibid*.

16. Monteze M. Snyder, Joyce Osland and Leslie Hunter, 'Developing Management Capacity in Latin America: A Comparative Survey of Public and Private Sector Students', *Public Administration Quarterly*, vol. 18 (Winter 1995), p. 431.

17. Monteze M. Snyder, Joyce Osland and Leslie Hunter, 'Personnel Practices in Careers of Women at the Top in Government and Business in Nicaragua and Costa Rica', *Public Administration and Development*, vol. 15 (October 1995), pp. 397–416.

18. Karen Ruffing Mangelsdorf and T. Zane Reeves, 'Implementing the Merit System in Ecuador', *Public Personnel Management*, vol. 18 (Summer 1989), p. 194.

19. George M. Guess, 'Transformation of Bureacratic States in Eastern Europe: Public Expenditure Lessons From Latin America', *International Journal of Public Administration*, vol. 20 (1997), p. 629.

20. M.D. Rowat, *op. cit.*, p. 404.

21. Peter Passell, 'How Chile Farms Out Nest Eggs: Can its Private Pension Plan Offer Lessons to the U.S.?', *The New York Times*, 21 March 1997, p. D.1.

# Part III
# Future Directions

# 12 What Lies Ahead for the Administrative State?

Gerald E. Caiden

What may well be in store for the administrative state can be deduced from the United Nations General Assembly Resolution 50/225, and from the deliberations of the latest meetings of experts in public administration and finance convened by the United Nations. On 19 April 1996, the resumed session on Public Administration and Development of the United Nations General Assembly adopted GA Resolution 50/225, which (a) reaffirmed that democracy and transparent and accountable governance and administration in all sectors of society were indispensable foundations for social and people-centred sustainable development; (b) recognised that there was a need for public administration systems to be sound, efficient and equipped with the appropriate capacities and capabilities; (c) reaffirmed that governments in all countries should promote and protect all human rights and fundamental freedoms, including the right to development; and (d) reconfirmed the importance of and called for the enhancement of the effectiveness of United Nations activities in the area of public administration and development, particularly

(a) strengthening government capacity for policy development, administrative restructuring, civil service reform, human-resources development and public-administration training;
(b) improving performance in the public sector;
(c) financial management;

295

(d)  public–private interaction;
(e)  social development;
(f)  developing infrastructure and protecting the environment;
(g)  government legal capacity;
(h)  post-conflict rehabilitation and reconstruction of government machinery; and
(i)  management of development programmes.

In this context, the United Nations was to carry out these activities through pooling and facilitating access to information in public administration, promoting training and research in public administration and finance at all levels, advocacy and exchange of experiences, advisory services, technical assistance, capacity-building and human-resources development. Its adoption followed a week of deliberations in which almost all member states participated. It had been preceded by an International Technical Forum attended by some 300 participants from institutions, associations and organisations of public administration, featuring a private-sector colloquium on public–private relations and a professional colloquium on public management.

What was all the fuss about? The General Assembly had never before had the opportunity of discussing public administration and development, and a week-long discussion had given member states the opportunity to air their views. At first glance, it may well appear that Resolution 50/225 affirms the current actions of the international community to strengthen public administration and management, suggests some areas that need special attention, and expresses support for continuing international technical cooperation for member states that feel this need. Otherwise, it could be taken as business as usual.

But such a complacent view would be mistaken. Member states were not so disinterested or unconcerned. On the contrary, they were most concerned that the public sector not be left lagging behind private-sector progress, that public administration not be thrown to the wolves of privatisation, and that investment in administrative reform not be shrunken but actually increased to improve state/public operations. They set forth the idea that development could not proceed as the exclusive domain of either the public or private sector, but should be fostered as a partnership between both, with neither one getting too far ahead of the other in disjointed development. The administrative state as the engine of development could be too overbearing and repressive, while the free market could be too exploitative and inequitable. Both have their rightful places and one should not be sacrificed for the other.

Where once the international community had pushed the state as the engine of development, there was now the danger of going too far in the other direction and abandoning the state's role in development altogether, reducing its activities, shrinking its size, eliminating public enterprise, deregulating, and eliminating basic welfare and social services. While this might be possible in advanced states and rich societies, many developing countries and poor societies had not yet been able to develop an economic, efficient or effective administrative state capable of carrying out the normal functions of government, let alone providing underlying infrastructures on which private enterprise could depend. Instead, they depended on international institutions to survive as independent agents; they were prey to international exploitation and organised crime against which they were ill-protected; and they were beset with so many internal weaknesses that government was ineffective outside the reach of the capital city. Their situation was quite different from other states which perhaps could afford to streamline a clumsy state bureaucracy, encourage people to move out of a bloated public sector into a thriving private sector, divest themselves of unprofitable public businesses, purge their welfare rolls of cheats and parasites, reduce heavy tax burdens, redress inequalities, and lessen military expenditures. The world has come to realise that every stage of development has its own requirements and its own needs, different problems, and quite different social objectives. When a country is poor, it needs everything. When a country is rich, it can afford to be more selective. It also faces the problems of affluence and excess. No one set of universal solutions can possibly fit these different situations. Moreover, in a global society no nation can act on its own behalf without taking into consideration its impact on others. Many of the world's most pressing problems need world approaches, global action and mutual cooperation. What may have worked on an individual basis in the past is no longer valid in the contemporary world. In addition to individual solutions to individual problems, there have now to be multinational solutions to multinational problems, which have been neglected for too long in the study of national public administration. The study and practice of public administration has to be internationalised and globalised where it can, without the promise of universal formulae and without losing sight of the fact that every national system will reflect its own idiosyncracies.

## A WATERSHED?

Will the world come to look back on Resolution 50/225 as some kind of significant turning point in the study and practice of public administration? It appears pretty innocuous. It seems to reaffirm what has been happening over the past few decades, and it suggests some new directions that might be followed. But read together with the discussions among the different parties, it was intended to be much more than that. It called for a thorough review of the status quo and its underlying assumptions. It implied dropping much of what had not really worked in the past or worked too poorly for comfort. Rarely had technical cooperation in public administration or even comparative studies made any appreciable impact on the course of any member state. Would the fate of any country have been otherwise had international efforts in public administration been absent? In some cases, things would undoubtedly have been far worse off. But again, in other cases countries might have been better off if they had not been subject to so much external interference, so many doubtful development theories, so many projects that helped the donors more than they seem to have helped the recipients, so few foreign ideas that actually worked in different surroundings. Soul searching should result in the jettisoning of much needless intellectual baggage and much unnecessary external interference from people who really do not seem to know what they are about, no matter how well meaning they might be.

Ridding public administration of its surplus baggage would clear the way for a reappraisal of what is now considered workable and – better still – what seems to work well in many different situations. There are many unsung projects that have improved public administration and management all over the world, but because they lacked the publicity, backing and propaganda of the most important players on the international scene, they have gone unheeded. The stage has been captured too long by the stars who have pursued their own self-interested schemes, sometimes to the detriment of recipients, and certainly not in their best interests. Projects have been put in place that have not been sustainable or economic and which have made the recipients dependent on the continuing goodwill of the donors. The donors have often been more interested in stability, or law and order, or ideological conformity, or pushing their own investments and investors than in the well-being of recipients, and in turn have been seen by recipients as an updated version of neo-colonialism. An honest appraisal or reevaluation might reveal many initiatives that have succeeded or at least done better in the long run, over and against the tainted or suspect self-evaluations of biased donors which have distorted the reality of international cooperation in favour of certain instruments and certain institutions which, if the truth were known, should not be so proud or aggressive or virtuous. But if the evaluators are the same as those who helped create some of the mess the world now finds itself in, then their solutions are likely to be equally biased and distorted.

A more realistic appraisal by experts willing to take a stand rather than worrying about securing their next international consultancy would also point to a reordering of priorities – or at least a rearrangement in current efforts. But such efforts may be made moot by the reduction in international technical cooperation, aid and relief now taking place among donors, with the rest of the world having to take only what is left when the cutbacks are completed. Most recipients will be thrown back on their own efforts and will have to rethink their own priorities, which from a global perspective might be something that they should have done long ago. Because of the resentment of poor people in rich countries to what they believe has been a favouring of international aid to rich people in poor countries, or parasitic bureaucrats in international organisations, donors and international organisations alike are having to reappraise what they have been doing and what they have been planning to do. They too are under pressure to alter their priorities and to be more realistic about what really works and for whom.

None of these efforts diverts from the pressing need to anticipate future and emerging needs in international public administration. Clearly, some regions require more help than others, and within regions some countries need more help than others. Sub-Saharan Africa – possibly the poorest region in the world and one in which much international help has failed to improve development prospects – will continue to command attention. It contains several countries that barely govern themselves and others where the administrative state has collapsed.

However, there are other regions and countries where trouble is brewing and where international intervention is unavoidable. Who is going to assume the leadership of such intervention? What is the international community prepared to do? How is the world to manage such intervention better than it has done in the past? Who is to be accountable for rapid response, value for money, transparency in operations, accurate reporting, and the many other issues about which the world has been too neglectful in the past? There is a new agenda here that calls out for creative and insightful thinking; an agenda that cannot afford to be mired down in infighting, ideological strife, complacency and bad execution. Much more than lip service, pious declarations and good intentions are required. Implementation, action and intended results are the keys – all of which are in the domain of public administration alone.

## RECONFIGURATION OF THE ADMINISTRATIVE STATE

Confidence in the capacity of the administrative state to lead in development has been severely undermined by the collapse of communist regimes, the questioning of socialist myths and the many failures of transitional economies. It had already been badly shaken when previously postcolonial regimes had bred corrupt autocratic bureaucracies intent on feeding from the public trough without commensurate political, economic and social gains. Even in countries where the administrative state had succeeded, grave misgivings had developed over its diminishing returns, its inability to exercise sufficient fiscal discipline, its questionable productivity and investment returns, and its unquenchable thirst for funds to support its ever-widening scope and activities. What exactly was the administrative state best fitted to do? Which activities could it safely divest or contract out to other institutions and organisations? What did it not need to do anymore? Had it overreached itself? Could it be downsized without much loss? Could other institutions perform any of its activities better?

Clearly, there were many activities that only the government, the public sector or the administrative state could be allowed to perform; no other body could be permitted to undertake them. Then there were other activities which for the sake of uniformity, egality, equity, universal access, monopoly or emergency could or should be best entrusted to the administrative state. In addition, the administrative state over the years had taken on much more. It had picked up where private initiatives and enterprise had left off. It had undertaken massive development projects because of their sheer costs and risks. It had come to rescue failing industries, failed businesses, wanton disregard of the public interest and the public good, and reckless ventures that had promised too much. But times had changed. Public opinion had changed. Momentum had been lost. Bureaupathologies had become entrenched. Several state ventures had lost their way. In short, there was some sorting out to do. What was to be retained? What needed tossing out? What should be kept under the condition that it would be repaired, updated, refurbished? What could be given to a new management?

The administrative state – far from being reckless – had been notoriously conservative and slow-moving. Once it acquired a new activity, it rarely relinquished it, and people got used to state performance. Rarely did it do so obviously badly that people demanded immediate privatisation or denationalisation or decentralisation; rather, state performance declined slowly, almost imperceptibly, until suddenly people woke up to the fact that its performance was no longer acceptable or tolerable. In the meantime, people had accustomed themselves to state performance and built up their expectations about its continuation. In time, vested interests in the *status quo* and state performers had become adept at protecting their turf. Most had lost sight of any possible alternative arrangements and could not conceive of anything different being done. Complacency had set in, until a rude shock – a sudden emergency, a new invention, a serious accident, failure under growing pressure – set people thinking that something had to be done: something radical, not incremental; some reinventing, not just some piecemeal reform. Yet public authorities failed to see what others had seen, or had no idea how to respond other than issuing tokens of reassurance and resorting to temporary holding actions until the alarm was over and people had forgotten what the fuss had been about. The result was much the same: nothing had really changed although it should have.

Every so often, the slow-moving administrative state does need a swift kick in the pants to remind itself that these days one has to change even to stay in the same place. But what should be done? Countries are at such different stages of development and are so diverse in resources. Moreover, they have quite different objectives and values. Each one has to decide for itself what has to be done to rethink or refigure or reconstruct its administrative state. First come countries where the administrative state barely exists or has collapsed altogether. In them, their governments (where they still exist), their public sectors, and their public bureaucracies lack sufficient resources to perform even at the barest acceptable levels. Their public leaders and officials lack sufficient competence, experience, integrity, vision and skills to manage public organisations, enforce public laws and implement public policies. They are soft states. Far from divesting themselves or downsizing, they need to be helped to create or recreate a proper functioning administrative state. They require external assistance to provide themselves with qualified public servants in virtually every state activity from diplomacy to tax collection, from public health specialists to firefighters. They also need experts in institution-building and capacity-enhancement to design and maintain properly functioning administrative systems. And they will probably need such external assistance for more than a generation, certainly long-term.

Second, countries should be considered where the administrative state is getting by, but barely coping with extra demands placed on them. In some areas, they do what they do well. In other areas, they resemble their backward neighbours in lacking sufficient competence. They, too, need external help in their weakest administrative systems, for they cannot take from their better systems without harming them. Nevertheless, in them there is indigenous administrative capacity; there are islands of excellence; there are models; there is hope. But their situation is tenuous and fragile. Come the unforeseen, they struggle. They do not need the same kind of technical assistance as the first category of countries which do not really function, but possibly an international clearing house of the best attainable technical expertise, reinforced with temporary international assignments lasting from a few days to several years, depending on specific needs. They also need regular regional and international meetings to learn of the latest developments, to know about other countries' experiments in improving the capacity of the administrative state, and share experiences, even passing on a few tips of their own. They will need more help when they have to revitalise outdated administrative systems, overcome exceptional in-house bureaucratic resistance, raise new public capital, increase the appeal of public service, or find partners for new ventures.

A third category of countries contains those where the administrative state may have been too successful: rather than risking all in some new experiment in governing or reinventing or reengineering, they overprotect old well-tried formulae. They have reliable public goods and services; they have competent administrators; they have few compelling problems with lack of accountability or integrity. Their administrative systems work well – so well that they can almost be taken for granted. Even in emergencies they rise to the occasion. But they are no longer pathfinders. They are not at the cutting edge of research. Rather than finding new answers to new problems, they adapt old solutions that will do but will not overcome. In the meantime, other institutions have improved so well that they now can give the administrative state a good run, if not outperform public administration. These countries can afford the risks of innovation. They can go beyond administrative reform without jeopardising much. They are fortunate to be able to look a generation ahead and take steps now that will transform their ways of doing public business a decade hence. They can divest themselves of some traditional state/public activities while preparing themselves for the wave of the future in new areas such as enforcing human rights, protecting the environment, switching from curative to preventative health measures, and restoring individual rather than community initiatives. Again, they could benefit from an international clearing house in innovative public administration and frequent exchanges among researchers, experimenters and evaluators.

## MORE THAN ADMINISTRATIVE REFORM

Few countries do not claim a campaign to improve the performance of their administrative state. Administrative reform has become quite popular. The world's leading management consulting and accounting firms have a thriving business advising countries how their public sectors could adopt more businesslike methods and a more businesslike managerial ethos. Public administration advisory services, likewise, are kept busy helping clients to improve public-sector performance and overhaul public administrative systems. International donors of technical cooperation and assistance cannot meet the demand to help public agencies improve themselves. Every week somewhere in the world there is a gathering of international experts to discuss ways of dealing with some particular public-sector management question. The newest crop of public administration textbooks now include discussion of administrative reform or the new (public sector) managerialism or dealing with corruption and other bureaupathologies. In short, there is growing international recognition that administrative reform should not be seen as an unfortunate periodic incident, but as a necessary ingredient in administrative policy and managerial practice.

This new emphasis on administrative reform is, however, accompanied by warnings that administrative reform is not enough. The administrative state should not be improved at the neglect of other social instrumentalities. That had been a mistake in the past, when too often administrative reform produced poorly-performing bureaucratic states which had dominated development and suffocated other possible development instrumentalities. Too much had been made of the state as the engine of development to the detriment of any alternatives. While administrative reform is desirable and to be welcomed, it should not be allowed to starve other development instrumentalities of scarce resources. No one instrumentality should be allowed to dominate all others. Rather, they should all be seen as partners in a common or joint enterprise, each having its own role to play. To prevent administrative reform from resulting in domineering public bureaucracies bordering on a bureaucratic polity, efforts should be made to strengthen other instrumentalities so that they too keep pace, thus presenting a choice and better protecting society against an overreliance on the performance of a favoured instrumentality. The private sector, non-governmental organisations (NGOs), and volunteerism all had their different roles to play in national development, and should not be eclipsed by an overburdened administrative state.

This more even-handed approach to development also recognises the possibility of negative consequences should any particular instrumentality fail to perform its proper part. The administrative state itself is jeopardised if the NGOs or private sector fail. The administrative state cannot do everything. In overreaching, something must give. Its weakest areas get exposed and the whole cannot cope adequately with mounting pressure. Although the right combination in any country is anyone's guess, disjointed development – that is, the obvious undervaluing of any sector – should be corrected as soon as it becomes apparent. The smothering of alternatives to the administrative state actually weakens it. A better course of action is to encourage alternatives while still retaining the capacity to supplement their efforts and even supplant them temporarily should they fail, until something better can be devised.

Another lesson learned from past experience is that administrative reform should not be allowed to upset the balance of political arrangements by making the state bureaucracy too powerful. Strengthening the administrative state entails strengthening other branches of government too, such as politicians who should retain control of the state and who should not allow it to be hijacked by domineering experts and bureaucrats; judges who should be able to challenge questionable and doubtful acts of the administrative state and hold the offending public authorities accountable; and independent bodies, such as public auditors and complaint receivers (ombudsmanlike offices), to check on the financial integrity and administrative fairness of public officials.

Administrative reform needs to be accompanied – or even preceded – by constitutional, political, legal and military reforms. Administrative reform by itself is insufficient to improve the performance of the administrative state, unless something is also done about corrupt politicians, biased judges, unfit auditors and overbearing generals. Hence, the tendency to prefer the term 'governance' to 'government', to indicate that reforms in government should not just be confined to the public or civil service, but should include all other branches of government and should be matched also by like reforms in all social sectors and development instrumentalities. Indeed, the attempt should be made to open up all development instrumentalities, to ensure that they are run on client-friendly lines, to encourage and strengthen civil society, to incorporate volunteerism or some greater measure of direct public involvement, and to soften the impact of the military and police on people. In short, administrative reform should be seen as only one part – and not necessarily the most important part – of restoring and rebuilding the public's confidence in, and the credibility of, all social institutions not just the administrative state.


EFFECTIVE GLOBAL POLICY-MAKING

Too much stress in international circles has been placed on the management and training side of public administration. It was safer to keep out of the public-policy side altogether lest countries complained that their internal affairs were being compromised by foreigners. By concentrating on the mechanics of the administrative side, other equally important aspects tended to be neglected or obscured. This avoidance of the political sphere threw off the whole balance of public administration and made the discussion of certain topics off-limits. However, now it is increasingly recognised that improving the operations of the administrative state cannot be divorced from improving the aims or objectives or the results of governance. Doing the wrong things well may be worse than doing the right things badly. But often governments do not know that they are doing the wrong things. Many do not even know how well or how badly they are performing administratively, let alone substantively. The result is that they lurch from crisis to crisis and are prisoners to events. They believe they are doing the best they can under the circumstances, because they have no means of knowing differently. They are largely predictable simply because they rarely depart from narrow guidelines. Rarely do they learn from their mistakes because they have no way they can learn. They rarely stop to think deeply about what they are trying to do. Some critics believe that they rarely stop to think at all because the thinking part of government is deficient and has been neglected for too long.

Fortunately, the policy sciences and studies of public-policy formation have made so much progress in the past 30 years that thinking about the mechanics of public policy-making does not entail international interference with the substance of national policy-making and implementation. Greater emphasis can be placed on this neglected dimension in international public administration without compromising national honour or embarrassing any regime. Recognising the importance of the mechanics of policy-formation (as contrasted to the mechanics of administration) probably requires different emphases, different materials and different professional education and training, with less stress on policy-implementation and getting things done, and more on policy-creation and designing alternative futures instead of alternative administrative systems and methods. It probably involves greater political controversy because it is concerned with values, radical choices and outcomes (as opposed to outputs). The international community has tended to avoid it, but in so doing it has virtually divorced the operations of government from its substance and made the study of public management too routinised, too impersonal, too bureaucratic, too process-oriented, even too dull and sterile without its political dimensions.

But there are those in the international community who would like to go much further than this. They would welcome more emphasis on public policy, particularly international public-policy issues. They would encourage debate on major global issues, the end result being practical international policies to which international organisations would subscribe. They do not think that enough has been done to study such issues as global peacekeeping, world disarmament and the elimination of atomic, biological and chemical weapons, reduction of genocide and terrorism, protection of migrants and refugees, international crime and money laundering, black markets and underground economies, underemployment and unemployment, child labour, epidemics, environmental protection, slum clearance, the world's homeless and disaster prevention. They worry that typical 'beggar thy neighbour' policies at national level only exacerbate world problems. They claim that the global society requires global policies for their effective implementation. This may well require the reformulation and restructuring of international organisations and the strengthening of international public administration. The ending of the cold war should be seized as an opportunity for rethinking how the world community operates – not only the role of public administration in development – and to deliver global public goods and services that other social institutions cannot.

## SEEKING COMMON SOLUTIONS

Irrespective of whether the policy side of public administration receives more attention, the management side has many common problems that require immediate action before they get completely out of hand. Most countries, rich and poor alike, are seeking solutions to them. The feeling is that countries should not struggle on their own but join in multinational efforts to seek practical solutions to them and share their experiences. Some success has been made in the past decade in the area of privatisation of profitable state/public enterprises and in anticorruption strategies. Similar success is being achieved in court administration, customs administration and tax administration. Although it is still too early to tell, success is also expected in civil service reform, management training, public/private partnerships, information systems, human-resources management, complaint-handling mechanisms and contract administration. But there are several areas troubling to all that require concentrated international attention.

**Public Finance**

Probably at the top of everyone's list is money trouble. Many governments overspend and find their public debts keep rising without much relief. The poorest countries have been promised some little relief by the World Bank, but the International Monetary Fund (IMF) seems as remorseless as ever in insisting on structural adjustments detrimental to the public sector whenever governments try to borrow more money. They need to borrow because taxes and other receipts do not cover their expenditures (including interest payments on public debts), and they cannot raise much from taxation because many people are just too poor and those who can afford to pay would be taxing themselves. What taxes are imposed tend to be regressive. Raising more money is a bleak prospect. It is becoming harder to collect more money even in richer countries. Creative financing is the order of the day, but it is only a temporary answer and ways must be found of tackling the income side of government.

In the meantime, the expenditure side is easier to tackle. However, downsizing is only a temporary solution because there are limits to how far the administrative state can be cut without crippling government activities. Obvious targets are excessive military expenditures, white-elephant development projects, expensive welfare services, corrupt programmes that divert public money into the wrong hands or give low returns or are just too costly, and bloated bureaucracies. The World Bank and the IMF together with the regional development banks have been trying to force their members into greater financial discipline, but there are limits to what they can do – the World

Bank and IMF themselves being blameworthy for turning a blind eye to excesses that often contribute to runaway inflation.

The expansion of the world economy and more favourable trade terms for the poor countries would help relieve the situation as the public sector would automatically benefit from higher national incomes. But some way has to be found to discourage governments from spending as if there were no tomorrow and to encourage better value for (public) money (VFM). Before substantial public monies are committed, the VFM auditors will have to be brought in early and they will have to play a more public part in going about their business, inevitably clashing with policy-makers and public managers. Likewise, public budgeting generally will have to be overhauled to provide incentives to save rather than spend public money, to economise on budgeting and accounting procedures, to experiment with multi-year budgets and to track through monies as they pass through different public agencies and contractors. Even so, financial management will continue to be a nightmare, for the possibilities for misuse and abuse are endless, and rogues can always be found exploiting any loopholes.

**Debureaucratisation**

Several governments have launched ambitious debureaucratisation schemes in the past only to find that they hardly made any appreciable dent and they lost heart. The problem of excessive bureaucratisation and overabundance of bureaupathologies has not gone away. If anything, it has got worse. The slimming of the administrative state and the streamlining of administrative processes obviously cut down the complexity, but they do not get to the fundamentals of excessive bureaucratisation and red tape, the bane of everyone's dealings with the administrative state. Probably every country is worried about the alienation of its public from the administrative state generally, and public bureaucracy specifically. Nobody seems to have come up with the right answers yet. Perhaps this should head the list of priorities for future international research on public administration.

One place to start is with obvious public maladministration that harms people even if they are unsure quite how. Even so, knowledge that somebody else has been harmed is disturbing to everyone else. Only a small percentage of those harmed complains publicly and many who do, do not know how or where to obtain redress. No administrative system is perfect; all make mistakes, some minor, some major. Everyone in public administration should be concerned to see that they are minimised by attacking the bureaupathologies that cause them. The task ahead is to design practical guidelines for remedial action and also appropriate compensation for victims. International experience has long demonstrated that sick administrative systems do respond to professional treatment. Public-relations experts have been devising ways for public bureaucracies to deal with their clients, and they have helped reduce any unpleasantness that people might feel when confronting public employees. Much more needs to be done along these lines, irrespective of the nature of the political regime in which the public bureaucracy operates.

Corruption, or the belief that corruption is widespread, is largely responsible for the poor image of public administration. This complicated bureaupathology has long been the focus of the international community through the regular meetings of the International Conference Against Corruption (ICAC) and the work of the United Nations Criminal Justice Department located in Vienna. At last their efforts are beginning to receive increasing international support, even from some major international organisations that for ages had little to do with them. The United Nations General Assembly adopted Resolution 1995/14 against corruption in December 1995, and since then similar pledges of increased action against international corruption have been adopted by the World Trade Organization (January 1996), OECD (April 1996), the G7 (June 1996 and April 1997) and the Council of Europe (June 1997). Their studies of administrative corruption have invariably spread to other forms of social corruption and gone well beyond public administration to cover governance and business too. Clearly, a narrower focus fails to deal with the heart of corruption and other bureaupathologies, and something more than administrative reform is needed to tackle them effectively. Public administration can only do so much. Nonetheless, it can and should do far more. The best remedy for public maladministration is better performance by all social institutions.

**Proving Worth**

Too often the public sector asks to be taken on trust, but a suspicious if not disillusioned public, the victim of public maladministration, is no longer prepared to give it the benefit of the doubt. Insiders know how important public administration is to society and to development prospects, but they have difficulty convincing outsiders of its worth. They cannot as yet produce sufficient easily understandable indicators of worth. They tend to be modest or self-effacing folk, reluctant to take front-stage and boast of their successes which they take as self-evident or too much for granted. Whatever the reasons, they fail to produce enough solid evidence of their worth to society. They need to convincingly show how much they contribute to improving government and the quality of life.

Without such convincing evidence, public administration continues to be subject to a barrage of unjust and biased criticism and deprived of sufficient resources to do a better job. Much is offensive and degrading, certainly demoralising. The result, intended or not, is a decline in the status of public service careers – and indeed, a demotion of the whole idea of public service. It has also led to the inability of the public sector to attract and retain its rightful share of talent. Too many competent, experienced and valuable public employees are lured away by superior employment conditions elsewhere. None of this bodes well for the future prospects of public administration. Concerted efforts are needed to reverse this unfortunate state of affairs. In 1989, the National (Volcker) Commission on the Public Service in the United States pointed out this need to restore prestige to the idea of public service and to rebuild leadership for governance, enrich the talent pool and inculcate a culture of performance. Its agenda was quite independent of administrative reform, modernisation, streamlining, better training and like devices to improve public-sector performance, which overlook the ever-continuing need for competent, fairly treated, wisely handled and professionally-led staff.

Equally disconcerting is the growing estrangement between public officials and the public. Hence, there is firm international support to reduce formal barriers between them, anything that impedes public access to public goods and services, blocks information channels between them, and denies public participation in decision-making. Besides expecting public officials to be more courteous, they should be encouraged to open administrative processes and to see their clients as partners in the improvement of public administration. Likewise, the public should be encouraged and educated to participate more in public affairs and to work with public officials to improve government performance. These are the twin objectives in democratisation and in attempts to develop the civil culture where the governed are too distant from the governors. The administrative state has to learn to listen and communicate more and to respect and protect the rights of individuals and groups. It must have public servants responsive and accountable to the people, with policy and decision-making processes transparent and open to public participation and review.

## REDEFINING THE INTERNATIONAL AGENDA

Resolution 50/225 recognised that what was needed was not less government but better and different government. The respective spheres of public and non-public actors had to be redefined and reworked. Mechanisms for better interaction and cooperation had to be devised and built. Enabling-frameworks of clear, understandable laws and regulations that generated stability, confidence and predictability and supported individual initiatives had to be strengthened with a greater ability to enforce them, particularly in the areas of property rights, fair market competition, public complaint-handling and labour safety and protection. Indeed, in framing a resolution that would be acceptable to all member states and that would cover all their demands, the General Assembly probably tried to include too much and obscured what steps the international community had to take to implement it.

Heading priorities is the need for international agencies to practice what they preach. They should set an example of proper administrative and managerial practices. They need to reform their own administrative systems to rid themselves of obvious bureaupathologies such as rigidity, excessive secrecy, fraud, waste, overstaffing, patronage and corruption. During 1996, the new head of the World Bank began to overhaul the organisation and to simplify its administrative processes, and in July 1997 a major reorganisation was put into operation. In early 1997, the new Secretary General began a similar task in the United Nations organisation, building upon work which had been in progress for several years. Other bodies within the United Nations family also instigated and strengthened administrative reforms to restore the original conception of a competent, professional international civil service envisaged some 50 years earlier, which unfortunately had been compromised in the meantime by cold war competition, in-breeding and secrecy. A new International Code of Conduct for Public Officials was adopted by the United Nations in 1997.

Not far behind reorganisation comes the recognition that delivering technical assistance and cooperation in public administration and development to member states is or should be a shared task. Although the predominance of the United Nations had already been eroded by severe cuts in its funding, other international bodies, such as the International Institute of Administrative Sciences, the Commonwealth Secretariat, the European Center for Public Administration and Transparency International, had assumed increased responsibilities, and they were ready to increase their efforts once resources could be found. They understood that there were advantages in specialisation and diversification, and in drawing on different resources and experiences, and they would be less encumbered by restrictions imposed by the United Nations itself. A new international partnership is in the offing among the different public-administration advisory and consulting services around the world.

During the first half of the 1990s, following several global conferences sponsored by the United Nations, tentative plans were being considered to map out new roles and activities for international public administration, each drawing on a concerted global strategy to tackle crucial international problems. In time, they are expected to receive full international backing with funds allotted for their implementation. When that happens, a new chapter will open in international public administration. Clearly, this is probably the wave of the future and the international public administration has been wise to anticipate it. Once again, it will alter relations between the international sphere and the national sphere so that national administrations will need to adjust and prepare themselves and their publics in advance.

These predictions were very much confirmed at the Thirteenth Meeting of Experts on the United Nations Programme in Public Administration and Finance, held in New York on 27 May–4 June 1997. The theme was redefining the state for socioeconomic development, specifically:

(a) promoting an enabling environment for sound governance,
(b) enhancing the professionalism, ethical values and image of the public service,
(c) rethinking the state for socioeconomic development,
(d) creating an enabling environment for private sector development, and
(e) strengthening governmental capacity in the mobilisation, management and accountability of financial resources.

Strong markets and strong states were truly complementary and necessary conditions for economic prosperity and social justice. Major global trends were redefining the role of the state and public sector and changing the nature of governance. One such trend was the growing momentum of globalisation that was rapidly changing the ways in which the economy and markets operate. Another was the progress of science and technology which was transforming the methods of production, service delivery, transportation, communications and information management. Yet a third trend was the emergence of a vibrant civil society as a dynamic partner in the conduct of public affairs and economic activity, nationally and internationally.

Governments that once viewed themselves as foremost actors in the direct production of goods and services now see their role very largely in terms of creating and sustaining an enabling environment for private-sector development. They are actively seeking partnerships with business and NGOs and other civil society actors in the pursuit of economic growth and socially worthwhile objectives. Debureaucratisation, decentralisation and devolution of power to lower-level actors, as well as to civil society, have gained new prominence in administrative reform, although experience shows that wider diffusion of power is not without its problems, tending to favour corrupt practices, clientelism and local elites. To yield beneficial results, decentralisation and deregulation should be combined with measures that safeguard transparency and accountability. Only then can they help to realize social, people-centred and people-driven development.

Allied to these concerns is the need to arrest and reverse a perilous trend which has seriously widened the gap between the rich and the poor, the skilled and the unskilled, the powerful and the weak. Only a strong active state can promote social justice, ensure universal access to quality services, and safeguard the rule of law and respect for human rights in the terms of Resolution 50/225. A strong state is required to lobby for the poor and for the future, neither of which has a voice. The need to re-design a strong strategic state does not entail big government, but is fully compatible with steps to encourage cost-consciousness, fiscal responsibility and sound financial management. What this requires are properly organised and duly-equipped public administration systems that encompass structures and policies that can attract, retain, develop and motivate high-calibre personnel. Professionalism, merit and an enforceable code of ethics are the essential ingredients of a much needed strategy to restore and enhance the image of the public service.

In turn, this strategy calls for capacity-building activities – a judicious combination of institution-building and human-resources development clearly recognised in Resolution 50/225. The Thirteenth Meeting of Experts recommended that – as a core component of the economic and social sector of the United Nations – the Programme in Public Administration and Finance should focus on promoting and monitoring the implementation of Resolution 50/225, advancing global strategies and country-specific approaches that contribute to sound governance, institutional reinforcement and management development, as well as to the enhancement of ethical standards and professionalism in the public service. To these ends, the Programme should serve as a forum for the global exchange of information on policies, best practices and methods among governments, intergovernmental and non-governmental institutions, as well as providing advisory services to interested governments.

# Index

321